Contemporary Philosophy of Religion

Contemporary
Philosophy of Religion

Edited by

Steven M. Cahn
David Shatz

New York   Oxford
OXFORD UNIVERSITY PRESS
1982

Copyright © 1982 by Oxford University Press, Inc.

Library of Congress Cataloging in Publication Data
Main entry under title:
Contemporary philosophy of religion.
Bibliography: p.
Contents: Preface / Steven M. Cahn and David
Shatz—The problem of evil / Richard Swinburne
—Cacodaemony / Steven M. Cahn—Suffering and
evil / George N. Schlesinger—[etc.]
1. Religion—Philosophy—Addresses, essays, lectures.
I. Cahn, Steven M.   II. Shatz, David.
BL51.C637   200'.1   81–38380
ISBN 0–19–503009–5   AACR2

Printing (last digit): 9 8 7 6 5 4 3 2 1

Printed in the United States of America

Preface

Philosophy of religion is an ancient branch of inquiry, extending back prior to the time of Socrates. Through the centuries some have employed the tools of philosophy in an effort to support religion, while others have used these same tools with opposite aims in mind. What unites all philosophers of religion, however, is a concern for clarifying religious beliefs and subjecting them to critical scrutiny.

A survey of the field today will surprise those who assume that contemporary philosophers are uniformly hostile to religion and do nothing more than repeat well-known criticisms of a limited set of familiar religious claims. In fact, recently the situation has been quite the contrary. Many of the most highly regarded scholars in the field are themselves religious believers. In numerous books and articles they have sharpened many traditional doctrines and provided sophisticated defenses of them, thus posing a formidable challenge to those who do not share their commitments. Not only have these works enlivened debate about conventional topics, but they have widened the scope of the discipline, focusing attention on important issues that had previously received little attention from twentieth-century philosophers.

This volume contains many of the provocative essays that have recently enriched the field. Of the twenty-one selections all but five have been published since 1971. Some of these articles are sympathetic to religion, others sharply critical. By collecting them all in one volume we hope to convey the novelty, variety, and richness of contemporary work in the philosophy of religion.

A cornerstone of many religions is belief in God. But through the centuries philosophers have been forced to grapple with numerous difficulties that beset any attempt to describe God's attributes. One traditional quandary is the problem of evil: How can God be all-powerful, all-knowing, and all-good if there is evil in the world? In the first essay Richard Swinburne offers a new defense of the classic view that evil is necessary so that human beings can bear moral responsibility for their actions. In the next selection, however, Steven M. Cahn points out a neglected line of argument that may undermine Swinburne's attempted theodicy. Cahn argues that every attempt to view evil as part of a greater good can be met by viewing goodness as part of a greater evil. George N. Schlesinger then offers a novel approach to the entire problem by questioning the commonly held assumption that God is morally obligated to render human existence as desirable as he can.

The remaining essays in Section I discuss other difficulties related to the attributes of God. Anne C. Minas maintains that an all-knowing, all-good being cannot forgive those who sin. Peter Geach claims that although God is almighty, he is not omnipotent, since a perfectly good being lacks the power to perform a wrong action. Nelson Pike defends the view that there is an incompatibility between the claim that God is omniscient and the claim that persons have free will. Nicholas Wolterstorff, developing a theme touched on by Pike, argues that the biblical God exists within time rather than outside it as many have claimed. In the concluding essay of the section, Paul Helm contends that if the arguments of Wolterstorff and others against the timelessness of God are sound, so are parallel arguments against the view that God is spaceless. All these articles vividly illustrate the challenges of providing a coherent, convincing account of the nature of God.

The essays in Section II highlight ways in which religious belief can affect one's understanding of human experience. How are we to interpret and evaluate the reports of those who claim to have undergone mystical encounters or witnessed miraculous events? The essays by Richard M. Gale, William J. Wainwright, and Paul J. Dietl probe the many complexities inherent in formulating satisfactory answers to these questions. How are we to understand the actions of those who perform religious rituals or engage in other acts of worship? Gareth Matthews offers a rationale for such activities, maintaining that ritual is a dramatic rehearsal of the tenets of one's faith. James Rachels, however, finds the concept of worship objectionable on the grounds that a worshiper must abandon the role of an autonomous moral agent. A final issue discussed in this section is whether it is reasonable to believe in an afterlife. Terence Penelhum argues that the notion of postmortem disembodied existence is unintelligible and that difficulties also plague the doctrine of bodily resurrection. Such skepticism about resurrection is explored by George Mavrodes, who argues that the difficulties inherent in the doctrine also hamper the skeptic's own attempt to formulate criteria for identity and spatio-temporal continuity. The articles in Section II all make clear how believers and non-believers differ in their interpretations of human experience.

The essays in the first two sections subject religious beliefs and activities to rational assessment. But philosophers have often asserted that the nature of religious faith makes such inquiry inappropriate. The influential arguments for this position developed by the Danish existentialist philosopher, Søren Kierkegaard (1813–55) are explored in the essay by Robert Merrihew Adams. He maintains that Kierkegaard assumes a flawed conception of religiosity and overlooks an important sort of objective reasoning, that which focuses on prudential considerations for belief. James Cargile examines this type of reasoning as it is found in its classic presentation by the French philosopher Blaise Pascal (1623–62). Cargile argues that Pascal's celebrated "wager" fails in its attempt to persuade the skeptic to accept theism.

Another response to those who judge religious beliefs by ordinary canons of reasoning has been provided by followers of the Austrian philosopher Ludwig Wittgenstein (1889–1951). They argue that religion has its own internal standards of rationality and, therefore, cannot be criticized or even understood by nonbelievers. Kai Nielsen's essay attacks this position. Aspects of the debate about the concept of rationality are further developed in the article by Alvin Plantinga. He maintains that religious beliefs are rational even in the absence of supporting evidence because, like beliefs of common sense, they form part of the foundation of an individual's system of beliefs.

But regardless of whether it is appropriate to judge religious tenets in the light of ordinary canons of evidence, how are we to adjudicate the apparently conflicting claims of the world's diverse religions? Can their views be harmonized or are the doctrines of one religion incompatible with those of others? In the concluding papers John Hick and Ninian Smart present opposing answers to these critical questions.

A final note. This volume does not contain selections opposing or defending traditional proofs for the existence of God; nor does it emphasize discussions of the language of religious discourse. Interesting work continues to be produced in these areas, but many other collections of articles are devoted exclusively to these topics. We have chosen to emphasize other equally important and fascinating issues that deserve to share the center of attention in contemporary philosophy of religion.

New York   S. M. C.
September 1981   D. S.

Contents

III. FAITH, RATIONALITY, AND WORLD RELIGIONS

FAITH

RELIGION + REASON RELIGIONS

RELIGIONS

PART I

THE ATTRIBUTES
OF GOD

The Problem of Evil

RICHARD SWINBURNE

God is, by definition, omniscient, omnipotent, and perfectly good. By "omniscient" I understand "one who knows all true propositions." By "omnipotent" I understand "able to do anything logically possible."[1] By "perfectly good" I understand "one who does no morally bad action," and I include among actions omissions to perform some action. The problem of evil is then often stated as the problem whether the existence of God is compatible with the existence of evil. Against the suggestion of compatibility, an atheist often suggests that the existence of evil entails the nonexistence of God. For, he argues, if God exists, then being omniscient, he knows under what circumstances evil will occur, if he does not act; and being omnipotent, he is able to prevent its occurrence. Hence, being perfectly good, he will prevent its occurrence and so evil will not exist. Hence the existence of God entails the nonexistence of evil. Theists have usually attacked this argument by denying the claim that necessarily a perfectly good being, foreseeing the occurrence of evil and able to prevent it, will prevent it. And indeed, if evil is understood in the very wide way in which it normally is understood in this context, to include physical pain of however slight a degree, the cited claim is somewhat implausible. For it implies that if through my neglecting frequent warnings to go to the dentist, I find my-

---

1. This account of omnipotence will do for present purposes. But a much more careful account is needed to deal with other well-known difficulties. I have attempted to provide such an account in my "Omnipotence," *American Philosophical Quarterly*, 10 (1973), 231–237.

self one morning with a slight toothache, then necessarily, there does not
exist a perfectly good being who foresaw the evil and was able to have prevented it. Yet it seems fairly obvious that such a being might well choose
to allow me to suffer some mild consequences of my folly—as a lesson for
the future which would do me no real harm.

The threat to theism seems to come, not from the existence of evil as
such, but rather from the existence of evil of certain kinds and degrees—
severe undeserved physical pain or mental anguish, for example. I shall
therefore list briefly the kinds of evil which are evident in our world, and
ask whether their existence in the degrees in which we find them is compatible with the existence of God. I shall call the man who argues for
compatibility the theodicist, and his opponent the antitheodicist. The theodicist will claim that it is not morally wrong for God to create or permit the
various evils, normally on the grounds that doing so is providing the logically necessary conditions of greater goods. The antitheodicist denies these
claims by putting forward moral principles which have as consequences
that a good God would not under any circumstances create or permit the
evils in question. I shall argue that these moral principles are not, when
carefully examined, at all obvious, and indeed that there is a lot to be said
for their negations. Hence I shall conclude that it is plausible to suppose
that the existence of these evils is compatible with the existence of God.[2]

Since I am discussing only the compatibility of various evils with the
existence of God, I am perfectly entitled to make occasionally some (non-
self-contradictory) assumption, and argue that if it was true, the compatibility would hold. For if p is compatible with q, given r (where r is not
self-contradictory), then p is compatible with q simpliciter. It is irrelevant
to the issue of compatibility whether these assumptions are true. If, however, the assumptions which I make are clearly false, and if also it looks as
if the existence of God is compatible with the existence of evil *only* given
those assumptions, the formal proof of compatibility will lose much of interest. To avoid this danger, I shall make only such assumptions as are not
clearly false—and also in fact the ones which I shall make will be ones to
which many theists are already committed for entirely different reasons.

What then is wrong with the world? First, there are painful sensations,
felt both by men, and, to a lesser extent, by animals. Second, there are
painful emotions, which do not involve pain in the literal sense of this
word—for example, feelings of loss and failure and frustration. Such suffering exists mainly among men, but also, I suppose, to some small extent
among animals too. Third, there are evil and undesirable states of affairs,
mainly states of men's minds, which do not involve suffering. For example,

2. Some of what I have to say will not be especially original. The extensive writing
on this subject has of course been well described in John Hick, *Evil and the God
of Love* (London, 1966).

there are the states of mind of hatred and envy; and such states of the world as rubbish tipped over a beauty spot. And fourth, there are the evil actions of men, mainly actions having as foreseeable consequences evils of the first three types, but perhaps other actions as well—such as lying and promise breaking with no such foreseeable consequences. As before, I include among actions, omissions to perform some actions. If there are rational agents other than men and God (if he exists), such as angels or devils or strange beings on distant planets, who suffer and perform evil actions, then their evil feelings, states, and actions must be added to the list of evils.

I propose to call evil of the first type physical evil, evil of the second type mental evil, evil of the third type state evil, and evil of the fourth type moral evil. Since there is a clear contrast between evils of the first three types, which are evils that happen to men or animals or the world, and evils of the fourth type, which are evils that men do, there is an advantage in having one name for evils of any of the first three types—I shall call these passive evils.[3] I distinguish evil from mere absence of good. Pain is not simply the absence of pleasure. A headache is a pain, whereas not having the sensation of drinking whiskey is, for many people, mere absence of pleasure. Likewise, the feeling of loss in bereavement is an evil involving suffering, to be contrasted with the mere absence of the pleasure of companionship. Some thinkers have, of course, claimed that a good God would create a "best of all (logically) possible worlds"[4] (i.e., a world than which no better is logically possible), and for them the mere absence of good creates a problem since it looks as if a world would be a better world if it had that good. For most of us, however, the mere absence of good seems less of a threat to theism than the presence of evil, partly because it is not at all clear whether any sense can be given to the concept of a best of all possible worlds (and if it cannot then of logical necessity there will be a better world than any creatable world) and partly because even if sense can be given to this concept it is not at all obvious that God has an obligation to create such a world[5]—to whom would he be doing an injustice if he did not? My concern is with the threat to theism posed by the existence of evil.

Now much of the evil in the world consists of the evil actions of men

---

3. In discussion of the problem of evil, terminology has not always been very clear or consistent. See Gerald Wallace, "The Problems of Moral and Physical Evil," *Philosophy*, 46 (1971), 349–351.

4. Indeed they have often made the even stronger claim that a good God would create *the* best of all (logically) possible worlds—implying that necessarily there was just one possible world better than all others. There seem to me no grounds at all for adopting this claim.

5. That he has no such obligation is very well argued by Robert Merrihew Adams, "Must God Create the Best?" *Philosophical Review*, 81 (1972), 317–332.

and the passive evils brought about by those actions. (These include the evils brought about intentionally by men, and also the evils which result from long years of slackness by many generations of men. Many of the evils of 1975 are in the latter category, and among them many state evils. The hatred and jealousy which many men and groups feel today result from an upbringing consequent on generations of neglected opportunities for reconciliations.) The antitheodicist suggests as a moral principle (P1) that a creator able to do so ought to create only creatures such that necessarily they do not do evil actions. From this it follows that God would not have made men who do evil actions. Against this suggestion the theodicist naturally deploys the free-will defense, elegantly expounded in recent years by Alvin Plantinga.[6] This runs roughly as follows: it is not logically possible for an agent to make another agent such that necessarily he freely does only good actions. Hence if a being G creates a free agent, he gives to the agent power of choice between alternative actions, and how he will exercise that power is something which G cannot control while the agent remains free. It is a good thing that there exist free agents, but a logically necessary consequence of their existence is that their power to choose to do evil actions may sometimes be realized. The price is worth paying, however, for the existence of agents performing free actions remains a good thing even if they sometimes do evil. Hence it is not logically possible that a creator create free creatures "such that necessarily they do not do evil actions." But it is not a morally bad thing that he create free creatures, even with the possibility of their doing evil. Hence the cited moral principle is implausible.

The free-will defense as stated needs a little filling out. For surely there could be free agents who did not have the power of moral choice, agents whose only opportunities for choice were between morally indifferent alternatives—between jam and marmalade for breakfast, between watching the news on BBC 1 or the news on ITV. They might lack this power either because they lacked the power of making moral judgments (i.e., lacked moral discrimination); or because all their actions which were morally assessable were caused by factors outside their control; or because they saw with complete clarity what was right and wrong and had no temptation to do anything except the right.[7] The free-will defense must claim, however, that it is a good thing that there exist free agents with the power and opportunity of choosing between morally good and morally evil actions,

6. See Alvin Plantinga, "The Free Will Defence," in Max Black, ed., *Philosophy in America* (London, 1965); *God and Other Minds* (Ithaca, N.Y., and London, 1967), chaps. 5 and 6; and *The Nature of Necessity* (Oxford, 1974), chap. 9.
7. In the latter case they would have, in Kant's terminology, holy wills. I argue that God must be such an agent in my "Duty and the Will of God," *Canadian Journal of Philosophy*, 4 (1974), 213–227.

agents with sufficient moral discrimination to have some idea of the difference and some (though not overwhelming) temptation to do other than
the morally good. Let us call such agents humanly free agents. The defense must then go on to claim that it is not logically possible to create humanly free agents such that necessarily they do not do morally evil actions.
Unfortunately, this latter claim is highly debatable, and I have no space to
debate it.[8] I propose therefore to circumvent this issue as follows. I shall
add to the definition of humanly free agents, that they are agents whose
choices do not have fully deterministic precedent causes. Clearly then it
will not be logically possible to create humanly free agents whose choices
go one way rather than another, and so not logically possible to create humanly free agents such that necessarily they do not do evil actions. Then
the free-will defense claims that (P1) is not universally true; it is not morally wrong to create humanly free agents—despite the real possibility that
they will do evil. Like many others who have discussed this issue, I find
this a highly plausible suggestion. Surely as parents we regard it as a good
thing that our children have power to do free actions of moral significance—
even if the consequence is that they sometimes do evil actions. This conviction is likely to be stronger, not weaker, if we hold that the free actions
with which we are concerned are ones which do not have fully deterministic precedent causes. In this way we show the existence of God to be
compatible with the existence of moral evil—but only subject to a very big
assumption—that men are humanly free agents. If they are not, the compatibility shown by the free-will defense is of little interest. For the agreed
exception to (P1) would not then justify a creator making men who did
evil actions; we should need a different exception to avoid incompatibility.
The assumption seems to me not clearly false, and is also one which most
theists affirm for quite other reasons. Needless to say, there is no space to
discuss the assumption here.

All that the free-will defense has shown so far, however (and all that
Plantinga seems to show), is grounds for supposing that the existence of
moral evil is compatible with the existence of God. It has not given grounds
for supposing that the existence of evil consequences of moral evils is compatible with the existence of God. In an attempt to show an incompatibility,
the antitheodicist may suggest instead of (P1), (P2)—that a creator able to
do so ought always to ensure that any creature whom he creates does not
cause passive evils, or at any rate passive evils which hurt creatures other
than himself. For could not God have made a world where there are humanly free creatures, men with the power to do evil actions, but where

8. For the debate see Antony Flew, "Divine Omnipotence and Human Freedom,"
in Antony Flew and Alasdair MacIntyre, eds., New Essays in Philosophical Theology; John L. Mackie, "Evil and Omnipotence," Mind, 64 (1955), 200–212; and
Plantinga, "Free Will Defence."

those actions do not have evil consequences, or at any rate evil consequences which affect others—e.g., a world where men cannot cause pain and distress to other men? Men might well do actions which are evil either because they were actions which they believed would have evil consequences or because they were evil for some other reason (e.g., actions which involved promise breaking) without them in fact having any passive evils as consequences. Agents in such a world would be like men in a simulator training to be pilots. They can make mistakes, but no one suffers through those mistakes. Or men might do evil actions which did have the evil consequences which were foreseen but which damaged only themselves. Some philosophers might hold that an action would not be evil if its foreseen consequences were ones damaging only to the agent, since, they might hold, no one has any duties to himself. For those who do not hold this position, however, there are some plausible candidates for actions evil solely because of their foreseeable consequences for the agent—e.g., men brooding on their misfortunes in such a way as foreseeably to become suicidal or misanthropic.

I do not find (P2) a very plausible moral principle. A world in which no one except the agent was affected by his evil actions might be a world in which men had freedom but it would not be a world in which men had responsibility. The theodicist claims that it would not be wrong for God to create interdependent humanly free agents, a society of such agents responsible for each other's well-being, able to make or mar each other.

Fair enough, the antitheodicist may again say. It is not wrong to create a world where creatures have responsibilities for each other. But might not those responsibilities simply be that creatures had the opportunity to benefit or to withhold benefit from each other, not a world in which they had also the opportunity to cause each other pain? One answer to this is that if creatures have only the power to benefit and not the power to hurt each other, they obviously lack any very strong responsibility for each other. To bring out the point by a caricature—a world in which I could choose whether or not to give you sweets, but not whether or not to break your leg or make you unpopular, is not a world in which I have a very strong influence on your destiny, and so not a world in which I have a very full responsibility for you. Further, however, there is a point which will depend on an argument which I will give further on. In the actual world very often a man's withholding benefits from another is correlated with the latter's suffering some passive evil, either physical or mental. Thus if I withhold from you certain vitamins, you will suffer disease. Or if I deprive you of your wife by persuading her to live with me instead, you will suffer grief at the loss. Now it seems to me that a world in which such correlations did not hold would not necessarily be a better world than the world in which they do. The appropriateness of pain to bodily disease or deprivation, and of mental evils to various losses or lacks of a more spiritual kind, is something for which I shall argue in detail a little later.

So then the theodicist objects to (P2) on the grounds that the price of possible passive evils for other creatures is a price worth paying for agents to have great responsibilities for each other. It is a price which (logically) must be paid if they are to have those responsibilities. Here again a reasonable antitheodicist may see the point. In bringing up our own children, in order to give them responsibility, we try not to interfere too quickly in their quarrels—even at the price, sometimes, of younger children getting hurt physically. We try not to interfere, first, in order to train our children for responsibility in later life and second because responsibility here and now is a good thing in itself. True, with respect to the first reason, whatever the effects on character produced by training, God could produce without training. But if he did so by imposing a full character on a humanly free creature, this would be giving him a character which he had not in any way chosen or adopted for himself. Yet it would seem a good thing that a creator should allow humanly free creatures to influence by their own choices the sort of creatures they are to be, the kind of character they are to have. That means that the creator must create them immature, and allow them gradually to make decisions which affect the sort of beings they will be. And one of the greatest privileges which a creator can give to a creature is to allow him to help in the process of education, in putting alternatives before his fellows.

Yet though the antitheodicist may see the point, in theory, he may well react to it rather like this. "Certainly some independence is a good thing. But surely a father ought to interfere if his younger son is really getting badly hurt. The ideal of making men free and responsible is a good one, but there are limits to the amount of responsibility which it is good that men should have, and in our world men have too much responsibility. A good God would certainly have intervened long ago to stop some of the things which happen in our world." Here, I believe, lies the crux—it is simply a matter of quantity. The theodicist says that a good God could allow men to do to each other the hurt they do, in order to allow them to be free and responsible. But against him the antitheodicist puts forward as a moral principle (P3) that a creator able to do so ought to ensure that any creature whom he creates does not cause passive evils as many and as evil as those in our world. He says that in our world freedom and responsibility have gone too far—produced too much physical and mental hurt. God might well tolerate a boy hitting his younger brothers, but not Belsen.

The theodicist is in no way committed to saying that a good God will not stop things getting too bad. Indeed, if God made our world, he has clearly done so. There are limits to the amount and degree of evil which are possible in our world. Thus there are limits to the amount of pain which a person can suffer—persons live in our world only so many years and the amount which they can suffer at any given time (if mental goings-on are in any way correlated with bodily ones) is limited by their physiology. Further, theists often claim that from time to time God intervenes in the natural order which he has made to prevent evil which would otherwise occur. So the theodicist can certainly claim that a good God stops too much sufferings—it is just that he and his opponent draw the line in different places. The issue as regards the passive evils caused by men turns ultimately to the quantity of evil. To this crucial matter I shall return toward the end of the paper.

We shall have to turn next to the issue of passive evils not apparently caused by men. But, first, I must consider a further argument by the theodicist in support of the free-will defense and also an argument of the anti-theodicist against it. The first is the argument that various evils are logically necessary conditions for the occurrence of actions of certain especially good kinds. Thus for a man to bear his suffering cheerfully there has to be suffering for him to bear. There have to be acts which irritate for another to show tolerance of them. Likewise, it is often said, acts of forgiveness, courage, self-sacrifice, compassion, overcoming temptation, etc., can be performed only if there are evils of various kinds. Here, however, we must be careful. One might reasonably claim that all that is necessary for some of these good acts (or acts as good as these) to be performed is belief in the existence of certain evils, not their actual existence. You can show compassion toward someone who appears to be suffering, but is not really; you can forgive someone who only appeared to insult you, but did not really. But if the world is to be populated with imaginary evils of the kind needed to enable creatures to perform acts of the above specially good kinds, it would have to be a world in which creatures are generally and systematically deceived about the feelings of their fellows—in which the behavior of creatures generally and unavoidably belies their feelings and intentions. I suggest, in the tradition of Descartes (*Meditations* 4, 5 and 6), that it would be a morally wrong act of a creator to create such a deceptive world. In that case, given a creator, then, without an immoral act on his part, for acts of courage, compassion, etc., to be acts open to men to perform, there have to be various evils. Evils give men the opportunity to perform those acts which show men at their best. A world without evils would be a world in which men could show no forgiveness, no compassion, no self-sacrifice. And men without that opportunity are deprived of the opportunity to show themselves at their noblest. For this reason God might well allow some of his creatures to perform evil acts with passive evils as consequences, since these provide the opportunity for especially noble acts.

Against the suggestion of the developed free-will defense that it would be justifiable for God to permit a creature to hurt another for the good of his or the other's soul, there is one natural objection which will surely be made. This is that it is generally supposed to be the duty of men to stop other men hurting each other badly. So why is it not God's duty to stop men hurting each other badly? Now the theodicist does not have to maintain that it is never God's duty to stop men hurting each other; but he does have to maintain that it is not God's duty in circumstances where it clearly is our duty to stop such hurt if we can—e.g., when men are torturing each other in mind or body in some of the ways in which they do this in our world and when, if God exists, he does not step in.

Now different views might be taken about the extent of our duty to interfere in the quarrels of others. But the most which could reasonably be claimed is surely this—that we have a duty to interfere in three kinds of circumstances—(1) if an oppressed person asks us to interfere and it is probable that he will suffer considerably if we do not, (2) if the participants are children or not of sane mind and it is probable that one or other will suffer considerably if we do not interfere, or (3) if it is probable that considerable harm will be done to others if we do not interfere. It is not very plausible to suppose that we have any duty to interfere in the quarrels of grown sane men who do not wish us to do so, unless it is probable that the harm will spread. Now note that in the characterization of each of the circumstances in which we would have a duty to interfere there occurs the word "probable," and it is being used in the "epistemic" sense—as "made probable by the total available evidence." But then the "probability" of an occurrence varies crucially with which community or individual is assessing it, and the amount of evidence which they have at the time in question. What is probable relative to your knowledge at t_1 may not be at all probable relative to my knowledge at t_2. Hence a person's duty to interfere in quarrels will depend on their probable consequences relative to that person's knowledge. Hence it follows that one who knows much more about the probable consequences of a quarrel may have no duty to interfere where another with less knowledge does have such a duty—and conversely. Hence a God who sees far more clearly than we do the consequences of quarrels may have duties very different from ours with respect to particular such quarrels. He may know that the suffering that A will cause B is not nearly as great as B's screams might suggest to us and will provide (unknown to us) an opportunity to C to help B recover and will thus give C a deep responsibility which he would not otherwise have. God may very well have reason for allowing particular evils which it is our bounden duty to attempt to stop at all costs simply because he knows so much more about them than we do. And this is no ad hoc hypothesis—it follows directly from the characterization of the kind of circumstances in which persons have a duty to interfere in quarrels.

We may have a duty to interfere in quarrels when God does not for a very different kind of reason. God, being our creator, the source of our beginning and continuation of existence, has rights over us which we do not have over our fellow-men. To allow a man to suffer for the good of his or someone else's soul one has to stand in some kind of parental relationship toward him. I don't have the right to let some stranger Joe Bloggs suffer for the good of his soul or of the soul of Bill Snoggs, but I do have *some* right of this kind in respect of my own children. I may let the younger son suffer *somewhat* for the good of his and his brother's soul. I have this right because in small part I am responsible for his existence, its beginning and continuance. If this is correct, then a fortiori, God who is, ex hypothesi, so much more the author of our being than are our parents, has so many more rights in this respect. God has rights to allow others to suffer, while I do not have those rights and hence have a duty to interfere instead. In these two ways the theodicist can rebut the objection that if we have a duty to stop certain particular evils which men do to others, God must have this duty too.

In the free-will defense, as elaborated above, the theist seems to me to have an adequate answer to the suggestion that necessarily a good God would prevent the occurrence of the evil which men cause—if we ignore the question of the quantity of evil, to which I will return at the end of my paper. But what of the passive evil apparently not due to human action? What of the pain caused to men by disease or earthquake or cyclone, and what too of animal pain which existed before there were men? There are two additional assumptions, each of which has been put forward to allow the free-will defense to show the compatibility of the existence of God and the existence of such evil. The first is that, despite appearances, men are ultimately responsible for disease, earthquake, cyclone, and much animal pain. There seem to be traces of this view in Genesis 3:16-20. One might claim that God ties the goodness of man to the well-being of the world and that a failure of one leads to a failure of the other. Lack of prayer, concern, and simple goodness lead to the evils in nature. This assumption, though it may do some service for the free-will defense, would seem unable to account for the animal pain which existed before there were men. The other assumption is that there exist humanly free creatures other than men, which we may call fallen angels, who have chosen to do evil, and have brought about the passive evils not brought about by men. These were given the care of much of the material world and have abused that care. For reasons already given, however, it is not God's moral duty to interfere to prevent the passive evils caused by such creatures. This defense has recently been used by, among others, Plantinga. This assumption, it seems to me, will do the job, and is not *clearly* false. It is also an assumption which was part of the Christian tradition long before the free-will defense was put forward in any logically rigorous form. I believe that this assumption may indeed be indispensable if the theist is to reconcile with the existence of God the existence of passive evils of certain kinds, e.g., certain animal pain. But I do not think that the theodicist need deploy it to deal with the central cases of passive evils not caused by men—mental evils and the human pain that is a sign of bodily malfunctioning. Note, however, that if he does not attribute such passive evils to the free choice of some other agent, the theodicist must attribute them to the direct action of God himself, or rather, what he must say is that God created a universe in which passive evils must necessarily occur in certain circumstances, the occurrence of which is necessary or at any rate not within the power of a humanly free agent to prevent. The antitheodicist then naturally claims, that although a creator might be justified in allowing free creatures to produce various evils, nevertheless (P4) a creator is never justified in creating a world in which evil results except by the action of a humanly free agent. Against this the theodicist tries to sketch reasons which a good creator might have for creating a world in which there is evil not brought about by humanly free agents. One reason which he produces is one which we have already considered earlier in the development of the free-will defense. This is the reason that various evils are logically necessary conditions for the occurrence of actions of certain especially noble kinds. This was adduced earlier as a reason why a creator might allow creatures to perform evil acts with passive evils as consequences. It can also be adduced as a reason why he might himself bring about passive evils—to give further opportunities for courage, patience, and tolerance. I shall consider here one further reason that, the theodicist may suggest, a good creator might have for creating a world in which various passive evils were implanted, which is another reason for rejecting (P4). It is, I think, a reason which is closely connected with some of the other reasons which we have been considering why a good creator might permit the existence of evil.

A creator who is going to create humanly free agents and place them in a universe has a choice of the kind of universe to create. First, he can create a finished universe in which nothing needs improving. Humanly free agents know what is right, and pursue it; and they achieve their purposes without hindrance. Second, he can create a basically evil universe, in which everything needs improving, and nothing can be improved. Or, third, he can create a basically good but half-finished universe—one in which many things need improving, humanly free agents do not altogether know what is right, and their purposes are often frustrated; but one in which agents can come to know what is right and can overcome the obstacles to the achievement of their purposes. In such a universe the bodies of creatures may work imperfectly and last only a short time; and creatures may be morally ill-educated, and set their affections on things and persons which are taken from them. The universe might be such that it requires long generations of cooperative effort between creatures to make perfect. While not wishing to deny the goodness of a universe of the first kind, I suggest that to create a universe of the third kind would be no bad thing, for it gives to creatures the privilege of making their own universe. Genesis 1 in telling of a God who tells men to "subdue" the earth pictures the creator as creating a universe of this third kind; and fairly evidently—given that men are humanly free agents—our universe is of this kind.

Now a creator who creates a half-finished universe of this third kind has a further choice as to how he molds the humanly free agents which it contains. Clearly he will have to give them a nature of some kind, that is, certain narrow purposes which they have a natural inclination to pursue until they choose or are forced to pursue others—e.g., the immediate attainment of food, sleep, and sex. There could hardly be humanly free agents without some such initial purposes. But what is he to do about their knowledge of their duty to improve the world—e.g., to repair their bodies when they go wrong, so that they can realize long-term purposes, to help others who innot get food to do so, etc.? He could just give them a formal hazy knowledge that they had such reasons for action without giving them any strong inclination to pursue them. Such a policy might well seem an excessively laissez-faire one. We tend to think that parents who give their children no help toward taking the right path are less than perfect parents. So a good creator might well help agents toward taking steps to improve the universe. We shall see that he can do this in one of two ways.

An action is something done for a reason. A good creator, we supposed, will give to agents some reasons for doing right actions—e.g., that they are right, that they will improve the universe. These reasons are ones of which men can be aware and then either act on or not act on. The creator could help agents toward doing right actions by making these reasons more effective causally; that is, he could make agents so that by nature they were inclined (though not perhaps compelled) to pursue what is good. But this would be to impose a moral character on agents, to give them wide general purposes which they naturally pursue, to make them naturally altruistic, tenacious of purpose, or strong-willed. But to impose a character on creatures might well seem to take away from creatures the privilege of developing their own characters and those of their fellows. We tend to think that parents who try too forcibly to impose a character, however good a character, on their children, are less than perfect parents.

The alternative way in which a creator could help creatures to perform right actions is by sometimes providing additional reasons for creatures to do what is right, reasons which by their very nature have a strong causal influence. Reasons such as improving the universe or doing one's duty do not necessarily have a strong causal influence, for as we have seen crea-

tures may be little influenced by them. Giving a creature reasons which by
their nature were strongly causally influential on a particular occasion on
any creature whatever his character, would not impose a particular character on a creature. It would, however, incline him to do what is right on
that occasion and maybe subsequently too. Now if a reason is by its nature
to be strongly causally influential it must be something of which the agent
is aware which causally inclines him (whatever his character) to perform
some action, to bring about some kind of change. What kind of reason
could this be except the existence of an unpleasant feeling, either a sensation such as a pain or an emotion such as a feeling of loss or deprivation?
Such feelings are things of which agents are conscious, which cause them
to do whatever action will get rid of those feelings, and which provide reason for performing such action. An itch causally inclines a man to do whatever will cause the itch to cease, e.g., scratch, and provides a reason for doing that action. Its causal influence is quite independent of the agent—
saint or sinner, strong-willed or weak-willed, will all be strongly inclined
to get rid of their pains (though some may learn to resist the inclination).
Hence a creator who wished to give agents some inclination to improve the
world without giving them a character, a wide set of general purposes
which they naturally pursue, would tie some of the imperfections of the
world to physical or mental evils.

To tie desirable states of affairs to pleasant feelings would not have the
same effect. Only an existing feeling can be causally efficacious. An agent
could be moved to action by a pleasant feeling only when he had it, and
the only action to which he could be moved would be to keep the world as
it is, not to improve it. For men to have reasons which move men of any
character to actions of perfecting the world, a creator needs to tie its imperfections to unpleasant feelings, that is, physical and mental evils.

There is to some considerable extent such tie-up in our universe. Pain
normally occurs when something goes wrong with the working of our body
which is going to lead to further limitation on the purposes which we can
achieve; and the pain ends when the body is repaired. The existence of the
pain spurs the sufferer, and others through the sympathetic suffering which
arises when they learn of the sufferer's pain, to do something about the
bodily malfunctioning. Yet giving men such feelings which they are inclined to end involves the imposition of no character. A man who is inclined to end his toothache by a visit to the dentist may be saint or sinner,
strong-willed or weak-willed, rational or irrational. Any other way of which
I can conceive of giving men an inclination to correct what goes wrong,
and generally to improve the universe, would seem to involve imposing a
character. A creator could, for example, have operated exclusively by threats
and promises, whispering in men's ears, "unless you go to the dentist, you
are going to suffer terribly," or "if you go to the dentist, you are going to

feel wonderful." And if the order of nature is God's creation, he does indeed often provide us with such threats and promises—not by whispering
in our ears but by providing inductive evidence. There is plenty of inductive evidence that unattended cuts and sores will lead to pain; that eating
and drinking will lead to pleasure. Still, men do not always respond to
threats and promises or take the trouble to notice inductive evidence (e.g.,
statistics showing the correlation between smoking and cancer). A creator
could have made men so that they naturally took more account of inductive evidence. But to do so would be to impose character. It would be to
make men, apart from any choice of theirs, rational and strong-willed.

Many mental evils too are caused by things going wrong in a man's
life or in the life of his fellows and often serve as a spur to a man to put
things right, either to put right the cause of the particular mental evil or
to put similar things right. A man's feeling of frustration at the failure of
his plans spurs him either to fulfill those plans despite their initial failure
or to curtail his ambitions. A man's sadness at the failure of the plans of his
child will incline him to help the child more in the future. A man's grief at
the absence of a loved one inclines him to do whatever will get the loved
one back. As with physical pain, the spur inclines a man to do what is
right but does so without imposing a character—without, say, making a
man responsive to duty, or strong-willed.

Physical and mental evils may serve as spurs to long-term cooperative
research leading to improvement of the universe. A feeling of sympathy
for the actual and prospective suffering of many from tuberculosis or cancer leads to acquisition of knowledge and provision of cure for future sufferers. Cooperative and long-term research and cure is a very good thing,
the kind of thing toward which men need a spur. A man's suffering is
never in vain if it leads through sympathy to the work of others which
eventually provides a long-term cure. True, there could be sympathy without a sufferer for whom the sympathy is felt. Yet in a world made by a
creator, there cannot be sympathy on the large scale without a sufferer, for
whom the sympathy is felt, unless the creator planned for creatures generally to be deceived about the feelings of their fellows; and that, we have
claimed, would be morally wrong.

So generally many evils have a biological and psychological utility in
producing spurs to right action without imposition of character, a goal
which it is hard to conceive of being realized in any other way. This point
provides a reason for the rejection of (P4). There are other kinds of reason
which have been adduced reasons for rejecting (P4)—e.g., that a creator
could be justified in bringing about evil as a punishment—but I have no
space to discuss these now. I will, however, in passing, mention briefly one
reason why a creator might make a world in which certain mental evils
were tied to things going wrong. Mental suffering and anguish are a man's

proper tribute to losses and failures, and a world in which men were im-munized from such reactions to things going wrong would be a worse world than ours. By showing proper feelings a man shows his respect for himself and others. Thus a man who feels no grief at the death of his child or the seduction of his wife is rightly branded by us as insensitive, for he has failed to pay the proper tribute of feeling to others, to show in his feeling how much he values them, and thereby failed to value them properly—for valuing them properly involves having proper reactions of feeling to their loss. Again, only a world in which men feel sympathy for losses experi-enced by their friends, is a world in which love has full meaning.

So, I have argued, there seem to be kinds of justification for the evils which exist in the world, available to the theodicist. Although a good cre-ator might have very different kinds of justification for producing, or allow-ing others to produce, various different evils, there is a central thread run-ning through the kind of theodicy which I have made my theodicist put forward. This is that it is a good thing that a creator should make a half-finished universe and create immature creatures, who are humanly free agents, to inhabit it; and that he should allow them to exercise some choice over what kind of creatures they are to become and what sort of universe is to be (while at the same time giving them a slight push in the direction of doing what is right); and that the creatures should have power to affect not only the development of the inanimate universe but the well-being and moral character of their fellows, and that there should be opportunities for creatures to develop noble characters and do especially noble actions. My theodicist has argued that if a creator is to make a universe of this kind, then evils of various kinds may inevitably—at any rate temporarily—belong to such a universe; and that it is not a morally bad thing to create such a universe despite the evils.

Now a morally sensitive antitheodicist might well in principle accept some of the above arguments. He may agree that in principle it is not wrong to create humanly free agents, despite the possible evils which might result, or to create pains as biological warnings. But where the crunch comes, it seems to me, is in the amount of evil which exists in our world. The antitheodicist says, all right, it would not be wrong to create men able to harm each other, but it would be wrong to create men able to put each other in Belsen. It would not be wrong to create backaches and headaches, even severe ones, as biological warnings, but not the long severe incurable pain of some diseases. In reply the theodicist must argue that a creator who allowed men to do little evil would be a creator who gave them little responsibility; and a creator who gave them only coughs and colds, and not cancer and cholera would be a creator who treated men as children instead of giving them real encouragement to subdue the world. The argu-ment must go on with regard to particular cases. The antitheodicist must sketch in detail and show his adversary the horrors of particular wars and diseases. The theodicist in reply must sketch in detail and show his adversary the good which such disasters make possible. He must show to his opponent men working together for good, men helping each other to overcome disease and famine; the heroism of men who choose the good in spite of temptation, who help others not merely by giving them food but who teach them right and wrong, give them something to live for and something to die for. A world in which this is possible can only be a world in which there is much evil as well as great good. Interfere to stop the evil and you cut off the good.

Like all moral arguments this one can be settled only by each party pointing to the consequences of his opponent's moral position and trying to show that his opponent is committed to implausible consequences. They must try, too, to show that each other's moral principles do or do not fit well with other moral principles which each accepts. The exhibition of consequences is a long process, and it takes time to convince an opponent even if he is prepared to be rational, more time than is available in this paper. All that I claim to have *shown* here is that there is no *easy proof* of incompatibility between the existence of evils of the kinds we find around us and the existence of God. Yet my sympathies for the outcome of any more detailed argument are probably apparent, and indeed I may have said enough to convince some readers as to what that outcome would be.

My sympathies lie, of course, with the theodicist. The theodicist's God is a god who thinks the higher goods so worthwhile that he is prepared to ask a lot of man in the way of enduring evil. Creatures determining in cooperation their own character and future, and that of the universe in which they live, coming in the process to show charity, forgiveness, faith, and self-sacrifice is such a worthwhile thing that a creator would not be unjustified in making or permitting a certain amount of evil in order that they should be realized. No doubt a good creator would put a limit on the amount of evil in the world and perhaps an end to the struggle with it after a number of years. But if he allowed creatures to struggle with evil, he would allow them a real struggle with a real enemy, not a parlor game. The antitheodicist's mistake lies in extrapolating too quickly from *our* duties when faced with evil to the duties of a creator, while ignoring the enormous differences in the circumstances of each. Each of us at one time can make the existing universe better or worse only in a few particulars. A creator can choose the kind of universe and the kind of creatures there are to be. It seldom becomes us in our ignorance and weakness to do anything more than remove the evident evils—war, disease, and famine. We seldom have the power or the knowledge or the right to use such evils to forward deeper and longer-term goods. To make an analogy, the duty of the weak and ignorant is to eliminate cowpox and not to spread it, while the doctor has a duty to spread it (under carefully controlled conditions). But a creator who made or permitted his creatures to suffer much evil and asked them to suffer more is a very demanding creator, one with high ideals who expects a lot. For myself I can say that I would not be too happy to worship a creator who expected too little of his creatures. Nevertheless such a God does ask a lot of creatures. A theodicist is in a better position to defend a theodicy such as I have outlined if he is prepared also to make the further additional claim—that God knowing the worthwhileness of the conquest of evil and the perfecting of the universe by men, shared with them this task by subjecting himself as man to the evil in the world. A creator is more justified in creating or permitting evils to be overcome by his creatures if he is prepared to share with them the burden of the suffering and effort.

Cacodaemony

STEVEN M. CAHN

For many centuries philosophers have grappled with what has come to be known as "the problem of evil." Succinctly stated, the problem is: could a world containing evil have been created by an omnipotent, omniscient, omnibenevolent being?

Considering the vast literature devoted to this issue, it is perhaps surprising that there has been little discussion of an analogous issue which might appropriately be referred to as "the problem of goodness." Succinctly stated, the problem is: could a world containing goodness have been created by an omnipotent, omniscient, omnimalevolent being?

This paper has two aims. The first is to provide a reasonable solution to the problem of goodness. Traditional theists, of course, find the hypothesis of creation by a benevolent deity far more plausible than the hypothesis of creation by a malevolent demon, and they may, therefore, believe the problem of goodness to be irrelevant to their commitments. My second aim is to demonstrate that this belief is mistaken.

Before proceeding it would be well to restate the problem of goodness in more formal fashion.

(1) Assume that there exists an omnipotent, omniscient, omnimalevolent Demon who created the world.

(2) If the Demon exists, then there would be no goodness in the world.

(3) But there is goodness in the world.

(4) Therefore, the Demon does not exist.

Since the conclusion of the argument follows from the premisses, those who wish to deny the conclusion must deny one of the premisses. No demonist (the analogue to a theist) would question premiss (1), so in

Reprinted from *Analysis* 37 (1977) by permission of the author.

order to avoid the conclusion of the argument, an attack would have to be launched against either premiss (2) or premiss (3).

What if a demonist attempted to deny premiss (3)? Suppose it were claimed that goodness is an illusion, that there is nothing of this sort in the world. Would this move solve the problem?

I think not, for such a claim is either patently false or else involves a distortion of the usual meaning of the term "good." If the word is being used in its ordinary sense, then acts of kindness, expressions of love, and creations of beauty *are* good. But since obviously such things do occur, there is goodness in the world.

If one insists that such things are not good, then the expression "good" is being used eccentrically, and the claim loses its import. It is as though one were to defend the view that all men are pigs by defining "men" as "omnivorous hoofed mammals of the family Suidae." Such "men" are no men at all, and similarly a supposedly omnimalevolent Demon who cherishes personal affection and great works of art is certainly not omnimalevolent and is probably no demon.

Premiss (3) can thus be adequately defended, and if the demonist is to find an answer to the problem of goodness, he must attack premiss (2). But how can there be goodness in the world if the creator is omnimalevolent and possesses the power and the knowledge to carry out his evil intentions? To paraphrase Epicurus, is the Demon willing to prevent good, but not able? Then he is impotent. Is he able, but not willing? Then he is benevolent. Is he both able and willing? Whence then is goodness?

At this point it may appear to be a hopeless task to justify the Demon's malevolence in the face of the fact of goodness, an enterprise appropriately referred to as "cacodaemony" (the analogue of "theodicy"). But a sophisticated demonist would realize that there is much play left in his position. He would not agree that just because there is goodness in the world, it could not have been created by the omnimalevolent Demon. After all, isn't it possible that whatever goodness exists is logically necessary for this to be the most evil world that the Demon could have created? Not even an omnipotent being can contravene the laws of logic, for such a task is senseless, and so if each and every good in the world were logically tied to the achievement of the greatest evil, the omnimalevolent Demon, in order to bring about the greatest possible evil, would have been forced to allow the existence of these goods.

The demonist thus rejects premiss (2) of the argument and argues instead for premiss (2′):

(2′) If the Demon exists, then every good in the world is logically necessary in order for this to be the most evil world that the Demon could have created.

Now if we substitute premiss (2′) for premiss (2) in the original argument, that argument falls apart, for the conclusion no longer follows from the premisses. One can affirm without contradiction both the existence of an omnipotent, omniscient, omnimalevolent Demon who created the world and the existence of goodness in the world, so long as one also affirms that every good is logically necessary in order for this to be the most evil world the Demon could have created. The demonist thus appears to have escaped the force of the problem of goodness.

But things are not so simple, for now the demonist is faced by yet another argument that challenges his belief.

(1) Assume that there exists an omnipotent, omniscient, omnimalevolent Demon who created the world.

(2) If the Demon exists, then every good in the world is logically necessary in order for this to be the most evil world that the Demon could have created.

(3) But there is strong reason to believe that not every good in the world is logically necessary in order for this to be the most evil world the Demon could have created.

(4) Therefore, there is strong reason to believe that the Demon does not exist.

This second argument, unlike the first, does not claim that belief in the Demon is illogical; rather, it claims that such belief is unreasonable. Beautiful mountain ranges, spectacular sunsets, the plays of Shakespeare, and the quartets of Beethoven do not seem in any way to enhance the evils of the world. Acts of altruism, generosity, and kindheartedness certainly do not appear to increase the world's sinister aspects. In other words, this argument challenges the demonist to suggest plausible reasons for his view that every good in the world makes possible a world containing even greater evils that would be possible without these goods.

The reader will, of course, have observed that thus far the discussion of the problem of goodness exactly parallels traditional discussions of the problem of evil; all the arguments and counterarguments that have been presented are equally applicable *mutatis mutandis* to either problem. What may be somewhat surprising, however, is that classic arguments in defence of the view that every evil in the world makes possible a world containing even greater goods can be exactly paralleled by arguments in defence of the view that every good in the world makes possible a world containing even greater evils. To illustrate this point, I shall proceed to construct a cacodaemony along the identical lines of the well-known theodicy constructed by John Hick.[1]

We begin by dividing all goods into two sorts: moral goods and physi-

1. See his *Philosophy of Religion,* 2nd ed. (Englewood Cliffs, N.J.: Prentice-Hall, Inc., 1973), pp. 36–43.

cal goods. Moral goods are those human beings do for each other; physical goods are those to be found in the human environment.

The justification of moral goods proceeds by logically tying the existence of such goods to man's free will. Surely, performing a bad act freely is more evil than performing such an act involuntarily. The Demon could have ensured that human beings would always perform bad actions, but such actions would not have been free, since the Demon would have ensured their occurrence.[2] And since the actions would not have been free, their performance would not have produced the greatest possible evil, since greater evil can be produced by free persons than by unfree ones. The Demon thus had to provide human beings with freedom, so that they might perform their bad actions voluntarily, thus maximizing evil.

As for the justification of physical goods, we should not suppose that the Demon's purpose in creating the world was to construct a mere chamber of tortures in which the inhabitants would be forced to endure a succession of unrelieved pains. The world can be viewed, instead, as a place of "soul-breaking," in which free human beings, by grappling with the exhausting tasks and challenges of their existence in a common environment, can thereby have their spirits broken and their wills-to-live destroyed.

This conception of the world can be supported by what, following Hick, we may call "the method of negative cacodaemony." Suppose, contrary to fact, that this world were so arranged that nothing could ever go well. No one could help anyone else, no one could perform a courageous act, no one could complete any worthwhile project. Presumably, such a world could be created through innumerable acts of the Demon that would continually alter the laws of nature as necessary.

It is evident that our present ethical concepts would be useless in such a world, for "ought" implies "can," and if no good acts could be performed, it would follow that none ought to be performed. The whole notion of "evil" would seem to drop out, for to understand and recognize evils we must have some idea of goods. Consequently, such a world, however efficiently it might promote pains, would be ill-adapted for the development of the worst qualities of the human personality.

At this point, this cacodaemony, just as Hick's theodicy, points forward in two ways to the subject of life after death. First, although there are many striking instances of evil being brought forth from good through a person's reaction to it (witness the pollution of beautiful lakes or the slashing of great paintings), still there are many other cases in which the opposite has happened. Therefore, it would seem that any demonic purpose of soul-

---

2. I here assume without argument that freedom and determinism are incompatible. Those who believe these two doctrines to be compatible have a far more difficult time resolving the problem of goodness (or the problem of evil).

breaking that is at work in earthly history must continue beyond this life if it is ever to achieve more than a very partial and fragmentary success.

Second, if we ask whether the business of soul-breaking is so evil as to nullify all the goodness to be found in human life, the demonist's answer must be in terms of a future evil great enough to justify all that has happened on the way to it.

Have we now provided an adequate cacodaemony? It is, I think, just as strong as Hick's theodicy, but neither in my view is successful. Nor do I see any plausible ways of strengthening either one. What reason is there to believe in an afterlife of any particular sort? What evidence is there that the world would be either better without the beauty of a sunset or worse without the horrors of bubonic plague? What evidence is there either that the free will of a Socrates achieved greater evil than would have been achieved by his performing wrong actions involuntarily or that the free will of a Hitler achieved greater good than would have been achieved by his performing right actions involuntarily?

The hypothesis that all the good in the world is a necessary part of this worst of all possible worlds is not contradictory; nevertheless, it is highly unlikely. Similarly, the hypothesis that all the evil in the world is a necessary part of this best of all possible worlds is not contradictory; but it too is highly unlikely. But if this is neither the worst of all possible worlds nor the best of all possible worlds, then it could not have been created by either an all-powerful, all-evil demon or an all-powerful, all-good deity. Thus, although the problem of goodness and the problem of evil do not show either demonism or theism to be impossible views, they show them both to be highly improbable. If demonists or theists can produce any other evidence in favour of their positions, they may be able to increase the plausibility of their views, but unless they can produce such evidence, the reasonable conclusion is that neither the Demon nor God exists.

Suffering and Evil

GEORGE N. SCHLESINGER

I

The world is full of suffering. God is either helpless to prevent it, in which case He is not all-powerful, or does not choose to prevent it, in which case He is not all-good. For generations this has been regarded as the most effective argument against the belief that an omnipotent and omnibenevolent being exists. Naturally, theists have tried their hardest to come up with an adequate reply.

Among the numerous suggestions as to how to meet the atheistic challenge we find some that contain important religious ideas yet, unfortunately, do not mitigate the problem. Many of us have heard it said that (1) we must not take for granted all the joy and moral beauty in the world, which by far outstrips the amount of existing pain and moral ugliness; or that (2) all suffering ultimately brings about a greater good and hence is not to be regarded as evil.

There is wisdom in these sayings, but they are irrelevant to the problem of evil. Multiply or divide the amount of pain in the world by a billion, and its incompatibility with divine goodness and omnipotence is not affected. If even a single individual had to endure unnecessarily a slight inconvenience for a brief moment, the problem, although it would not hurt so much or possibly not even be noticed by anyone, would be logically just as real.[1] And without wishing to deny the truth of point (2) or its opti-

---

1. Some people fail to realize this simple truth. There are theologians who have claimed that the unprecedented atrocities of Auschwitz have created insurmountable difficulties for theism, which now needs to be revised radically. Now, admittedly,

Published for the first time.

mistic implication, it cannot contribute anything to the solution of our problem. For we may ask: why did God in His omnipotence not create for us all the benefits referred to in (2) without our having to pay for them first in pain?

Another suggestion, no longer very much discussed, is that suffering is always chastisement for transgressions and hence is well-deserved and does not amount to evil. One of the objections a sceptic may raise against this is: why have opportunities to sin been created? In an attempt to defend himself, the theist might wish to claim that human free will is very precious and that we cannot have it unless people are free to sin. This attempt can be defeated by pointing out that it would be possible to have a world in which there are free agents but no one is punished, for God could have created free agents who He knows prior to their birth will freely refrain from sinning.

Let me very briefly point out that one of the most discussed problems in the philosophy of religion in the last few years has been whether such a world is possible. Some very elaborate arguments have been advanced to show that it is logically impossible for God to create free agents who He can be certain will not sin. These prolonged debates provide striking illustration of the fascination that complex arguments may hold for some philosophers, who debate them with such zest that it never even occurs to them to pause and ask themselves: is there any point to these arguments? Indeed, it seems quite evident that they have no point at all. Suppose we ask: why did we have to have monsters like Hitler or Stalin? The theist would answer, according to the line of thought just reviewed, that God would not have prevented their coming into being unless He had made sure that there were no free agents at all. The creation of free agents inevitably carries the risk of some very wicked people being born.

But the atheist need not trouble himself to examine the soundness of the various arguments leading to this conclusion, since it is in any case of no help to the theist. He can readily grant that since the existence of free agents is an indispensable part of the Divine scheme of things, the birth of some vicious people is unavoidable. Still, a competent psychologist could have determined while Hitler was still an adolescent that he had a nefarious character and would be likely, if given the opportunity, to inflict much pain on others. It is reasonable to maintain that God could do this even earlier. Why then did a benevolent God not liquidate him or render him harmless by any other means at His disposal as soon as the wicked nature of Hitler became evident?

---

the horrors of Auschwitz are unprecedented, but this has no effect on the status of the problem of evil. Either we can show that suffering is not incompatible with divine goodness and, therefore, the problem does not arise in any possible situation, or we cannot, in which case the slightest amount of suffering creates a problem.

It may also be mentioned that the claim that all suffering is punishment for sins runs into another difficulty, since it cannot account for the suffering of innocent babies.

II

In order to gain real insight into the nature of Divine benevolence, we have to start from the beginning and ask: is there indeed evil in the world? Suffering unquestionably exists, but can this be construed as the existence of evil? Before one can answer this question one must assess the moral status of divine acts. It is generally agreed that divine acts are assessed by the same criterion as human acts; otherwise the notions of "good" and "bad" would not retain their normal meanings. What then are evil human acts? As a rule they are acts which contravene moral obligations. This brings us to the question which must be answered first: what are my obligations toward my fellow man? On the surface, it may seem that my obligation toward another is to make him as happy as I can, provided this does not interfere with the welfare of others. Upon reflection, however, this appears inadequate.

Suppose I have under my care a child of very low intelligence but of very happy disposition. Provided his basic bodily needs are minimally taken care of, he enjoys lying on his back all day long and staring into the air. A minor operation, I am assured by the best medical authorities, would spectacularly raise his intelligence and render him capable of creative achievements as well as the appreciation of music, art, literature, and science. Naturally, if his intelligence were raised he would be vulnerable to the frustrations, disappointments, and anxieties most of us are subject to from time to time. Nevertheless, I believe it will be agreed that I should be reprehensible if I refrained from letting the child have the operation, even if I insured to the best of my ability that his physical needs would always be taken care of.

But why is it not good enough that I am keeping him in a state of maximum happiness? Apparently, the degree of desirability of a state is not a simple function of a single factor—namely, the degree to which one's wants are satisfied—but is also dependent on the kind of being one is. The somewhat less happy but intelligent child is ultimately better off than the happy idiot because, although the amount of happiness is less in his case, he is more than compensated for this by having become a preferable kind of person.

Thus, my moral obligations do not consist simply in having to endeavor to raise the amount of happiness a certain being is granted to enjoy. These obligations are somewhat more complex and consist in my having to raise the degree of desirability of his state, a two-valued function depending both on the potentials of the individual and the extent to which his needs are being taken care of. The idea may be illustrated as follows. In recent years much has been heard about machines that electrically stimulate the pleasure centers of one's brain. Once a person's brain is connected to the machine, he becomes completely captivated by the experience it provides and desires absolutely nothing but the passive enjoyment of the sublime pleasures it induces. But I believe that most would condemn me if, without prior consultation, I hooked up A, a normal person, to this machine and thus caused him to become addicted to it for the rest of his life. This would be so even if I provided an attendant to look after A's vital physical needs. I should, I believe, be severely condemned, even though A's addiction has no ill after-effects. But A, previously a normal person, has had his usual ups and downs, while now he is in a continual state of "bliss." Shouldn't I be praised for having eliminated the large gap between his potential and actual amounts of happiness by having satiated him with pleasure?

The answer, I believe, is no, and not merely because I have rendered A a less useful member of society. Even if the needs of others are not taken into account, it will be agreed by most that by inducing in A a permanent state of euphoria I have not done a good thing to him. This is so because I have reduced the desirability of A's state. The latter is not solely a function of how satiated A is with pleasure but also of the kind of being he is. A was, prior to my interference, capable of a great variety of response, of interaction with others, of creativity and self-improvement, while now he is reduced to a completely inactive, vegetable-like existence. The great increase in the factor of happiness is insufficient to make up for the great loss in the second factor, A's being lowered from the state of a normal human being to the state of an inferior quasi-hibernating inert existence.

The general ethical view I am trying to explain, and which is quite widely accepted, is well-reflected in the famous dictum, "Better Socrates dissatisfied than the fool satisfied; better the fool dissatisfied than the pig satisfied." It suggests that given two different creatures A and B, with different capacities and appetites and different potentials for suffering and happiness, it may turn out that although A is satisfied with his lot while B is complaining, B is in a more desirable state than A. Accordingly, one of the universal rules of ethics is not, "if everything else is equal increase the state of happiness of A," but rather, "if everything is equal increase the degree of desirability of the state of A by as much as possible." It may be pointed out that generally I have far more opportunities to affect A's happiness than to affect the other factor which determines the degree of desirability of his state. It should also be noted that it is by no means always clear how much increase in one factor makes up for a given decrease in the other factor.

Now I take it that conceptually there is no limit to the degree which the desirability of state may reach. One can easily conceive a super-Socrates who has a much higher intelligence and many more than five senses through which to enjoy the world and who stands to Socrates as the latter stands to the pig. And there is the possibility of a super-super-Socrates and so on *ad infinitum*. Given this last supposition about an infinite hierarchy of possible beings and hence the limitlessness of the possible increase in the degree of desirability of state, how does the aforementioned universal ethical rule, ". . . increase the degree of desirability of state as much as possible," apply to God? After all, no matter to what degree it is increased it is always logically possible to increase it further. A mortal's possibilities are physically limited, hence in his case there is a natural limit to the principle; but there is no limit to what God can do. It is therefore logically impossible for Him to fulfill the ethical principle, i.e., to do enough to discharge His obligation to do more and further increase the degree of desirability of state. But what is logically impossible to do cannot be done by an omnipotent being either, and it is agreed by practically all philosophers that God's inability to do what is logically impossible does not diminish His omnipotence. Just as it is logically impossible to name the highest integer, it is impossible to grant a creature a degree of desirability of state higher than which is inconceivable; thus it is logically impossible for God to fulfill what is required by the universal ethical principle, and therefore He cannot fulfill it, and so is not obliged to fulfill it. There is no room for complaint, seeing that God has not fulfilled the ethical principle which mortals are bound by and has left His creatures in various low states of desirability. Thus the problem of evil vanishes.

III

The reader may want to raise a number of objections. Let me consider two of these.

Admittedly, it is impossible that the Almighty should place everybody, or for that matter anybody, in a state better than which is inconceivable. Yet He could improve the state of everybody and make it better than it is now. The problem of evil may thus be stated not as the problem of why things are not so good that they could not be better, but why things are not better than they actually are.

The answer is that one is justified in complaining about an existing state of affairs only if what one is complaining about is not logically inherent in every state of affairs, that is, if the situation could be changed into another in which the reason for complaint would be removed. If, however, it is clear now that no matter what changes are introduced, in any new situation there is exactly as much reason to complain as before, then there is no right to demand that the old situation be replaced by another. In our case it is clear that, no matter by how much the degree of desirability of the state of an individual be increased, it would still be just as short as it is now of being so large that larger it could not be. Therefore, in any improved situation, there is objectively as much reason for complaint as in the present situation. So while the situation of creatures could be so changed as to make them cease to complain, nothing could be done to mitigate the objective situation and remove the objective grounds on which to complain, namely, that things are less good than they could be. The reason for this complaint remains constant through all changes; there is, therefore, no objective justification for demanding any changes.

Another objection a sceptic might want to raise is that while nobody can reach the logical limit of happiness, there seem to be no conceptual obstacles against at least eliminating all possible misery. He could therefore challenge the theist and say that if God were good, then at least He should not have permitted any creature, however exalted or humble its kind, to be positively distressed at any time.

But once we have agreed on the reasonableness of the value judgment expounded in the previous section, it necessarily follows that it is possible for A to be really much better off than B even though A is dissatisfied and B satisfied. For A, who may be deficient in one of the ingredients that contribute to the desirability of his condition—namely in happiness, may have been more than sufficiently compensated by having been granted the other ingredient in abundance, i.e., by having been allotted a much higher rank in the hierarchy of beings. Thus we can see the absurdity of the sceptic's position. Confronted with B, he sees no grounds to question Divine goodness, since B does not suffer. But should God *improve* B's lot and raise the degree of the desirability of his state to be equal to that of A, this he would regard as evil!

I shall not discuss here any more objections[2] but point out that it is not surprising that upon hearing my solution for the first time the reader should feel a certain amount of uneasiness. This is to a certain degree due to the fact that it seems paradoxical that an omnipotent being is capable of doing less than a human being, that is, that the former cannot, while the latter can, follow the important ethical rule to increase everybody's degree of desirability of state to the utmost of one's ability. In fact, however, this should not look so strange when we remember that it is also true that an omnipotent being, unlike a human being, is incapable of putting together a weight which he cannot lift.

Another source of dissatisfaction may be the fact that my solution of-

2. I discuss ten objections in chapter 10 of my *Religion and Scientific Method* (D. Reidel, 1977).

fers no solace for another one's grief. Indeed, it would be most callous of me to tell a victim of a series of disasters, "You have no grounds for lamentation. Even if nothing unpleasant had ever happened, in which case you would not be complaining, objectively speaking you would still be as far from having the maximum degree of desirability of state as you are now. So what is the point of your complaints?" It must, however, be realized that the important psychological task of providing comfort for the sufferer and the logical task of demonstrating the failure of the alleged proof of the inconsistency of theism are two different tasks. It may well be that the first task is more urgently needed. Still, defending theism against the attempt to dismiss it as incoherent has value of its own.

God and Forgiveness

ANNE C. MINAS

To err is human, to forgive, divine. Most of us tend to believe this whether or not we also believe in the actual existence of a divine being. The non-believer reasons that if there were such a being he would forgive the wrong-doings of mortals, and insofar as he himself exercises forgiveness his nature approaches that which believers attribute to a deity. There is supposed to be something about being divine that makes a deity especially capable of exercising forgiveness; and, conversely, it is human frailty which prevents us from this exercise on occasions when we ought to forgive.

This belief in a connection between forgiving and being divine I want to show is mistaken, in a radical way. Far from its being the case that divine nature makes its possessor especially prone to forgive, such a nature makes forgiveness impossible. Such a being logically cannot forgive, since possession of divine attributes logically precludes conditions which are necessary for forgiveness. So, far from its being the case that human frailty makes forgiveness difficult or impossible, it is the possession of distinctly human, non-divine characteristics, that makes forgiveness appropriate for human beings. Only a human being can forgive—a divine being cannot.

In my discussion, I shall be assuming mainly that a divine being (if there is one) is perfect. He has a perfect moral sense, a perfect moral will, perfect knowledge, and perfect benevolence. I shall try not to make too many assumptions about the nature of forgiveness. The definitions given in the *Oxford English Dictionary* and the uses made of the word "forgiveness" are varied enough to rule out any assumption that forgiveness amounts to one kind of thing in all circumstances. So I shall instead take up various

Reprinted from *The Philosophical Quarterly* 25 (1975) by permission of *The Philosophical Quarterly* and the author.

kinds of actions forgiveness is, or might be, and show that not one of them is an action that could be performed by a perfect being.

I

The *OED* in some of its definitions of "forgive" directs forgiveness upon actions that are wrong. Part of definition 3 of "forgive" is "to give up resentment or claim to requital for, pardon (an offence)." In this connection it mentions Hobbes' writing on "An Authority to Forgive, or Retain Sins," in *Leviathan* (III xlii 274); and *Isaiah* xxxiii 24, about forgiving iniquities. So let us suppose that forgiveness of one kind involves the forgiver's believing that the person forgiven has done something wrong and that it is this wrong action that the forgiveness is being directed upon.

Forgiveness of this sort may simply be retraction or modification of a previous adverse moral judgment about the act in question. The eloping couple might be forgiven in this way by their parents. The parents, in their shock and dismay when first hearing the news, censure the action harshly. Later, however, they realize that their judgment about the elopement was too severe and so they modify or abandon it, and so forgive the couple.

Now with human beings this reversal or modification of moral judgment is sometimes laudable, sometimes not. It depends on whether the original judgment was correct, or whether the person who made the judgment had good reason to believe it correct. If the parents changed their minds about the elopement, that would probably be laudable, since presumably elopement is not wrong (or not *very* wrong) and the parents had no good reason to think it was. But suppose a son had asked his parents to reverse their censure of his having murdered his sister. There would be no cause to praise them if they somehow deluded themselves into believing that the son had not done anything really wrong. They would then apparently have lost all sense of right and wrong, at least as regards their son, not to mention any special feelings they might have had about this particular victim, their daughter. Forgiveness, in the sense of reversal of moral judgment, is not always in order for human beings.

But when it is a deity considering an action, reversal of moral judgment is never in order. When contradictory judgments are made about the same action, one of them is wrong, and a being with a perfect moral sense cannot (logically cannot) make wrong moral judgments. If he was right in his second appraisal of the situation, he was wrong in his first and vice versa. And this is quite aside from the difficulty of how a being who is not in time can reverse his judgments, having no time in which to do so.

The situation is not appreciably changed if forgiveness, in the sense of reversal of judgment, is granted because new facts have come to light which

should affect an assessment of the situation. One human being may be forgiven by another for this reason. "I didn't understand the situation fully,"
the forgiver says. "At first I could see no reason for your firing Smith. But
since then I have learned he has had his hand in the till, and has been ma-
licious towards his subordinates, etc. I now see you were quite right in letting him go." It is fine for a human being to make a new assessment of an
action when new facts come to light. It is impossible for an omniscient
deity, however, because, being omniscient, he always knows all the facts.
For him, there can be no such thing as learning something new. And, of
course, for such a being there can be no such thing as a temporary lapse of
consciousness where he overlooks, or temporarily fails to remember, a relevant fact. So such things cannot be reasons for reversal of judgment in a
deity, although they certainly can be for us. For this reason it is a little
hard to see how some one can argue with a deity that he or someone else
ought to be forgiven, by trying to bring certain facts to his attention. One
of the last things Jesus said was "Father, forgive them, for they know not
what they do." But how could Jesus have been trying to draw a certain
fact to God's attention when God, being (as we sometimes say) omnipercipient, must have all facts in his attention all the time? He is also supposed to show perfect moral judgment in weighing facts, so it is equally
insulting or, more accurately, blasphemous, to try to argue with God that
a fact should have a particular moral-weight in his consideration.

Sometimes it is thought that people ought to be forgiven for doing
wrong for special considerations pertaining to their case. Such considerations include the motives of the agent (he stole the loaf of bread to feed
his starving children), or special difficulties in which he found himself (he
shot the burglar in self-defence), or any other special characteristics of the
action (he went through the red light at 4 a.m. when the streets were virtually deserted). According to the rule (moral, legal, or whatever) he did
something wrong, but the wrongness seems to be mitigated by special circumstances. But in cases like these, the fact of the matter is that the rule
is too crude, or too general, to take the special circumstances into account.
What someone who appeals to mitigating circumstances is arguing is that
while the action is wrong according to the rule, it is not wrong (or not as
wrong) in a more general, all things considered, sort of way. Forgiveness
in this sense is really a kind of moral judgment; a recognition that the rule
has only limited application to the assessment and that other factors must
also be taken into account.

It is very difficult to see how God could make this kind of judgment,
for what would the defective rule be for him? It could hardly be one of his
own, one of the rules which he makes to define right and wrong (if this is
indeed what he does) for why should he make a defective one? His only
motivation, as far as I can see, would be considerations of simplicity and

ease of understanding for human beings. This, however, would only function as a reason for giving human beings defective rules, and not for using them himself. Complexities being no problem for a perfectly omniscient being, he would, if he used rules at all to make moral assessments, use ones which had the degree of complexity necessary to take into account *all* morally relevant factors in a situation to be judged. Our rules would only be crude approximations to these perfectly accurate divine rules, and thus while it might appear to us as if God is making an exception to his own rules (not judging an action wrong which is wrong by our crude rules) this appearance would be delusory.

Finally, a human being may *condone* offences by others, meaning, according to *OED*, "to forgive or overlook (an offence) so as to treat it as non-existent." This is especially appropriate with minor wrongdoings. For I take it that the idea of condoning is that of refusing to form an adverse moral judgment of an action, even though there may be some reason to do so. One overlooks, refuses to take account of, the immoral aspects of an action. Essentially, it is making an exception for a particular case for no reason. If this is a kind of forgiveness, as the definition suggests, it is again difficult to see how it is something a divine being can do. Being omniscient, he knows everything there is to be known, and is not able to overlook it, in the sense of refusing to know it. So in particular, he cannot do this with moral aspects of an action. In addition, condoning may show a certain lack of moral sense and so there is a second reason why a deity cannot do it. This is most clear when the immoral aspects are fairly substantial. Someone who condones mass murders shows a significant moral blindness, to say the least.

II

Reversing moral judgments, exhibiting moral blindness, and making exceptions to moral rules being impossible for perfect beings, it is time to consider other types of actions which might merit the name "forgiveness." In the passage quoted earlier, the *OED* mentioned giving up a claim to requital for an offence. When requital or punishment is remitted or reduced because of a new, more favourable judgment about the moral aspects of the case, then such cases become instances of the kinds discussed in the first part of this paper. This includes cases where special circumstances merit a special kind of judgment about the action. These are simply ways of forming judgments where all relevant circumstances are considered.[1]

1. Alwynne Smart makes essentially this point in connection with mercy ("Mercy," in *The Philosophical Quarterly*, 17 (1967), 345–59). She argues that remission or modification of punishment in the light of special circumstances surrounding the crime is not a genuine exercise of mercy, but making a judgment about the appropriate punishment taking *all* relevant considerations into account.

But there are also cases where punishment is remitted without reversing or modifying a judgment about the wrongdoing the punishment was supposed to be punishment for. This kind of forgiveness is akin to clemency exercised by a judge in the courts, or pardon by a high official. Someone who is in a position to mete out punishment for a wrongdoing decides to give less punishment than what is called for by the nature of the wrongdoing, or no punishment at all.

It is easy to envisage the deity in the role of a judge who makes decisions about punishments and rewards. For it is he who decides the lots of humans in life after death and these lots are often conceived of as rewards or punishments. People who are good or bad in this life get good or bad lots, respectively, in the afterlife. In addition, it is often thought that virtue is rewarded and vice punished by the deity in this life. Misfortunes, for instance, are sometimes thought of as being sent by God as a punishment for wrongdoing.

What is not so easy to envisage, however, is how a perfectly just God can remit punishment. In the first place, what would be the mechanism by which the punishment was originally assigned which was then remitted by God? With human beings the assignment and remission typically is done by two separate agencies, the remitting agency taking precedence over the assigning one. A judge (the remitter) gives a lighter punishment than that prescribed by law (the assigner). Or a high political official, a governor, say, remits a punishment assigned by the courts. But who or what assigns punishments which God then remits? God himself? He then appears to be something of a practical joker, assigning punishments which he, with perfect foreknowledge, knows he is going to remit, perhaps doing this to scare some virtue into sinners. If not he but his laws assign the original punishment, essentially the same problem arises, namely why God makes laws that he knows he is going to override.

Other problems would appear here as well. One concerns the question of whether the punishment over which the sinner is being forgiven by God was what the sinner justly deserved. If it was, then in remitting him this punishment God is not giving the sinner what he deserves, and thus not behaving in a way consistent with his being a perfectly just being. If, on the other hand, the sinner did not deserve the punishment, then it was an unjust mechanism which assigned such punishment. If this mechanism were God's laws or decrees, then once again he would not be a perfectly just being, although he certainly would be more just in remitting one of his own unjust sentences than in letting it stand. If the mechanism assigning the punishment were, on the other hand, a human one, it is difficult to see why God should pay any attention to it. Ignoring this punishment would be a much more appropriate attitude than remitting it.

Another problem has to do with God's absolving only some sinners from their punishments. For either God forgives everyone or he does not. If he only forgives some people, and not others, then he might be behaving unjustly towards those whose punishment he allows to stand. If he picks out people to forgive for no special reason, then he is acting arbitrarily and immorally. A just God does not play favourites with rewards and punishments.

So is there a reason God might have for remitting punishment in some cases but not in others? We have been assuming that these are all cases where God does not reverse his moral condemnation of the actions, so this cannot be a reason. But one reason that is often cited is repentance on the part of the sinner. This repentance would be an overt expression of the agent's realization of having done wrong, his having the appropriate feelings about his actions, and his resolve not to repeat them. So in asking for forgiveness with this attitude, the penitent is not asking God for a new judgment on his actions—as noted earlier, this smacks of blasphemy—but rather a new and more favourable judgment on *him,* as an agent. He is not the wrongdoer he once was, but has a new, reformed, character.

We, as human beings, revise our judgments about people's characters in the light of evidence that they are repentant about their past misdeeds. But for an omniscient being, such revision would not be possible. In his omniscience, God would be able to foreknow the repentance of the agent; therefore he need not make, and could not have made, a judgment about the agent's character which did not take this act of repentance into account. It is difficult to see, moreover, why God should count the end of the agent's life, the post-repentance period, more heavily than the beginning in his final assessment of the agent's character. Because God is omniscient and outside time, all parts of a human life are known to him in exactly the same way, known to him much as a number series is known to us. We do not attach any special significance to the later numbers in the series just because they are later, nor do we believe they are better representatives of the series. Similarly God should not regard an agent's later character as the best representative of his total character.

We, on the other hand, do attach special significance to an agent's later character, for at least two reasons. One is that it is the man's most recent character with which we are (presently) confronted, and with which we have to deal. And the other is that insofar as we need, or want to make, predictions about his future character, the most recent evidence will tend to be the most reliable. These two reasons have importance in a utilitarian justification of infliction or withholding of punishment. The utilitarian treats punishment as a method for obtaining good results, one of the foremost being improvement of the agent's character, behaviour and motivation. Punishment is only justified to the extent it is effective in these areas. So a utilitarian would not be able to derive this kind of justification when he is considering punishing an already reformed character. The effect already having been gained, the punishment is superfluous as a method, and hence unjustified.

A utilitarian can thus consider withholding or remitting punishment for repentant, reformed agents. Now the question is, can God be such a utilitarian, consistently with his perfection, and thus exercise forgiveness in this particular way? He would be a God who uses threats and bribes to get people to behave themselves, threatening them with punishment if they misbehave, bribing them with forgiveness, remission of punishment, if they decide to behave.

It seems to me that this portrayal of God the manipulator is inconsistent with the image of divine perfection. There must be better, fairer, and more effective ways to instil into human beings a sense of right and wrong and a will to do the right. Moreover, the whole exercise of threats and bribes would presumably become inoperative at the end of an individual's life. Since he has no more opportunities to choose the wrong, there is no longer a utilitarian reason for punishing him as a threat. To condemn him to the eternal flames just as an example to mortals still on earth is not, I think, something that a just God could contemplate, particularly since these mortals seem to have no good way of knowing who has been condemned and who has not. So everyone would have to have his punishment remitted at the end of this life, i.e., everyone would have to be forgiven, a possibility that was mentioned, but not discussed, a little earlier. But then the whole activity of threats and bribes during an individual's life becomes meaningless, a little game God plays with us where everything comes out all right in the end anyway. The juiciest rewards and the most terrible punishments he can mete out would be those in the after-life, and it is just these that he can have no utilitarian reasons for conferring.

Nor, I believe, can God remit punishment for a repentant sinner for non-utilitarian reasons, as has already been noted, although he must take reformed periods of the agent's life into account in making his judgment. But to weigh (in some non-utilitarian way) the amount of punishment, if any, due to a repentant character and give him just that much would be to disregard the pre-repentance period of the agent's life and this, I have argued, a just omniscient god could not do. Far from having the special significance which they are sometimes thought to have, death-bed confessions and pleas for forgiveness would be pretty useless. If the agent spent ten minutes of his life reformed, and seventy years of his life unreformed, the seventy years should count much more heavily when God is considering what kinds of punishment to mete out.

III

The kinds of forgiveness so far considered have been essentially ones involving either a reversal of moral judgment on the actions forgiven or a
reversal of judgment about punishing the agent. It may be felt that the
discussion so far has missed the most central kinds of forgiveness, those, for
instance, fitting this definition in the OED: "4. To give up resentment
against, pardon (an offender)." Although pardoning an offender may mean
remission of punishment, which I have already discussed, giving up resentment seems to be something different. Resentment being a kind of feeling
or attitude, to give it up would be to change a feeling or attitude. This
would not necessarily involve reversing a judgment. The change may be
partly, or even wholly, non-cognitive.

Joseph Butler devotes two sermons to a discussion of resentment and
forgiveness, viewing forgiveness as an avoidance of the abuses of resentment. He defines resentment thus: "the natural object or occasion of settled resentment then being injury as distinct from pain or loss . . . but
from this [sudden anger], deliberate anger or resentment is essentially distinguished, as the latter is not naturally excited by, or intended to prevent
mere harm without the appearance of wrong or injustice."[2] Resentment is
a moral feeling or attitude whose object must be an action believed wrong
or unjust, and not just any harm. Giving up of resentment might then
mean giving up or reversing the belief that the action was wrong, as discussed in Part I of this paper; or it might mean merely giving up part or
all of an accompanying feeling or attitude toward the action, while retain-
ing the belief that it was wrong. It is forgiveness of this second sort that I
want now to discuss.

Such seems to be the case of the forgiving father of the Prodigal Son.
Presumably the father did not reverse his judgment of the son's prodigality,
deciding that the son's actions were not so bad after all. Rather, it was in
spite of this judgment that he was able to forgive him.

Something of this sort seems to be the kind of forgiveness Butler urges.
He does not think we ought to reverse our moral judgments about those
who have wronged us (except in instances where the evidence warrants it).
Nor does he recommend giving up what he calls "a due, natural sense of
the injury." Some moral attitudes and feelings toward a wrongdoing may
be appropriate to retain in forgiveness. What has to be given up, according
to Butler, seems to be what we might call taking the wrongdoing personally.
For to forgive, according to him, is just "to be affected towards the injurious

2. Joseph Butler, Fifteen Sermons Preached at the Rolls Chapel (London, 1967),
pp. 125 ff.

person in the same way any good men, uninterested in the case, would be, if they had the same just sense, which we have supposed the injured person to have, of the fault, after which there will yet remain real goodwill towards the offender."[3] To forgive is just to cease to have any personal interest in the injury. It is to regard it as if it had happened to someone else in whom we have no special interest, other than the general interest we have in all human beings. So the father might forgive his prodigal son by ceasing to take the son's prodigality personally. He regards it no longer as a wasting of *his* money, as something *his* son has done to *him,* but instead as a mere wasting of someone's good money.

How and why can this change in feeling happen? One suggestion is that the personal feelings are gradually forgotten, or wear off in some natural manner. "Forgive and forget" is what is sometimes said, and one possibility is that forgiving is forgetting. It could be argued that personal feelings only last naturally for so long and then wear off, unless the person makes a determined effort to retain or renew them, or as Butler puts it, "resentment has taken possession of the temper and will not quit its hold," suggesting that the mechanism by which this happens is "bare obstinacy."[4]

This may be true of human beings, but it cannot be true of God, and thus this kind of forgiveness is not open to him to exercise. An omniscient being cannot (logically) forget anything, so cannot in particular forget his feelings. And all his feelings are equally alive to him at all times, this being, I think, part of what is meant in calling him omnipercipient. In perceiving situations, he knows them in a way in which they are fully real to him, meaning that he reacts not just by forming judgments, but also with all appropriate feelings. Then, to be omnipercipient is to have all reactions to all situations equally vivid, regardless of when they happened. So the reactions of omnipercipient beings cannot change over time. So even if God were subject to change, and this change could take place in time (even though he is supposed to exist outside time) he would not be able to change in this particular way, since this change involves a dimming of feeling.

Let us then consider a different kind of situation where resentment, in the sense of taking an injury personally, is dispelled, not through forgetting or some other kind of natural erosion, but as a result of conscious effort on the part of the forgiver. What reasons would he have for making this kind of effort?

When an injury is taken personally, the result is a certain breach between the injured person and the person who has injured him. This breach is not wholly due to the nature of the injury, nor to the injured person's re-

3. Butler, op. cit., p. 143.
4. Butler, op. cit., p. 129 ff.

actions by way of judgment or sense of wrongness of the action. Other people could have these same reactions without such a breach occurring. Friends of the father of the Prodigal Son could agree with him in his judgments of the son's behaviour and could react with moral indignation at the son's waste without such reactions causing estrangement from the son. They have not themselves been injured, so there is no reason to take the prodigality personally. And also their relations with the boy are not such as to be affected by resentment in the way the father's are, since he is much more involved with the boy. This involvement, I think, also makes it more important for the father that this breach should be healed.

The father's motivation for forgiveness is thus to heal the breach, and this breach presumably is virtually intolerable because of his relationship with the boy. His involvement in and regard for the relationship require that he should not spoil it by feelings of personal injury.[5] Abandoning his feelings of personal injury is also required by a regard for the injuring party as a human being. Presumably more things should be taken into account in forming an attitude toward him than the injury he has caused. The trouble with a sense of personal injury is that it tends to swamp other considerations in the formation of attitudes. The person tends to be seen just as the agent of the injury and nothing else.

A final reason for trying to get rid of feelings of personal injury as soon as possible is that harbouring such feelings tends to be bad for the person who refuses to forgive. At least, this is what the psychologists tell us—that it is unhealthy to harbour and brood over personal resentments.

A change in attitude becomes particularly appropriate when the offender repents, shows remorse for his wrong-doing.[6] If the remorse is genuine he has dissociated himself from the wrong-doing in the sense that if he had it to do over again he would refrain, and he censures himself for having done it in the same way as if the agent had been someone else. So, since he is no longer the kind of person who would commit such an injury, an attitude that presupposes that he is such a person is inappropriate. And a sense of personal injury is, I think, just such an attitude since it is an attitude toward a person as the agent of a certain deed. Repentance as an overt sign of remorse makes such a difference in forgiveness (as an abandonment of a sense of personal injury) that it is sometimes difficult to see

5. Thus R. S. Downic argues ("Forgiveness," in *The Philosophical Quarterly*, 15 (1965), 128–34) that an injury severs the relationship of *agape* with the person injured, forgiveness restores it.

6. In fact, Strawson makes repentance, in the sense of repudiation of the injury, a necessary condition for forgiveness (P. F. Strawson, "Freedom and Resentment," in *Studies in the Philosophy of Thought and Action*, ed. Strawson [Oxford, 1968]) since he defines forgiveness thus: "and to forgive is to accept the repudiation and to forswear the resentment." In this paper Strawson makes a number of interesting comments about resentment, too many for me to discuss here.

how forgiveness can take place without it. The parent who is willing to forgive a child anything, despite the fact that the child shows absolutely no signs of remorse, can be regarded as indulgent at best, and, at worst, as lacking a certain sense of appropriateness in his/her relations with the child. Too much of a readiness to forgive without repentance indicates a certain lack of awareness of personal injury, which in turn indicates a general lack of awareness in personal relations. Or sometimes the injuries are so great that the person really has no redeeming features which will outbalance them. Take the operators of the furnaces at Buchenwald, for example: if they are unrepentant what possible reasons could we have for forgiving them? In the absence of remorse there may not be any basis for realigning one's attitude toward the offender. The best one can do is just forget about him, taking the method of forgiveness I previously suggested.

Now, how could God figure in this kind of forgiveness? Since it presupposes a sense of taking an injury personally (it is this attitude that is remitted in forgiveness) it is very difficult to see how God could forgive in this way. For I think it is fairly clear that taking an injury personally, as opposed to having a general sense of its wrongness, is a distinctly human failing, an imperfection. Try to imagine a god sulking or brooding, perhaps plotting revenge because someone has, say, made off with the treasure in one of his churches, and you have imagined a less than perfect being. The Olympian gods and goddesses were noted for their pettiness in their relations with each other, with regard to injuries, real or imagined, and this is one good reason why they were not and are not regarded as perfect. A god whose perspective of another god or a person is distorted by a sense of personal injury—I argued earlier that this was an accompaniment of, if not part of, resentment and so was one reason for human forgiveness, getting rid of this attitude—is at the very least not omnipercipient, and probably also not just in his assessment of the human being who committed the injury. Relations with the injuring party are also severed, I maintained, by this attitude, and surely a perfect being could not allow this to happen. And the third reason for our getting rid of feelings of personal injury also serves as a reason for God's not having them at all. They are detrimental to one's psychological wellbeing, and in extreme cases make a person a candidate for the psychiatrist's couch. This sort of thing obviously cannot (logically) happen to a perfect being.

God, then, cannot forgive personal injuries where what is given up is personal resentment (OED—for "forgive"—"1. To give up, cease to harbour (resentment, wrath)") since he cannot have such feelings. But, it is sometimes said, God forgives us before we ask for forgiveness, sometimes even before we do wrong. Such a line of thinking perhaps would mean that God forgives before he resents, gives up the resentment before he has it, thus skipping the resentment phase of the process. More simply, he decides, wills not to harbour resentment. But the problem here is whether it makes any sense to make decisions where there is only one logically possible alternative. It is a little peculiar for me to make a decision about whether I am going to be the number 2, since I have only one alternative which is logically possible, and that is not to be the number 2. God presumably is in the same position with regard to harbouring resentment. Only the alternative of not harbouring it is logically open to him.

It is, however, sometimes maintained that God has all his perfections because he wills to have them, and so has made a meaningful decision in choosing them. If this is true, it would apply to a decision not (ever) to harbour resentment. But I think there are nonetheless good reasons not to count this as real forgiveness, since forgiveness has to be a giving up of something, and no one can give up something he never had. It would be as if I decided as a New Year's resolution to give up gambling, when I had never gambled. Also, repentance and remorse would lose their connection with God's forgiveness. Since he harbours no resentment anyway, there would be no point in setting matters straight by repenting. The only likely function repentance could have, in restoring a relationship with God which had been severed by a misdeed, would be if the injury made some change in the *sinner's* attitude toward God which had severed the relationship, and if this attitude could be changed back by repentance. This may well happen (although I cannot understand just how the mechanism would work), but it is clearly not a case of God's forgiving, since it is not a case of God's doing anything. Everything that is done is done by the sinner, and it is in him that the changes take place.

IV

It is, moreover, only harm, or supposed harm, to himself that a person can take personally. Even if others are harmed as well, it is only the concomitant, or resultant, harm to oneself that causes feelings of personal resentment. If a son takes insults about his parents personally, for instance, this is because he believes that, when they are insulted, he is as well. Thus, forgiveness as a ceasing to hold personal resentment can only be directed toward actions which have wronged the forgiver (or which he believes have wronged him). And I think this is true of any kind of forgiveness—it is appropriately directed only toward actions which have wronged the forgiver. It would be a bit high-handed of me, for instance, to forgive someone else's husband's excessive drinking and womanizings when his wife felt not the least inclined in that direction—high-handed because I would have to construe his behaviour as wronging me rather than her. Only in certain restricted cases can one person forgive wrongs to another by proxy, as it were. Typically this happens only when the forgiver bears a special relationship to the wronged person and the wronged person is dead. I could, for instance, conceivably forgive a wrong done to one of my dead ancestors if my relationship to him/her were such that if I were not to forgive the action, it would never be forgiven.

The implications here for God are that he can only forgive wrongs, sins, that are injuries to him. If he has universal powers of forgiveness, for all sins, sins must all have this characteristic.

Several problems arise immediately. One is how it is possible to wrong, to injure, a perfect being. His very perfection should make him immune from the kind of injury which makes forgiveness appropriate. The other problem is how even an imperfect being could construe as primarily wrongs to himself actions which seem mainly to harm someone else. On such a construction the person stolen from, raped, injured, killed, enslaved, is not really wronged at all, or at least the injury done him is rather minimal compared to that done to God by breaking his laws, contravening his wishes, or whatever. But this would have to be true if God is to forgive these actions, and especially if he is to forgive them independently of whether they have been forgiven by the ostensible injured party. To give God the first or primary right to forgive is to view him as the primary injured party.

Finally, I want to mention a kind of forgiveness which God alone is supposed to be able to exercise, which is associated with the washing away of one's sins. The idea, as nearly as I have been able to make out, is that before God forgives there are a certain number of wrongs which the person committed. Afterwards there are none. He did the actions all right, but after God's forgiveness, they are no longer wrong.

This is a little like a child's plea that a parent make things all right. The child imagines that rightness and wrongness depend wholly on the parent's say-so. So an action, or anything, might be changed from wrong to right, while remaining otherwise unchanged, because the parent first said it was wrong and then later says it is right. I think we sometimes expect God to set things right in the same way and we call this "forgiveness."

But much as we would like sometimes to retreat into these childhood fancies where God as parent makes things all right by some kind of magic, I think they embody too many confusions to make them worth considering. The first is the idea that the rightness or wrongness of an action can change without anything else about it changing. And another is the dependence of right or wrong on God's say-so. For in a situation like the ones being described it is not as if God gave us general precepts by which to live and they were right because they were expressions of the will of God. Many people have objections to the view that God's will has anything to do with right or wrong. But quite aside from these general objections, there is the problem that a god like the one being described does not impart to his decrees any generality. He literally changes wrong to right from one day to the next. This absence of generality, I think, disqualifies these change-able decrees from being *ethical* precepts. It also gives human beings con-siderable motivation for disobedience to God's will. If there is no telling how God is going to regard an action from one day to the next, then some-one might want to take his chances on disobedience, figuring that what contravenes God's will one day will be favourably regarded the next.

With some actions, a necessary condition for their being wrong is an unfavourable reaction by someone affected by the action. So if the person ceases to show the reaction, the action is no longer wrong. The person to whom a promise is made can make a broken promise cease to be wrong by welcoming the fact that it was broken. The masochist, by welcoming in-juries to himself, makes them cease to be injuries. Thus, if (1) all wrongs are injuries to God only and (2) they are the kind of wrongs which God eventually shows a favourable reaction to, God might be able to set all wrongs right.

I have already commented on (1) above, maintaining that it is very difficult to take the point of view that God is always the only one injured in a wrong-doing. (2), I think, is even more absurd. How could a morally sensitive and just God welcome human beings torturing, maiming, killing and causing suffering to one another?

So we cannot without logical and/or moral absurdity say of a fully di-vine being that it forgives in any sense I have been able to give to "for-give." Whether this is because divine forgiveness is beyond the scope of human understanding is another question, not the concern of this paper. I have only tried to show that divine forgiveness does appear absurd to the human understanding, or at least to mine.

Omnipotence

PETER GEACH

It is fortunate for my purposes that English has the two words "almighty"
and "omnipotent," and that apart from any stipulation by me the words
have rather different associations and suggestions. "Almighty" is the familiar word that comes in the creeds of the Church; "omnipotent" is at home
rather in formal theological discussions and controversies, e.g. about miracles and about the problem of evil. "Almighty" derives by way of Latin
"omnipotens" from the Greek word *"pantokratōr"*; and both this Greek
word, like the more classical *"pankratēs,"* and "almighty" itself suggest
God's having power *over* all things. On the other hand the English word
"omnipotent" would ordinarily be taken to imply ability to *do* everything;
the Latin word "omnipotens" also predominantly has this meaning in
Scholastic writers, even though in origin it is a Latinization of *"pantocra-
tōr."* So there already is a tendency to distinguish the two words; and in
this paper I shall make the distinction a strict one. I shall use the word
"almighty" to express God's power over all things, and I shall take "omnipotence" to mean ability to do everything.

I think we can in a measure understand what God's almightiness implies, and I shall argue that almightiness so understood must be ascribed
to God if we are to retain anything like traditional Christian belief in God.
The position as regards omnipotence, or as regards the statement "God can
do everything," seems to me to be very different. Of course even "God
can do everything" may be understood simply as a way of magnifying
God by contrast with the impotence of man. McTaggart described it as "a
piece of theological etiquette" to call God omnipotent: Thomas Hobbes,

Reprinted from *Philosophy* 48 (1973) by permission of Cambridge University Press.
© The Royal Institute of Philosophy 1973.

out of reverence for his Maker, would rather say that "omnipotent" is an attribute of honour. But McTaggart and Hobbes would agree that "God is omnipotent" or "God can do everything" is not to be treated as a proposition that can figure as premise or conclusion in a serious theological argument. And I too wish to say this. I have no objection to such ways of speaking if they merely express a desire to give the best honour we can to God our Maker, whose Name only is excellent and whose praise is above heaven and earth. But theologians have tried to prove that God can do everything, or to derive conclusions from this thesis as a premise. I think such attempts have been wholly unsuccessful. When people have tried to read into "God can do everything" a signification not of Pious Intention but of Philosophical Truth, they have only landed themselves in intractable problems and hopeless confusions; no graspable sense has ever been given to this sentence that did not lead to self-contradiction or at least to conclusions manifestly untenable from a Christian point of view.

I shall return to this; but I must first develop what I have to say about God's almightiness, or power over all things. God is not just more powerful than any creature; no creature can compete with God in power, even unsuccessfully. For God is also the source of all power; any power a creature has comes from God and is maintained only for such time as God wills. Nebuchadnezzar submitted to praise and adore the God of heaven because he was forced by experience to realize that only by God's favour did his wits hold together from one end of a blasphemous sentence to the other end. Nobody can deceive God or circumvent him or frustrate him; and there is no question of God's trying to do anything and failing. In Heaven and on Earth, God does whatever he will. We shall see that some propositions of the form "God cannot do so-and-so" have to be accepted as true; but what God cannot be said to be able to do he likewise cannot will to do; we cannot drive a logical wedge between his power and his will, which are, as the Scholastics said, really identical, and there is no application to God of the concept of trying but failing.

I shall not spend time on citations of Scripture and tradition to show that this doctrine of God's almightiness is authentically Christian; nor shall I here develop rational grounds for believing it is a true doctrine. But it is quite easy to show that this doctrine is indispensable for Christianity, not a bit of old metaphysical luggage that can be abandoned with relief. For Christianity requires an absolute faith in the promises of God: specifically, faith in the promise that some day the whole human race will be delivered and blessed by the establishment of the Kingdom of God. If God were not almighty, he might will and not do; sincerely promise, but find fulfilment beyond his power. Men might prove untamable and incorrigible, and might kill themselves through war or pollution before God's salvific plan for them could come into force. It is useless to say that after the end of this earthly life men would live again; for as I have argued elsewhere, only the promise of God can give us any confidence that there will be an after-life for men, and if God were not almighty, this promise too might fail. If God is true and just and unchangeable and almighty, we can have abso-lute confidence in his promises: otherwise we cannot—and there would be an end of Christianity.

A Christian must therefore believe that God is almighty; but he need not believe that God can do everything. Indeed, the very argument I have just used shows that a Christian must not believe that God can do every-thing: for he may not believe that God could possibly break his own word. Nor can a Christian even believe that God can do everything that is logi-cally possible; for breaking one's word is certainly a logically possible feat.

It seems to me, therefore, that the tangles in which people have en-meshed themselves when trying to give the expression "God can do every-thing" an intelligible and acceptable content are tangles that a Christian believer has no need to enmesh himself in; the spectacle of others en-meshed may sadden him, but need not cause him to stumble in the way of faith. The denial that God is omnipotent, or able to do everything, may seem dishonouring to God; but when we see where the contrary affirma-tion, in its various forms, has led, we may well cry out with Hobbes: "Can any man think God is served with such absurdities? . . . As if it were an acknowledgment of the Divine Power, to say, that which is, is not; or that which has been, has not been."

I shall consider four main theories of omnipotence. The first holds that God can do everything absolutely; everything that can be expressed in a string of words that makes sense; even if that sense can be shown to be self-contradictory, God is not bound in action, as we are in thought, by the laws of logic. I shall speak of this as the doctrine that God is *absolutely* omnipotent.

The second doctrine is that a proposition "God can do so-and-so" is true when and only when "so-and-so" represents a logically consistent description.

The third doctrine is that "God *can* do so-and-so" is true just if "God does so-and-so" is logically consistent. This is a weaker doctrine than the second; for "God is doing so-and-so" is logically consistent only when "so-and-so" represents a logically consistent description, but on the other hand there may be consistently describable feats which it would involve contradiction to suppose done *by God*.

The last and weakest view is that the realm of what can be done or brought about includes all future possibilities, and that whenever "God *will* bring so-and-so about" is logically possible, "God *can* bring so-and-so about" is true.

The first sense of "omnipotent" in which people have believed God to

be omnipotent implies precisely: ability to do absolutely everything, every-   FIRST
thing describable. You mention it, and God can do it. McTaggart insisted   THEORY
on using "omnipotent" in this sense only; from an historical point of view   ↓
we may of course say that he imposed on the word a sense which it, and
the corresponding Latin word, have not always borne. But Broad seems to
me clearly unjust to McTaggart when he implies that in demolishing this
doctrine of omnipotence McTaggart was just knocking down a man of
straw. As Broad must surely have known, at least one great philosopher,
Descartes, deliberately adopted and defended this doctrine of omnipotence:
what I shall call the doctrine of absolute omnipotence.

As Descartes himself remarked, nothing is too absurd for some philosopher to have said it some time; I once read an article about an Indian
school of philosophers who were alleged to maintain that it is only a delu-
sion, which the wise can overcome, that anything exists at all—so perhaps
it would not matter all that much that a philosopher is found to defend
absolute omnipotence. Perhaps it would not matter all that much that the
philosopher in question was a very great one; for very great philosophers
have maintained the most preposterous theses. What does make the denial
of absolute omnipotence important is not that we are thereby denying what
a philosopher, a very great philosopher, thought he must assert, but that
this doctrine has a live influence on people's religious thought—I should of
course say, a pernicious influence. Some naive Christians would explicitly
assert the doctrine; and moreover, I think McTaggart was right in believing that in popular religious thought a covert appeal to the doctrine is
sometimes made even by people who would deny it if it were explicitly
stated to them and its manifest consequences pointed out.

McTaggart may well have come into contact with naive Protestant defenders of absolute omnipotence when he was defending his atheist faith
at his public school. The opinion is certainly not dead, as I can testify from
personal experience. For many years I used to teach the philosophy of
Descartes in a special course for undergraduates reading French; year by
year, there were always two or three of them who embraced Descartes' defence of absolute omnipotence *con amore* and protested indignantly when
I described the doctrine as incoherent. It would of course have been no
good to say I was following Doctors of the Church in rejecting the doctrine; I did in the end find a way of producing silence, though not, I fear,
conviction, and going on to other topics of discussion; I cited the passages
of the Epistle to the Hebrews which say explicitly that God cannot swear
by anything greater than himself (vi. 13) or break his word (vi. 18). For-
tunately none of them ever thought of resorting to the ultimate weapon
which, as I believe George Mavrodes remarked, is available to the defender
of absolute omnipotence; namely, he can always say: "Well, you've stated
a difficulty, but of course being omnipotent God can overcome that diffi-

culty, though I don't see how." But what I may call, borrowing from C. S. Lewis's story, victory by the Deplorable Word is a barren one; as barren as a victory by an incessant demand that your adversary should prove his premises or define his terms.

Let us leave these naive defenders in their entrenched position and return for a moment to Descartes. Descartes held that the truths of logic and arithmetic are freely made to be true by God's will. To be sure we clearly and distinctly see that these truths are necessary; they are necessary in our world, and in giving us our mental endowments God gave us the right sort of clear and distinct ideas to see the necessity. But though they are necessary, they are not necessarily necessary; God could have freely chosen to make a different sort of world, in which other things would have been necessary truths. The possibility of such another world is something we cannot *comprehend,* but only dimly *apprehend;* Descartes uses the simile that we may girdle a tree-trunk with our arms but not a mountain—but we can *touch* the mountain. Proper understanding of the possibility would be possessed by God, or, no doubt, by creatures in the alternative world, who would be endowed by God with clear and distinct ideas corresponding to the necessities of their world.

In recent years, unsound philosophies have been defended by what I may call shyster logicians: some of the more dubious recent developments of modal logic could certainly be used to defend Descartes. A system in which "possibly p" were a theorem—in which everything is possible—has indeed never been taken seriously; but modal logicians have taken seriously systems in which "possibly possibly p," or again "it is not necessary that necessarily p," would be a theorem for arbitrary interpretation of "p." What is more, some modern modal logicians notoriously take possible worlds very seriously indeed; some of them even go to the length of saying that what you and I vulgarly call the actual world is simply the world we happen to live in. People who take *both* things seriously—the axiom "possibly possibly p" and the ontology of possible worlds—would say: You mention any impossibility, and there's a possible world in which that isn't impossible but possible. And this is even further away out than Descartes would wish to go; for he would certainly not wish to say that "It is possible that God should not exist" is even *possibly* true. So *a fortiori* a shyster logician could fadge up a case for Descartes. But to my mind all that this shows is that modal logic is currently a rather disreputable discipline: not that I think modal notions are inadmissible—on the contrary, I think they are indispensable—but that current professional standards in the discipline are low, and technical ingenuity is mistaken for rigour. On that showing, astrology would be rigorous.

Descartes' motive for believing in absolute omnipotence was not contemptible: it seemed to him that otherwise God would be *subject to the* inexorable laws of logic as Jove was to the decrees of the Fates. The nature of logical truth is a very difficult problem, which I cannot discuss here. The easy conventionalist line, that it is our arbitrary way of using words that makes logical truth, seems to me untenable, for reasons that Quine among others has clearly spelled out. If I could follow Quine further in regarding logical laws as natural laws of very great generality—revisable in principle, though most unlikely to be revised, in a major theoretical reconstruction—then perhaps after all some rehabilitation of Descartes on this topic might be possible. But in the end I have to say that as we cannot say how a non-logical world would look, we cannot say how a supra-logical God would act or how he could communicate anything to us by way of revelation. So I end as I began: a Christian need not and cannot believe in absolute omnipotence.

It is important that Christians should clearly realize this, because otherwise a half-belief in absolute omnipotence may work in their minds subterraneously. As I said, I think McTaggart was absolutely right in drawing attention to this danger. One and the same man may deny the doctrine of absolute omnipotence when the doctrine is clearly put to him, and yet reassure himself that God can certainly do so-and-so by using *merely* the premise of God's omnipotence. And McTaggart is saying this is indefensible. At the very least this "so-and-so" must represent a logically consistent description of a feat; and proofs of logical consistency are notoriously not always easy. Nor, as we shall see, are our troubles at an end if we assume that God *can* do anything whose description is logically consistent.

Logical consistency in the description of the feat is certainly a *necessary* condition for the truth of "God can do so-and-so": if "so-and-so" represents an inconsistent description of a feat, then "God can do so-and-so" is certainly a false and impossible proposition, since it entails "It could be the case that so-and-so came about"; so, by contraposition, if "God can do so-and-so" is to be true, or even logically possible, then "so-and-so" must represent a logically consistent description of a feat. And whereas only a minority of Christians have explicitly believed in absolute omnipotence, many have believed that a proposition of the form "God can do so-and-so" is true whenever "so-and-so" represents a description of a logically possible feat. This is our second doctrine of omnipotence. One classic statement of this comes in the *Summa Theologica* Ia q. xxv art. 3. Aquinas rightly says that we cannot explain "God can do everything" in terms of what is within the power of some agent; for "God can do everything any created agent can do," though true, is not a comprehensive enough account of God's power, which exceeds that of any created agent; and "God can do everything God can do" runs uselessly in a circle. So he puts forward the view that if the description "so-and-so" is in itself possible through the relation of the terms involved—if it does not involve contradictories' being true together—then

"God can do so-and-so" is true. Many Christian writers have followed Aquinas in saying this; but it is not a position consistently maintainable. As we shall see, Aquinas did not manage to stick to the position himself.

Before I raise the difficulties against this thesis, I wish to expose a common confusion that often leads people to accept it: the confusion between self-contradiction and gibberish. C. S. Lewis in *The Problem of Pain* says that meaningless combinations of words do not suddenly acquire meaning simply because we prefix to them the two other words "God can," and Antony Flew has quoted this with just approval. But if we take Lewis's words strictly, his point is utterly trivial, and nothing to our purpose. For gibberish, syntactically incoherent combination of words, is quite different from self-contradictory sentences or descriptions; the latter certainly have an intelligible place in our language.

It is a common move in logic to argue that a set of premises A, B, C together yield a contradiction, and that therefore A and B as premises yield as conclusion the contradictory of C; some logicians have puritanical objections to this manoeuvre, but I cannot stop to consider them; I am confident, too, that neither Aquinas nor Lewis would share these objections to *reductio ad absurdum*. If, however, a contradictory formula were gibberish, *reductio ad absurdum* certainly would be an illegitimate procedure—indeed it would be a nonsensical one. So we have to say that when "so-and-so" represents a self-contradictory description of a feat, "God can do so-and-so" is likewise self-contradictory, but that being self-contradictory it is *not* gibberish, but merely false.

I am afraid the view of omnipotence presently under consideration owes part of its attractiveness to the idea that then "God can do so-and-so" would never turn out *false,* so that there would be no genuine counterexamples to "God can do everything." Aquinas says, in the passage I just now cited: "What implies contradiction cannot be a word, for no understanding can conceive it." Aquinas, writing seven centuries ago, is excusable for not being clear about the difference between self-contradiction and gibberish; we are not excusable if we are not. It is not gibberish to say "a God can bring it about that in Alcalá there lives a barber who shaves all those and only those living in Alcalá who do not shave themselves"; this is a perfectly well-formed sentence, and not on the face of it self-contradictory; all the same, the supposed feat notoriously is self-contradictory, so this statement of what God can do is not nonsense but false.

One instance of a description of a feat that is really but not overtly self-contradictory has some slight importance in the history of conceptions of omnipotence. It appeared obvious to Spinoza that *God can bring about everything that God can bring about,* and that to deny this would be flatly incompatible with God's omnipotence (*Ethics* I.17, scholium). Well, the italicized sentence is syntactically ambiguous. "Everything that God can bring about God can bring about" is one possible reading of the sentence, and this is an obvious, indeed trivial predication about God, which must be true if there is a God at all. But the other way of taking the sentence relates to a supposed feat of *bringing about everything that God can bring about—all* of these bringable-about things *together*—and it says that God is capable of *this* feat. This is clearly the way Spinoza wishes us to take the sentence. But taken this way, it is not obvious at all; quite the contrary, it's obviously false. For among the things that are severally possible for God to bring about, there are going to be some pairs that are not *com*possible, pairs which it is logically impossible should both come about; and then it is beyond God's power to bring about such a pair together—let alone, to bring about all the things together which he can bring about severally.

This does not give us a description of a *logically possible* feat which God cannot accomplish. However, there is nothing easier than to mention feats which are logically possible but which God cannot do, if Christianity is true. Lying and promise-breaking are logically possible feats: but Christian faith, as I have said, collapses unless we are assured that God cannot lie and cannot break his promises.

This argument is an *ad hominem* argument addressed to Christians; but there are well-known logical arguments to show that on any view there must be some logically possible feats that are beyond God's power. One good example suffices: making a thing which its maker cannot afterwards destroy. This is certainly a possible feat, a feat that some human beings have performed. Can God perform the feat or not? If he cannot there is already some logically possible feat which God cannot perform. If God can perform the feat, then let us suppose that he does: *ponatur in esse,* as medieval logicians say. Then we are supposing God to have brought about a situation in which he *has* made something he cannot destroy; and in that situation destroying this thing is a *logically* possible feat that God cannot accomplish, for we surely cannot admit the idea of a creature whose destruction is logically *im*possible.

There have been various attempts to meet this argument. The most interesting one is that the proposition "God cannot make a thing that he cannot destroy" can be turned round to "Any thing that God can make he can destroy"—which does not even look like an objection to God's being able to do everything logically possible. But this reply involves the very same bracketing fallacy that I exposed a moment ago in Spinoza. There, you will remember, we had to distinguish two ways of taking "God can bring about everything that God can bring about":

A. Everything that God can bring about, God can bring about.

B. God can bring about the following feat: to bring about everything that God can bring about.

And we saw that A is trivially true, given that there *is* a God, and B certainly false. Here, similarly, we have to distinguish two senses of "God cannot make a thing that its maker cannot destroy":

A. Anything that its maker cannot destroy, God cannot make.
B. God cannot bring about the following feat: to make something that its maker cannot destroy.

And here A does contrapose, as the objectors would have it, to "Anything that God can make, its maker can destroy," which on the face of it says nothing against God's power to do anything logically possible. But just as in the Spinoza example, the B reading purports to describe a single feat, *bringing about everything that God can bring about* (this feat, I argued, is impossible for God, because logically impossible): so in our present case, the B reading purports to describe a single feat, *making something that its maker cannot destroy*. This, as I said, is a logically possible feat, a feat that men sometimes do perform; so we may press the question whether this is a feat God can accomplish or not; and either way there will be some *logically possible* feat God cannot accomplish. So this notion of omnipotence, like the Cartesian idea of absolute omnipotence, turns out to be obviously incompatible with Christian faith, and moreover logically untenable.

Let us see, then, if we fare any better with the third theory: the theory that the only condition for the truth of "God can do so-and-so" is that "God does so-and-so" or "God is doing so-and-so" must be logically possible. As I said, this imposes a more restrictive condition than the second theory: for there are many feats that we can consistently suppose to be performed but cannot consistently suppose to be performed by God. This theory might thus get us out of the logical trouble that arose with the second theory about the feat: *making a thing that its maker cannot destroy*. For though this is a logically possible feat, a feat some creatures do perform, it might well be argued that *"God has made a thing that its maker cannot destroy"* is a proposition with a buried inconsistency in it; and if so, then on the present account of omnipotence we need not say "God *can* make a thing that its maker cannot destroy."

This suggestion also, however, can easily be refuted by an example of great philosophical importance that I borrow from Aquinas. "It comes about that Miss X never loses her virginity" is plainly a logically possible proposition: and so also is "God brings it about that Miss X never loses her virginity." All the same, if it so happens that Miss X already has lost her virginity, "God *can* bring it about that Miss X never loses her virginity" is false (Ia q. xxv art. 4 ad 3 um). Before Miss X had lost her virginity, it would have been true to say this very thing; so what we can truly say about what God can do will be different at different times. This appears to imply a change in God, but Aquinas would certainly say, and I think rightly, that it doesn't really do so. It is just like the case of Socrates coming to be shorter than Theaetetus because Theaetetus grows up; here, the change is on the side of Theaetetus not of Socrates. So in our case, the change is really in Miss X not in God; something about her passes from the realm of possibility to the realm of *fait accompli*, and thus *no longer* comes under the concept of the accomplishable—*deficit a ratione possibilium* (Aquinas, loc. cit., ad 2 um). I think Aquinas's position here is strongly defensible; but if he does defend it, he has abandoned the position that God can do everything that it is not a priori impossible *for God to do,* let alone the position that God can bring about everything describable in a logically consistent way.

Is it a priori impossible for God to do something wicked? And if not, could God do something wicked? There have been expressed serious doubts about this: I came across them in that favourite of modern moral philosophers, Richard Price. We must distinguish, he argues, between God's natural and his moral attributes: if God is a free moral being, even as we are, it must not be absolutely impossible for God to do something wicked. There must be just a chance that God should do something wicked: no doubt it will be a really infinitesimal chance—after all, God has persevered in ways of virtue on a vast scale for inconceivably long—but the chance must be there, or God isn't free and isn't therefore laudable for his goodness. The way this reverend gentleman commends his Maker's morals is so startling that you may suspect me of misrepresentation; I can only ask any sceptic to check in Daiches Raphael's edition of Price's work! Further comment on my part is I hope needless.

A much more restrained version of the same sort of thing is to be found in the Scholastic distinction between God's *potentia absoluta* and *potentia ordinata*. The former is God's power considered in abstraction from his wisdom and goodness, the latter is God's power considered as controlled in its exercise by his wisdom and goodness. Well, as regards a man it makes good sense to say: "He has the bodily and mental power to do so-and-so, but he certainly will not, it would be pointlessly silly and wicked." But does anything remotely like this make sense to say about Almighty God? If not, the Scholastic distinction I have cited is wholly frivolous.

Let us then consider our fourth try. Could it be said that the "everything" in "God can do everything" refers precisely to things that are not in the realm of *fait accompli* but of futurity? This will not do either. If God can promulgate promises to men, then as regards any promises that are not yet fulfilled we know that they certainly will be fulfilled: and in that case God clearly has not a *potentia ad utrumque*—a two-way power of either actualizing the event that will fulfil the promise or not actualizing it. God can then only do what will fulfil his promise. And if we try to evade this by denying that God can make promises known to men, then we have once

[margin note: FOURTH THEORY ↓]

more denied something essential to Christian faith, and we are still left with something that God cannot do.

I must here remove the appearance of a fallacy. God cannot but fulfil his promises, I argued; so he has not a two-way power, *potentia ad utrumque,* as regards these particular future events. This argument may have seemed to involve the fallacy made notorious in medieval logical treatises, of confusing the necessity by which something follows—*necessitas consequentiae*—with the necessity of that very thing which follows—*necessitas consequentis.* If it is impossible for God to promise and not perform, then if we know God has promised something we may infer with certainty that he will perform it. Surely, it may be urged, this is enough for Christian faith and hope; we need not go on to say that God *cannot not* bring about the future event in question. If we do that, are we not precisely committing the hoary modal fallacy I have just described?

I answer that there are various senses of "necessary." The future occurrence of such-and-such, when God has promised that such-and-such shall be, is of course not logically necessary; but it may be necessary in the sense of being, as Arthur Prior puts it, now unpreventable. If God *has* promised that Israel shall be saved, then there is nothing that anybody, even God, can do about that; this past state of affairs is now unpreventable. But it is also necessary in the same way that if God has promised then he will perform; God cannot do anything about that either—cannot make himself liable to break his word. So we have as premises "Necessarily p" and "Necessarily if p then q," in the same sense of "necessarily"; and from these premises it not merely necessarily follows that q—the conclusion in the necessitated form, "Necessarily q" with the same sense of "necessarily," follows from the premises. So if God has promised that Israel shall be saved, the future salvation of Israel is not only certain but inevitable; God must save Israel, because he cannot not save Israel without breaking his word given in the past and he can neither alter the past nor break his word.

Again, in regard to this and other arguments, some people may have felt discomfort at my not drawing in relation to God the sort of distinction between various applications of "can" that are made in human affairs: the "can" of knowing how to, the "can" of physical power to, the "can" of opportunity, the "can" of what fits in with one's plans. But of course the way we make these distinct applications of "he can" to a human agent will not be open if we are talking about God. There is no question of God's knowing how but lacking the strength, or being physically able to but not knowing how; moreover (to make a distinction that comes in a logical example of Aristotle's) though there is a right time when God may bring something about, it is inept to speak of his then having the opportunity to do it. (To develop this distinction: if "x" stands for a finite agent and "so-and-so" for an act directly in x's power, there is little difference between "At time t it is suitable for x to bring so-and-so about" and "It is suitable for x to bring so-and-so about at time t"; but if "x" means God, the temporal qualification "at time t" can attach only to what is brought about; God does not live through successive times and find one more suitable than another.)

These distinct applications of "can" are distinct only for finite and changeable agents, not for a God whose action is universal and whose mind and character and design are unchangeable. There is thus no ground for fear that in talking about God we may illicitly slip from one sort of "can" to another. What we say God can do is always in respect of his changeless supreme power.

All the same, we have to assert different propositions at different times in order to say truly what God can do. What is past, as I said, ceases to be alterable even by God; and thus the truth-value of a proposition like "God can bring it about that Miss X never loses her virginity" alters once she has lost it. Similarly, God's promise makes a difference to what we can thereafter truly say God can do; it is less obvious in this case that the real change involved is a change in creatures, not in God, than it was as regards Miss X's virginity, but a little thought should show that the promulgation or making known of God's intention, which is involved in a promise, is precisely a change in the creatures to whom the promise is made.

Thus all the four theories of omnipotence that I have considered break down. Only the first overtly flouts logic; but the other three all involve logical contradictions, or so it seems; and moreover, all these theories have consequences fatal to the truth of Christian faith. The last point really ought not to surprise us; for the absolute confidence a Christian must have in God's revelation and promises involves, as I said at the outset, both a belief that God is almighty, in the sense I explained, and a belief that there are certain describable things that God cannot do and therefore will not do.

If I were to end the discussion at this point, I should leave an impression of Aquinas's thought that would be seriously unfair to him; for although in the passage I cited Aquinas appears verbally committed to our second theory of omnipotence, it seems clear that this does not adequately represent his mind. Indeed, it was from Aquinas himself and from the *Summa Theologica* that I borrowed an example which refutes even the weaker third theory, let alone the second one. Moreover, in the other Summa (Book II, c. xxv) there is an instructive list of things that *Deus omnipotens* is rightly said not to be able to do. But the mere occurrence of this list makes me doubt whether Aquinas can be said to believe, in any reasonable interpretation, the thesis that God can do everything. That God is almighty in my sense Aquinas obviously did believe; I am suggesting that here his "omnipotens" means "almighty" rather than "omnipotent." Aquinas does not say or even imply that he has given an *exhaustive* list of kinds of case in which "God can do so-and-so" or "God can make so-and-so" turns out false; so what he says here does not commit him to "God can do everything" even in the highly unnatural sense "God can do everything that is not excluded under one or other of the following heads."

I shall not explore Aquinas's list item by item, because I have made open or tacit use of his considerations at several points in the foregoing and do not wish to repeat myself. But one batch of items raises a specially serious problem. My attention was drawn to the problem by a contribution that the late Mr. Michael Foster made orally during a discussion at the Socratic Club in Oxford. Aquinas tells us that if "doing so-and-so" implies what he calls passive potentiality, then "God can do so-and-so" is false. On this ground he excluded all of the following:

> God can be a body or something of the sort.
> God can be tired or oblivious.
> God can be angry or sorrowful.
> God can suffer violence or be overcome.
> God can undergo corruption.

Foster pointed out that as a Christian Aquinas was committed to asserting the contradictory of all these theses. *Contra factum non valet ratio;* it's no good arguing that God cannot do what God has done, and in the Incarnation God did do all these things Aquinas said God cannot do. The Word that was God *was* made flesh (and the literal meaning of the Polish for this is: The Word became a body!); God the Son *was* tired and did sink into the oblivion of sleep; he *was* angry and sorrowful; he was bound like a thief, beaten, and crucified; and though we believe his Body did not decay, it suffered corruption in the sense of becoming a corpse instead of a living body—Christ in the Apocalypse uses of himself the startling words "I became a corpse," "*egenomēn nekros,*" and the Church has always held that the dead Body of Christ during the *triduum mortis* was adorable with Divine worship for its union to the Divine Nature.

Foster's objection to Aquinas is the opposite kind of objection to the ones I have been raising against the various theories of omnipotence I have discussed. I have been saying that these theories say by implication that God *can* do certain things which Christian belief requires one to say God *cannot* do; Foster is objecting that Aquinas's account says God *cannot* do some things which according to Christian faith God *can* do and has in fact done.

It would take me too far to consider how Aquinas might have answered this objection. It would not of course be outside his intellectual milieu; it is the very sort of objection that a Jew or Moor might have used, accepting Aquinas's account of what God cannot do, in order to argue against the Incarnation. I shall simply mention one feature that Aquinas's reply would have had: it would have to make essential use of the particle "as," or in

Latin *"secundum quod."* God did become man, so God can become man
and have a human body; but God *as* God cannot be man or have a body.

The logic of these propositions with "as" in them, reduplicative propositions as they are traditionally called, is a still unsolved problem, although
as a matter of history it was a problem raised by Aristotle in the *Prior
Analytics.* We must not forget that such propositions occur frequently in
ordinary discourse; we use them there with an ill-founded confidence that
we know our way around. Jones, we say, is Director of the Gnome Works
and Mayor of Middletown; he gets a salary *as* Director and an expense
allowance *as* Mayor; he signs one letter *as* Director, another *as* Mayor. We
say all this, but how far do we understand the logical relations of what we
say? Very little, I fear. One might have expected some light and leading
from medieval logicians; the theological importance of reduplicative propositions did in fact lead to their figuring as a topic in medieval logical
treatises. But I have not found much that is helpful in such treatments as
I have read.

I hope to return to this topic later. Meanwhile, even though it has
nothing directly to do with almightiness or omnipotence, I shall mention
one important logical point that is already to be found in Aristotle. A
superficial grammatical illusion may make us think that "A as P is Q" attaches the predicate "Q" to a complex subject "A as P." But Aristotle
insists, to my mind rightly, on the analysis: "A" subject, "is as P, Q" predicate—so that we have not a complex subject-term, but a complex predicate-
term; clearly, this predicate entails the simple conjunctive predicate "is
both P and Q" but not conversely. This niggling point of logic has in fact
some theological importance. When theologians are talking about Christ as
God and Christ as Man, they may take the two phrases to be two logical
subjects of predication, if they have failed to see the Aristotelian point; and
then they are likely to think or half think that Christ as God is one entity
or *Gegenstand* and Christ as Man is another. I am sure some theologians
have yielded to this temptation, which puts them on a straight road to the
Nestorian heresy.

What Aquinas would have done, I repeat, to meet Foster's objection in
the mouth of a Jew or Moor is to distinguish between what we say God
can do, *simpliciter,* and what we say God *as* God can do, using the reduplicative form of proposition. Now if we do make such a distinction, we
are faced with considerable logical complications, particularly if we accept
the Aristotelian point about the reduplicative construction. Let us go back
to our friend Jones: there is a logical difference between:

1. Jones as Mayor can attend this committee meeting.
2. Jones can as Mayor attend this committee meeting.

as we may see if we spell the two out a little:

1. Jones as Mayor has the opportunity of attending this committee meeting.

2. Jones has the opportunity of (attending this committee meeting as Mayor).

We can easily see now that 1 and 2 are logically distinct: for one thing, if Jones is not yet Mayor but has an opportunity of becoming Mayor and *then* attending the committee meeting, 2 would be true and 1 false. And if we want to talk about what Jones as Mayor *cannot* do, the complexities pile up; for then we have to consider how the negation can be inserted at one or other position in a proposition of one of these forms, and how all the results are logically related.

All this is logical work to be done if we are to be clear about the implications of saying that God can or cannot do so-and-so, or again that God *as God* can or cannot do so-and-so. It is obvious, without my developing the matter further, that the logic of all this will not be simple. It's a far cry from the simple method of bringing our question "Can God do so-and-so?" under a reassuring principle "God can do *everything*." But I hope I have made it clear that any reassurance we get that way is entirely spurious.

Divine Omniscience and
Voluntary Action

NELSON PIKE

In Part V, Section III of his *Consolatio Philosophiae,* Boethius entertained
(though he later rejected) the claim that if God is omniscient, no human
action is voluntary. This claim seems intuitively false. Surely, given only a
doctrine describing God's *knowledge,* nothing about the voluntary status
of human actions will follow. Perhaps such a conclusion would follow from
a doctrine of divine omnipotence or divine providence, but what connection could there be between the claim that God is *omniscient* and the claim
that human actions are determined? Yet Boethius thought he saw a problem here. He thought that if one collected together just the right assumptions and principles regarding God's knowledge, one could derive the conclusion that if God exists, no human action is voluntary. Of course, Boethius
did not think that all the assumptions and principles required to reach
this conclusion are true (quite the contrary), but he thought it important
to draw attention to them nonetheless. If a theologian is to construct a doctrine of God's knowledge which does not commit him to determinism, he
must first understand that there is a way of thinking about God's knowledge which would so commit him.

    In this paper, I shall argue that although his claim has a sharp counter-
intuitive ring, Boethius was right in thinking that there is a selection from
among the various doctrines and principles clustering about the notions of
knowledge, omniscience, and God which, when brought together, demand
the conclusion that if God exists, no human action is voluntary. Boethius,
I think, did not succeed in making explicit all of the ingredients in the

Reprinted from *The Philosophical Review* 74 (1965) by permission of *The Philosophical Review* and the author.

problem. His suspicions were sound, but his discussion was incomplete. His argument needs to be developed. This is the task I shall undertake in the pages to follow. I should like to make clear at the outset that my purpose in rearguing this thesis is not to show that determinism is true, nor to show that God does not exist, nor to show that either determinism is true or God does not exist. Following Boethius, I shall not claim that the items needed to generate the problem are either philosophically or theologically adequate. I want to concentrate attention on the implications of a certain set of assumptions. Whether the assumptions are themselves acceptable is a question I shall not consider.

I

A. Many philosophers have held that if a statement of the form "A knows X" is true, then "A believes X" is true and "X" is true. As a first assumption, I shall take this partial analysis of "A knows X" to be correct. And I shall suppose that since this analysis holds for all knowledge claims, it will hold when speaking of God's knowledge. "God knows X" entails "God believes X" and " 'X' is true."

Secondly, Boethius said that with respect to the matter of knowledge, God "cannot in anything be mistaken."[1] I shall understand this doctrine as follows. Omniscient beings hold no false beliefs. Part of what is meant when we say that a person is omniscient is that the person in question believes nothing that is false. But, further, it is part of the "essence" of God to be omniscient. This is to say that any person who is not omniscient could not be the person we usually mean to be referring to when using the name "God." To put this last point a little differently: if the person we usually mean to be referring to when using the name "God" were suddenly to lose the quality of omniscience (suppose, for example, He came to believe something false), the resulting person would no longer be God. Although we might call this second person "God" (I might call my cat "God"), the absence of the quality of omniscience would be sufficient to guarantee that the person referred to was not the same as the person formerly called by that name. From this last doctrine it follows that the statement "If a given person is God, that person is omniscient" is an a priori truth. From this we may conclude that the statement "If a given person is God, that person holds no false beliefs" is also an a priori truth. It would be conceptually impossible for God to hold a false belief. " 'X' is true" follows from "God believes X." These are all ways of expressing the same principle—the principle expressed by Boethius in the formula "God cannot in anything be mistaken."

1. *Consolatio Philosophiae*, Bk. V, sec. 3, par. 6.

A second principle usually associated with the notion of divine omniscience has to do with the scope or range of God's intellectual gaze. To say that a being is omniscient is to say that he knows everything. "Everything" in this statement is usually taken to cover future, as well as present and past, events and circumstances. In fact, God is usually said to have had foreknowledge of everything that has ever happened. With respect to anything that was, is, or will be the case, God knew, *from eternity*, that it would be the case.

The doctrine of God's knowing everything from eternity is very obscure. One particularly difficult question concerning this doctrine is whether it entails that with respect to everything that was, is, or will be the case, God knew *in advance* that it would be the case. In some traditional theological texts, we are told that God is *eternal* in the sense that He exists "outside of time," that is, in the sense that He bears no temporal relations to the events or circumstances of the natural world.[2] In a theology of this sort, God could not be said to have known that a given natural event was going to happen before it happened. If God knew that a given natural event was going to occur *before* it occurred, at least one of God's cognitions would then have occurred before some natural event. This, surely, would violate the idea that God bears no temporal relations to natural events.[3] On the other hand, in a considerable number of theological sources, we are told that God *has always* existed—that He existed long *before* the occurrence of any natural event. In a theology of this sort, to say that God is eternal is not to say that God exists "outside of time" (bears no temporal relations to natural events), it is to say, instead, God has existed (and will continue to exist) at each moment.[4] The doctrine of omniscience which goes with this second understanding of the notion of eternity is one in which it is affirmed that God *has always* known that what was going to happen in the natural world. John Calvin wrote as follows:

> When we attribute foreknowledge to God, we mean that all things have ever been and perpetually remain before, his eyes, so that to his knowledge nothing is future or past, but all things are present; and present in such manner, that he does not merely conceive of them from ideas formed in his

2. This position is particularly well formulated in St. Anselm's *Proslogium,* ch. xix and *Monologium,* chs. xxi–xxii; and in Frederich Schleiermacher's *The Christian Faith,* Pt. I, sec. 2, par. 51. It is also explicit in Boethius, op. cit., secs. 4–6, and in St. Thomas' *Summa Theologica,* Pt. I, Q. 10.

3. This point is explicit in Boethius, op. cit., secs. 4–6.

4. This position is particularly well expressed in William Paley's *Natural Theology,* ch. xxiv. It is also involved in John Calvin's discussion of predestination, *Institutes of the Christian Religion,* Bk. III, ch. xxi; and in some formulations of the first cause argument for existence of God, e.g., John Locke's *Essay Concerning Human Understanding,* Bk. IV, ch. x.

mind, as things remembered by us appear to our minds, but really he holds
and sees them as if (*tanquam*) actually placed before him.[5]

All things are "present" to God in the sense that He "sees" them as if
(*tanquam*) they were actually before Him. Further, with respect to any
given natural event, not only is that event "present" to God in the sense
indicated, it has *ever been and has perpetually remained* "present" to Him
in that sense. This latter is the point of special interest. Whatever one
thinks of the idea that God "sees" things as if "actually placed before him,"
Calvin would appear to be committed to the idea that God has *always
known* what was going to happen in the natural world. Choose an event
(*E*) and a time (T_2) at which *E* occurred. For any time (T_1) prior to T_2
(say, five thousand, six hundred, or eighty years prior to T_2), God knew
at T_1 that *E* would occur at T_2. It will follow from this doctrine, of course,
that with respect to any human action, God knew well in advance of its
performance that the action would be performed. Calvin says, "when God
created man, He foresaw what would happen concerning him." He adds,
"little more than five thousand years have elapsed since the creation of the
world."[6] Calvin seems to have thought that God foresaw the outcome of
every human action well over five thousand years ago.

In the discussion to follow, I shall work only with this second interpretation of God's knowing everything *from eternity*. I shall assume that
if a person is omniscient, that person has always known what was going to
happen in the natural world—and, in particular, has always known what
human actions were going to be performed. Thus, as above, assuming that
the attribute of omniscience is part of the "essence" of God, the statement
"For any natural event (including human actions), if a given person is
God, that person would always have known that that event was going to
occur at the time it occurred" must be treated as an a priori truth. This is
just another way of stating a point admirably put by St. Augustine when
he said: "For to confess that God exists and at the same time to deny that
He has foreknowledge of future things is the most manifest folly. . . .
One who is not prescient of all future things is not God."[7]

B. Last Saturday afternoon, Jones mowed his lawn. Assuming that
God exists and is (essentially) omniscient in the sense outlined above, it
follows that (let us say) eighty years prior to last Saturday afternoon, God
knew (and thus believed) that Jones would mow his lawn at that time.
But from this it follows, I think, that at the time of action (last Saturday

5. *Institutes of the Christian Religion*, Bk. III, ch. xxi; this passage trans. by John
Allen (Philadelphia, 1813), II, 145.
6. Ibid., p. 144.
7. *City of God,* Bk. V, sec. 9.

afternoon)˙ Jones was not *able*—that is, it was not *within Jones's power*—to refrain from mowing his lawn.[8] If at the time of action, Jones had been able to refrain from mowing his lawn, then (the most obvious conclusion would seem to be) at the time of action, Jones was able to do something which would have brought it about that God held a false belief eighty years earlier. But God cannot in anything be mistaken. It is not possible that some belief of His was false. Thus, last Saturday afternoon, Jones was not able to do something which would have brought it about that God held a false belief eighty years ago. To suppose that it was would be to suppose that, at the time of action, Jones was able to do something having a conceptually incoherent description, namely something that would have brought it about that one of God's beliefs was false. Hence, given that God believed eighty years ago that Jones would mow his lawn on Saturday, if we are to assign Jones the power on Saturday to refrain from mowing his lawn, this power must not be described as the power to do something that would have rendered one of God's beliefs false. How then should we describe it vis-à-vis God and His belief? So far as I can see, there are only two other alternatives. First, we might try describing it as the power to do something that would have brought it about that God believed otherwise than He did eighty years ago; or, secondly, we might try describing it as the power to do something that would have brought it about that God (Who, by hypothesis, existed eighty years earlier) did not exist eighty years earlier—that is, as the power to do something that would have brought it about that any person who believed eighty years ago that Jones would mow his lawn on Saturday (one of whom was, by hypothesis, God) held a false belief, and thus was not God. But again, neither of these latter can be accepted. Last Saturday afternoon, Jones was not able to do something that would have brought it about that God believed otherwise than He did eighty years ago. Even if we suppose (as was suggested by Calvin) that eighty years ago God knew Jones would mow his lawn on Saturday in the sense that He "saw" Jones mowing his lawn as if this action were occurring

8. The notion of someone being *able* to do something and the notion of something being *within one's power* are essentially the same. Traditional formulations of the problem of divine foreknowledge (e.g., those of Boethius and Augustine) made use of the notion of what is (and what is not) *within one's power*. But the problem is the same when framed in terms of what one is (and one is not) *able* to do. Thus, I shall treat the statements "Jones was able to do X," "Jones had the ability to do X," and "It was within Jones's power to do X" as equivalent. Richard Taylor, in "I Can," *Philosophical Review*, LXIX (1960), 78–89, has argued that the notion of ability or power involved in these last three statements is incapable of philosophical analysis. Be this as it may, I shall not here attempt such an analysis. In what follows I shall, however, be careful to affirm only those statements about what is (or is not) within one's power that would have to be preserved on any analysis of this notion having even the most distant claim to adequacy.

before Him, the fact remains that God knew (and thus believed) eighty years prior to Saturday that Jones would mow his lawn. And if God held such a belief eighty years prior to Saturday, Jones did not have the power on Saturday to do something that would have made it the case that God did not hold this belief eighty years earlier. No action performed at a given time can alter the fact that a given person held a certain belief at a time prior to the time in question. This last seems to be an a priori truth. For similar reasons, the last of the above alternatives must also be rejected. On the assumption that God existed eighty years prior to Saturday, Jones on Saturday was not able to do something that would have brought it about that God did not exist eighty years prior to that time. No action performed at a given time can alter the fact that a certain person existed at a time prior to the time in question. This, too, seems to me to be an a priori truth. But if these observations are correct, then, given that Jones mowed his lawn on Saturday, and given that God exists and is (essentially) omniscient, it seems to follow that at the time of action, Jones did not have the power to refrain from mowing his lawn. The upshot of these reflections would appear to be that Jones's mowing his lawn last Saturday cannot be counted as a voluntary action. Although I do not have an analysis of what it is for action to be *voluntary*, it seems to me that a situation in which it would be wrong to assign Jones the *ability* or *power* to do *other* than he did would be a situation in which it would also be wrong to speak of his action as voluntary. As a general remark, if God exists and is (essentially) omniscient in the sense specified above, no human action is voluntary.[9]

As the argument just presented is somewhat complex, perhaps the following schematic representation of it will be of some use.

1. "God existed at T_1" entails "If Jones did X at T_2, God believed at T_1 that Jones would do X at T_2."
2. "God believes X" entails " 'X' is true."
3. It is not within one's power at a given time to do something having a description that is logically contradictory.
4. It is not within one's power at a given time to do something that would bring it about that someone who held a certain belief at a

9. In Bk. II, ch. xxi, secs. 8–11 of the *Essay*, John Locke says that an agent is not *free* with respect to a given action (i.e., that an action is done "under necessity") when it is not within the agent's power to do otherwise. Locke allows a special kind of case, however, in which an action may be *voluntary* though done under necessity. If a man chooses to do something without knowing that it is not within his power to do otherwise (e.g., if a man chooses to stay in a room without knowing that the room is locked), his action may be voluntary though he is not free to forbear it. If Locke is right in this (and I shall not argue the point one way or the other), replace "voluntary" with (let us say) "free" in the above paragraph and throughout the remainder of this paper.

time prior to the time in question did not hold that belief at the time prior to the time in question.

5. It is not within one's power at a given time to do something that would bring it about that a person who existed at an earlier time did not exist at that earlier time.

6. If God existed at T_1 and if God believed at T_1 that Jones would do X at T_2, then if it was within Jones's power at T_2 to refrain from doing X, then (1) it was within Jones's power at T_2 to do something that would have brought it about that God held a false belief at T_1, or (2) it was within Jones's power at T_2 to do something which would have brought it about that God did not hold the belief He held at T_1, or (3) it was within Jones's power at T_2 to do something that would have brought it about that any person who believed at T_1 that Jones would do X at T_2 (one of whom was, by hypothesis, God) held a false belief and thus was not God—that is, that God (who by hypothesis existed at T_1) did not exist at T_1.

7. Alternative 1 in the consequent of item 6 is false (from 2 and 3).

8. Alternative 2 in the consequent of item 6 is false (from 4).

9. Alternative 3 in the consequent of item 6 is false (from 5).

10. Therefore, if God existed at T_1 and if God believed at T_1 that Jones would do X at T_2, then it was not within Jones's power at T_2 to refrain from doing X (from 6 through 9).

11. Therefore, if God existed at T_1, and if Jones did X at T_2, it was not within Jones's power at T_2 to refrain from doing X (from 1 and 10).

In this argument, items 1 and 2 make explicit the doctrine of God's (essential) omniscience with which I am working. Items 3, 4, and 5 express what I take to be part of the logic of the concept of ability or power as it applies to human beings. Item 6 is offered as an analytic truth. If one assigns Jones the power to refrain from doing X at T_2 (given that God believed at T_1 that he would do X at T_2), so far as I can see, one would have to describe this power in one of the three ways listed in the consequent of item 6. I do not know how to argue that these are the only alternatives, but I have been unable to find another. Item 11, when generalized for all agents and actions, and when taken together with what seems to me to be a minimal condition for the application of "voluntary action," yields the conclusion that if God exists (and is essentially omniscient in the way I have described) no human action is voluntary.

C. It is important to notice that the argument given in the preceding paragraphs avoids use of two concepts that are often prominent in discussions of determinism.

In the first place, the argument makes no mention of the *causes* of Jones's action. Say (for example, with St. Thomas)[10] that God's foreknowledge of Jones's action was, itself, the cause of the action (though I am really not sure what this means). Say, instead, that natural events or circumstances caused Jones to act. Even say that Jones's action had no cause at all. The argument outlined above remains unaffected. If eighty years prior to Saturday, God believed that Jones would mow his lawn at that time, it was not within Jones's power at the time of action to refrain from mowing his lawn. The reasoning that justifies this assertion makes no mention of a causal series preceding Jones's action.

Secondly, consider the following line of thinking. Suppose Jones mowed his lawn last Saturday. It was then *true* eighty years ago that Jones would mow his lawn at that time. Hence, on Saturday, Jones was not able to refrain from mowing his lawn. To suppose that he was would be to suppose that he was able on Saturday to do something that would have made false a proposition that was *already true* eighty years earlier. This general kind of argument for determinism is usually associated with Leibniz, although it was anticipated in Chapter IX of Aristotle's *De Interpretatione*. It has been used since, with some modification, in Richard Taylor's article, "Fatalism."[11] This argument, like the one I have offered above, makes no use of the notion of causation. It turns, instead, on the notion of its being *true eighty years ago* that Jones would mow his lawn on Saturday.

I must confess that I share the misgivings of those contemporary philosophers who have wondered what (if any) sense can be attached to a statement of the form "It was true at T_1 that E would occur at T_2."[12] Does this statement mean that had someone believed, guessed, or asserted at T_1 that E would occur at T_2, he would have been right?[13] (I shall have something to say about this form of determinism later in this paper.) Perhaps it means that at T_1 there was sufficient evidence upon which to pre-

10. *Summa Theologica*, Pt. I, Q. 14, a. 8.

11. *Philosophical Review*, LXXI (1962), 56–66. Taylor argues that if an event E fails to occur at T_2, then at T_1 it was true that E would fail to occur at T_2. Thus, at T_1, a necessary condition of anyone's performing an action sufficient for the occurrence of E at T_2 is missing. Thus at T_1, no one could have the power to perform an action that would be sufficient for the occurrence of E at T_2. Hence, no one has the power at T_1 to do something sufficient for the occurrence of an event at T_2 that is not going to happen. The parallel between this argument and the one recited above can be seen very clearly if one reformulates Taylor's argument, pushing back the time at which it was true that E would not occur at T_2.

12. For a helpful discussion of difficulties involved here, see Rogers Albritton's "Present Truth and Future Contingency," a reply to Richard Taylor's "The Problem of Future Contingency," both in the *Philosophical Review*, LXVI (1957), 1–28.

13. Gilbert Ryle interprets it this way. See "It Was To Be," *Dilemmas* (Cambridge, 1954).

dict that E would occur at T_2.[14] Maybe it means neither of these. Maybe it means nothing at all.[15] The argument presented above presupposes that it makes straightforward sense to suppose that God (or just anyone) held a true belief eighty years prior to Saturday. But this is not to suppose that *what* God believed *was true eighty years prior to Saturday*. Whether (or in what sense) it was true eighty years ago that Jones would mow his lawn on Saturday is a question I shall not discuss. As far as I can see, the argument in which I am interested requires nothing in the way of a decision on this issue.

II

I now want to consider three comments on the problem of divine foreknowledge which seem to be instructively incorrect.

A. Leibniz analyzed the problem as follows:

> They say that what is foreseen cannot fail to exist and they say so truly; but it follows not that what is foreseen is necessary. For necessary truth is that whereof the contrary is impossible or implies a contradiction. Now the truth which states that I shall write tomorrow is not of that nature, it is not necessary. Yet, supposing that God foresees it, it is necessary that it come to pass, that is, the consequence is necessary, namely that it exist, since it has been foreseen; for God is infallible. This is what is termed a *hypothetical necessity*. But our concern is not this necessity; it is an *absolute* necessity that is required, to be able to say that an action is necessary, that it is not contingent, that it is not the effect of free choice.[16]

The statement "God believed at T_1 that Jones would do X at T_2" (where the interval between T_1 and T_2 is, for example, eighty years) does not entail "'Jones did X at T_2' is necessary." Leibniz is surely right about this. All that will follow from the first of these statements concerning "Jones did X at T_2" is that the latter is *true*, not that it is *necessarily true*. But this observation has no real bearing on the issue at hand. The following passage from St. Augustine's formulation of the problem may help to make this point clear.

> Your trouble is this. You wonder how it can be that these two propositions are not contradictory and incompatible, namely that God has fore-

14. Richard Gale suggests this interpretation in "Endorsing Predictions," *Philosophical Review*, LXX (1961), 378–385.

15. This view is held by John Turk Saunders in "Sea Fight Tomorrow?" *Philosophical Review*, LXVII (1958), 367–378.

16. *Théodicée*, Pt. I, sec. 37. This passage trans. by E. M. Huggard (New Haven, 1952), p. 144.

knowledge of all future events, and that we sin voluntarily and not by necessity. For if, you say, God foreknows that a man will sin, he must necessarily sin. But if there is necessity there is no voluntary choice of sinning, but rather fixed and unavoidable necessity.[17]

In this passage, the term "necessity" (or the phrase "by necessity") is not used to express a modal-logical concept. The term "necessity" is here used in contrast with the term "voluntary," not (as in Leibniz) in contrast with the term "contingent." If one's action is necessary (or by necessity), this is to say that one's action is not voluntary. Augustine says that if God has foreknowledge of human actions, the actions are necessary. But the form of this conditional is "P implies Q," not "P implies N (Q)." "Q" in the consequent of this conditional is the claim that human actions are not voluntary—that is, that one is not able, or does not have the power, to do other than he does.

Perhaps I can make this point clearer by reformulating the original problem in such a way as to make explicit the modal operators working within it. Let it be *contingently* true that Jones did X at T_2. Since God holds a belief about the outcome of each human action well in advance of its performance, it is then *contingently* true that God believed at T_1 that Jones would do X at T_2. But it follows from this that it is *contingently* true that at T_2 Jones was not able to refrain from doing X. Had he been (contingently) able to refrain from doing X at T_2, then either he was (contingently) able to do something at T_2 that would have brought it about that God held a false belief at T_1, or he was (contingently) able to do something at T_2 that would have brought it about that God believed otherwise than He did at T_1, or he was (contingently) able to do something at T_2 that would have brought it about that God did not exist at T_1. None of these latter is an acceptable alternative.

B. In *Concordia Liberi Arbitrii*, Luis de Molina wrote as follows:

It was not that since He foreknew what would happen from those things which depend on the created will that it would happen; but, on the contrary, it was because such things would happen through the freedom of the will, that He foreknew it; and that He would foreknow the opposite if the opposite was to happen.[18]

Remarks similar to this one can be found in a great many traditional and contemporary theological texts. In fact, Molina assures us that the view

17. *De Libero Arbitrio*, Bk. III. This passage trans. by J. H. S. Burleigh, *Augustine's Earlier Writings* (Philadelphia, 1955).
18. This passage trans. by John Mourant, *Readings in the Philosophy of Religion* (New York, 1954), p. 426.

expressed in this passage has always been "above controversy"—a matter of "common opinion" and "unanimous consent"—not only among the Church fathers, but also, as he says, "among all catholic men."

One claim made in the above passage seems to me to be truly "above controversy." With respect to any given action foreknown by God, God would have foreknown the opposite if the opposite was to happen. If we assume the notion of omniscience outlined in the first section of this paper, and if we agree that omniscience is part of the "essence" of God, this statement is a conceptual truth. I doubt if anyone would be inclined to dispute it. Also involved in this passage, however, is at least the suggestion of a doctrine that cannot be taken as an item of "common opinion" among *all* catholic men. Molina says it is not because God foreknows what He foreknows that men act as they do: it is because men act as they do that God foreknows what He foreknows. Some theologians have rejected this claim. It seems to entail that men's actions determine God's cognitions. And this latter, I think, has been taken by some theologians to be a violation of the notion of God as self-sufficient and incapable of being affected by events of the natural world.[19] But I shall not develop this point further. Where the view put forward in the above passage seems to me to go wrong in an interesting and important way is in Molina's claim that God can have foreknowledge of things that will happen "through the freedom of the will." It is this claim that I here want to examine with care.

What exactly are we saying when we say that God can know in advance what will happen *through the freedom of the will?* I think that what Molina has in mind is this. God can know in advance that a given man is going to *choose* to perform a certain action sometime in the future. With respect to the case of Jones mowing his lawn, God knew at T_1 that Jones would *freely decide* to mow his lawn at T_2. Not only did God know at T_1 that Jones would mow his lawn at T_2, He also knew at T_1 that this action would be performed *freely*. In the words of Emil Brunner, "God knows that which will take place in freedom in the future as something which happens in freedom."[20] What God knew at T_1 is that Jones would *freely* mow his lawn at T_2.

I think that this doctrine is incoherent. If God knew (and thus believed) at T_1 that Jones would *do* X at T_2,[21] I think it follows that Jones was not able to do other than X at T_2 (for reasons already given). Thus, if God knew (and thus believed) at T_1 that Jones would *do* X at T_2, it would follow that Jones did X at T_2, but *not freely*. It does not seem to be possible that God could have believed at T_1 that Jones would freely do X

19. Cf. Boethius' *Consolatio*, Bk. V, sec. 3, par. 2.
20. *The Christian Doctrine of God*, trans. by Olive Wyon (Philadelphia, 1964), p. 262.
21. Note: no comment here about *freely* doing X.

at T_2. If God believed at T_1 that Jones would do X at T_2, Jones's action at T_2 was not free; and if God *also* believed at T_1 that Jones would freely act at T_2, it follows that God held a false belief at T_1—which is absurd.

C. Frederich Schleiermacher commented on the problem of divine foreknowledge as follows:

> In the same way, we estimate the intimacy between two persons by the foreknowledge one has of the actions of the other, without supposing that in either case, the one or the other's freedom is thereby endangered. So even the divine foreknowledge cannot endanger freedom.[22]

St. Augustine made this same point in *De Libero Arbitrio*. He said:

> Unless I am mistaken, you would not directly compel the man to sin, though you knew beforehand that he was going to sin. Nor does your prescience in itself compel him to sin even though he was certainly going to sin, as we must assume if you have real prescience. So there is no contradiction here. Simply you know beforehand what another is going to do with his own will. Similarly God compels no man to sin, though he sees beforehand those who are going to sin by their own will.[23]

If we suppose (with Schleiermacher and Augustine) that the case of an intimate friend having foreknowledge of another's action has the same implications for determinism as the case of God's foreknowledge of human actions, I can imagine two positions which might then be taken. First, one might hold (with Schleiermacher and Augustine) that God's foreknowledge of human actions cannot entail determinism—since it is clear that an intimate friend can have foreknowledge of another's voluntary actions. Or, secondly, one might hold that an intimate friend cannot have foreknowledge of another's voluntary actions—since it is clear that God cannot have foreknowledge of such actions. This second position could take either of two forms. One might hold that since an intimate friend *can* have foreknowledge of another's actions, the actions in question cannot be voluntary. Or, alternatively, one might hold that since the other's actions *are* voluntary, the intimate friend cannot have foreknowledge of them.[24] But what I propose to argue in the remaining pages of this paper is that Schleiermacher and Augustine were mistaken in supposing that the case of an intimate friend having foreknowledge of other's actions has the same implications for determinism as the case of God's foreknowledge of hu-

22. *The Christian Faith,* Pt. I, sec. 2, par. 55. This passage trans. by W. R. Matthew (Edinburgh, 1928), p. 228.
23. Loc. cit.
24. This last seems to be the position defended by Richard Taylor in "Deliberation and Foreknowledge," *American Philosophical Quarterly,* I (1964).

man actions. What I want to suggest is that the argument I used above to show that God cannot have foreknowledge of voluntary actions cannot be used to show that an intimate friend cannot have foreknowledge of another's actions. Even if one holds that an intimate friend *can* have foreknowledge of another's voluntary actions, one ought not to think that the case is the same when dealing with the problem of divine foreknowledge.

Let Smith be an ordinary man and an intimate friend of Jones. Now, let us start by supposing that Smith believed at T_1 that Jones would do X at T_2. We make no assumption concerning the truth or falsity of Smith's belief, but assume only that Smith held it. Given only this much, there appears to be no difficulty in supposing that at T_2 Jones was able to do X and that at T_2 Jones was able to do not-X. So far as the above description of the case is concerned, it might well have been within Jones's power at T_2 to do something (namely, X) which would have brought it about that Smith held a true belief at T_1, and it might well have been within Jones's power at T_2 to do something (namely, not-X) which would have brought it about that Smith held a false belief at T_1. So much seems apparent.

Now let us suppose that Smith *knew* at T_1 that Jones would do X at T_2. This is to suppose that Smith correctly believed (with evidence) at T_1 that Jones would do X at T_2. It follows, to be sure, that Jones *did* X at T_2. But now let us inquire about what Jones was *able* to do at T_2. I submit that there is nothing in the description of this case that requires the conclusion that it was not within Jones's power at T_2 to refrain from doing X. By hypothesis, the belief held by Smith at T_1 was true. Thus, by hypothesis, Jones did X at T_2. But even if we assume that the belief held by Smith at T_1 was *in fact* true, we can add that the belief held by Smith at T_1 *might have* turned out to be false.[25] Thus, even if we say that Jones *in fact* did X at T_2, we can add that Jones *might not* have done X at T_2—meaning by this that it was within Jones's power at T_2 to refrain from doing X. Smith held a true belief which might have turned out to be false, and, correspondingly, Jones performed an action which he was able to refrain from performing. Given that Smith correctly believed at T_1 that Jones would do X at T_2, we can still assign Jones the *power* at T_2 to refrain from doing X. All we need add is that the power in question is one which Jones *did not exercise*.

These last reflections have no application, however, when dealing with God's foreknowledge. Assume that God (being essentially omniscient) existed at T_1, and assume that He believed at T_1 that Jones would do X at

25. The phrase "might have" as it occurs in this sentence does not express mere *logical* possibility. I am not sure how to analyze the notion of possibility involved here, but I think it is roughly the same notion as is involved when we say, "Jones might have been killed in the accident (had it not been for the fact that at the last minute he decided not to go)."

T_2. It follows, again, that Jones did X at T_2. God's beliefs are true. But now, as above, let us inquire into what Jones was *able* to do at T_2. We cannot claim now, as in the Smith case, that the belief held by God at T_1 was *in fact* true but *might have* turned out to be false. No sense of "might have" has application here. It is a conceptual truth that God's beliefs are true. Thus, we cannot claim, as in the Smith case, that Jones *in fact* acted in accordance with God's beliefs but had the *ability* to refrain from so doing. The ability to refrain from acting in accordance with one of God's beliefs would be the ability to do something that would bring it about that one of God's beliefs was false. And no one could have an ability of this description. Thus, in the case of God's foreknowledge of Jones's action at T_2, if we are to assign Jones the ability at T_2 to refrain from doing X, we must understand this ability in some way other than the way we understood it when dealing with Smith's foreknowledge. In this case, either we must say that it was the ability at T_2 to bring it about that God believed otherwise than He did at T_1; or we must say that it was the ability at T_2 to bring it about that any person who believed at T_1 that Jones would do X at T_2 (one of whom was, by hypothesis, God) held a false belief and thus was not God. But, as pointed out earlier, neither of these last alternatives can be accepted.

The important thing to be learned from the study of Smith's foreknowledge of Jones's action is that the problem of divine foreknowledge has as one of its pillars the claim that truth is *analytically* connected with God's *beliefs*. No problem of determinism arises when dealing with human knowledge of future actions. This is because truth is not analytically connected with human belief even when (as in the case of human knowledge) truth is contingently conjoined to belief. If we suppose that Smith knows at T_1 that Jones will do X at T_2, what we are supposing is that Smith believes at T_1 that Jones will do X at T_2 and (as an additional, contingent, fact) that the belief in question is true. Thus having supposed that Smith knows at T_1 that Jones will do X at T_2, when we turn to a consideration of the situation of T_2 we can infer (1) that Jones *will* do X at T_2 (since Smith's belief is true), and (2) that Jones does not have the power at T_2 to do something that would bring it about that Jones did not *believe* as he did at T_1. But paradoxical though it may seem (and it seems paradoxical only at first sight), Jones can have the power at T_2 to do something that would bring it about that Smith did not have *knowledge* at T_1. This is simply to say that Jones can have the *power* at T_2 to do something that would bring it about that the belief held by Smith at T_1 (which was, in fact, true) was (instead) false. We are required only to add that since Smith's belief was in fact true (that is, was knowledge) Jones *did not* (in fact) *exercise* that power. But when we turn to a consideration of God's foreknowledge of Jones's action at T_2 the elbowroom between belief and truth disappears and, with it, the possibility of assigning Jones even the *power* of doing other than he does at T_2. We begin by supposing that God *knows* at T_1 that Jones will do X at T_2. As above, this is to suppose that God believes at T_1 that Jones will do X at T_2, and it is to suppose that this belief is true. But it is *not* an additional, contingent fact that the belief held by God is true. "God believes X" entails "X is true." Thus, having supposed that God knows (and thus believes) at T_1 that Jones will do X at T_2, we can infer (1) that Jones *will do* X at T_2 (since God's belief is true); (2) that Jones does not have the power at T_2 to do something that would bring it about that God did not hold the belief He held at T_1, and (3) that Jones does not have the power at T_2 to do something that would bring it about that the belief held by God at T_1 was false. This last is what we could *not* infer when truth and belief were only factually connected—as in the case of Smith's knowledge. To be sure, "Smith knows at T_1 that Jones will do X at T_2" and "God knows at T_1 that Jones will do X at T_2" both entail "Jones will do X at T_2" ("A knows X" entails "'X' is true"). But this similarity between "Smith knows X" and "God knows X" is not a point of any special interest in the present discussion. As Schleiermacher and Augustine rightly insisted (and as we discovered in our study of Smith's foreknowledge) the mere fact that someone knows in advance how another will act in the future is not enough to yield a problem of the sort we have been discussing. We begin to get a glimmer of the knot involved in the problem of divine foreknowledge when we shift attention away from the *similarities* between "Smith knows X" and "God knows X" (in particular, that they both entail "'X' is true") and concentrate instead on the logical *differences* which obtain between Smith's knowledge and God's knowledge. We get to the difference which makes the difference when, after analyzing the notion of knowledge as true belief (supported by evidence) we discover the radically dissimilar relations between truth and belief in the two cases. When truth is only factually connected with belief (as in Smith's knowledge) one can have the power (though, by hypothesis, one will not exercise it) to do something that would make the belief false. But when truth is analytically connected with belief (as in God's belief) no one can have the power to do something which would render the belief false.

To conclude: I have assumed that any statement of the form "A knows X" entails a statement of the form "A believes X" as well as a statement of the form "'X' is true." I have then supposed (as an analytic truth) that if a given person is omniscient, that person (1) holds no false beliefs, and (2) holds beliefs about the outcome of human actions in advance of their performance. In addition, I have assumed that the statement "If a given person is God that person is omniscient" is an a priori statement. (This last I have labeled the doctrine of God's essential omniscience.) Given these items (plus some premises concerning what is and what is not within one's power), I have argued that if God exists, it is not within one's power to do other than he does. I have inferred from this that if God exists, no human action is voluntary.

As emphasized earlier, I do not want to claim that the assumptions underpinning the argument are acceptable. In fact, it seems to me that a theologian interested in claiming both that God is omniscient and that men have free will could deny any one (or more) of them. For example, a theologian might deny that a statement of the form "A knows X" entails a statement of the form "A believes X" (some contemporary philosophers have denied this) or, alternatively, he might claim that this entailment holds in the case of human knowledge but fails in the case of God's knowledge. This latter would be to claim that when knowledge is attributed to God, the term "knowledge" bears a sense other than the one it has when knowledge is attributed to human beings. Then again, a theologian might object to the analysis of "omniscience" with which I have been working. Although I doubt if any Christian theologian would allow that an omniscient being could believe something false, he might claim that a given person could be omniscient although he did not hold beliefs about the outcome of human actions *in advance* of their performance. (This latter is the way Boethius escaped the problem.) Still again, a theologian might deny the doctrine of God's essential omniscience. He might admit that if a given person is God that person is omniscient, but he might deny that this statement formulates an a priori truth. This would be to say that although God is omniscient, He is not *essentially* omniscient. So far as I can see, within the conceptual framework of theology employing any one of these adjustments, the problem of divine foreknowledge outlined in this paper could not be formulated. There thus appears to be a rather wide range of alternatives open to the theologian at this point. It would be a mistake to think that commitment to determinism is an unavoidable implication of the Christian concept of divine omniscience.

But having arrived at this understanding, the importance of the preceding deliberations ought not to be overlooked. There is a pitfall in the doctrine of divine omniscience. That knowing involves believing (truly) is surely a tempting philosophical view (witness the many contemporary philosophers who have affirmed it). And the idea that God's attributes (including omniscience) are essentially connected to His nature, together with the idea that an omniscient being would hold no false beliefs and would hold beliefs about the outcome of human actions in advance of their performance, might be taken by some theologians as obvious candidates for inclusion in a finished Christian theology. Yet the theologian must approach these items critically. If they are embraced together, then if one affirms the existence of God, one is committed to the view that no human action is voluntary.

God Everlasting

NICHOLAS WOLTERSTORFF

All Christian theologians agree that God is without beginning and without end. The vast majority have held, in addition, that God is *eternal,* existing outside of time. Only a small minority have contended that God is *everlasting,* existing within time.[1] In what follows I shall take up the cudgels for that minority, arguing that God as conceived and presented by the biblical writers is a being whose own life and existence is temporal.

The biblical writers do not present God as some passive factor within reality but as an agent in it. Further, they present him as acting within *human* history. The god they present is neither the impassive god of the Oriental nor the nonhistorical god of the Deist. Indeed, so basic to the biblical writings is their speaking of God as agent within history that if one viewed God as only an impassive factor in reality, or as one whose agency does not occur within human history, one would have to regard the biblical speech about God as at best one long sequence of metaphors pointing to a reality for which they are singularly inept, and as at worst one long sequence of falsehoods.

More specifically, the biblical writers present God as a redeeming God. From times most ancient, man has departed from the pattern of responsibilities awarded him at his creation by God. A multitude of evils has followed. But God was not content to leave man in the mire of his misery.

---

1. The most noteworthy contemporary example is Oscar Cullmann, *Christ and Time* (Eng. tr., Philadelphia, 1950).

From *God and the Good: Essays in Honor of Henry Stob,* edited by Clifton J. Orlebeke and Lewis B. Smedes. Copyright © 1975 Wm. B. Eerdmans Publishing Company. Used by permission.

Aware of what is going on, he has resolved, in response to man's sin and its resultant evils, to bring about renewal. He has, indeed, already been acting in accord with that resolve, centrally and decisively in the life, death, and resurrection of Jesus Christ.

What I shall argue is that if we are to accept this picture of God as acting for the renewal of human life, we must conceive of him as everlasting rather than eternal. God the Redeemer cannot be a God eternal. This is so because God the Redeemer is a God who *changes*. And any being which changes is a being among whose states there is temporal succession. Of course, there is an important sense in which God as presented in the Scriptures is changeless: he is steadfast in his redeeming intent and ever faithful to his children. Yet, *ontologically*, God cannot be a redeeming God without there being changeful variation among his states.

If this argument proves correct the importance of the issue here confronting us for Christian theology can scarcely be exaggerated. A theology which opts for God as eternal cannot avoid being in conflict with the confession of God as redeemer. And given the obvious fact that God is presented in the Bible as a God who redeems, a theology which opts for God as eternal cannot be a theology faithful to the biblical witness.

Our line of argument will prove to be neither subtle nor complicated. So the question will insistently arise, why have Christian theologians so massively contended that God is eternal? Why has not the dominant tradition of Christian theology been that of God everlasting?

Our argument will depend heavily on taking with seriousness a certain feature of temporality which has been neglected in Western philosophy. But the massiveness of the God eternal tradition cannot, I am persuaded, be attributed merely to philosophical oversight. There are, I think, two factors more fundamental. One is the feeling, deep-seated in much of human culture, that the flowing of events into an irrecoverable and unchangeable past is a matter for deep regret. Our bright actions and shining moments do not long endure. The gnawing tooth of time bites all. And our evil deeds can never be undone. They are forever to be regretted. Of course, the philosopher is inclined to distinguish the mere fact of temporality from the actual pattern of the events in history and to argue that regrets about the latter should not slosh over into regrets about the former. The philosopher is right. The regrettableness of what transpires in time is not good ground for regretting that there is time. Yet where the philosopher sees the possibility and the need for a distinction, most people have seen none. Regrets over the pervasive pattern of what transpires within time have led whole societies to place the divine outside of time—freed from the "bondage" of temporality.

But I am persuaded that William Kneale is correct when he contends that the most important factor accounting for the tradition of God eternal within Christian theology was the influence of the classical Greek philosophers on the early theologians.[2] The distinction between eternal being and everlasting being was drawn for the first time in the history of thought by Plato (*Timaeus* 37–38), though the language he uses is reminiscent of words used still earlier by Parmenides. Plato does not connect eternity and divinity, but he does make clear his conviction that eternal being is the highest form of reality. This was enough to influence the early Christian theologians, who did their thinking within the milieu of Hellenic and Hellenistic thought, to assign eternity to God. Thus was the fateful choice made.

A good many twentieth-century theologians have been engaged in what one might call the dehellenization of Christian theology. If Kneale's contention is correct, then in this essay I am participating in that activity. Of course, not every bit of dehellenization is laudatory from the Christian standpoint, for not everything that the Greeks said is false. What is the case, though, is that the patterns of classical Greek thought are incompatible with the pattern of biblical thought. And in facing the issue of God everlasting versus God eternal we are dealing with the fundamental pattern of biblical thought. Indeed, I am persuaded that unless the tradition of God eternal is renounced, fundamental dehellenizing will perpetually occupy itself in the suburbs, never advancing to the city center. Every attempt to purge Christian theology of the traces of incompatible Hellenic patterns of thought must fail unless it removes the roadblock of the God eternal tradition. Around this barricade there are no detours.

I

Before we can discuss whether God is outside of time we must ask what it would be for something to be outside of time. That is, before we can ask whether God is eternal we must ask what it would be for something to be eternal. But this in turn demands that we are clear on what it would be for something to be a temporal entity. We need not be clear on all the features which something has by virtue of being temporal—on all facets of temporality—but we must at least be able to say what is necessary and sufficient for something's being in time.

For our purposes we can take as the decisive feature of temporality the exemplification of the temporal ordering-relations of precedence, succession, and simultaneity. Unless some entities did stand to each other in one or the other of these relations, there would be no temporal reality. Conversely, if there is temporal reality then there are pairs of entities whose members stand to each other in the relation of one occurring before (prece-

2. William Kneale, "Time and Eternity in Theology," *Proceedings of the Aristotelian Society* (1961).

dence) or one occurring after (succession) or one occurring simultaneously with (simultaneity) the other.

We must ask in turn what sort of entity is such that its examples can stand to each other in the relations of precedence, succession, and simultaneity. For not every sort of entity is such. The members of a pair of trees cannot stand in these relations. The golden chain tree outside my back door neither occurs before nor after nor simultaneously with the shingle oak outside my front door. Of course, *the sprouting of the former* stands in one of these relations to *the sprouting of the latter;* and so too does *the demise of the latter* to *the demise of the former.* But the trees themselves do not. They do not occur at all.

We have in this example a good clue, though, as to the sort of entity whose examples can stand in the relations of precedence, succession, and simultaneity. It is just such entities as *the demise of my golden chain tree* and *the sprouting of my shingle oak.* It is, in short, what I shall call events that stand in these relations.

As I conceive of an event, it consists in something's actually having some property, or something's actually performing some action, or something's actually standing in some relation to something. Events as I conceive them are all actual occurrences. They are not what *can have* occurrences. They are, rather, themselves occurrences. Furthermore, as I conceive of events, there may be two or more events consisting in a given entity's having a given property (or performing a given action). For example, my golden chain tree flowered last spring and is flowering again this spring. So there are two events each consisting in the flowering of my golden chain tree. One began and ended last year. The other began and will end this year.

Such events as I have thus far offered by way of example are all temporally limited, in the sense that there are times at which the event is not occurring. There are times at which it has not yet begun or has already ended. Last year's flowering of my golden chain tree is such. It began at some time last spring and has now for about a year or so ceased. But there are other events which are not in this way temporally limited; *3's being prime,* for example. If time itself begins and ends, then this event, too, occurs wholly within a finite interval. Yet even then there is no time at which it does not occur.

I said that every event consists in something's actually having some property, actually performing some action, or actually standing in some relation to something. So consider some event *e* which consists in some entity *a* having some property or performing some action or standing in some relation. Let us call *a,* a *subject* of *e.* And let us call *e* an *aspect* of *a.* A given event may well have more than one subject. For example, an event consisting of my sitting under my shingle oak has both me and the shingle oak as subjects. Indeed, I think it can also be viewed as having the relation of *sitting under* as subject. I see nothing against regarding an event consisting of my sitting under my shingle oak as identical with an event consisting of the relation of *sitting under* being exemplified by me with respect to my shingle oak.

Now consider that set of a given entity's aspects such that each member bears a temporal order-relation to every member of the set and none bears a temporal order-relation to any aspect not a member of the set. Let us call that set, provided that it is not empty, the *time-strand* of that entity. I assume it to be true that every entity has at most one time-strand. That is, I assume that no entity has two or more sets of temporally interrelated aspects such that no member of the one set bears any temporal order-relation to any member of the other. I do not, however, assume that each of the aspects of every entity which has a time-strand belongs to the strand. And as to whether every entity has at least one time-strand—that of course is involved in the question as to whether anything is eternal.

Consider, next, a set of events such that each member stands to every member in one of the temporal order-relations, and such that no member stands to any event which is not a member in any of these relations. I shall call such a set a *temporal array*. A temporal array is of course just the union of a set of time-strands such that every member of each member strand bears some temporal order-relation to every member of every other member strand, and such that no member of any member strand bears any temporal order-relation to any member of any strand which is not a member of the set. In what follows I assume that there is but one temporal array. I assume, that is, that every member of every time-strand bears a temporal order-relation to every member of every time-strand.

Now suppose that there is some entity all of whose aspects are such that they are to be found in no temporal array whatsoever. Such an entity would be, in the most radical way possible, outside of time. Accordingly, I shall define "eternal" thus:

> Def. 1: x is eternal if and only if x has no aspect which is a member of the temporal array.

An alternative definition would have been this: "x is eternal if and only if x has no time-strand." The difference between the two definitions is that, on the latter, an entity is eternal if none of its aspects bears any temporal order-relation to any of those events which are *its* aspects; whereas on the former, what is required of an entity for it to be eternal is that none of its aspects be related by any temporal order-relation to *any event whatsoever*. Of course, if every event which bears any temporal order-relation to any event whatsoever is also simultaneous with itself, then everything which fails to satisfy the "temporal array" definition of "eternal" will also fail to satisfy the "time-strand" definition.

At this point, certain ambiguities in the concepts of precedence, succession, and simultaneity should be resolved. By saying that event e_1 occurs *simultaneously with* event e_2, I mean that there is some time at which both e_1 and e_2 are occurring. I do *not* mean—though indeed this might reasonably also have been meant by the words—that there is *no* time at which one of e_1 and e_2 is occurring and the other is not. When two events stand in that latter relation I shall say that they are *wholly simultaneous*. By saying that e_1 *precedes* e_2, I mean that there is some time at which e_1 but not e_2 is occurring, which precedes all times at which e_2 is occurring. I do not mean that every time at which e_1 occurs precedes every time at which e_2 occurs. When e_1 stands to e_2 in this latter relationship, I shall say that *it wholly precedes* e_2. Lastly, by saying that e_1 *succeeds* e_2, I mean that there is some time at which e_1 but not e_2 is occurring which succeeds all times at which e_2 is occurring. This, as in the case of precedence, allows for overlap. And, as in the case of precedence, an overlapping case of succession may be distinguished from a case in which one event *wholly succeeds* another.

When "simultaneity," "precedence," and "succession" are understood thus, they do not stand for exclusive relations. An event e_1 may precede, occur simultaneously with, and succeed, another event e_2. But of course e_1 cannot *wholly* precede e_2 while also being *wholly* simultaneous with it, and so forth for the other combinations.

Reflecting on the consequences of the above definitions and explanations, someone might protest that the definition of eternal is altogether too stringent. For consider, say, the number 3. This, no doubt, was referred to by Euclid and also by Cantor. So, by our explanation of "aspect," *3's being referred to by Euclid* was an aspect of the number 3, and *3's being referred to by Cantor* was another aspect thereof. And of course the former preceded the latter. So, by our definition, 3 is not eternal. But—it may be protested—the fact that something is successively referred to should not be regarded as ground for concluding that it is not eternal. For after all, successive references to something do not produce any change in it. Although they produce variation among its aspects, they do not produce a changeful variation among them.

In response to this protest it must be emphasized that the concept of an eternal being is not identical with the concept of an unchanging being. The root idea behind the concept of an eternal being is not that of one which does not change but rather that of one which is outside of time. And a question of substance is whether an unchanging being may fail to be eternal. The most thoroughgoing and radical way possible for an entity to be outside of time is that which something enjoys if it satisfies our definition of "eternal." And it must simply be acknowledged that if an entity is successively referred to, then it is not in the most thoroughgoing way outside of time. There is temporal succession among its aspects.

However, the idea of change could be used by the protester in another way. It is indeed true that not every variation among the aspects of an entity constitutes change therein. Only variation among some of them—call them its *change-relevant* aspects—does so. So on the ground that the change-relevant aspects of an entity are more basic to it, we might distinguish between something being *fundamentally* noneternal and something being *trivially* noneternal. Something is *fundamentally* noneternal if it fails to satisfy the concept of being eternal by virtue of some of its change-relevant aspects. Something is *trivially* noneternal if its failure to satisfy the concept of being eternal is not by virtue of any of its change-relevant aspects.

Now in fact it will be change-relevant aspects of God to which I will appeal in arguing that he is not eternal. Thus my argument will be that God is *fundamentally* noneternal.

II

In order to present our argument that God is fundamentally noneternal we must now take note of a second basic feature of temporality; namely, that all temporal reality comes in the three modes of past, present, and future.[3]

An important fact about the temporal array is that some events within it are *present*: they *are occurring*; some are *past*: they *were occurring*; some are *future*: they *will be occurring*. Indeed, every event is either past or present or future. And not only *is* this the case now. It always was the case in the past that every event was either past or present or future. And it always will be the case in the future that every event is either past or present or future. Further, every event in the array is such that it either was present or is present or will be present. No event can be past unless it was present. No event can be future unless it will be present. Thus the present is the most basic of the three modes of temporality. To be past is just to have been present. To be future is just to be going to be present. Further, if an event is past, it *presently* is past. If an event is future, it *presently* is future. In this way, too, the present is fundamental.

The reason every event in the temporal array is either past, present, or

3. There are two other basic features of temporality: one is the phenomenon of temporal location—the fact that events occur at or within intervals. The other is the phenomenon of temporal duration—the fact that intervals have lengths. In our preceding discussion we repeatedly made appeal to the phenomenon of temporal location without calling attention to our doing so.

future is as follows: in order to be in the array at all, an event must occur either before or after or at the same time as some other event. But then, of course, it must occur sometime. And when an event is occurring it is present. So consider any event *e* which is to be found in the temporal array. If *e* is occurring, *e* is present. If, on the other hand, *e* is not occurring, then *e* either precedes or succeeds what is occurring. For *some* event is presently occurring. And every event in the array either precedes or succeeds or is wholly simultaneous with every other. But if *e* were wholly simultaneous with what is occurring, *e* itself would be occurring. So *e* either succeeds or precedes what is occurring if it is not itself occurring. Now for any event *x* to precede any event *y* is just for *x* sometime to be past when *y* is not past. So if *e* precedes what is occurring and is not itself occurring, then *e* is past. On the other hand, for any event *x* to succeed any event *y* is just for *x* sometime to be future when *y* is not future. So if *e* succeeds what is occurring and is not itself occurring, then *e* is future. Hence everything to be found in the temporal array is either past, present, or future.

In contemporary Western philosophy the phenomenon of temporal modality has been pervasively neglected or ignored in favor of the phenomena of temporal order-relationships, temporal location, and temporal duration. Thus time has been "spatialized." For though space provides us with close analogues to all three of these latter phenomena, it provides us with no analogue whatever to the past/present/future distinction.[4]

Perhaps the most fundamental and consequential manifestation of this neglect is to be found in the pervasive assumption that all propositions expressed with tensed sentences are mode-indifferent and dated. Consider for example the tensed sentence "My golden chain tree is flowering." The assumption is that what I would assert if I now (June 5, 1974) assertively uttered this sentence with normal sense is *that my golden chain tree is or was or will be flowering on June 5, 1974*. And that the proposition I would be asserting if I assertively uttered the same sentence on June 4, 1975, is *that my golden chain tree is or was or will be flowering on June 4, 1975*. And so forth.

In order to see clearly what the assumption in question comes to, it will be helpful to introduce a way of expressing tenses alternative to that found in our natural language.[5] We begin by introducing the three tense operators, *P*, *T*, and *F*. These are to be read, respectively, as "it was the case

---

4. A recent example of the neglect of temporal modality in favor of temporal location is to be found in David Lewis, "Anselm and Actuality," *NOÛS*, 4 (May 1970). Concluding several paragraphs of discussion he says, "If we take a timeless view and ignore our own location in time, the big difference between the present time and other times vanishes."

5. See the writings of Arthur Prior, especially *Time and Modality* (Oxford, 1957); *Past, Present and Future* (Oxford, 1967); and *Time and Tense* (Oxford, 1968).

that," "it is the case that," and "it will be the case that." They are to be attached as prefixes either to sentences in the present tense which lack any
such prefix,[6] or to compound sentences which consist of sentences in the
present tense with one or more such prefixes attached. And the result of
attaching one such operator to a sentence is to yield a new sentence. For
example: P (my golden chain tree is flowering), to be read as, *"it was the
case that my golden chain tree is flowering."* And: F[P (my golden chain
tree is flowering)], to be read as: *"it will be the case that it was the case
that my golden chain tree is flowering."*

So consider any sentence *s* which is either a present tense sentence with
no operators prefixed or a compound sentence consisting of a present tense
sentence with one or more operators prefixed. The proposition expressed
by P(*s*) is true if and only if the proposition expressed by *s* was true (in
the past). The proposition expressed by T(*s*) is true if and only if the
proposition expressed by *s* is true (now, in the present).[7] And the proposition expressed by F(*s*) is true if and only if the proposition expressed by *s*
will be true (in the future).

Any proposition expressed by a tensed sentence from ordinary speech
can be expressed by a sentence in this alternative language. Thus "My
golden chain tree was flowering" has as its translational equivalent "P (my
golden chain tree is flowering)." And "My golden chain tree will have
been flowering" has as its translational equivalent "F[P (my golden chain
tree is flowering)]."

Let us now introduce a fourth tense operator, D, defining this one in
terms of the preceding three thus:

Def. 2: D(. . .), if and only if P(. . .) or T(. . .) or F(. . .).

And let us read it as: "It was or is or will be the case that. . . ." Let us
call this the *tense-indifference* tense operator. And, correspondingly, let us
call a sentence which has at least one tense operator and all of whose tense
operators are tense-indifferent, a *wholly tense-indifferent* sentence. Furthermore, as the ordinary language counterpart to the tense-indifferent operator
let us use the verb in its present tense with a bar over it, thus: "My golden
chain tree is flowering." Or "My golden chain tree flowers."

Finally, let us add to our linguistic stock a certain set of modifiers of
these tense operators—modifiers of the form "at *t*," "before *t*," and "after *t*,"
where *t* stands in for some expression designating a time which is such that

6. This reflects the fact that the past is what was *present*; the future what will be
present.
7. Thus, strictly speaking, the T operator is unnecessary. Attaching T to any sentence *s* always yields a sentence which expresses the same proposition as does *s* by
itself. This reflects the fact that what is past is *presently* past, what is future is
presently future, and, of course, what is present is *presently* present.

that expression can be used to designate that time no matter whether that time is in the past, present, or future. These modifiers are to be attached to our tense operators, thus: *P at 1974* (. . .). The result of attaching one to an operator is to yield an operator of a new form—what one might call a *dated* tense operator. The proposition expressed by a sentence of the form *P at t(s)* is true if and only if the proposition expressed by *s* was true at or within time *t*. The proposition expressed by *T at t(s)* is true if and only if the proposition expressed by *s* is true at or within time *t*. And the proposition expressed by *F at t(s)* is true if and only if the proposition expressed by *s* will be true at or within time *t*. Thus the proposition expressed by "P at 1973 (my golden chain tree is flowering)" is true if and only if my golden chain tree was flowering at or within 1973. Similarly, the proposition expressed by a sentence of the form *P before t(s)* is true if and only if the proposition expressed by *s* was true before *t*; likewise for *T before t(s)* and *F before t(s)*. And the proposition expressed by a sentence of the form *P after t(s)* is true if and only if the proposition expressed by *s* was true after *t*; likewise for *T after t(s)* and *F after t(s)*. Let us call a sentence which has tense operators and all of whose tense operators are dated ones, a *fully dated* sentence.

The assumption underlying a great deal of contemporary philosophy can now be stated thus: every proposition expressed by a sentence which is not wholly tense-indifferent and not fully dated is a proposition which can be expressed by some sentence which is wholly tense-indifferent and fully dated. Consider, for example, the sentence "T (my golden chain tree is flowering)"—the translational equivalent of the ordinary sentence, "My golden chain tree is flowering." Suppose that I assertively utter this sentence on June 5, 1974. The assumption is that the proposition I assert by uttering this sentence is that which is expressed by "D at June 5, 1974 (my golden chain tree is flowering)." And in general, where *s* is some present tense sentence, the assumption is that the proposition asserted by assertively uttering *s* at time *t* is just that which would be asserted by assertively uttering *D at t(s)*. Similarly, it is assumed that the proposition asserted by assertively uttering *P(s)* at time *t* is that which would be asserted by assertively uttering *D before t(s)*. And it is assumed that the proposition asserted by assertively uttering *F(s)* at time *t* is that which would be asserted by assertively uttering *D after t(s)*.

On this view, tense-committed sentences are characteristically used to assert different propositions on different occasions of use. For example, if the sentence "My golden chain tree is flowering" is assertively uttered on June 5, it is being used to assert that it is or was or will be the case on June 5 that my golden chain tree is flowering; whereas, if uttered on June 4, it is being used to assert that it is or was or will be the case on June 4 that my golden chain tree is flowering. Whether this view is correct will be considered shortly. If it is, then tense-committed sentences are in that way different from wholly tense-indifferent sentences. For these latter are used to assert the same proposition on all occasions of utterance.

I think we now have the assumption in question clearly enough before us to weigh its acceptability. It is in fact clearly false. To see this, suppose that I now (June 5, 1974) assertively utter the sentence "My golden chain tree is flowering" and "*D at June 5, 1974 (my golden chain tree is flowering).*" The proposition asserted with the former entails that the flowering of my golden chain tree is something that *is* occurring, *now*, *presently*. But the latter does not entail this at all. In general, if someone assertively utters a present tense sentence *s* at *t*, what he asserts is true if and only if the proposition "*D at t(s)*" is true. Yet "*s*" and "*D at t(s)*" are distinct propositions. So also, if I now assertively utter "My golden chain tree was flowering," what I assert entails that the flowering of my golden chain tree is something that *did* take place, in the past. Whereas the proposition asserted with "*D before June 5, 1974 (my golden chain tree is flowering)*" does not entail this. And this nonidentity of the propositions holds even though it is the case that if someone assertively utters *P(s)* at *t*, what he asserts is true if and only if the proposition *D before t(s)* is true.

Just as a wholly tense-indifferent sentence is used to assert the same proposition no matter what the time of utterance, so, too, the proposition asserted with such a sentence does not vary in truth value. If it is ever true, it is always true, that *D at June 5, 1974 (my golden chain tree is flowering)*. And if it is ever false, it is always false. Such a proposition is constant in its truth value. But an implication of the failure of the contemporary assumption is that the same cannot be said for the propositions expressed by tense-committed sentences. At least some of these are such that they are sometimes true, sometimes false. They are variable in their truth value. For example, "My golden chain tree is flowering" is now true; but two weeks ago it was false.

So the situation is not that in successively uttering a tense-committed sentence we are asserting distinct propositions, each of which is constant in truth value and each of which could also be expressed with wholly tense indifferent, fully dated, sentences. The situation is rather that we are repeatedly asserting a proposition which is variable in its truth value. Contemporary philosophers, along with assuming the dispensability of the temporal modes, have assumed that all propositions are constant in truth value. Plato's lust for eternity lingers on.

Though philosophers have ignored the modes of time in their theories, we as human beings are all aware of the past/present/future distinction. For without such knowledge we would be lost in the temporal array. Suppose one knew, for each event *x*, which events $\overline{occur}$ simultaneously with *x*, which $\overline{occur}$ before *x*, and which $\overline{occur}$ after *x*. (Recall the significance of the bar over a present-tense verb.) Then with respect to, say, Luther's posting of his theses, one would know which events $\overline{\text{occur}}$ simultaneously therewith, which $\overline{\text{occur}}$ before it, and which $\overline{\text{occur}}$ after it. And so forth, for all other temporal interrelations of events. There would then still be something of enormous importance which one would not on that account know. One would not know where we are in the array of temporally ordered events. For one would not know which events are occurring, which were occurring, and which will be occurring. To know this it is not sufficient to know, with respect to every event, which events $\overline{\text{occur}}$ simultaneously therewith, which $\overline{\text{occur}}$ before, and which $\overline{\text{occur}}$ after.

Nor, as we have seen above, is such knowledge gained by knowing what $\overline{\text{occurs}}$ at what time. If all I know with respect to events $e_1 \ldots e_n$ is that they all $\overline{\text{occur}}$ at the time, say, of the inauguration of the first post-Nixon President, then I do not yet know whether those events are in the past, in the present, or in the future. And if all my knowledge with respect to every event and every interval is of that deficient sort, I do not know where we are in the temporal array. For I do not know which events are present, which are past, and which are future.

III

It might seem obvious that God, as described by the biblical writers, is a being who changes, and who accordingly is fundamentally noneternal. For God is described as a being who *acts*—in creation, in providence, and for the renewal of mankind. He is an agent, not an impassive factor in reality. And from the manner in which his acts are described, it seems obvious that many of them have beginnings and endings, that accordingly they stand in succession relations to each other, and that these successive acts are of such a sort that their presence and absence on God's time-strand constitutes changes thereon. Thus it seems obvious that God is fundamentally noneternal.

God is spoken of as calling Abraham to leave Chaldea and later instructing Moses to return to Egypt. So does not the event of *God's instructing Moses* succeed that of *God's calling Abraham*? And does not this sort of succession constitute a change on God's time-strand—not a change in his "essence," but nonetheless a change on his time-strand? Again, God is spoken of as leading Israel through the Red Sea and later sending his Son into the world. So does not his doing the latter succeed his doing the former? And does not the fact of this sort of succession constitute a change along God's time-strand?

In short, it seems evident that the biblical writers regard God as having a time-strand of his own on which actions on his part are to be found, and that some at least of these actions vary in such a way that there are changes along the strand. It seems evident that they do not regard changes on time-strands as confined to entities in God's creation. The God who acts, in the way in which the biblical writers speak of God as acting, seems clearly to change.

Furthermore, is it not clear from how they speak that the biblical writers regarded many of God's acts as bearing temporal order-relations to events which are not aspects of him but rather aspects of the earth, of ancient human beings, and so forth? The four cited above, for example, seem all to be described thus. It seems obvious that God's actions as described by the biblical writers stand in temporal order-relations to all the other events in our own time-array.

However, I think it is not at all so obvious as on first glance it might appear that the biblical writers do in fact describe God as changing. Granted that the language they use suggests this. It is not at once clear that this is what they wished to say with this language. It is not clear that this is how they were describing God. Let us begin to see why this is so by reflecting on the following passage from St. Thomas Aquinas:

> Nor, if the action of the first agent is eternal, does it follow that His effect is eternal, . . . God acts voluntarily in the production of things, . . . God's act of understanding and willing is, necessarily, His act of making. Now, an effect follows from the intellect and the will according to the determination of the intellect and the command of the will. Moreover, just as the intellect determines every other condition of the thing made, so does it prescribe the time of its making; for art determines not only that this thing is to be such and such, but that it is to be at this particular time, even as a physician determines that a dose of medicine is to be drunk at such and such a particular time, so that, if his act of will were of itself sufficient to produce the effect, the effect would follow anew from his previous decision, without any new action on his part. Nothing, therefore, prevents our saying that God's action existed from all eternity, whereas its effect was not present from eternity, but existed at that time when, from all eternity, He ordained it (*Summa Contra Gentiles* II.35; cf. II.36, 4).

Let us henceforth call an event which neither begins nor ends an *everlasting event*. And let us call an event which either begins or ends, a *temporal* event. In the passage above, St. Thomas is considering God's acts of bringing about temporal events. So consider some such act; say, that of God's bringing about Israel's deliverance from Egypt. The temporal event in question, Israel's deliverance from Egypt, occurred (let us say) in 1225 B.C. But from the fact that what God brought about occurred in 1225 it does not follow, says Aquinas, that God's act of bringing it about occurred in 1225. In fact, it does not follow that this act had any beginning or ending whatsoever. And in general, suppose that God brings about some temporal event *e*. From the fact that *e* is temporal it does not follow, says Aquinas, that God's act of bringing about *e*'s occurrence is temporal. The temporality of the event which God brings about does not infect God's act of bringing it about. God's act of bringing it about may well be everlasting. This can perhaps more easily be seen, he says, if we remember that God, unlike us, does not have to "take steps" so as to bring about the occurrence of some event. He need only will that it occur. If God just wants it to be the case that *e* occur at *t*, *e* occurs at *t*.

Thus God can bring about changes in our history without himself changing. The occurrence of the event of Israel's deliverance from Egypt constitutes a change in our history. But there is no counterpart change among God's aspects by virtue of his bringing this event about.

Now let us suppose that the four acts of God cited above—instructing Moses, calling Abraham, leading Israel through the Red Sea, and sending his Son into the world—regardless of the impression we might gain from the biblical language used to describe them, also have the structure of God's bringing about the occurrence of some temporal event. Suppose, for example, that God's leading Israel through the Red Sea has the structure of God's bringing it about that Israel's passage through the Red Sea occurs. And suppose Aquinas is right that the temporality of Israel's passage does not infect with temporality God's act of bringing about this passage. Then what is strictly speaking the case is not that God's leading Israel through the Red Sea occurs during 1225. What is rather the case is that Israel's passage through the Red Sea occurs during 1225, and that God brings this passage about. And the temporality of the passage does not entail the temporality of God's bringing it about. This latter may be everlasting. So, likewise, the fact that the occurrence of this passage marks a change in our history does not entail that God's bringing it about marks a change among God's aspects. God may unchangingly bring about historical changes.

It is natural, at this point, to wonder whether we do not have in hand here a general strategy for interpreting the biblical language about God acting. Is it not perhaps the case that all those acts of God which the biblical writers speak of as beginning or as ending really consist in God performing the everlasting event of bringing about the occurrence of some temporal event?

Well, God does other things with respect to temporal events than bringing about their occurrence. For example, he also *knows* them. Why then should it be thought that the best way to interpret all the temporal-event language used to describe God's actions is by reference to God's action of bringing about the occurrence of some event? May it not be that the best way to interpret what is said with some of such language is by reference to one of those other acts which God performs with respect to temporal events? But then if God is not to change, it is not only necessary that the temporality of e not infect God's act of *bringing about* the occurrence of e, but also that *every* act of God such that he performs it with respect to e not be infected by the temporality of e. For example, if God *knows* some temporal event e, his knowledge of e must not be infected by the temporality of e.

So the best way of extrapolating from Aquinas' hint would probably be along the lines of the following theory concerning God's actions and the biblical speech about them. All God's actions are everlasting. None has either beginning or ending. Of these everlasting acts, the structure of some consists in God's performing some action with respect to some event. And at least some of the events that God acts with respect to are temporal events. However, in no case does the temporality of the event that God acts with respect to infect the event of his acting. On the contrary, his acting with respect to some temporal event is itself invariably an everlasting event. So whenever the biblical writers use temporal-event language to describe God's actions, they are to be interpreted as thereby claiming that God acts with respect to some temporal event. They are not to be interpreted as claiming that God's acting is itself a temporal event. God as described by the biblical writers is to be interpreted as acting, and as acting with respect to temporal events. But he is not to be interpreted as changing. All his acts are everlasting.

This, I think, is a fascinating theory. If true, it provides a way of harmonizing the fundamental biblical teaching that God is a being who acts in our history, with the conviction that God does not change. How far the proposed line of biblical interpretation can be carried out, I do not know. I am not aware of any theologian who has ever tried to carry it out, though there are a great many theologians who might have relieved the tension in their thought by developing and espousing it. But what concerns us here is not so much what the theory can adequately deal with as what it cannot adequately deal with. Does the theory in fact provide us with a wholly satisfactory way of harmonizing the biblical presentation of God as acting in history with the conviction that God is fundamentally eternal?

Before we set about looking for a refutation of the theory it should be observed, though, that even if the theory were true God would still not be eternal. For consider God's acts of bringing about Abraham's leaving of Chaldea and of bringing about Israel's passage through the Red Sea. These would both be, on the theory, *everlasting* acts. Both are always occurring. Hence they occur simultaneously. They stand to each other in the temporal order-relation of simultaneity. And since both are aspects of God, God accordingly has a time-strand on which these acts are to be found. Hence God is not eternal. Further, these are surely change-relevant aspects of God. Hence God is fundamentally noneternal.[8]

Though I myself think that this argument is sound, it would not be decisive if presented to Aquinas. For Aquinas held that God is simple. And an implication of this contention on his part is that all aspects of God are identical. Hence in God's case there are no two aspects which are simultaneous with each other; for there are no two aspects at all.

A reply is possible. For consider that which is, on Aquinas' theory, God's single aspect; and refer to it as you will—say, as *God's being omnipotent*. This aspect presumably occurs at the same time as itself. Whenever it occurs, it is itself occurring. It is simultaneous with itself. Furthermore, it occurs simultaneously with every temporal event whatsoever. Since God's being omnipotent is always occurring, it "overlaps" all temporal events whatsoever. So once again we have the conclusion: God is noneternal, indeed, he is fundamentally noneternal.

It is true, though, that even if Aquinas were to accept this last argument he would not *say*, in conclusion, that God was noneternal. For Aquinas defined an eternal being as one which is without beginning and without end, and which has no *succession* among its aspects (*Summa Theologica*, I.I q 10 a 1). Thus as Aquinas defined eternal, an eternal being may very well have aspects which stand to each other in the temporal order-relation of simultaneity. What Aquinas ruled out was just aspects standing in the temporal order-relation of succession. Our own definition of "eternal," which disallows simultaneity as well as succession, is in this way more thoroughgoing than is Aquinas'. For a being at least one of whose aspects occurs simultaneously with some event is not yet, in the most radical way possible, outside of time. However, in refutation of the extrapolated Thomistic theory sketched out above I shall now offer an argument against God's being eternal which establishes that there is not only simultaneity but succession among God's aspects, and not just succession but *changeful* succession. This argument will be as relevant to the issue of God's being eternal on Aquinas' definition of eternal as it is on my own definition.

To refute the extrapolated Thomistic theory we would have to do one or the other of two things. We would have to show that some of the temporal-event language the biblical writers use in speaking of God's actions cannot properly be construed in the suggested way—that is, cannot be con-

8. By a similar argument the number 3 can be seen to be fundamentally noneternal. Surely *3's being odd* and *3's being prime* are both change-relevant aspects of 3. If either of these were for a while an aspect of 3 and then for a while not, we would conclude that 3 had changed. But these two aspects occur simultaneously with each other. They stand to each other in the temporal order-relation of simultaneity. Hence 3 is fundamentally noneternal.

strued as used to put forth the claim that God acts in some way with respect to some temporal events. Or, alternatively, we would have to show that some of the actions that God performs with respect to temporal events are themselves temporal, either because they are infected by the temporality of the events or for some other reason.

One way of developing this latter alternative would be to show that some of God's actions must be understood as a response to the free actions of human beings—that what God does he sometimes does in response to what some human being does. I think this is in fact the case. And I think it follows, given that all human actions are temporal, that those actions of God which are "response" actions are temporal as well. But to develop this line of thought would be to plunge us deep into questions of divine omniscience and human freedom. So I shall make a simpler, though I think equally effective objection to the theory, arguing that in the case of certain of God's actions the temporality of the event that God acts on infects his own action with temporality.

Three such acts are the diverse though similar acts of knowing about some temporal event that it is occurring (that it is *present*), of knowing about some temporal event that it was occurring (that it is *past*), and of knowing about some temporal event that it will be occurring (that it is *future*). Consider the first of these. No one can know about some temporal event *e* that it is occurring except when it is occurring. Before *e* has begun to occur one cannot know that it is occurring, for it is not. Nor after *e* has ceased to occur can one know that it is occurring, for it is not. So suppose that *e* has a beginning. Then P's knowing about *e* that it is occurring cannot occur until *e* begins. And suppose that *e* has an ending. Then P's knowing about *e* that it is occurring cannot occur beyond *e*'s cessation. But every temporal event has (by definition) either a beginning or an ending. So every case of knowing about some temporal event that it is occurring itself either begins or ends (or both). Hence the act of knowing about *e* that it is occurring is infected by the temporality of *e*. So also, the act of knowing about *e* that it *was* occurring, and the act of knowing about *e* that it *will be* occurring, are infected by the temporality of *e*.

But God, as the biblical writers describe him, performs all three of these acts, and performs them on temporal events. He knows what is happening in our history, what has happened, and what will happen. Hence, some of God's actions are themselves temporal events. But surely the nonoccurrence followed by the occurrence followed by the nonoccurrence of such knowings constitutes a change on God's time-strand. Accordingly, God is fundamentally noneternal.[9]

9. This line of argument is adumbrated by Arthur Prior here and there in his essay "Formalities of Omniscience," in *Time and Tense*. It is also adumbrated by Norman Kretzmann, "Omniscience and Immutability," *Journal of Philosophy*, 63 (1966).

It is important, if the force of this argument is to be discerned, that one distinguish between, on the one hand, the act of knowing about some event *e* that it $\overline{occurs}$ at some time *t* (recall the significance of the bar) and, on the other hand, the act of knowing about *e* that it is occurring or of knowing that it was occurring or of knowing that it will be occurring. Knowing about *e* that it $\overline{occurs}$ at *t* is an act not infected by the temporality of the event known. *That Calvin's flight from Geneva $\overline{occurs}$ in 1537* is something that can be known at any and every time whatsoever. For it is both true, and constant in its truth value. But *that Calvin's flight from Geneva is occurring* is variable in its truth value. It once was true, it now is false. And since one can know only what is true, this proposition cannot be known at every time. It cannot be known now. God can know, concerning every temporal event whatsoever, what time that event $\overline{occurs}$ at, without such knowledge of his being temporal. But he cannot know concerning any temporal event whatsoever that it is occurring, or know that it was occurring, or know that it will be occurring, without that knowledge being itself temporal.

Similarly, we must distinguish between, on the one hand, the act of knowing about some temporal event *e* that it $\overline{occurs}$ simultaneously with events $e_1 \ldots e_n$, after events $f_1 \ldots f_n$, and before events $g_1 \ldots g_n$; and, on the other hand, the act of knowing about *e* that it is occurring or of knowing that it was occurring or of knowing that it will be occurring. Knowledge of the former sort is not infected by the temporality of the event whose temporal order-relationships are known. Knowledge of the latter sort is. I know now that Calvin's flight from Geneva $\overline{occurs}$ after Luther's posting of his theses $\overline{occurs}$. But once again, I do not and cannot now know that Calvin's flight *is* occurring. Because it is not. So too, God once knew that Calvin's flight from Geneva was occurring. But he no longer knows this. For he, too, does not know that which is not so. Thus, in this respect his knowledge has changed. But God always knows that Calvin's flight from Geneva $\overline{occurs}$ after Luther's posting of his theses $\overline{occurs}$. Only if time lacked modes and only if propositions were all constant in truth value could God's knowledge be unchanging—assuming that God's knowledge comprises temporal as well as everlasting events.

The act of *remembering* that *e* has occurred is also an act infected by the temporality of *e* (remembering is, of course, a species of knowing). For one can only remember that *e* has occurred after *e* has occurred. "P

The essence of the argument is missed in discussions of Kretzmann's paper by Hector Castaneda, "Omniscience and Indexical Reference," *Journal of Philosophy*, 64 (1967); and Nelson Pike, *God and Timelessness* (New York, 1970), ch. 5. Castaneda and Pike fail to take the *modes* of time with full seriousness; as a partial defense of them it should perhaps be admitted as not wholly clear that Kretzmann himself does so.

remembers that e $\overline{\text{occurs}}$" entails that e has occurred. So if e is an event that has a beginning, then the act of remembering that e has occurred has a beginning. But some events with beginnings are such that God remembers their occurrence. Consequently this act on God's part is also a temporal event. It too cannot be everlasting.

God is also described by the biblical writers as planning that he would bring about certain events which he does. This, too, is impossible if God does not change. For consider some event which someone brings about, and suppose that he planned to bring it about. His planning to bring it about must occur before the planned event occurs. For otherwise it is not a case of planning.

So in conclusion, if God were eternal he could not be aware, concerning any temporal event, that it is occurring nor aware that it was occurring nor aware that it will be occurring; nor could he remember that it has occurred; nor could he plan to bring it about and do so. But all of such actions are presupposed by, and essential to, the biblical presentation of God as a redeeming God. Hence God as presented by the biblical writers is fundamentally noneternal. He is fundamentally in time.

IV

As with any argument, one can here choose to deny the premises rather than to accept the conclusion. Instead of agreeing that God is fundamentally noneternal because he changes with respect to his knowledge, his memory, and his planning, one could try to save one's conviction that God is eternal by denying that he knows what is or was or will be occurring, that he remembers what has occurred, and that he brings about what he has planned. It seems to me, however, that this is clearly to give up the notion of God as a redeeming God; and in turn it seems to me that to give this up is to give up what is central to the biblical vision of God. To sustain this latter claim would of course require an extensive hermeneutical inquiry. But lest someone be tempted to go this route of trying to save God's eternity by treating all the biblical language about God the redeemer as either false or misleadingly metaphorical, let me observe that if God were eternal he could not be the object of any human action whatsoever.

Consider, for example, my act of referring to something, X. The event consisting of *my referring to* X is a temporal event. It both begins and ends, as do all my acts. Now the event of *my referring to* X is identical with the event of X's *being referred to by me*. And this event is an aspect both of X and of me. So if X is a being which lasts longer than my act of referring to X does, then for a while X has this aspect and for a while not. And thus X would have *succession* on its time-strand. And so X would not be eternal. Thus if God were eternal, no human being could ever refer to him—or perform any other temporal act with respect to him. If he were eternal, one could not know him. In particular, one could not know that he was eternal, or even believe that he was. Indeed, if God were eternal one could not predicate of him that he is eternal. For predicating is also a temporal act. So this is the calamitous consequence of claiming of God that he is eternal: if one predicates of him that he is eternal, then he is not.

V

I have been arguing that God as described by the biblical writers is a being who changes. That, we have seen, is not self-evidently and obviously so, though the mode of expression of the biblical writers might lead one to think it was. Yet it is so nonetheless.

But are there not explicit statements in the Bible to the effect that God does not change? If we are honest to the evidence, must we not acknowledge that on this matter the biblical writers contradict each other? Let us see.

Surprisingly, given the massive Christian theological tradition in favor of God's ontological immutability, there are only two passages (to the best of my knowledge) in which it is directly said of God that he does not change. One of these is Malachi 3:6. The prophet has just been saying to the people that God is wearied by their hypocrisy; however (he goes on), God will send his messenger to clear a path before him; and "he will take his seat, refining and purifying." As a result of this cleansing, the "offerings of Judah and Jerusalem shall be pleasing to the Lord as they were in days of old." And then comes this assurance: "I am the Lord, unchanging; and you, too, have not ceased to be sons of Jacob. From the days of your forefathers you have been wayward and have not kept my laws. If you will return to me, I will return to you, says the Lord of Hosts" (NEB).

Surely it would be a gross misinterpretation to treat the prophet here as claiming that God is ontologically immutable. What he says, on the contrary, is that God is faithful to his people Israel—that he is unchanging in his fidelity to the covenant he has made with them. All too often theologians have ontologized the biblical message. Malachi 3:6 is a classic example of a passage which, cited out of context, would seem to support the doctrine of God's ontological immutability. Read in context, however, it supports not that but rather the doctrine of God's unswerving fidelity. No ontological claim whatever is being made.

The other passage in which it is said of God that he is unchanging is to be found in Psalm 102:27. Again we must set the passage in its context:

> My strength is broken in mid course;
> the time allotted me is short.

> Snatch me not away before half my days are done,
>   for thy years last through all generations.
> Long ago thou didst lay the foundations of the earth,
>   and the heavens were thy handiwork.
>
> They shall pass away, but thou endurest;
>   like clothes they shall all grow old;
>   thou shalt cast them off like a cloak,
>   and they shall vanish;
> but thou art the same and thy years shall have no end;
>   thy servants' children shall continue,
> and their posterity shall be established in thy presence (NEB).

Here, too, it would be a gross misinterpretation to regard the writer as teaching that God is ontologically immutable. The Psalmist is making an ontological point of sorts, though even so the ontological point is set within a larger context of religious reflection. He is drawing a contrast between God on the one hand and his transitory creation on the other. And what he says about God is clearly that God is without end—"Thy years shall have no end." He does not say that God is ontologically immutable.

In short, God's ontological immutability is not a part of the explicit teaching of the biblical writers. What the biblical writers teach is that God is faithful and without beginning or end, not that none of his aspects is temporal. The theological tradition of God's ontological immutability has no explicit biblical foundation.[10]

VI

The upshot of our discussion is this: the biblical presentation of God presupposes that God is everlasting rather than eternal. God is indeed without beginning and without end. But at least some of his aspects stand in temporal order-relations to each other. Thus God, too, has a time-strand. His life and existence is itself temporal. (Whether his life and existence always was and always will be temporal, or whether he has taken on temporality, is a question we have not had time to consider.) Further, the events to be found on God's time-strand belong within the same temporal array as that which contains our time-strands. God's aspects do not only bear temporal order-relations to each other but to the aspects of created entities as well. And the aspects and succession of aspects to be found on God's time-

10. "I am that I am" (Exod. 3:13) has also sometimes been used to support the doctrine of God's immutability. However, this is one of the most cryptic passages in all of Scripture; and—to understate the point—it is not in the least clear that what is being proclaimed is God's ontological immutability. There is a wealth of exegetical material on the passage, but see especially the comments by J. C. Murray, *The Problem of God* (New Haven, 1967), ch. 1.

strand are such that they constitute *changes* thereon. God's life and existence incorporates changeful succession.

Haunting Christian theology and Western philosophy throughout the centuries has been the picture of time as bounded, with the created order on this side of the boundary and God on the other. Or sometimes the metaphor has been that of time as extending up to a horizon, with all creaturely reality on this side of the horizon and God on the other. All such metaphors, and the ways of thinking that they represent, must be discarded. Temporality embraces us along with God.

This conclusion from our discussion turns out to be wholly in accord with that to be found in Oscar Cullmann's *Christ and Time*. From his study of the biblical words for time Cullmann concluded that, in the biblical picture, God's "eternity" is not qualitatively different from our temporality. Cullmann's line of argument (though not his conclusion) has been vigorously attacked by James Barr on the ground that from the lexicographical patterns of biblical language we cannot legitimately make inferences as to what was being said by way of that language.[11] Verbal similarities may conceal differences in thought, and similarities in thought may be clothed with verbal differences. Barr's objection is *apropos*. But though we have traveled a very different route from Cullmann's we have come out at the same place. We have not engaged in any word studies. Yet, by seeing that God's temporality is presupposed by the biblical presentation of God as redeemer, we too have reached the conclusion that we share time with God. The lexicographical and philosophical cases coincide in their results.

Though God is within time, yet he is Lord of time. The whole array of contingent temporal events is within his power. He is Lord of what occurs. And that, along with the specific pattern of what he does, grounds all authentically biblical worship of, and obedience to, God. It is not because he is outside of time—eternal, immutable, impassive—that we are to worship and obey God. It is because of what he can and does bring about within time that we mortals are to render him praise and obedience.

11. *Biblical Words for Time* (London, 1962).

God and Spacelessness

PAUL HELM

In recent years the doctrine that God exists in a timeless eternity has achieved something of the status of philosophical heterodoxy, if not of downright heresy. The arguments against the idea of God's timeless eternity come from two sources. The first of these is Professor Kneale's paper "Time and Eternity in Theology" (*Proceedings of the Aristotelian Society* 61, 1960–61) in which, alluding to the famous definition of eternity by Boethius as "the complete possession of eternal life at once" Professor Kneale confesses "I can attach no meaning to the word 'life' unless I am allowed to suppose that what has life acts . . . life must at least involve some incidents in time and if, like Boethius, we suppose the life in question to be intelligent, then it must involve also awareness of the passage of time" (p. 99).

This argument is taken up and embellished by J. R. Lucas in *A Treatise on Time and Space* (London: Methuen, 1973) in which he says that "To say that God is outside time, as many theologians do, is to deny, in effect, that God is a person" (p. 300). According to Mr. Lucas since minds are necessarily in time but only contingently in space it is reasonable to suppose that everything that exists is present to God spacelessly, but not timelessly (p. 304). This argument against the timelessness of God has recently been endorsed by Professor Swinburne (*The Coherence of Theism,* Oxford: Clarendon Press, 1977, Ch. 12). Let us call this *the argument from personality.*

The source of the other argument against the idea of God's timelessness is A. N. Prior's paper "The Formalities of Omniscience" (*Time and Tense,*

Reprinted from *Philosophy* 55 (1980) by permission of Cambridge University Press. © The Royal Institute of Philosophy 1980.

Oxford: Clarendon Press, 1968) in which he claims that a proposition such as "It is raining now" is not equivalent in meaning to "It is raining on Tuesday," and that an omniscient individual who knew the latter would not necessarily know the former, and would necessarily not know it if he were timeless, since he could not be *present* on the occasion on which it was raining. This argument of Prior's has been taken up by Norman Kretzmann ("Omniscience and Immutability," *Journal of Philosophy* 1966) and by Nicholas Wolterstorff ("God Everlasting" in *God and the Good,* Orlebeke and Smedes (eds.), Grand Rapids: Eerdman, 1975) [this volume, pp. 77–98—Eds.]. The effectiveness of this argument has been denied by H.–N. Castaneda ("Omniscience and Indexical Reference," *Journal of Philosophy* 1967), Nelson Pike (*God and Timelessness,* London: Routledge and Kegan Paul, 1970, Ch. 5), and Professor Swinburne (op. cit., 162ff.). Let us call this *the argument from indexicals.*

In this paper I shall not attempt to defend the idea of divine timelessness, but to argue that the considerations which are used to cast doubt on it have parallels which cast equal doubt on the idea of divine spacelessness. I shall do this by considering the two arguments just noted. Then I shall consider the question of whether any individual who is in space must be finite. If the answer to this question is "Yes" it will then appear that the arguments used to show that God is in time in effect support the view that he is finite, and so anyone who wishes to maintain that God is infinite, as a traditional theist does, will either have to find other arguments for the view that God is in time, arguments which do not also show that God is in space, or eschew the idea of God being in time altogether.

I

I shall consider first the argument from indexicals, in the particularly clear version of it given by Nicholas Wolterstorff. Wolterstorff argues, briefly, that to replace the present tense of a verb by a tense-indifferent use of the same verb together with a designator of time is to construct a wholly new proposition. That is, while from

(1) The kettle is boiling

we can infer

(2) The kettle is boiling at present

from

(3) The kettle boils on 19th January

we cannot infer (2). (1) conveys something that (3) does not convey, namely the presentness of the kettle's boiling. Without the ability to distinguish between the presentness, pastness and futurity of facts we would not know where we are in the sequence of events. The significant fact about propositions like (1) is that they can only be known to be true when they are true.

The application to the idea of timeless knowledge is quickly made. Take God's knowledge of the fact that the kettle is boiling. He cannot know this until it is true, and so God's coming to know that the kettle is boiling is synchronous with the onset of the kettle's boiling:

> But every temporal event has (by definition) either a beginning or an ending. So every case of knowing about some temporal event that it is occurring itself either begins or ends (or both). Hence the act of knowing about *e* that it is occurring is infected by the temporality of *e*. So also, the act of knowing about *e* that it *was* occurring, and the act of knowing about *e* that it *will be* occurring, are infected by the temporality of *e* (Wolterstorff, op. cit., 198) [this volume, p. 93—Eds.].

So if God were timelessly eternal there are matters that he could never know, nor remember, nor plan. Hence the character of God, particularly the God of Christian theism who judges and redeems, is radically compromised.

As was noted earlier some writers, for example Nelson Pike, have rejected this type of argument. They claim that it rests on a confusion between an utterance and a proposition, and that though God could not know that the kettle is boiling he could know the fact expressed by "the kettle is boiling." However for the purposes of this paper I shall take it that there is a distinction of meaning between (1) and (3), and in particular that (3) could be known when (1) was not known.

But a precisely parallel argument can be constructed for space. It is of course not an accident that ways of constructing future and past tenses of verbs are well entrenched in a natural language such as English while there are no "tenses" for expressing distance in space. The reason has something to do with the fact that time is only one-dimensional whereas space concerns not only distance but direction. However vague a thing it is to say "He will be coming" it is precise to the extent of fixing his coming in the future, whereas to say "He is there" is hopelessly vague until accompanied by gestures or directions of other kinds.

Still, the fact that there are no "space tenses" as there are "time tenses" need not worry us. The argument can proceed without them. While from

(4) The kettle is boiling here

we can infer

(5) The kettle is boiling at this place, i.e., where I am or we are

we cannot infer (5) from

(6) The kettle is boiling in the Old Kent Road.

For (5) conveys something that (6) does not convey, namely the fact that the kettle is boiling at the place where the utterer of the proposition happens to be. Further, if all we had to use in expressing the places at which events took place were proper names or certain definite descriptions for places (those that made no use of indexicals for space) then we would not know where we are in relation to the total array of places.

Now we might suppose that God knows that the kettle is boiling here. He cannot know this except where it is true. He cannot know this until he occupies a place in the Old Kent Road near to where the kettle is boiling if so be that the kettle is boiling in the Old Kent Road. So God cannot know that the kettle is boiling here until he arrives at or near the place where the kettle is boiling. That is, God's coming to know that the kettle is boiling here cannot occur until he arrives at the Old Kent Road, unless of course we suppose that he is already there.

So if God is spacelessly present in his creation there are matters that he cannot know. But just as the Bible, for example, portrays God as knowing when things take place so he is portrayed as knowing where they take place. Accordingly we must conclude that if the earlier argument establishes the presence of God in time this argument establishes the presence of God in space.

Wolterstorff also argues that if God were timelessly eternal he could not be the object of any human act whatever, since to suppose that he could would be to suppose that God changed, changed from not being referred to, or worshipped, by Smith to being referred to or worshipped by Smith. This argument can be rebutted by distinguishing between different kinds of change, between what Geach has called "real" and "merely Cambridge" changes (*God and the Soul*, London: Routledge and Kegan Paul, 1969, 71–72). "Merely Cambridge" changes are, roughly, changes in the relations that a logical subject has. The distinction between a "real" and a "merely Cambridge" change is a difficult one to express exactly. If for that reason we were to suppose that Wolterstorff's argument cannot be rebutted by employing the distinction, then the parallel argument with regard to space would be: if God were spaceless no human being would be able to refer to him, for to refer to God is to establish spatial relations between the referrer and God. Hence if God can be referred to he must be in space.

Although we noted earlier that Swinburne rejects the argument from indexicals he does employ another argument to show the incoherence of the idea of God being timeless which has certain features in common with the argument from indexicals. It makes no use of the supposition that a timeless individual knows about events in a temporal sequence, but otherwise similar sorts of considerations apply. Let us call this subargument of the argument from indexicals *the argument from simultaneity*. It can be stated as follows:

(7) God exists timelessly.

(8) God exists simultaneously at all moments of human time (from 1).

(9) God is simultaneously present at what I did yesterday, am doing today, and will do tomorrow.

(10) If time t_1 is simultaneous with time t_2, and t_2 is simultaneous with t_3, then t_1 is simultaneous with t_3.

(11) If God is simultaneously present at what I did yesterday and am doing today then yesterday and today are simultaneous (from 9 and 10).

(12) But the idea that yesterday and today are simultaneous is absurd.

(13) Therefore (7) is incoherent.

As previously, when we were discussing Wolterstorff's argument, I shall assume the soundness of this argument. A precisely parallel argument can be constructed to show the incoherence of the idea of God's spacelessness, as follows:

(14) God is spaceless.

(15) God is wholly spatially present at different places.

(16) God is wholly spatially present at what I am doing here and you are doing there.

(17) If an individual is wholly spatially present with another individual, and that individual is wholly spatially present with a third individual then the first individual is wholly spatially present with the third individual.

(18) Thus if God is wholly spatially present at what I am doing here and you are doing there then where you are and where I am are the same place.

(19) But the idea that this place and that place are the same place is absurd.

(20) Therefore (14) is incoherent.

So if the timeless existence of God is incoherent then so is the spaceless existence of God. It ought to be stressed that in these arguments I have not assumed, nor argued, that space and time are in all respects analogous, but that they are analogous in those respects that are relevant for the propounding of these arguments. The exact extent to which time can be regarded as similar to space is a matter of controversy into which I do not go. (See, for example, G. Schlesinger, "The Similarities Between Space and Time," *Mind*, April 1975, and the literature cited there.) But we can see that Wolterstorff is mistaken when he writes:

> In contemporary Western philosophy the phenomenon of temporal
> modality has been pervasively neglected or ignored in favour of the
> phenemena of temporal order-relationships, temporal location, and tem-
> poral duration. Thus time has been 'spatialized'. For though space
> provides us with close analogues to all three of these latter phenomena,
> it provides us with no analogue whatever to the past/present/future
> distinction (p. 188) [this volume, p. 188—Eds.].

This is not so. There is *some* analogue of the past, present and future
distinction provided by the spatial distinction between here and there, and
before and behind. There are spatial modalities just as there are temporal
modalities. Suppose that we introduce two spatial operators "It is the case
that here" (H) and "It is the case that there" (TH). The verb "to be" in
these operators is of course to be understood tense-indifferently. Then "The
kettle is boiling here" comes to be H (The kettle is boiling), "It is raining
here and it is snowing there" comes to be H (It is raining) and TH (It is
snowing). This is pretty unilluminating stuff by comparison with Prior's
Past, Present and Future (I doubt very much that there is a book waiting
to be written entitled *Here, There and Everywhere*). But all that this
shows is that the modalities of time are philosophically more interesting
than the modalities of place.

II

Let us now consider the argument from personality. The two arguments
are connected in the following way. The argument from personality, if it
is regarded as sound, provides a reason for treating the argument from
indexicals as relevant to the issue of God's timelessness, since otherwise it
could be argued that the indexical argument is beside the point because
God only needs to know the truth of tense-indifferent propositions. The
reason why it is thought that God needs to know more than the truth of
tense-indifferent propositions is that he observes and initiates changes in
the universe. That is, he is a person.

Kneale claims that to act purposefully is to act with thought of what
will come about after the beginning of the action, and that therefore
Boethius's definition of eternity as "the complete possession of eternal life
all at once" is a contradiction in terms. But though this consideration is
relevant to timelessness as such, to whether or not there could be a
timeless conscious agent, it is not quite what is relevant to the question of
whether or not God is timeless. For the question here is not whether

(a) Whatever has life must have an awareness of time

but whether

(b) Whatever consciously brings about changes in the states of things in time must have an awareness of being in time

and if (b) whether

(c) Whatever consciously brings about changes in the states of things in space must have an awareness of being in space.

So in saying that the agent in question must have an awareness of time Kneale seems to mean more than that the agent must have the concept of time. It obviously does not follow that if one has the concept of something temporal or spatial that one is at that time or that place. It is possible for a person to have the concept of being somewhere else than the place he is at present, but it would be absurd to suppose that one had to be somewhere other than one was at present in order to have this concept.

In a similar way Lucas's claim that minds are necessarily in time but only contingently in space does not meet the case in hand because the question is not whether God is a mind, and therefore possibly in time but not in space, but whether God has knowledge of, and acts within, a spatial universe. Lucas has to show not merely that minds are contingently in space, and that therefore it is possible that God is spaceless, but that minds that bring about changes in the states of things in space are possibly not in space themselves. But let us look at his argument more closely.

(21) I cannot conceive of a mind being conscious of something about whom the question "When?" does not arise.

(22) There are many states of consciousness for which the question "Where?" does not arise.

(23) Therefore, minds are contingently in space, necessarily in time.

A number of questions arise about this. (21) is unclear, in at least two respects. If it is a proposition about the *contents* of minds then it is obviously false. There are many objects of consciousness for which the question "When?" does not make sense. If a person is conscious of the proposition that seven and five make twelve it makes no sense to ask when seven and five first made twelve. By (21) Lucas must mean something like

(21a) I cannot conceive of a mind being conscious of something about which the question "When did you first conceive of that thing?" does not arise.

"Does not arise" here presumably means "is not capable of being given a positive answer, i.e. a named date." If so then (21a) would rule out not only the idea of an eternal, timeless mind, but also a sempiternal mind as well. For it is possible that there should be a sempiternal being that had a belief that it never acquired, i.e. a being such that it had existed for all time and there was no time at which it failed to have the belief. In which case the question "When did you first have that belief?" would not arise. But perhaps "Always" would be a satisfactory answer to that question. Let us, then, accept (21a). What has to be compared to it for the purpose of considering Lucas's argument is not (22) but (22a).

>(22a) I can conceive of a mind being conscious of something about which the question "Where did you conceive of that thing?" does not arise.

Let us take it that (23) follows from (21a) and (22a). It follows then that it is possible that there is a mind that is not in space. But what precisely does this mean? And, more particularly, what does it mean to say that God is spaceless? Let us look briefly at each of these.

To say that a mind exists that is not in space may mean that the mind does not occupy any *area* of space. Presumably it means at least that. Does it also mean that there is no point of space at which the mind exists? If so, this seems to amount either to the view that such a mind exists nowhere, or that it exists everywhere. The second possibility seems absurd, except in the case of God, and we shall look at that possibility in a moment. But with regard to the first possibility it is hardly intelligible to suppose that there is a mind that is conscious of things happening in space and yet is nowhere. But perhaps the supposition is that there could only be a spaceless mind if there was no space. I have no idea whether this is intelligible or not, or how to decide the question.

Some of the things that Lucas means by saying that God is spaceless are that (a) God possesses all space, (b) nothing can be dim or distant or remote from God, and (c) God's relation to space is non-token-reflexive. (*A Treatise on Time and Space*, 304–305.) Let us examine (b). (b) cannot mean that nothing is spatially more distant from God than another thing. For if neither of two things in a given direction is more distant than the other from an individual then they are equidistant from that individual in that direction. So that if nothing in a given direction is more distant from God than anything else in that direction then everything in that direction is in the same place. But perhaps what Lucas means is that nothing is either distant or near as far as God is concerned.

Further, either (a)–(c) are true of every mind that is spaceless or they are not. If they are true of only some spaceless minds then the negations of (a)–(c) are presumably true of the rest. If they are true then for a mind that is spaceless everything in a given direction is in the same place. If they are not true then for a mind that is spaceless some things are more spatially distant than others. If it is only in the case of God that an individual can be spacelessly present to the whole of space, whereas in the case of minds other than God spacelessness is possible only if there is no space to be located in, then it seems that "spaceless" does not mean quite the same when applied to God and when applied to other minds.

Even if it is possible to sort out all these points and to answer them satisfactorily, there is still the earlier problem of what to say about the claim that God, who brings about changes in space, is not himself in any spatial relations to the changes in space, i.e. in the states of individuals in space, that he brings about. The chief problem here is: if God is not in spatial relations with the individuals in space whom he affects how does he know where to bring about the changes? If God wishes to bring about certain changes in the Red Sea, how does he know where the Red Sea is? Two answers seem possible. Perhaps he just does know where the Red Sea is just as we know, without observation (mostly) what the positions of our limbs are. Alternatively, perhaps he knows by means of using proper names and non-indexical definite descriptions. Perhaps so. But it will not have escaped attention that these two answers are also open to the advocate of God's eternal timelessness.

III

What I have argued so far is that two sorts of argument against the timelessness of God—the argument from indexicals, and the argument from personality—are also arguments against the spacelessness of God. If the conclusion of these arguments is that God is in time then, *pari passu,* God is in space. This conclusion might well be welcomed by someone who argues that God is in time, even though, as we have seen, it is not welcome to everyone who argues that God is in time. To see whether it *ought* to be welcome I want to explore some of the consequences of saying that God is in space. I want to suggest a number of things that it does mean and a number of other things that it need not mean.

One thing it seems to mean is that God has some spatial perspective, as he has some temporal perspective if he is in time. That is to say God will be positioned in space and know things from some spatial perspective or other. Take a biblical story about Elijah, (1 Kings xix.9). Elijah flees and God finds him. He says to Elijah "What doest thou here, Elijah?" Taken literally and in accordance with the conclusions of the previous arguments what God says is "What are you doing where I am, Elijah?" To say that God must have some spatial perspective it does not follow that he has only one spatial perspective at once. Yet we must not be misled by the analogy of a person in a control room watching a series of television screens relaying pictures from differently positioned cameras. The cameras each have a different spatial perspective, but the person in the control room has one perspective. To have more than one perspective in the sense that interests us must be to have more than one position—in effect be a scattered object.

A second thing that it seems to mean is that God cannot be wholly present at two or more separated places at once. It seems to be a conceptual truth about any individual in space that it cannot be wholly present in two places at once.

A third thing that it means is that if God is capable of being at two places at once, then God is spatially divisible. For if God can be at two places at once, though not wholly at two places at once, then it would seem to follow that he can only be in two or more places at once by having a part of him in one place and a part of him in each of the other places where he is. Hence it seems to follow that God has parts, proper parts that is, and is not simple, as has traditionally been thought.

But the main difficulty with supposing that God is an individual in space, at least on the reasons considered earlier, can be expressed as follows. Suppose God says

(24) Elijah is here.

Suppose further the truth of the doctrine we might call the omnispatiality or spacefulness of God, the doctrine that at any time God occupies (in some sense) all the spaces in the universe that there are. It follows from

(25) God is omnispatial

that

(26) Of every space at a given time God can truly say both "I am here" and "I am there."

That is, take any particular place, say the Old Kent Road. Then God can say, with respect to the Old Kent Road, "I am here" and also, since he is omnispatial, he can say with respect to the Marble Arch, "I am there." But given the truth of (24), (26) contradicts it, for by (26) God can also say, with respect to the place where Elijah is,

(27) Elijah is there.

Given the truth of (24), (27) cannot be true since an individual who is here cannot be there. What might be true is not (27) but

(28) I am where Elijah regards as there

or

(29) I am at the place which is there for Elijah.

But both (28) and (29) mean something different from (27). So God cannot occupy all space. If (24) is true (25) must be false.

The basic point can be expressed as follows. Either the "heres" and "theres" are *ordinary* spatial indexicals, in which case God is bounded in space, for on the ordinary meaning of these expressions "I am here and I am there" is a self-contradiction except perhaps where the "here" and "there" refer to places where parts of one's body are. Alternatively the "heres" and "theres" are peculiar and extraordinary "heres" and "theres" according to which it is consistent to assert "I am both here and there." But in this case the way in which God is in space differs from the way in which other individuals are in space.

Perhaps the matter can be put more simply, as follows. Suppose that God knows that Elijah is here. If he knows that Elijah is here then he also knows that Elijah is not there. If he knows that Elijah is not there he knows that Elijah is not at a certain place distant from both Elijah and himself. If he knows that Elijah is not at a certain place distant from himself then there is such a place distant from him. If there is a place distant from him then he is bounded by space, and if he is bounded by space then he is finite.

In Chapter 8 of *God and Timelessness*, Nelson Pike considers the question of whether or not the timeless eternity of God is entailed by the Anselmian claim that God is a being than which no greater can be conceived. He concludes that it is not entailed by it, and thus that the doctrine of God's timeless eternity is not something that is *required* by theism (p. 165). But if, as we have argued earlier, the arguments currently used to establish that God is in time are strictly parallel to arguments that would establish that God is in space, and if it follows that if God is in space in the sense that he can properly use ordinary spatial indexicals then he is enclosed by space, there is here a reason for thinking that such a God is a being than which a greater *can* be conceived, namely a being that is not bounded by space but who is otherwise as similar as can be to the God who is in space. Hence an infinite God must be spaceless. And if we come to this conclusion on the basis of arguments about space then there is no good reason to withhold the conclusion that God is outside time, since the arguments that establish the one are strictly parallel to the arguments that establish the other.

Thus theism seems to require that God be spaceless. The spacelessness of God seems to involve denying the soundness of the sorts of arguments considered earlier. If these arguments are unsound there is no reason why the parallel arguments about the timeless eternity of God ought not to be judged unsound. Or at least a reason must be given why the parallel does not hold. Failing such a reason we can say that even if Pike is correct that theism does not directly require divine timeless eternity, it indirectly requires it.

In saying that we ought to conclude that if God exists he is outside space and time I am by no means claiming that I fully understand what these propositions amount to. Perhaps the best way to grasp what they mean, or to try to grasp what they mean, is to use models or analogies. And then again, perhaps not. All that I am claiming is that the spacelessness of God seems to be a requirement of traditional theism and hence that the timelessness of God does.

From this conclusion at least three alternative consequences follow. The first would be to say that all that the argument just given shows is that theism is more incoherent than was previously thought, in that it requires unintelligibilities such as timeless *and* spaceless existence. The second reaction would be to say that if the current arguments against time-lessness are also in effect arguments against spacelesness then there must be something wrong with those arguments, since theism is coherent and theism entails divine spacelessness. A third reaction would be to supply an argument against timelessness that does not have a spatial parallel. Nothing in the argument of this paper requires one of these consequences as against either of the other two to be the correct one.

PART II

GOD AND
HUMAN EXPERIENCE

Mysticism and Philosophy

RICHARD M. GALE

This paper will be an attempt to deal with the key problems which mysticism poses for philosophy, these being the alleged ineffability of mystical experiences, the relation between the so-called eternal and temporal orders of being and the objectivity of mystical experiences. We will use Professor Walter Stace's *Time and Eternity* as a springboard for our own critical analysis of these problems.

1. ALLEGED INEFFABILITY OF MYSTICAL EXPERIENCES

Basic to Professor Stace's thesis is his claim that mystical experiences, unlike all other types of experience, are completely ineffable, or non-conceptualizable. From this it follows that nothing revealed through mystical experience could possibly be either proved or disproved by anything known through the intellect, which is the process of understanding objects by means of concepts. His discussion, however, is marred by a failure to state clearly in exactly what sense mystical experiences are ineffable. I believe that a careful reading of the book will reveal that four different criteria or senses of ineffability are appealed to. It will be necessary to discuss each one of these four senses separately to determine, first, whether mystical experiences are ineffable in any of these senses, and, second, if they are ineffable in any sense, whether this sense is trivial, i.e., one which would apply equally well to certain non-mystical experiences.

(1) *Within the mystical experience there is an undifferentiated unity, affording no foothold for any concept.* During the mystical experience, as viewed phenomenologically from the standpoint of the experient, there is

Reprinted from *The Journal of Philosophy* 57 (1960) by permission of *The Journal of Philosophy* and the author.

a dissolution of the dualism between subject and object as well as a unification of what was originally a multiplicity of objects. For this reason mystical experiences are ineffable.

In opposition to this it can be maintained that mystics as a matter of fact *do* manage to conceptualize their mystical experiences when they are outside them. By applying concepts such as "the undifferentiated unity," "the dissolution of the personal ego," "non-temporal and non-spatial," "the sense of peace and sacredness," etc. to their experiences they succeed in distinguishing mystical from non-mystical experiences.

Professor Stace's counter to this would be that *within* the mystical experience the mystic cannot conceptualize his experience because the use of any concept presupposes a multiplicity of objects as well as the subject-object dualism, and this is just what is wiped out during the experience. In claiming that mystical experiences are ineffable because they cannot be conceptualized by the mystic *while he is within* the experience, Professor Stace seems to be appealing to the following criterion of ineffability: *An experience is ineffable if a proposition describing this experience cannot be either formulated, consciously considered, or verified by the experient during the time that he is actually having the experience.* I will attempt to show that this sense of ineffability is trivial because many non-mystical experiences would equally well qualify as candidates for the title of ineffable.

We would all agree that the experience of wrestling with an alligator is conceptualizable. However, the proposition, "Tarzan is wrestling with an alligator," could not possibly be either formulated, consciously considered, or verified by Tarzan while he is actually having the experience described by the proposition. Similarly, and for slightly different practical reasons, Schnabel is not capable of formulating or verifying the proposition, "Schnabel is concentrating *solely* on interpreting Beethoven's 14th Sonata," while he is actually engaged in performing the sonata; for if he were to attempt to verify this proposition while he was performing the Sonata he would automatically render it false, because that would mean that he could not possibly be concentrating *solely* on interpreting the Sonata.

Because an experience, whether of the mystical or the Tarzan-Schnabel type, is not conceptualizable by the experient while he is having the experience, it does not follow that a third person cannot describe the experience at the very moment the experient is having his experience, or that the experient himself cannot conceptualize his experience after the experience is over.

Professor Stace's answer to this argument would be that there still is a significant difference between mystical experiences and the Schnabel-Tarzan type of experiences, for only in the former is there a complete dissolution of the personal ego. Whether the mystic actually experiences the dissolution of his own ego is open to some doubts, for if this were so how would it be possible for the mystic to remember that *he* had had such an experience? In what sense could it be said to be *his* experience? How can someone experience the dissolution of his ego? But if we waive these difficulties and grant Professor Stace his point that there actually is such a dissolution of the personal ego, this would have no logical relevance to the claim that mystical experiences are ineffable in some unique sense. It would show only that there are different practical reasons why the mystic cannot conceptualize his experience when inside the experience than why Tarzan and Schnabel cannot.

(2) *Mystical experiences are unique, being totally different from all other types of experience.* Mystics themselves claim that they cannot find adequate words to describe their experiences. They have not been able to invent a new language in which their experiences would no longer be ineffable.

However, against this, it can be said that many mystics have been autobiographical mystics. Such mystics manage to communicate the nature of their experience not only to fellow mystics but to many non-mystics as well. When we read the descriptions of mystical experience given by an Eckhart or a Suzuki we seem to know what they are talking about. If we should be soaking in a hot bath one night and suddenly have an experience in which our personal ego was dissolved by melting into an infinite ocean which was an undifferentiated unity and which furthermore gave us a sense of peace and sacredness far transcending anything previously experienced, we would leap to our feet saying with great excitement, "Why that Eckhart wasn't just pulling our leg! There really are such experiences and I just had one!"

There is something woefully inconsistent in Professor Stace's saying, in one breath, that mystical experiences are ineffable—that no concepts can be used to describe them—and, in the next breath, that there is unanimity among the mystics—that all mystics describe their experiences in pretty much the same way. If one of these claims is true then the other must be false.[1] Also, if mystical experiences were as ineffable as mystics claim they are, then what sense could we make of their claim that their experiences are in principle verifiable if the proper steps are taken? What kind of an experience would serve as a confirming instance?

1. I believe that Professor Stace, in accordance with his latest formulation of the empirical theory of meaning, put forth in "Some Misinterpretations of Empiricism" (*Mind,* 1958), would be forced to attribute empirical meaning to mystical propositions. There he states that a word or sentence has empirical meaning if it refers to some specific but unanalyzable experiential datum or if it is amenable to a process of analysis, the end-terms of which will be such experiential data.

To say that mystical experiences are ineffable in the sense of not being adequately described by language is to make a trivial claim. No concepts can completely describe any direct experience; they can never serve as substitutes for such experiences. My concept of a loud, deafening noise is not itself a loud, deafening noise. Our experience of yellow is just as unique and ineffable as a mystical experience; we cannot define the color yellow in terms of anything more simple or basic. But this does not mean that we cannot conceptualize our direct experience of yellow and communicate with others about it. If the experience of the color yellow were unique, and accessible to only one person in the universe, then it would be impossible for this person to communicate with others about this experience. What is presupposed in communicating propositions about simple color experiences as well as mystical experiences is an experiential awareness on the part of the addressee of the experience referred to by the proposition.

I believe that the real reason for the mystic's claiming some sort of unique ineffability for his experience is to be found in the inestimable significance and value which the experience has for him. It seems that the more highly we prize some experience the more we shun applying concepts to it. Like the composer who shuns writing program notes for his symphony because he fears, and rightly so, that eventually the reading of the program notes will take the place of the direct listening experience of the music, the mystic is afraid that the concepts by which he describes his experience will become surrogates for the experience itself. Both men are telling us by their refusal to conceptualize their experience that it is the direct experience itself which counts and that language is a very poor substitute.

(3) *Propositions describing mystical experiences contain self-contradictions.*[2] Professor Stace finds the basic paradox of the Divine in the contradiction between the positive and negative conceptions of the Divine. "The latter denies all predicates of Him, even that of existence; whereas, the former says that He is the fullness of Being, the ultimate reality" (p. 34).

It seems to me that this alleged contradiction between the positive and negative conceptions of the Divine rests on the equivocation of the term "exist." When in the negative conception of the Divine the mystic denies that God *exists,* he means, by "exist," "to be a fact in a spatio-temporal order"; whereas, when from the positive conception of the Divine he claims that God *exists* or *Is,* he means now, by "exist," "to be an eternal or timeless Being," which is supposedly apprehended through mystical experiences. If

2. Paul Henle, in his excellent article, "Mysticism and Semantics" (*Philosophy and Phenomenological Research,* 1949), claims that the mystic is not entitled to claim that his mystical utterances are ineffable in regard to all symbolism, possible as well as actual. In principle we cannot know that any utterance is ineffable in any possible symbol system; for, in order to know that a certain utterance is ineffable, we should have to find a new symbolism for expressing what is now ineffable.

we distinguish between these two different meanings of "exist" the alleged contradiction between the positive and negative conception of the Divine disappears.

This still does not explain away many seemingly self-contradictory statements made by mystics. They refer to their experience as being at once passive and active, personal and impersonal, full and empty, containing a multiplicity of objects and still being a Oneness without parts, etc. What I will try to show is that such statements are not literal self-contradictions because the law of contradiction does not apply to them. The function of mystical statements is not the cognitive one of literally describing facts in space and time, but rather that of evoking in the addressee certain feelings and emotions in the same way that esthetic language does. In the following discussion we will consider *only* propositions having some sort of empirical meaning, i.e., propositions referring to something which is a content of a direct experience. Mystical propositions, while not having existential import in the strictest sense since they do not refer to facts in space and time, still come under the heading of propositions having empirical meaning, since, as we tried to prove, they do have experiential import.

Now in regard to propositions having empirical meaning we can say that one proposition contradicts another proposition only if we first know the time factor of the two propositions.[3] The law of contradiction has application only to those empirical propositions in which the time factor can be specified. For this reason *we can never say that two mystical propositions are contradictories because the time factor of the two propositions can never be specified.* The reason why the time factor of a mystical proposition can never be specified is that such a proposition refers to an experience which is, as the mystic himself claims, phenomenologically atemporal, containing within itself no change and therefore no relations of before and after. Therefore when we read in the *Isa Upanishad,* "It (the Self) stirs and it stirs not," we cannot say that such a proposition is a self-contradiction because the mystic can never tell us whether it stirs and also stirs not *at one and the same moment of time.* He cannot supply us with this information because his experience is atemporal.

The conclusion to be drawn from this analysis is that mystical propositions cannot be said to be literally self-contradictory.[4] The law of contradic-

3. In formulating the law of contradiction Aristotle wrote, "The same attribute cannot *at the same time* belong and not belong to the same subject in the same respect" (*Metaphysics,* 1005b, 17).

4. Professor Stace writes: "The Ultimate can be neither self-consistent nor self-contradictory, for both of these are logical categories. It is neither logical nor illogical, but alogical" (p. 153). This is in complete concordance with the conclusion reached in this paper. However, Professor Stace's claim that the Ultimate is alogical is obviously inconsistent with his assertion that there is a logical contradiction between the negative and positive conceptions of the Ultimate or Divine.

tion is a rule of discourse applying *only* to propositions having a cognitive function, i.e., propositions referring to events locatable in some definite region of space and time. The propositions of the mystics are alogical. They do not violate the law of contradiction—it simply does not apply to them. Professor Stace would agree with the end result of this analysis if not with the means by which it is achieved; for he has said that the function of mystical propositions is not cognitive, but rather that of *evoking* within us a certain type of experience (p. 120). But the evocative function of language is not unique to mystical symbolism; it is equally true of the esthetic use of language, so that we would not have shown that mystical experiences were ineffable in some unique sense. In describing my listening experience of the second movement of Beethoven's 7th Symphony I might say that it is the most tragic and yet the most joyous music I ever heard. If someone should then ask, "Do you mean at the same moment of time?," I would not know how to answer, for, as in the case of mystical propositions, I would not be able to specify the time factor. By describing the movement as being both tragic and joyous I am referring to an emotional quality which permeates the *entire* movement, and the function of my language is to evoke in the addressee an emotional experience of a similar type to the one I had when I listened to the movement.

(4) *Propositions describing mystical experiences contradict propositions describing non-mystical experiences.* This is unquestionably the case, for mystical propositions claim that space, time, and multiplicity are unreal; whereas propositions describing non-mystical experiences deny this. But it does not follow that mystical propositions are empirically meaningless, and consequently that mystical experiences are ineffable. We can understand the empirical meaning of each one of a pair of contradictory propositions; it is only the conjunction of these two contradictory propositions into a single proposition which becomes empirically meaningless. If our analysis has been correct, we understand what sort of experiences are being referred to by mystical propositions, and the fact that such propositions contradict propositions referring to non-mystical experiences does not render mystical experiences ineffable any more than it renders non-mystical experiences ineffable. Because mystical experiences are so different from the ordinary run-of-the-mill experiences, the mystic feels that these experiences are mysterious and paradoxical.

2. RELATION OF THE ETERNAL TO THE TEMPORAL ORDER OF BEING

During the mystical experience the mystic experiences only one order of being, the so-called eternal order. Within his experience there is no opposition between the eternal and temporal since the temporal world then simply does not exist for him; therefore, there is no contradiction for him to be puzzled over or to try and explain away. But most of the mystic's life is lived outside of the mystical moment, and it is then that he feels the contradiction between his mystical and non-mystical experiences. He may then even attempt to reconcile intellectually these two seemingly diametrically opposed realms of being, and so become involved in contradictions.

Professor Stace's answer to the seeming contradiction between the eternal and temporal order of being takes the form of an *exclusive* disjunction: *Either* we take our stand *outside* the mystical experience, as the naturalist does, in which case mystical experiences are purely subjective feelings and emotions; *or* we take our stand *inside* the mystical experience, in which case the natural world of space, time, and multiplicity is unreal or illusory. These two possible standpoints or perspectives are disjuncts in an exclusive disjunction, which means that *we cannot take both of these standpoints at the same time.* We must affirm one of these disjuncts and so deny the other.

However, in his theory of intersection Professor Stace makes this disjunction *inclusive.* The eternal and natural order intersect at each point of space and time. We know of such an intersection through the experience of the mystic. The mystic lives in both orders and at the moment of his mystical experience the two orders intersect. The point at which his experience takes place can be considered as a moment of time if viewed from the naturalistic standpoint, or it can be seen from within as the eternal Now-moment. "It is one and the same human consciousness which experiences both the temporal or natural and the eternal and infinite order which is disclosed in mystical illumination. Thus this identity of eternity with a temporal moment is an actual experienced fact, and this fact is what is metaphorically represented by the image of intersection" (p. 82).

Professor Stace's claim that the "identity of eternity with a temporal moment is an actual experienced fact" is ambiguous. It could mean: (1) that one and the same person has mystical experiences and *at other times* has experiences of a non-mystical variety; and (2) that the mystic experiences in the mystical experience the intersection of the two orders. In the case of (1) there is no direct experience of the intersection of the two orders; herein we are still left with an exclusive disjunction between the naturalistic and mystic standpoints. In the case of (2) the intersection is the content of a single direct intuitive experience.

I believe that the first interpretation is the only defensible one. It is certainly the case that one and the same person can have both mystical and non-mystical experiences, but it is not true that a person can have an experience which is *at once both* mystical and non-mystical. As the mystic himself has proclaimed, a person cannot at the same time experience both the eternal and the temporal; by definition it follows that if a person is having a mystical experience he cannot at the same time be having a non-

mystical experience. Therefore it is not possible for a person to have a single direct experience in which the temporal and timeless realms of being
intersect because for this to happen he would have to have an experience
which was at once both mystical and non-mystical, and by definition this
is impossible. The intersection of the eternal and the temporal is arrived
at through an intellectual interpretation, and can never be the content of
any direct experience.

In his theory of intersection, Professor Stace uses at the same time the
language of both mystic and naturalist, and in this way attempts to escape
the confines of his own exclusive disjunction. By saying that *at a moment
in time* a mystic experiences the *eternal* he is employing at the same time
the language of both mystic and nauralist, and thereby makes his disjunction inclusive by *adopting both standpoints at the same time*. But insofar
as we use the language of the naturalist we must describe the mystical experience as a subjective psychological event taking place at some moment
of time, and insofar as we adopt the mystical standpoint we must describe
the experience as union with the eternal or infinite and so deny that there
is a temporal order. From the latter standpoint there is no *moment in time*
at which the experience takes place.

3. OBJECTIVITY OF MYSTICAL EXPERIENCE

It may appear that we have been begging the question up to now by referring to mystical experiences as subjective psychological experiences
when viewed from the naturalistic standpoint. Some mystics would argue
that the same criterion by which we judge a sense experience to be veridical
or objective can be used to prove the objectivity of a mystical experience.
This is the argument: The criterion for objectivity in sense experience is
unanimity or agreement among observers; since there is unanimity among
mystics it follows by analogy with the criterion for objectivity in sense
experience that mystical experiences are objective. The fact that very few
persons have had mystical experiences is not evidence against the objectivity of such experiences; for a mystical proposition, like any non-mystical
one, is really a hypothetical statement saying what experiences a person
will have *if* certain verifying procedures are followed. However, in the case
of propositions about sense experience we can specify exactly what operations must be performed by the verifier; whereas, in the case of mystical
propositions, it is far more difficult to do this. The proper steps to be taken
by one who wishes to verify a mystical proposition may include living an
ascetic life for twenty years—staying out of bars, not watching television,
doing breathing exercises, etc. If after following the "mystic way" for
twenty years this poor chap still does not have a mystical experience there
is the tendency for the mystic to beg the question by definition by saying

that this only proves that this person has not taken the proper steps. In this case part of the very definition of what constitutes the proper steps is the stipulation that the verifier must have a mystical experience.

Waiving this difficulty and also granting the claim for unanimity among the mystics, we can still point to a basic flaw in this argument which is due to the fact that the criterion for objectivity which is appealed to is inadequate even in the realm of sense experience. Mere unanimity or agreement among observers is not a sufficient condition for objectivity. *Everybody* who presses his finger on his eyeball will see double, *everybody* who stands at a certain spot in the desert will see the mirage, etc. The true criterion for objectivity is the Kantian one: An experience is objective if its contents can be placed in a spatio-temporal order with other experiences in accordance with scientific laws. The objectivity of a sense experience means the verifiability of further possible sense experiences which are inferred from this experience in accordance with known scientific laws. In accordance with this criterion we would say that our sense experience of seeing things double when we press our finger on our eyeball is subjective—a mere illusion—because the inferences we make from this sense experience to other possible sense experiences do not hold. When we reach out to touch the two objects which we saw we find only one. There is, then, a rupture in the temporal continuity of our experience.

In accordance with this new criterion for objectivity we must classify mystical experiences as subjective because they represent a break in the temporal continuity of our experience. What we have in the case of mystical experience is a moment of eternity, i.e., phenomenological atemporality, suddenly appearing in the midst of a temporal sequence of events. When the mystic reports that during his experience all change and multiplicity were obliterated, we must, from the naturalistic standpoint, tell him that he was "seeing things." Because we cannot fit the content of mystical experiences into a temporal order with other experiences in accordance with scientific laws, we must call these experiences subjective.

Since Professor Stace defines God or the Eternal ostensively in terms of the content of the mystical experience itself, he is not claiming that a mystical experience is evidence for the existence of some Being or Reality which transcends the experience. By God we mean the mystical experience and *nothing more.* If we accept Professor Stace's ostensive definition of God in terms of the mystical experience itself, and if we grant the fact that there are mystical experiences, then it follows that God, *in his sense,* must exist. All of this is perfectly compatible with our classification of mystical experiences as subjective psychological experiences from the naturalistic standpoint. We cannot add to such psychological facts any existence claim; an existence claim cannot follow either deductively or inductively from a psychological claim. Since mystical experiences do not point beyond themselves to other facts they are irrefutable. We cannot dispute the claim of the mystic because, from the naturalistic standpoint, he is not making an existence claim—he is making only a psychological claim.

Professor Stace argues that each mystic experiences the same reality or Oneness. He states that since the mystic is identical with the One or God during his experience, his experience is identical with all other mystical experiences, whether of himself or of others, and this moment of time is identical with all other moments of time. "And hence there is, from within, no relation at all between one mystical experience and another and therefore no likeness or unlikeness" (p. 84). Professor Stace is writing here from the eternal standpoint; from this standpoint there is no problem of the identity of one mystical experience with another or of one moment of time with another simply because there are no other mystical experiences or moments of time. There is only the undifferentiated unity. But from the naturalistic standpoint it is not true that the moment of one mystical experience is identical with the moment of every other mystical experience. Two or more mystical experiences can be alike as two peas in a pod as far as the phenomenological content of the experiences are concerned, but they can still be distinguished from each other by the experient's position in space and time. The fact that two mystical experiences are phenomenologically identical is no more evidence for the objective existence of the content of these experiences than is the fact that two dreams are phenomenologically identical evidence for the objective existence of the content of the dreams.

What we are left with, then, is an exclusive disjunction between the mystical and naturalistic standpoint. There is no way of getting rid of the contradiction between the claim of the mystic and the naturalist. Such a dispute is not resolvable by any empirical means; for the very criterion for objectivity in terms of temporal continuity is made from the naturalistic standpoint, and so the mystic would accuse us of begging the question from the outset. The question, "Which is the *true* reality, the one revealed to us in mystical experiences or the one revealed to us in our non-mystical experiences?," is really a value question and cannot be settled by any logical means. What a man takes to be the *really* real is a value judgment expressive of what experiences have the greatest significance for him.

Mysticism and Sense Perception

WILLIAM J. WAINWRIGHT

I

In this paper I propose to examine the cognitive status of mystical experience.

There are, I think, (at least) three distinct but overlapping sorts of religious experience. (1) In the first place, there are two kinds of mystical experience. The extrovertive or nature mystic (in some sense) identifies himself with a world which is both transfigured and one. The introvertive mystic withdraws from the world and, after stripping the mind of concepts and images, experiences union with something which (in some respects at least) can be described as an undifferentiated unity. Introvertive mysticism is a more important phenomenon than extrovertive mysticism. (2) Numinous experiences are complex experiences involving dread, awe, wonder, and fascination. One (apparently) finds onself confronted with something which is radically unlike ordinary objects. Before its overwhelming majesty and power, one is nothing but dust and ashes. In contrasting oneself with its uncanny beauty and goodness, one experiences one's own uncleanness and ugliness. (3) The experiences bound up with the devotional life of the ordinary believer (gratitude, love, trust, filial fear, etc.) are also religious in character. Nevertheless these more ordinary experiences should, I think, be distinguished both from numinous experiences and from mystical experiences, for they do not appear to involve the sense of immediate presence which characterises the latter. For the same reason, there is no

Reprinted from *Religious Studies* 9 (1973) by permission of Cambridge University Press. © Cambridge University Press, 1973. Footnotes have been renumbered for convenience.

prima facie case for the supposition that these experiences provide an independent source of knowledge, that they involve a glimpse of reality or some aspect of reality which is normally hidden from us. (Even those who deny this would—most of them—agree that the salient features of numinous and mystical experience only occur in these more ordinary experiences in an embryonic form.) I think it is clear that we should focus our attention on the more extraordinary varieties of religious experience. If the latter have no cognitive value, it is highly unlikely that common garden variety religious experiences have any cognitive value.

While I intend most of my remarks to apply to numinous experiences as well as to mystical experiences, I will only discuss the latter. There are two connected reasons for this. In the first place there is a voluminous religious literature connected with mysticism and in the second place mysticism has been institutionalised in a way in which the experience of the numinous has not. Because of this, it is easier to discuss mystical experience than it is to discuss numinous experience. One has a better idea of exactly how the religious community deals with the experience, the criteria it uses for evaluating it and so on.

I propose to attack my question from a particular point of view. Mystical experience is often said to be a kind of "seeing" or "tasting" or "touching." We are told that mystical experience is a kind of "experiential knowledge" of the divine. Mystical experiences like numinous experiences are believed to involve a direct or immediate awareness of reality or some aspect of reality which is normally hidden from us. It is difficult to deny that some analogy with sense experience is intended and that part of what is implied in ascribing cognitive value to these peculiar kinds of experience is that these experiences are in some important respects like ordinary perceptual experience. In the opposite camp we find critics like C. B. Martin,[1] who assume that ordinary perceptual experiences provide us with the paradigm of a cognitive or perceptual experience and then proceed to argue that religious experiences cannot be cognitive or perceptual because they deviate in certain important ways from that paradigm.

The analogy (or lack of it) between mystical experience and sense experience appears, then, to be important both to those who ascribe cognitive value to mystical experiences and to those who refuse to do so. In the remainder of this paper I shall explore that analogy.[2]

---

1. "Seeing God" in *Religious Belief*.

2. For another (and different) exploration of the ways in which sense experiences and religious experiences are like and unlike each other see H. P. Owen, *The Christian Knowledge of God*, pp. 269–276. I became acquainted with Owen's very interesting book only after completing this paper. Though we touch on many of the same themes our treatment of these themes is quite different. I have indicated certain points of contact in footnotes in sections III and VI.

II

There are two respects in which mystical experiences and sense experiences are alike. (1) Both types of experience are noetic. (2) On the basis of both types of experience corrigible and independently checkable claims are made about something other than the experience itself, and in each case there are both tests for determining whether or not the object of the experience is real and tests for determining whether or not the apparent perception of that object is a genuine one.

A. Sense experiences (whether veridical or not) have a noetic quality. This involves two things. (1) The experiences have an object, i.e., they are experiences of something (real or imagined). In this respect sense experiences are unlike pains, feelings of depression and so on. The latter may have causes. They may be aroused or occasioned by certain kinds of events or objects but (in spite of certain continental philosophers) they are not experiences *of* those events or objects. (To the question "What is the object of a visual (auditory) experience?" we can reply "Colors and shapes (sounds)." The question "What is the object of a dull pain (a feeling of depression)?" cannot be answered so easily.) (2) Sense experience typically involves the conviction that the object on which the experience is focused is "really there," that it exists and that one is present to it. To use Berkeley's language, the experience has "outness."[3] This conviction should not be regarded as if it were only an interpretation placed upon the experience from outside. On the contrary, it is part of the experience itself.

In spite of the fact that some mystics speak as if their experiences transcended the subject-object structure of ordinary perceptual experience, many mystical experiences (and perhaps all of them) are noetic. (Mystics by and large agree that they experience something which transcends space and time, is devoid of distinctions, supremely valuable, etc.)

B. (1) No type of experience can be called cognitive if it typically induces those who have it to make false claims. Thus, the vision of a mirage, or the experiences one obtains by pressing the eyeball and seeing double and so on, can be called delusive because the very nature of these experiences is such that (until one learns better) one is likely to make false claims on the basis of them. (That water is really present or that there are two candles rather than just one.) I do not think that there is any very good reason to suppose that mystical experiences are delusive in this sense. The mystic does not make false empirical statements because he does not make any empirical statements at all. Rather he claims to know, on the basis of his experience, that God is real and present to him or that there

3. For Berkeley's usage see an unpublished paper by Nelson Pike entitled "The Modes of Mystical Union."

is an "uncreated, imperishable Beyond" or something of the sort. *These* are the kinds of statements which the experience induces those who have it to make, and it would seem that we are entitled to assert that the experience is delusive only if we have good independent reasons for believing that claims of this kind are false. It is by no means clear that we *do* have such reasons.

(2) The fact that experiences are not delusive in the sense we have just explained does not imply that they are cognitive. Pains are not delusive in this sense but they are not cognitive either. If we now turn to sense experiences (which are admitted to be cognitive experiences by all parties to the dispute) we see that not only do they not induce *false* claims, they also provide a basis for making *true* claims about something other than the experience itself.

Are mystical experiences like sense experiences in this respect? We can at least say this. On the basis of their experiences mystics do make claims about something other than their own experiences and (given that there is no disproof of God's existence or of the reality of the One, etc.) these claims are not clearly false.

(3) When someone claims to see or hear or touch something, his claim is not self-certifying. Things other than the experience itself are relevant to a determination of the truth or falsity of those claims, and one who makes these claims is normally aware that this is the case. C. B. Martin[4] and others have asserted that in this respect sense experiences are radically unlike mystical experiences, for (they say) when the mystic claims to experience God, his claims are not corrigible—there are (to use Martin's phrase) no independent tests and checkup procedures which he and others would regard as relevant to a determination of the truth or falsity of the claims he makes. As far as I can see this is simply false. C. B. Martin and others, have, I think, been misled by the fact that certain familiar tests (e.g., the appeal to the agreement of others) play a very minor role here, or no role at all, and have illicitly jumped to the conclusion that the mystic therefore dismisses all tests and checkup procedures as irrelevant and regards his claims as incorrigible.

Suppose someone claims to have seen an elephant in his backyard. There are at least two ways in which his claim might be attacked. One might try to show that no elephant was there at all, or one might try to show that he could not have seen it because, for example, he was not in a position to observe it, or because his sensory equipment was defective. When we turn to mystical experience we find both sorts of tests and checkup procedures (at least in a rough and ready way), i.e., we find inde-

4. Op. cit.

pendent procedures for determining whether or not the object is real and we also find procedures for determining whether or not the experience, the claims of which are in question, is indeed a genuine perception of that object.

(a) In the first place, even when claims about God and Nirvāna and so on are grounded in mystical consciousness, they are in fact not self-certifying. Things other than the experience itself are relevant to an evaluation of them. For example, considerations of logic are relevant. These claims cannot be true if the concepts of God or Nirvāna or what have you, are self-contradictory. Again, the considerations adduced in the controversy between those philosophers who espouse some form of naturalism and theistic philosophers would appear to have some bearing on the truth value of the claims in question. When the mystic asserts that he has experienced God (Nirvāna, Brahman) he implies that there is such a being and, if he has his wits about him, he will recognise that things other than his own experience are relevant to an evaluation of that claim. It is true that mystics are certain of the truth of the claims that they make but this is no more incompatible with a recognition of their corrigibility than the fact that I am certain that I now see a red pen is incompatible with a recognition of the fact that *that* particular claim is a corrigible one. In short claims about God, or Nirvāna or other things of that kind are not self-certifying and there seems to be no feature of the mystical experience which would prevent a mystic from acknowledging that fact. (Individual mystics might be confused on this point, but this can as easily be attributed to bad philosophy as to the experience itself.)

(b) Even if God exists and a direct experience of him is possible, it does not follow that every claim to be immediately aware of God is justified. How then do we distinguish those experiences of God which are veridical from those which are not? If we turn our attention to communities in which mysticism has flourished we find that various tests have been used to distinguish those experiences which genuinely involve a perception of the divine from those which do not. Each of the following six criteria is employed in the Christian (particularly the Catholic) community. Similar criteria are used in other communities.

(i) The consequences of the experience must be good for the mystic. The experience must lead to, or produce, or reinforce, a new life marked by such virtues as wisdom, humility, charity and so on. Let me make two comments at this point. (α) Sanity is a criterion which is often appealed to. It should, I think, be subsumed under the criterion which we are now considering. A genuine experience of God is believed to lead to, or produce, or reinforce, a life of rather extraordinary goodness. It seems reasonable to suppose that sanity is a necessary condition of such a life. (At least if we do not define "sanity" too narrowly.) (β) We can understand why people are bothered by the presence of certain kinds of causes. Many find it impossible to believe that the use of drugs, nervous and physical disorders and so on, can play a part in the best sort of life. Consequently, if they find that these things play a major role in the life of a mystic, they will tend to reject (or at least be suspicious of) his experiences—*not* because there is some reason for supposing that a genuine vision of God cannot have natural causes but because these particular natural causes are (rightly or wrongly) deemed to be incompatible with the best life—that kind of life which is believed to be bound up with, and to follow, a genuine vision of the divine.

(ii) One must consider the effect of the experience upon others. One should ask, for example, whether the actions of the mystic, his words and his example, tend to build up the community or to destroy it.

(iii) The depth, the profundity and the "sweetness" (Jonathan Edwards) of what the mystic says on the basis of his experience counts in favor of the genuineness of that experience. On the other hand, the insignificance, or the silliness of what he says counts against it. (On the basis of this criterion many would reject the claims of Margery Kempe. Cf. David Knowles, *The English Mystical Tradition,* Chapter VIII.)

(iv) We must examine what the mystic says on the basis of his experience and see whether it agrees or disagrees with orthodox talk.

(v) It will also be helpful to determine whether or not the experience in question resembles other mystical experiences which are regarded as paradigmatic within the religious community. (In the Roman Catholic church, experiences are often compared with the experiences of St. Teresa of Avila or St. John of the Cross.)

(vi) We must also take the pronouncements of authority into account. In some communities the word of the spiritual director, or guru or master is final. (This is clearly the case in Zen, and is true to some degree in other religious communities as well.) In other cases the relevant authority may be the community as a whole or some special organ of it (e.g., the college of bishops). In some cases all of these authorities may be relevant.

If I am correct the criteria we have just considered are similar to those we employ in ordinary cases to show, not that the object of the experience is real or unreal, but rather that the experience of it is or is not genuine (because of, e.g., the position of the observer, or the condition of his sensory equipment, etc.). Of course the *nature* of the tests is not much alike. Nevertheless, the point of them is. (One would not expect the nature of the tests to be much alike. In the case of mystical experience there is no sensory equipment which can go awry because no sense organs are involved. Nor does there appear to be anything which clearly corresponds to the position of the observer in the case of sense experience. And so on.)

III

Among the more important tests and check up procedures which are used to evaluate ordinary perceptual claims are the agreement and disagreement of those who occupy similar positions, and the success or failure of predictions based upon the experience whose claims are in question. Are similar tests used to determine the cognitive status of religious experience?

A. The claim that mystical experience is cognitive is often supported by appealing to the rather surprising amount of agreement that exists. Mystics can be found in radically different cultures, in places which have had little or no contact with each other, and in both ancient and modern times. Not only are the experiences of these mystics alike, they base remarkably similar claims upon their experiences.

(1) It would appear initially that some kinds of agreement are irrelevant in the present connection, that the presence of certain kinds of agreement has little or no tendency to show that the mode of experience whose claims are in question is either cognitive or non-cognitive.

(a) It is true that the visual and auditory experiences of persons from different cultures, with different social backgrounds, different psychological makeups, and so on, are quite similar. Analogously mystics from different cultures, with different social backgrounds, different psychological makeups, etc., can and do enjoy similar experiences. It is equally true that those who suffer from migraines or indigestion undergo similar experiences in spite of differences in culture, social background, psychological makeup and many other factors. Sense experiences are widespread and so are mystical experiences. But so also are migraines and stomach aches. Since migraines and stomach aches would seem to be paradigm cases of non-cognitive experience, the presence of this kind of agreement hardly provides a decisive reason for asserting that the mode of experience whose claims are in question, is cognitive.

(b) People who make visual (or auditory or tactual, etc.) observations can typically describe conditions under which others can obtain similar experiences. ("If you go into the room on the left, you will see the body." "If the telescope is trained on such and such a place at such and such a time, you will obtain a sighting of the moons of Jupiter.") Now the mystic can do something like this. He can prescribe a regimen, a mode of procedure, which is likely to lead to introvertive experiences. (These will include such things as postures and breathing techniques, moral behavior, meditation, ascetic practices of one kind or another, and so on. Sometimes the procedures are specified in great detail. Furthermore, in spite of some variation—particularly in the emphasis placed upon physical techniques—there is a great deal of agreement as to just what these procedures involve.)

We should notice three things about these procedures.

(i) The only agreement or disagreement which is directly relevant to an examination of the cognitive value of sense experiences, is agreement or disagreement among those who follow the prescribed procedures, who try to make the observation under the prescribed conditions. Agreement among those who fail to follow these procedures is not expected and, hence, its absence is regarded as beside the point. If sense experience provides the model for all cognitive modes of experience, then it would seem that the fact that most of us have never enjoyed mystical experience is irrelevant. For most of us, of course, have not subjected ourselves to the necessary discipline.

(ii) There is a closer connection between the use of the appropriate procedures and success in the case of sense perception than in the case of mysticism, i.e., one is more likely to obtain the relevant experience by employing the recommended techniques in the former case than in the latter case.

(iii) The presence of agreement among those who employ certain prescribed techniques to elicit the type of experience whose claims are in question, is not decisive. This kind of agreement can be found in the case of sense experience, but it can also be found in the case of other experiences which would almost universally be considered subjective. Thus it can be safely asserted that most of those who eat ten bratwurst sandwiches within twenty minutes will undergo strikingly similar and equally unpleasant digestive experiences. It would appear to follow that the fact that this kind of agreement can be found in the case of mysticism, is not of crucial importance.[5]

(c) We now come to the crucial point. Those who see, hear, touch, etc., base non-psychological claims (claims about something other than the experiences themselves) upon their experiences and the lack of agreement among those who follow the appropriate procedures is considered to have a special bearing on the truth of those claims.

Those who suffer from headaches or indigestion do not typically base non-psychological claims on those experiences and so do not consider the agreement or disagreement of others to be relevant to an examination of the truth of such claims.

Mystics, unlike those who suffer from headaches and indigestion, do base non-psychological claims upon their experiences. The question is, do they consider the agreement or disagreement of others to be relevant to those claims, i.e., do they take the fact that others have similar experiences (and thus say similar things) when following the appropriate procedures

5. R. M. Gale makes a point similar to this in the last section of a paper entitled "Mysticism and Philosophy" *Journal of Philosophy,* Volume 57, 1960 [this volume, pp. 113–22—Eds.]; Walter Stace also makes a similar point in *Mysticism and Philosophy,* pp. 135–9.

as counting *for* their claims, and do they take the fact that others do not have similar experiences when following these procedures (and so do not say similar things) as counting *against* their claims? If they do, then we have discovered what may be an important analogy between mystical experiences and sense experiences. If they do not, we have uncovered what is perhaps a significant disanalogy between the two modes of experience. Unfortunately the situation is ambiguous.

(2) Many mystics do, I think, believe that the fact that others have enjoyed similar experiences, and made similar claims, provides support for the claims which *they* base upon their experiences, and because of this agreement they are more confident of the cognitive value of their experiences than they would otherwise be. However, as far as I can see, no distinction is made between those experiences which are obtained by employing the appropriate techniques and those which are obtained in some other way. All similar experiences are thought to (equally) confirm the claims which are made or (what comes to more or less the same thing) the cognitive value of the experience upon which those claims are based.

It is not clear whether or not the mystic believes that disagreement (the failure of others to enjoy similar experiences) has any bearing upon the cognitive standing of his experiences. (*a*) Mystics are clearly not disturbed by the fact that most people never enjoy mystical experiences. Nor do they appear to be bothered by the fact that some of those who earnestly employ the appropriate techniques never achieve illumination or union. These points are not, however, decisive, for it might nonetheless be true that if there *was* more disagreement than in fact obtains (if, e.g., the mystic stood alone) the mystic would withdraw or qualify his claim. Disagreement is regarded as relevant if there is *any* degree of disagreement which *would* be taken as counting against the claim if it *were* to occur. (*b*) Suppose that the mystic were to discover that those who were believed to have achieved a unitive experience after employing the standard techniques had not really done so. Would he regard this discovery as counting against the cognitive value of his own experiences? Of course he might do so (particularly if he had used these techniques himself) but he might only conclude that the techniques were not as effective as he had believed them to be. (*c*) Suppose the mystic stood entirely alone. While it is by no means clear that the mystic would (or should) repudiate his experience under these conditions (it is, perhaps, too impressive for that) he might nevertheless be bothered by the absence of supporting claims. (There is some evidence that those who believe that their religious experiences are unique are more suspicious of them than those who are aware of the fact that others have enjoyed similar experiences.)

(3) What emerges from these considerations is this. The mystic bases non-psychological statements upon his experiences and believes that the

fact that others have similar experiences tends to confirm those claims (the veridical character of his own experience). It is possible that if others were to fail altogether to have similar experiences, he would take this fact as counting against the veridical character of his own experience. In these respects mystical experience appears to be more like sense experiences than like, e.g., feelings of nausea or depression.

On the other hand there are significant disanalogies. (a) *All* similar experiences are believed to confirm the mystic's claim. The fact that some of these experiences have not been obtained by employing the appropriate procedures is ignored. (b) Furthermore, it is not clear that a complete breakdown of the procedures for obtaining these experiences would induce the mystic to hedge his claims, though he might be bothered if no similar experiences occurred at all.

In both these respects mystical experience is unlike sense experience. In the latter case, the only relevant agreement is that which is found among those who satisfy certain appropriate conditions, and the failure to obtain similar experiences by employing the appropriate techniques is regarded as very bothersome indeed.

(c) Most significant, I think, is the fact that the presence of agreement or disagreement is not regarded as a crucial consideration by those who have had mystical experiences, or are interested in defending their cognitive value. It is not even clear to me that this consideration is believed to be important. In the case of sense experience, on the other hand, the presence or absence of agreement (among those who employ the appropriate procedures) is treated as important, and sometimes even as crucial.

B. (1) In evaluating a particular instance of sense experience, we take into account any predictions which have been based upon that experience. Successful predictions count for its veridicality and unsuccessful predictions count against it. Furthermore, if one were to attempt to justify the claim that sense experience is a cognitive *mode* of experience, he would undoubtedly appeal to the fact that large numbers of successful, and comparatively few unsuccessful, non-psychological predictions are based upon experiences of that kind.

(2) A few predictions do appear to be based upon mystical experience. (a) On the basis of their experience mystics often assert that the soul is immortal, and this, of course involves a prediction. (b) Mystics also sometimes claim that their experiences confirm theological systems which include certain predictions as an integral part. Thus, Christian mystics have sometimes become more deeply convinced of the truth of Christian dogma as a result of their experiences and the Christian dogmatic structure includes a belief in the general resurrection, the transfiguration of heaven and earth and so on. (c) A mystic may, on the basis of his experience, predict that if one subjects oneself to the appropriate discipline (e.g., recites

the Jesus prayer in the right way or follows the noble eight-fold path) he will obtain a vision of God or pass into Nirvāna or something of the sort.

(3) Many, perhaps most, of the predictions made by those who are subject to sense experiences of a certain type can be checked *both* by others who enjoy experiences of that type *and* by those who have never had that kind of experience. Thus suppose I see thunderclouds approaching and predict that it will rain. Someone who was blind would be unable to do this (though he might, of course, predict rain on the basis of other factors). He can, however, check this prediction. If it rains he will not be able to see it, but he will (if suitably situated) feel, hear, and perhaps even taste the rain. Again, if he fails to have these experiences he can (if suitably situated) conclude that my prediction was a failure.

The claim that we are immortal and the claim that human beings will be resurrected are, I think, verifiable (though not falsifiable). But the experiences which would justify them if they were to occur are (in the first case) post-mortem experiences, and (in the second case) post-Advent experiences. These claims cannot be verified in this life, or before the second Advent either by non-mystics or by other mystics. If one verified the third prediction one would be a mystic. The conclusion then is that none of these predictions can be checked in this life by the non-mystic and the first two predictions cannot be checked in this life by anyone at all. (Unless perhaps immortality and the possibility of the vision of God, etc., can be made out in this life by reason and authority. This would be a check of sorts, though not an experiential one.)

In so far as these predictions cannot be checked, they cannot be appealed to in order to establish the cognitive value of the mode of experience whose claims are in question, nor to establish the cognitive value of instances of that mode of experience. It would thus appear that a blind man may have a reason for ascribing cognitive value to visual experience (*qua mode* of experience) or to some particular visual experience, which the non-mystic does not have for ascribing cognitive value to mystical experience (*qua mode* of experience) or to some particular mystical experience, viz. that the blind man knows and the non-mystic does not, that the particular experience or mode of experience whose claims are in question leads to successful predictions. (Though, again, as I pointed out, someone might insist that he knows, upon the basis of reason and/or authority, that the predictions which the mystic makes are successful.) This difference is striking and some would think, deeply significant.

C. We have seen that a consideration of the presence of agreement or disagreement, and of the success or failure of any predictions which might have been based upon the experience do not play an important role in the evaluation of the cognitive status of mystical consciousness. Many think that they have explained these differences when they assert that sense experiences are cognitive and that mystical experiences are not. There is however another way to account for them. The differences can be explained by the fact that the objects of these two kinds of experience are radically different.

(1) Suppose[6] that God is the object of the experience (rather than Nirvāna or the Ātman, etc.). If God is what he is supposed to be—omnipotent, omniscient, mysterious, other, transcendent and so on, then whether or not one enjoys a vision of him will, in the last analysis, depend upon his will and there will be no set of procedures the correct use of which will invariably result in illumination or union. Hence while mystical experience may be repeatable in the weak sense that given exactly the same conditions (including the operation of God's grace), the same experience will occur, there is no reason to suppose that it will be repeatable in the strong sense, viz. that certain procedures or methods can be described which are such that (almost) all who correctly employ them will obtain the experience in question.

On the other hand, given the nature of physical objects (physical objects exhibit spatio-temporal continuity, are relatively accessible, behave in lawlike and regular ways, etc.) one reasonably supposes that if one's experience of the object is indeed veridical, others will enjoy similar experiences under similar conditions. One expects experiences of these objects to cohere and mutually support one another in certain familiar ways. However, if physical objects were not of this kind, these expectations would not be reasonable. If the nature of physical objects was different in certain ways, the experiences of these objects would not be repeatable in the strong sense, *even if the objects were real and experiences of them were genuine.* Thus suppose that mountains jumped about in a discontinuous fashion, randomly appeared and disappeared, and behaved in other lawless and unpredictable ways. If these conditions obtained, observation under similar conditions would not normally yield similar results even if mountains were real and experiences of them were genuine. There would be no reason to expect experiences in this area to cohere and support one another in the way in which they do.

The general point is this. The nature of the object should (at least in part) determine the tests for its presence.[7] Given the nature of physical objects it is reasonable to suppose that genuine experiences of these objects can be confirmed by employing certain appropriate procedures and obtaining similar experiences, and that non-genuine experiences can be disconfirmed by employing these same procedures and obtaining different ex-

6. The main point in this section (III C. (1)) can be found (in an abbreviated form) in William Alston's *Religious Belief and Philosophical Thought,* pp. 124–5. My discussion derives from his.

7. As H. P. Owen asserts in various places in *The Christian Knowledge of God.*

periences. But God's nature is radically different from that of physical objects and it is therefore, not so clearly reasonable to suppose that (apparent) experiences of God can be confirmed or disconfirmed in the same way.

The difference in the nature of their respective objects explains, then, why the presence or absence of agreement is an important test in the one case, but not in the other.

This difference also explains other disanalogies. God is not bound by our techniques. One person may employ these techniques and fail to obtain the desired experience while another who has never used them may experience (some degree of) enlightenment. It is therefore only to be expected that little distinction is made between similar experiences which are obtained by the use of these practices and similar experiences which are obtained without using them. Finally since God freely bestows the experience upon whom he will, we have no idea of just how many of these experiences to expect. Hence it is not clear at what point (if any) we should begin to be bothered by the absence of agreement. It should not therefore surprise us if we find ourselves unable to specify a degree of disagreement which is so great that in the face of it the mystic should withdraw his claim.

(2) Similar considerations explain why the disanalogy which was uncovered in section III B is not as significant as it might appear to be.

It is sometimes maintained that successful predictions—predictions which we can show to be successful—provide the only reason we *could* have for ascribing cognitive value to a mode of experience. However, it is not clear that we should accept this. (*a*) From the fact that successful predictions provide *a* reason for ascribing cognitive value to a mode of experience, it does not follow that they provide the *only* reason for doing so. (One would perhaps have a reason for ascribing cognitive value to mystical experience, (i) if there was a close analogy in other respects between mystical experience and the more ordinary sorts of cognitive experience and/or (ii) if the hypothesis that the experience involves contact with the transcendent were to provide the best explanation of all the relevant facts. (iii) Again, natural theology or revealed theology might provide the reason we are looking for.) (*b*) It might be reasonable to insist on successful predictions when the mode of experience in question is supposed to provide access to ordinary empirical objects—objects which exhibit spatial and/or temporal continuity, which are accessible, and which behave in lawlike and regular ways—for we rightly assume that testable predictions can be made about such objects. It is not however clear that such a demand is reasonable when the object in question is (like God) a-spatial, a-temporal (?), and neither accessible in the way in which ordinary objects are accessible nor lawlike and regular in its movements. (For this reason, I believe that the comparison which is sometimes drawn between mystical experiences and those psychic experiences (such as clairvoyance) which purport to provide extraordinary knowledge about perfectly ordinary events and objects, is less than apt. Since the objects of these two kinds of experience is radically different one would expect to find a corresponding difference in the appropriate tests and checkup procedures. The demand for a large number of clearly successful predictions is entirely appropriate, in the second case. I do not think that it is appropriate in the first case.)

(3) Summary. There is no reason to believe that genuine experiences of God will be supported by the experience of others in the way in which veridical sense experiences are supported by the experience of others, and there is no very good reason to believe that genuine experiences of this kind will provide data which can be used in predicting the future. Since this is the case it would seem unreasonable to suppose that a decisive consideration against the veridicality of mystical consciousness is provided by the fact that these experiences are not supported by the experience of others in the way in which veridical sense experiences are supported by the experience of others, and do not afford us a glimpse of the future.

IV

If a mode of experience is to be admitted as cognitive, more is necessary than that there be tests for evaluating the cognitive character of instances of that type of experience. It is also necessary that these tests be relevant to the cognitive status of these experiences, and that they be satisfied by many (most?) instances of that type of experience. Thus we would dismiss a test which specified that genuine experiences occur only in months the English name of which contains the letter r, on the ground that whether or not an experience occurs in those months has nothing to do with its cognitive status. Furthermore, if the relevant tests yielded negative results in almost all cases of a given type of experience we would not, I think, regard that mode of experience as cognitive. (Thus, if visual experiences normally conflicted with one another and generally proved a deceptive guide to future experience, we should not, I think, regard visual experience as cognitive.)

In the light of these considerations we can see that two significant sorts of disagreement are possible. People may disagree as to the relevance of the tests which are used to evaluate instances of the experience whose cognitive status is in question, and opinions may differ as to whether or not the appropriate tests are met with any degree of frequency.

A. Whether or not the appropriate tests are met depends, of course, upon just what the appropriate tests are. The six tests which we considered in section II B (3) (b) are met in many cases. On the other hand while mystical experiences do not lead to patently false predictions, the few predictions which are based upon them are not, perhaps, known to be true. Nor is it clear that mystical experiences agree and cohere in the way in which sense experiences agree and cohere. Nevertheless for the reasons given at the end of section III, these last two tests may not be particularly relevant to the evaluation of religious experience, and, if they are not, then the fact that experiences of this kind fail to satisfy these tests, or satisfy them very imperfectly, is of no particular importance. At least it is not crucial. (One might, of course, insist that the satisfaction of these two tests is *always* crucial, and if anyone does, then—since mystical experiences either fail to satisfy these tests or satisfy them very imperfectly—he will probably refuse to ascribe cognitive value to this peculiar mode of experience. That the satisfaction of these tests *is* always crucial appears to me, however, to be a mere dogma.)

B. Others refuse to ascribe cognitive value to mystical experience because, though they admit that there are tests for evaluating experiences of this kind, and that these tests are often satisfied, they deny that the tests are relevant. This, however, may be a mistake.

As we saw in section II, the tests for evaluating mystical experiences break down into two kinds—those tests which are used to determine the reality of the object of the experience and those which are used to determine the genuineness of the experience of that object.

In determining the truth of the claim that God is real, one may address oneself to considerations of logic, review the more telling points brought forward by theists and atheists and so on. (One would do similar, if not identical things, in order to determine the reality of the Brahman or Nirvāna, etc.) It would be generally agreed that this procedure is legitimate and that these considerations do bear on the truth or falsity of the claim that God is real. It is the other set of tests—those procedures which are used to determine the genuineness of the experience of the object— which create the most suspicion. Nevertheless, there are good reasons to believe that, at least under certain conditions, these tests are relevant.

(1 and 2) The first two tests are moral tests. A genuine experience is one which is fruitful and edifying both for the mystic himself and for others. If the (apparent) objects of these experiences is God (in which case the experience is only genuine if it is really and not only apparently an experience of God), then these tests are relevant. For, if God exists, is good, cares for his creatures, etc. (and these things are analytically connected with the notion of God) then one would expect a direct experience of him to be fruitful and edifying, to result in beauty, goodness, holiness and wisdom.

(3) The third test also appears to be relevant if God is the (apparent) object of the experience; for if God is all good, omniscient, omnipotent, necessary, the mysterium tremendum, holy, numinous, etc. (and again, all

of these attributes would seem to be analytically connected with the notion of God) then one would not expect a vision of him to lead to twaddle.
Quite the contrary.

(4) The fourth test is relevant to an evaluation of experiences which
seem to involve a direct awareness of God provided that (*a*) God is a God
of truth and (*b*) orthodox beliefs are true. If God is a God of truth and
orthodox beliefs are true, one would suppose that a genuine experience of
God would not lead to (very much) non-orthodox talk.

(5 and 6) The relevance of the fifth and sixth tests depends upon the
truth of doctrines concerning the holiness and authoritative character of
the individual or community which is in question. For example the claims
of the Christian community and its representatives would be supported by
an appeal to the notion that the Church is the Body of Christ and the
temple of the Holy Spirit, to the claim that its bishops possess teaching
authority, and so on.

The relevance of the first three tests depends upon the truth of certain
conditional propositions (viz. that *if* God exists and is good and cares for
his creatures, then genuine experiences of him will be fruitful and edifying for the mystic and for others, etc.). One may be uncertain as to
whether or not God exists and yet nonetheless admit that if a given experience really is an experience of God, it will be fruitful and that, therefore, there is a good reason to examine the consequences of the experience.
One need not be a theist to admit the relevance of these tests. The last
three tests, on the other hand, are relevant only if the specific tenets of
some particular religious community are true. One would have no reason
to compare the talk of the mystic whose claims are in question with orthodox Christian talk, or to stress the ways in which his experience is like and
unlike the experience of St. John of the Cross (rather than some Sufi or
Theravādin mystic) or to appeal to the consensus of the Church, if one
were not oneself a Christian.

A minor question remains. Agreement is sometimes appealed to, to
support the claims of mystical experience, though if I am correct this appeal is relatively unimportant. Now we have seen that because of the peculiar nature of the object of mystical experience, there is no reason to expect that genuine experiences will be confirmed by the experiences of
others in the way in which veridical sense experiences are confirmed by
the experiences of others, and having seen this, it may occur to us to ask
whether there is any logical connection at all between the presence of
agreement and the absence of disagreement on the one hand, and a genuine experience of God on the other. True, agreement is appealed to, and
the mystic might feel ill at ease in the absence of any agreement at all.
But it does not follow that agreement and disagreement have any logical

significance in the present connection. (Most of us take comfort in numbers and are uneasy if we find ourselves alone and there is nothing particularly significant in this fact.)

There are two considerations which suggest (but do not prove) that agreement and disagreement have some logical bearing upon the cognitive value of these experiences. (1) If God's behaviour were completely erratic and unpredictable, then perhaps agreement and disagreement should not count at all. However, though his behaviour does not possess the regularity and lawlike character which belongs to the behaviour of physical objects, it is not generally believed to be completely erratic and lawless either.

(2) The second consideration is this. Other things being equal, it *may* be reasonable to expect instances of a genuinely cognitive mode of experience to occur under radically different social and psychological conditions. (Similar visual experiences are of course, enjoyed by people with radically different natures and radically different backgrounds.) The presence of widespread agreement shows that this expectation is satisfied, and the complete absence of agreement would show that it was not satisfied. Neither of these considerations are, I think, decisive.

V

1. Consider the following argument:

(1) If the analogy between mystical experience and the more familiar modes of perceptual experience (= sense experience) is very close then we are (probably) justified in regarding mystical experience as a cognitive experience.

(2) The analogy is very close. (Both experiences are noetic. On the basis of both of these experiences corrigible and independently checkable claims are made about something other than the experience itself. In both cases there are tests for determining the reality of the object of the experience as well as tests for determining the genuineness of the apparent perception of that object. In both cases, the application of these tests yields positive results in a large number of cases.)

(3) Therefore, we are probably justified in regarding mystical experience as a cognitive experience.

There is a variation of this argument which may be more persuasive.

(1) The analogy between mystical experience and the more familiar modes of perceptual experience (= sense experience) is close enough to warrant the conclusion that mystical experiences are

cognitive *provided that* we have independent reasons for believing
mystics when they assert that they have directly experienced some
transcendent aspect of reality.

(2) Such and such a bit of natural theology (this would be filled in by
alluding to some "demonstration of the being and attributes of
God") and/or the sanity, sanctity and intelligence of the great
mystics provides us with such a reason.

(3) Therefore, we are warranted in drawing the conclusion that mystical experiences are cognitive.

2. The first premiss of the first argument is I think, a plausible one.
The plausibility of the second premiss of the second argument depends in
large measure upon the success or failure of natural theology, and here
opinions can and do differ.

The second premiss of the first argument and the first premiss of the
second argument involve the same kind of problem. One's opinion of these
premisses will be determined not only by one's estimate of the number of
respects in which sense experience and mystical experience are like and
unlike each other, but also by one's judgment as to the relative importance
of these resemblances and differences. (Thus, one's estimate of the significance of the fact that the presence or absence of agreement is regarded as
vitally important when evaluating sense experiences, but as relatively unimportant when evaluating mystical experiences will depend upon whether
or not one believes that the appeal to the presence or absence of agreement
is an appropriate test for the evaluation of mystical experience, upon
whether or not one thinks that this test *must* be among the tests used to determine the cognitive value of an experience, and so on.) There is no mechanical decision procedure which can be used to determine the truth
value of these premisses, just as there is no mechanical decision procedure
which can be appealed to, to determine what one should do when moral
obligations conflict, or how one should appraise a new style of art, or the
general plausibility of a world view. What is called for in all of these cases,
is a judgment and reasonable men may differ. (There are criteria, but it is
sometimes difficult to see whether or not they have been applied correctly.
Thus, in choosing a world view, we should attempt to determine which
view has the most explanatory power. But this itself is something which
calls for judgment.)

3. It is often assumed that no experience can be cognitive which is unlike sense experience in very many important respects. This is, of course,
quite vague. (What deviations are important and how many deviations
are very many?) There is however a more important point—it is by no
means clear that the assumption is true. As far as I can see, all that we
mean when we say that an experience is cognitive or perceptual, is that,

through this experience we come to know something which we could not know, or could not know as easily, in other ways, and (probably) that the knowledge in question is non-inferential. If this is even roughly correct, then I doubt that *x is a cognitive experience* entails *x is very much like sense experiences*. Of course, sense experiences clearly are cognitive experiences. Therefore, if we could show that some other mode of experience is very much like sense experience, we would have thereby provided a good (if not conclusive) reason for supposing that the mode of experience in question is cognitive. On the other hand, if something like the analysis I have provided is correct then the fact that a mode of experience is radically *unlike* sense experience would hardly appear to be decisive. (Perhaps it should be pointed out that from the fact (if it is a fact) that mystical experience is radically unlike so-called objective experiences (seeing, hearing, etc.) it does not follow that it is like paradigmatic cases of non-cognitive experiences (suffering, headaches, feeling depressed, etc.). It may be—as Stace suggests—that mystical experience is unlike *both* of these two types of experience.)

4. The arguments we have considered are not the only ones which might be employed in an attempt to establish the cognitive value of mystical experience. However these are the arguments which should concern us in this paper because they are the arguments which are directly based upon the analogy between mystical experience and sense experience.

VI

Flew (*God and Philosophy,* Chapter 6), Schmidt (*Religious Knowledge,* Chapter 8) and Hepburn (*Christianity and Paradox,* p. 37) all argue that any cognitive claims which are made for religious experience (or any other kind of praeternatural experience) must be certified by independent checks. Thus, according to Hepburn, even if we (and no one else?) saw a red circle in the air whenever John was angry, we would be entitled to claim that John was angry on the basis of this experience only if we had learned by ordinary procedures that the "code" was reliable (i.e., to justify these claims we would have to show that a correlation obtained between seeing the red circle and John's anger, the latter being established by normal criteria). Or again, Schmidt asks us to look at a case in which we judge that we have a cavity because we feel pain in one of our teeth. He suggests that this judgment is warranted only because we have independent criteria (criteria other than the toothache) by means of which we can establish the presence of a cavity and because we know (on the basis of past experience) that a correlation obtains between toothaches and cavities. Schmidt concludes that, in general, we can move from a first person psychological report about feelings (or some other kind of private experience) to a descriptive claim about some non-psychological entity or event only if we have independent criteria for determining the truth or falsity of that claim and have discovered by experience that there is a correlation between the presence of those feelings and its truth.

The implication of all this is, of course, that the mystic can legitimately base religious and metaphysical claims on his experience only if he has independent criteria for establishing the existence (or presence) of the supposed object of his experience, and if he can show that his experience and (the presence of) that object are correlated.

The first thing we should do is to notice exactly what is being demanded. We must distinguish (1) the demand that independent checks be provided for claims based on particular experiences of a given kind from (2) the demand that there be an independent certification of the claim that experiences of a certain kind (e.g., mystical ones) provide an adequate basis for cognitive claims (of a certain kind). (In the second case we are being asked to justify the cognitive status of a certain mode of experience. In the first case we are only being asked to justify the cognitive status of an *instance* of a certain kind of experience. An example of the second sort of demand would be the demand to justify the cognitive status of visual experience. An example of the first sort of demand would be a demand to justify the cognitive status of some particular visual experience.)

The first demand is rather easily met. Just as there are tests other than the visual experiences of someone who bases a cognitive claim upon one of those experiences (e.g., his own auditory and tactual experience, the sense experiences of others, etc.) so there are tests other than the mystical experiences of someone who bases cognitive claims on *those* particular experiences (e.g., his sanity, the similarity of his experiences to those of other mystics, etc.). But this is not what is at issue here. What is at issue is not the cognitive status of some particular mystical experience but the cognitive status of mystical experience in general; i.e., it is the second demand which is being made rather than the first.

For the sake of simplicity I will concentrate on Schmidt's remarks.

(1) There is something very wrong in supposing (as Schmidt and the others do) that "having certain feelings and sensations" is an adequate description of the subjective side of mystical experience. If our description is to be adequate we must at least mention the intentional character of the experience. As William James pointed out many years ago the experience is noetic. (It has an object and the conviction that one is in the presence of that object is an essential feature of the experience.) Having a mystical experience is not like feeling pain or being depressed. (None of this, of course, entails that mystical experiences are veridical.)

(2) In the second place there may in fact be independent reasons for thinking that God exists (the arguments for the existence of God) and

that there is a correlation between the presence of God and certain kinds of religious experience (such reasons might be provided by tradition and authority). It is true of course, that many (including Schmidt) would not accept these reasons. Again (though this is clearly not what Schmidt is looking for) one might suppose that a kind of independent certification of the cognitive character of mystical experience is provided by one or more of the arguments considered in section V.

(3) Perhaps some other kind of experience can be used to test the claims made for mystical experience (by showing that judgments based on mystical experience do or do not square with judgments based on this other sort of experience). It might, for example, be suggested that numinous experience corroborates mystical experience in the way in which auditory and tactual experience corroborates visual experience, or (and this is essentially the same point) that mystical experiences and numinous experiences support and reinforce one another in the way in which the various kinds of sense experience support and reinforce one another. Of course Schmidt will not accept this because he believes that numinous and mystical experiences are equally suspect. He is demanding that we justify the claim that religious experiences (of either or both kinds) involve an awareness of the presence of God (or some transcendent being or state) in precisely the way in which we would justify the claim that toothaches are a sign of cavities.

(4) It is not clear that this demand is reasonable. Suppose that someone asks us to justify the claim that "tree experiences" (those complex experiences involving visual, tactual . . . elements, which reveal the presence of trees) are experiences of something distinct from them, viz. trees. It is not clear that we would know how to satisfy this request. In particular, it should be noticed that we cannot independently (of those experiences) establish the existence of trees at certain times and places, and the occurrences of these experiences, and observe that the two are correlated. (To suppose that we could do this would be to suppose that there are tests for ascertaining the presence of trees which do not directly or indirectly rely on the tree experiences of ourselves and others, and as far as I can see there are none.) In short, while (a) the connection between mystical experiences and a transcendental object cannot be justified by the procedure which Schmidt suggests, it is also true that (b) the connection between tree experiences and trees cannot be justified by the procedure which Schmidt suggests. Since (b) does not entitle us to conclude that (c) tree experiences do not provide cognitive access to trees, it is unclear why (a) should entitle us to conclude that (d) mystical experiences do not provide cognitive access to a transcendent object. (Note: Schmidt's demand might be in order when we are dealing with experiences which are not "perception-like," e.g., toothaches, twinges, depression, etc. It is not

clear that it is in order when the experiences in question are "perception-like," e.g., visual and mystical experiences.[8])

(5) Schmidt might suggest (though he does not in fact do so) that the two cases are different in the following very important respect. When we learn the meaning of the word "tree" we learn what trees look like, what they feel like, what they sound like when the wind blows through them, etc., i.e., in learning the meaning of the word "tree" we learn the connection between these experiences and the presence of trees. On the other hand numinous and mystical experiences are not connected in this way with the meaning of "God" or "Brahman." Someone who has never had numinous or mystical experiences and has no idea of what they are like can learn the meaning of "God" or "Brahman." On the bases of these considerations we might conclude that tree experiences and trees are analytically connected, whereas mystical (numinous) experiences and God (Brahman) are not, and that therefore while some kind of independent justification must be provided to connect mystical (numinous) experiences and God (or Brahman), no such justification is needed to connect tree experiences and trees.

It seems to me that this move is plausible if statements about trees can be translated into statements about tree experiences (i.e., if phenomenalism is true) and if statements about God (Brahman) cannot be translated into statements about mystical and numinous experiences. In spite of claims made by Schleiermacher, John Wilson and others it is, I think, reasonably clear that God (Brahman) statements cannot be translated into statements about religious experience. A fair number of good philosophers have thought that statements about trees can be translated into statements about tree experiences. It is, however, by no means clear that they are correct.

(a) It is logically possible for trees to exist and for no one to have tree experiences just as it is logically possible for God to exist and for there to be no mystical or numinous experiences, and, as far as I can see, it is logically possible that there be tree experiences and religious experiences even if there were no trees and God did not exist. (b) However, while there is no necessary connection between the presence of trees and *actual* tree experiences, there may be a necessary connection between the presence of trees and the *possibility* of tree experiences, i.e., it may be necessarily true that if a tree exists, then, if a normal observer is present under standard conditions he will enjoy tree experiences. Unfortunately (for Schmidt) a parallel claim can be made about God and mystical experiences, viz., that it is necessarily true that if God exists, then if there is an adequately pre-

---

8. H. P. Owen makes a point similar to the one made in this paragraph in *The Christian Knowledge of God*, pp. 276–80.

pared mystic whom God chooses to visit, he will enjoy mystical experiences. (c) What I am getting at is that it is by no means clear that there is any significant difference in the logical relations which obtain between tree experiences and trees, and those which obtain between mystical (numinous) experiences and God (though on the other hand, I would admit that the fact that phenomenalism is more attractive in the one case than in the other, *might* indicate some underlying logical difference).

On Miracles

PAUL J. DIETL

Some of the most remarkable turns in recent philosophical discussion have been the resurrection of issues original readers of *Language, Truth, and Logic* would have thought forever dead. "Freewill" is no longer considered a pseudo-problem. There is serious controversy concerning the existence of God. Ethics is considered cognitively significant in respectable circles. In fact the concept of a miracle is probably the only concept left for resurrection. Here there is general agreement—among sophisticated theologians as well as militant atheists—that a priori rejection of claims is justified. Miracle claims, it is generally believed, could not be true because of the very nature of the concept of a miracle. Nonetheless I should like to argue for its vindication. The crucial issue is whether conditions could ever obtain which would justify one in applying "miracle" in any way resembling its standard historical use. I shall argue that there could be such conditions, that we could very well recognize them, so that we do know what miracles are, and therefore that miracle claims are at worst false.

Here as elsewhere Hume anticipated much later opinion, so it is reasonable to begin with his contribution. The difficulty is that in much of what he wrote on the subject Hume seemed to be arguing that the event which is supposed to have been an exception to a law of nature could not happen. The laws themselves are based on "a firm and unalterable experience" and "as a uniform experience amounts to a proof, there is here a direct and full proof, from the nature of the fact, against the existence of any miracle. . . ."[1] In at least one place, though, Hume does admit that bizarre events could occur.

1. David Hume, *An Enquiry Concerning Human Understanding*, sect. 10, pt. 1, p. 115 (references are to the L. A. Selby-Bigge edition entitled *Enquiries*).

Reprinted from *American Philosophical Quarterly* 5 (1968) by permission of *American Philosophical Quarterly* and Mrs. Jane Dietl.

> Suppose all authors, in all languages, agree that from the first of Jan-
> uary, 1600, there was total darkness over the whole earth for eight days;
> suppose that the tradition of this extraordinary event is still strong and
> lively among the people; that all travelers who return from foreign
> countries, bring us accounts of the same tradition without the least
> variation or contradiction—it is evident that our present philosophers,
> instead of doubting the fact, ought to receive it as certain and ought
> to search for the causes from whence it might be derived.[2]

Apparently the bizarre cannot be ruled out on the grounds that it is bizarre. Indeed, given the right circumstances, even the second-hand *reports*
of bizarre events are immune to the criticism that the claim must be false
on the grounds that it goes against laws of nature. Nevertheless, even
though it is possible that exceptions to established laws should occur, apparently we are never justified in describing the events as miraculous. One
looks in vain for Hume's reasons for this latter thesis.

P. H. Nowell-Smith has tried to defend this second view.[3] Nowell-
Smith repudiates the view that miracle-claims can be refuted on the
grounds that they are exceptions to laws of nature, but he cannot understand the difference between the natural and the supernatural upon which
the interpretation or explanation of a bizarre event as miraculous depends.[4]
Science, he reminds us, has come to explain things which at an earlier date
were beyond its very concepts. He claims that no matter what happens, if
it is explained at all, that explanation will take its place in some department of the university. Perhaps a new department will have to be created
to accommodate it but that the new department will be among the natural-
science faculties Nowell-Smith has no doubt. The point is that to describe
an event as miraculous is to say that it could never be explained in any
natural science whatsoever, and we can never say that. Not even science itself could show it.

> To say that it is inexplicable as a result of natural agents is already
> beyond the competence of any scientist as a scientist, and to say that
> it must be ascribed to supernatural agents is to say something that no
> one could possibly have the right to affirm on the evidence alone.[5]

Some would answer this charge by attempting to reconcile an event's being miraculous with its eventually being naturally explainable but, say,

2. Ibid., p. 128.
3. In "Miracles," reprinted in *New Essays in Philosophical Theology*, ed. A. Flew
and A. MacIntyre (London, 1955), pp. 243–253.
4. Ibid., p. 244.
5. Ibid., pp. 246–247.

highly coincidental.[6] That there is such a usage for "miracle" I do not contest, but I am interested in defending the concept Nowell-Smith is attacking. That there is also a usage of "miracle" according to which to call an
event a miracle is to attribute it to the will of a supernatural agent and to
claim that if the supernatural agent had not intervened that event would
not have taken place is, I think, equally clear. Indeed this latter usage is
unquestionably more frequent in the history of religion.

It follows that in the way in which I am using "miracle" miracle-claims
do have the implications Nowell-Smith envisages. "Supernatural" implies
that the agent be able to bring about events which are exceptions to physical laws. Nothing else about the agent is at issue, however. For example,
we are not concerned with questions of whether he is all-good or all-
powerful or eternal or even with the question of whether there is more
than one such being. But he must be a being who can control the laws of
nature. The question is whether or not any event would ever be rationally
described as a manifestation of power of such a being. It will only be such
if all causes other than such a being can be ruled out—which is precisely
what Nowell-Smith denied could be done.

Before I construct what I think is a counterexample to Nowell-Smith's
thesis, I want to call attention to two features of miracles. The first is simply that there is nothing amiss in one person having several miracles he
can perform. In the Book of Exodus, for example, Moses is given more
than a dozen miracles with which he attempts to melt the Pharaoh's heart.
He brings on several miraculous catastrophes and then stops them. The
Pharaoh's heart remains hard, and so Moses brings about several more.
The second feature of historical accounts to which I wish to call attention
is the rather elaborate circumstances in which they may take place. The
people who wrote the Old Testament quite obviously had some notion of
how to tell the real thing from a fake. Take the story about Elijah at Carmel (I Kings 18). Controversy had arisen whether prayer should be directed to the Lord God of the Jews or to Baal. Elijah took the people to
Mt. Carmel and said: "Let them . . . give us two bullocks; and let them
choose one bullock for themselves, and cut it to pieces, and lay it on wood."
The ministers of Baal took the meat from one animal and made a pile,
and Elijah called upon the ministers of Baal to ask Baal to cook their meat.
"But there was no voice, nor any that answered. And they leaped upon the
altar which was made. And it came to pass at noon, that Elijah mocked
them, and said, Cry aloud; for he is a god; either he is talking, or he is
pursuing, or he is on a journey, or peradventure he sleepeth, and must be
awakened. And they cried aloud, and cut themselves after their manner

6. For an interesting discussion of that concept of "miracle," see R. F. Holland, "The
Miraculous," *American Philosophical Quarterly* 2 (1965), pp. 43–51.

with knives and lances, till the blood gushed out upon them." But all this to no avail. Then Elijah stepped up and said: "Fill four barrels with water, and pour it on the burnt sacrifice, and on the wood." And he said, Do it the second time. And they did it the second time. And he said, Do it the third time. And they did it the third time. And the water ran round about the altar; and he filled the trench also with water. Then he called on God for fire and "Then the fire of the Lord fell, and consumed the burnt sacrifice, and the wood, and the stones, and the dust, and licked up the water that was in the trench."

We are given here, first of all, about as artificial a setting as any laboratory affords. The account also involves a random sampling of the material to be set on fire, a prediction that one pile will burn up and one will not, a prediction when the fire will start, and twelve barrels of precaution against earthly independent variables. There is obviously nothing wrong with applying somewhat sophisticated experimental design to miracles.

Now for the example. Its essential ingredients are simply a bundle of miracles no larger than Moses had and a randomizing technique just a little more complicated than Elijah's. Let us assume that a local prophet opens, or appears with the help of God to open, the mighty Schuylkill River. Two possibilities arise. The first is that the prophet does not figure causally in the natural explanation but that he notices a cue in the physical situation which indicates natural sufficient conditions. This is especially tempting because he might not be consciously aware of the cue and so might himself honestly believe in the miracle. This sort of explanation can be ruled out, however, if he is required to do miracles at random. Say he allows non-believers to pick twelve miracles and number them. Which one he will do will be determined by the roll of a pair of unloaded dice, and the hour of the day at which it will occur will be determined by a second roll. Rolling the dice without his prediction could establish that the dice had no efficacy and using the dice to randomize the predictions proves that the prophet does not predict on the basis of a natural cue.[7]

This randomizing also establishes that there is a cause at work other than would have operated if the prophet had not been there. But perhaps there is still some law covering the events. To see how vastly different this would be from an ordinary scientific law, however, one has only to realize that there would be no new scientific department on a par with, say, physics or chemistry, which included such laws. This would be a department which dealt with all the other sciences and had no laws of its own, except that when this prophet spoke, all laws, or any one of an indefinitely large number, are broken.

7. One might object to "proves," but such procedures eliminate candidates with as much certainty as any non-logical procedures ever could.

Odd, you might say, but not yet miraculous. Such a prophet might require a new metascientific department, but we still have not been forced to admit supernatural explanation. But this is so only because we have not yet looked at the *explanans* in these supposed scientific explanations. What could possibly be the natural conditions which this new department will ascertain to be necessary and sufficient for the unexpected events?

If the prophet prayed we might think that the prayer was connected in some curious way with the exceptions. But what if he does not pray? What if he just requests? Could it be the sounds of his words which have the extraordinary effect? Then let him predict in different languages. Might we mention language-independent brain processes as the sufficient conditions? Let him predict what will happen later when he is asleep—even drugged, or dead.

But surely it has become obvious that there is nothing which could be pinned down as the independent variable in a scientific explanation; for no conceivable candidate is necessary. The prophet asks God to do miracle No. 4 at midnight and then goes to sleep. Or he asks God to do whatever miracle turns up at whatever hour turns up and then dies. We are dealing with requests and answers—that is, thoughts, and thoughts not as psychological occurrences but as understood.

No natural law will do because only vehicles of thought could function as the natural *explanans* and no such vehicle is necessary. There would have to be one law connecting the acoustics of English with general law-breaking, another for French, and so on indefinitely—and when the prophet asks that whatever miracle turns upon the dice be performed and then goes to sleep before the dice are thrown, there just is not anything left except his request as understood.[8]

What is needed here is not a law but an understanding which can grasp the request and then bring it about that a physical law be broken. But an understanding physical-law breaker is a supernatural being, and that is why if a new department is set up it will not be with the science faculties at all. It will be a department of religion.

I should like here to attempt to forestall some foreseeable objections. The first one is that even if what I have said is all true, that still does not prove that there ever has been a miracle. Of course I agree with this objection. The sophistication of the experimental design of the Elijah account may be the progressive result of centuries of anxious parents trying to convince doubting children of false stories. The point is that the concept of miracle allowed such sophistication. What they *meant* to say was ascertainable, or at least they meant to *say* that it was ascertainable, in

---

8. Since in this case the prophet does not know what miracle will be asked for, pre-cognition is also ruled out.

principle. Whether or not their claims were actually true is another question.

A second criticism shows a hankering after a simple a priori disproof. Believing in miracles, it will be said, inevitably involves believing in the suspension of some physical law. We can always avoid this by doubting the data. Hallucinations do not rest on the suspension of such laws. The trouble with this sort of objection to the miraculous is that it can quickly be pushed to the point at which the very distinction between hallucinatory and veridical experiences breaks down. Faith, it has been said, can move mountains. Suppose that someone moved the Poconos to northern Minnesota. Thousands saw them flying through the air. Old maps showed them in Pennsylvania where we all remembered them to have been, and a thriving ski industry grows up where there had only been the exhausted open mines of the Mesabi Range. If that is a hallucination then everything is.

A third criticism is that the account of physical laws in this paper is hopelessly over-simple and crude. I agree. One must show, however, that the crudity and simplicity make a difference to the general thesis about miracles. As far as I can see, the introduction of statistics and probability, or the ideal nature of some or all laws, or of accounts of laws as models or inference tickets or as the designation of patterns we find intelligible, makes no difference. Specifically, the account offered here does not rest on belief in metaphysical connections between causes and effects. Of course, physical laws are only descriptive. But I take it that they do serve as bases for predictions and also for contrary-to-fact conditionals. They are not ontological, but they must be nomological. As long as according to the natural laws operative (e.g., gravity) and the state of the world at one time (e.g., including a free body) another state can be predicted to occur (e.g., the body's fall), then, even though there may never have been an exactly true formulation of the law or a perfect instantiation of the initial conditions (no body ever quite free), as long as the denial of the predicted event is internally coherent, to speak of exceptions is meaningful.

A fourth rejoinder to my arguments might be that even if I have proved that there could be conditions which, if you experienced them, would justify your belief in a miracle, and even though we might have reason to believe second-hand reports of bizarre phenomena, we could still never have better reasons to believe a second-hand miracle claim than to doubt the veracity of the man reporting it; and surely this is really all that Hume, if not Nowell-Smith, set out to prove. In answer let me say first that if you had good reason to believe that what the report describes as happening really did happen—and happened as the reports describe, viz., with randomizing and predictions—then it seems to me that you have good reasons to believe in supernatural intervention as an explanation of the events. But in any case remember Exodus once more. Moses had brought several miraculous plagues, then called them off, then brought down a new batch. Now say that you happened into Egypt during the second batch of catastrophes. Could you rule out a priori the possibility that there had been an earlier set? I think not.

Fifthly, one might object that even if I have shown that there could be evidence for miracles and even in the sense in which "miracle" implies supernatural intervention, this is still of no religious significance unless "miracle" also implies *divine* intervention. Miracles, as defined here, in short, do not tend to prove the existence of God. My only answer is that to prove the existence of a being who deserves some of the predicates which "God" normally gets would be to go some way toward proving the existence of *God*. The question whether the comprehensibility of miracle claims strengthens the position of the theologians or whether the paucity of latter-day evidence has the opposite effect, I leave to the theologians and more militant atheists.

A final criticism might be that calling an event a miracle appears to be offering an explanation for it, but is really not an explanation at all since explanations must always rest on laws. In fact, it might be held, this is the real dilemma behind miracle hypotheses. Either there are laws covering miracles or not. If there are no laws then miracles cannot be explanations: they are not hypotheses at all. But if there are laws, then there is no difference between natural and supernatural explanations. Nowell-Smith's argument goes:

(A) Calling an event a miracle is apparently to explain it.
(B) Explanations must rest on laws.
(C) If one has laws one can predict the events they explain.
(D) We cannot predict miracles, therefore calling an event a miracle has no (explanatory) meaning over and above a mere (descriptive) statement of the phenomena to be explained.[9]

Now, a prediction was involved in the Elijah story, and I do not see how one could pin down God as the independent variable unless predictions like those were possible. These predictions, however, were not made possible by anything Nowell-Smith would call a law. Indeed, that the prediction did not rest on the knowledge of a regularity between initial conditions and effect was the reason for looking to the supernatural. In other words, it cannot be objected that miracles are not explanations because miracles are not lawful until it has been proved that all explanations are lawful. This is all the more pressing since part of the point of interpreting an event as a miracle is to see it not as a natural event but as an action, or

9. Nowell-Smith, p. 250.

the result of an action, of an intelligent being.[10] That all intelligible *actions* are subsumable under laws is even less credible than that all *events* are. An action can be made intelligible by showing its *point* (for example, to bring wayward children back to the truth, to reward the holy, to save the chosen people, etc.), and showing the good of an action is not automatically to subsume it under a law.

I conclude that "miracle" is perfectly meaningful. To call an event a miracle is to claim that it is the result of supernatural intervention into the natural course of events. We could know that the supernatural agent was intelligent, but little else (though when and for whom he did miracles would be evidence about his character).[11]

---

10. This is the point of drawing an analogy between explanations in terms of miracles and human intervention into the course of nature. Whether or not such divine intervention would have to be in conformity to the laws of nature because human intervention apparently is would be a further question. Nowell-Smith seems to think that anyone who draws the analogy at all must admit that divine intervention would have to be in accordance with laws (p. 249).

11. This paper has profited from criticisms by Professors William Wisdom and Michael Scriven.

Ritual and the Religious Feelings

GARETH MATTHEWS

For when men pray they do with the members of their bodies what befits suppliants—when they bend their knees and stretch out their hands, or even prostrate themselves, and whatever else they do visibly, although their invisible will and the intention of their heart is known to God. Nor does He need these signs for the human mind to be laid bare to Him. But in this way a man excites himself to pray more and to groan more humbly and more fervently. I do not know how it is that, although these motions of the body cannot come to be without a motion of the mind preceding them, when they have been made, visibly and externally, that invisible inner motion which caused them is itself strengthened. And in this manner the disposition of the heart which preceded them in order that they might be made, grows stronger because they are made. Of course if someone is constrained or even bound, so that he cannot do these things with his limbs, it does not follow that, when he is stricken with remorse, the inner man does not pray and prostrate himself before the eyes of God in his most secret chamber.

AUGUSTINE, De cura pro mortuis 5.7

I

One smiles and tells the expert chef how good the sauce béarnaise is, not so much to inform him about the sauce (he knows better than we how good it is) as to assure him that we are enjoying it and that we appreciate his efforts. But when one kneels in one's pew and repeats a litany of thanksgiving it is not, it seems, that one means to be informing God of anything—not even of one's thankfulness. For God, unlike the chef, has no need of information.

This paper is a revised version of "Bodily Motions and Religious Feelings," *Canadian Journal of Philosophy* 1 (1971). Used by permission of the *Canadian Journal of Philosophy* and the author. The revised essay first appeared in Amélie Oksenberg Rorty (ed.), *Explaining Emotions* (University of California Press, 1980).

So why do religious people do all the things they do in prayer "with the members of their bodies"?

The answer Augustine gives in the above passage from his treatise, "On the Care of the Dead," is that the bodily performance of ritual has the effect of intensifying appropriate religious attitudes and affections. (". . . in this way a man excites himself to pray more and to groan more humbly and more fervently.") Yet Augustine is puzzled by his answer. "I do not know how it is," he says.[1]

And he should be puzzled. For, as Augustine conceives it, the intensification of a religious attitude or feeling by the performance of a ritualistic act is a case of movements of the body having the effect of moving the soul. (". . . when [these motions of the body] have been made, visibly and externally, that invisible inner motion which caused them is itself strengthened.") And this never happens—it cannot happen; for, according to Augustine, the soul, any soul, is superior to the body, any body (*Enarrationes in psalmos* 145.3 and *De musica* 6.5.8) and that which is inferior can never move that which is superior (*De genesi ad litteram* 12.16.33).

There would have been an even better reason for Augustinian puzzlement. Augustine, like Descartes, conceives the soul and the body as two different things of such disparate sorts that the idea of interaction between a body and a soul becomes incomprehensible. Augustine is presumably led to overlook this incomprehensibility by the (to him) very obvious fact that the soul does affect the body (see, e.g., *De genesi ad litteram* 12.19.41). Perhaps a similarly robust sense of fact leads him to throw out his metaphysical principle about the superior and the inferior and to concede that the actual performance of ritual often does intensify the attitudes and feelings that give rise to it.

Sometimes, of course, the reverse is true. A child who is made to say "Thank you" upon receipt of any and every benefaction may thereby be made more thankful; she may also be made more resentful. It all depends.

---

1. In a passage somewhat reminiscent of Augustine, Jonathan Edwards says this: "To instance in the duty of prayer: it is manifest that we are not appointed in this duty to declare God's perfections, His majesty, holiness, goodness, and all-sufficiency, and our meanness, emptiness, dependence, and unworthiness, and our wants and desires, to inform God of these things, or to incline His heart, and prevail with him to be willing to show us mercy; but suitably to affect our own hearts with the things we express, and so to prepare us to receive the blessings we ask. And such gestures and manner of external behaviour in the worship of God, which custom has made to be significations of humility and reverence, can be of no further use than as they have some tendency to affect our own hearts, or the hearts of others" (*The Religious Affections* 2.9). Edwards's suggestion that one reason for gesticulation is to affect the hearts of others seems a natural addition to what Augustine says. It is noteworthy, however, that Edwards, unlike Augustine, shows no puzzlement over the idea that "external behavior" might have "some tendency to affect our own hearts."

Some people are annoyed and offended by ritual. Even those for whom characteristically religious attitudes are enormously important may abhor ritual; indeed they may abhor ritual precisely because they feel it encourages the wrong feelings and attitudes.

Augustine can hardly have forgotten that it was Jesus who condemned the Pharisee's energetic recitation of public prayer. Jesus advised praying in secret, where concern with externals could be eliminated, or at least minimized. Perhaps this is a second reason for Augustine's embarrassment and puzzlement in the passage above. Aware that Jesus criticized ritualizers (see Augustine's *De sermone domini in monte* 1.3), Augustine nevertheless finds himself somewhat uneasily suggesting that the behavior of the outer man (*homo exterior*) often intensifies the spiritual motions of the inner man (*homo interior*).

II

Metaphysics and theology aside, it seems obviously true that sometimes and for some people participation in a liturgical rite nurtures certain religious attitudes and affections. But why? Well, if I refer to myself as a poor and miserable sinner often enough, I may come finally to believe that this is what I am. Is this not an honored truth of both pedagogy and propaganda?

Now suppose I bow or kneel. This in itself may have an important effect upon my attitudes (the primary meaning of "attitude" is relevant to this point), even though it does not involve making an assertion.

I suppose we might try to understand the effect of nonverbal gestures and ritualistic movements in terms of what they symbolize—what they "say."[2] Kneeling, for example, "says": "I am a suppliant."[3] Then we could add that the performance of these ritualistic acts, like the repetition of a statement, encourages one to believe what is hereby "said."

Yet this is all much too easy. Not just any old repetition of a statement encourages belief. Not just any old performance of a ritual instills the appropriate attitudes. The mocking repetition of a statement may undermine its credibility. And the self-righteous and hypocritical performance of ritual may discourage the favored attitudes. At most it is sincere, or at least apparently sincere, repetition that instills belief.

2. "No less than words, actions or gestures are also a type of language; they hold a message for us. They have a meaning which the person who sincerely wishes to pray the Liturgy must get to know. Whether used by man for practical or symbolical reasons, gestures or ceremonies help man to express himself better, make his thought and intent clearer and more vivid." (John H. Miller, C.S.C., *Fundamentals of the Liturgy* [Notre Dame, 1959], p. 188).
3. "In the Liturgy . . . kneeling was usually associated with fasting and was a penitential and suppliant posture" (ibid., p. 192).

Now, however, we have torn ourselves loose from the terms of Augustine's problem. His problem is how what the outer man does can affect the inner man—how the mere "motions of the body," motions that "cannot come to be without a motion of the mind preceding them," can affect the mind itself.

That Augustine identifies the outer man with the body, something merely physical, that "part" of a human being buried at death, is shown in this passage from *The City of God:*

> . . . a man is not just a body, or just a soul, but a being made up of body and soul. . . . The soul is not the whole man, but the better part of a man; the body is not the whole, but the inferior part of a man. When both are joined together they have the name "man," which, however, they do not either one lose when we speak of them singly. For who is prohibited from saying, in ordinary language, "That man is dead and is now in peace or in torment," though this can be said only of the soul; or "That man is buried in that place or in that," though this cannot be understood except as referring to the body alone? Will they say that Holy Scripture follows no such usage? On the contrary, it so thoroughly adopts it that even when a man is alive and his body and soul are joined together it calls each of them singly by the name "man," speaking of the soul as the "inner man" and the body as the "outer man"—as if there were two men, although both together are one man.
>
> *De civitate dei* 13.24.21

Now clearly a motion of the outer man (or body), so understood, cannot be either sincere or insincere, mocking or serious. It takes the action of the whole man—body and mind (or soul)—to be insincere. According to Augustine, its insincerity will lie in a certain discrepancy between what the outer man does and what the inner man does.

This means that our effort to understand a physical motion as "saying" something (e.g., "I am a suppliant") is misplaced. For a mere motion of an Augustinian body could not by itself have meaning in the way required.

Thus we cannot explain how the mere motion of the body in ritual inculcates religious attitudes and intensifies religious feelings because it is not the mere motion of the body that has this effect. What may have this effect is the sincere and understanding performance of ritual.

III

So the puzzle Augustine moves on to is a specious puzzle. What about the puzzle Augustine starts with? That is, what about the worry as to why one need pray outwardly when God knows already what is in one's heart? Augustine's answer to this worry—that the bodily performance of ritual may have the effect of intensifying appropriate religious attitudes and affections—suggests that Augustine's question ("Why need one pray outwardly?") is really two questions. One question is "Why pray, when God knows already everything one could possibly tell him?" and the other is "Why pray *outwardly*, with 'the members of the body,' when God knows already one's 'invisible will' and the 'intention of one's heart?' "

It seems perverse to run these two questions together. Surely one can't make a good judgment as to whether what Augustine offers us is a good reason for praying *outwardly* until one is reasonably clear about what a good reason for *praying* might be. And there is a further point. Suppose the reason for praying were Q. It might actually follow from Q (or perhaps from Q together with certain natural assumptions) that one ought to pray *outwardly*. So an answer to the first question might actually be all, or most, of an answer to the second.

Perhaps Augustine tends to conceive praying inwardly as simply having certain feelings and attitudes without expressing them, much as one might conceive giving alms inwardly as simply having feelings of charity. If this is the way Augustine conceives, or tends to conceive, inward praying, then the question "Why pray, when God knows already?" easily becomes the question "Why pray *outwardly*, when God knows already?"

I think that such is, in fact, the way Augustine conceives inward, versus outward, praying. That this is so can be seen at once from his use of the biblical locution "inner man" to mean simply *mind* or *soul* and "outer man" to mean simply *body*—as in the quotation from *The City of God* in the last section.

Augustine therefore looks upon inner acts and speeches as making up one's authentic mental and spiritual life. Outer acts and speeches, only contingently related to inner acts and speeches, may sometimes manifest the inner ones with a modest degree of accuracy; but they need not even do that. In any case, psychological descriptions (descriptions of one's thoughts, desires, intentions, attitudes, feelings, etc.) are really descriptions of the independent and self-sufficient inner man. With this sort of picture before us it is natural to suppose that the body's only functions are to manifest the soul's thoughts, to help gratify the soul's desires, and to help execute decisions made by the soul. And since ritual serves neither to advance practical ends nor to pass on information to God, the question arises, why engage in ritual?

That Augustine's dualism affords a mistaken basis for interpreting the biblical inner-outer contrast could be shown in detail; but I shall not attempt that here. Instead I shall just say, rather dogmatically, that when (to pick one example) the psalmist speaks of someone as blessing outwardly and cursing inwardly ("They bless with their mouth, but they curse inwardly" [Ps. 62:4]) he is describing the mock piety of an insincere person, not a merely physical movement of a body. As we have already noted, a merely physical movement is not either sincere or insincere.

Moreover, the inner-outer contrast one finds in the Bible, far from rendering problematic the importance of ritual to one's devotional life, in fact underlines its central significance. Corresponding to each inner act or gesture that one may be said to perform, there is a state, attitude, or feeling that all and only those who perform the inner act may be said to have. Thus, "He kneels inwardly" corresponds to the claim that he has contrition, or is contrite, or does something contritely, and "He gives alms inwardly" corresponds to the claim that he has charity, or is charitable, or does something charitably. In making use of an inner-man locution rather than the corresponding abstract substantive, adjective, or adverb, biblical writers remind us of the way of life in which typically religious attitudes and feelings take form.

Two caveats are in order. First, one's participation in this life of worship may be insincere. One's actions may then be said to be merely outward. (But that doesn't, of course, mean that they are merely physical.) Second, one may be faithful and God-fearing though one is either physically or psychologically unable to worship in standard, ritualistic ways. This inability may be only momentary, or it may be long-term. But in saying that one kneels (etc.) inwardly, the biblical writer reveals that it is by reference to the standard ritualistic case that he conceives and understands piety.

IV

Augustine's mind-body dualism may give rise to an even more basic puzzle than anything I have mentioned so far. This puzzle concerns nonreligious feelings as much as religious ones. Take, for example, gratitude.

Suppose my sister has foregone a chance to hear a concert so that I could hear it. Suppose, as would be likely, it is important to her that I be at least minimally grateful to her for what she has done. What exactly is it that is important to her? That I have a certain feeling, a certain mental datum? And how can that be seriously important to her? Or is what is important to her that I act toward her in a grateful way? But acting toward her in a grateful way may not please her at all, may even upset or annoy her, if she discovers that no feeling of gratitude accompanies my actions. So we are back to the feeling of gratitude. And how can it be important to her that I have a certain feeling?

Or take, for example, feeling sorry for having done someone a wrong.

Suppose my friend is prepared to forgive me a grave injustice I have done him if he knows I am sorry. How can it be so important to him that I have a certain feeling? Or is what is important to him that I behave in a contrite manner? But if he discovers that I behave as if appropriately contrite but do not really feel sorry, he may be even more upset than before. So it is, after all, my feeling sorry that counts. But how can it be so important to him that I have a certain feeling?

What generates this puzzle is the notion that a feeling of gratitude or sorrow is basically an inner event—what Augustine calls "an invisible inner motion." In fact, other-directed feelings such as these, whether religious or not, are much more complex and interesting than the notion of an "invisible inner motion" would suggest. Gratitude, for example, carries with it the recognition of what one takes to be a benefaction and a disposition to look favorably on one's putative benefactor. There is no such thing as having the feeling without recognizing the (putative) benefaction and being disposed to look favorably on the (putative) benefactor.

What my sister wants, in the above situation, is not simply that there be within me an invisible mental motion, perhaps something like a sensation of warmth. What she wants is that I recognize her benefaction (already something complex and far-ranging) and that I be moved by that recognition to look favorably on her as a benefactor.

Something similar is true of sorrow at having wronged another. Such sorrow carries with it the recognition that one has wronged another and the disposition to behave toward that person in a compensatory way. What my friend wants, in the situation just described, is not especially that there be within me some mental motion (say, something like an unpleasant sensation). What he wants is for me to recognize that I have wronged him and for me to take certain steps toward effecting a reconciliation. (What some of those steps might be I shall detail in a moment.)

These points apply to religious, as well as nonreligious, feelings. But before we can see how they are relevant to Augustine's worry about why one should pray outwardly, when God knows already what is in one's heart, we need to deal directly with the apparent disanalogy between God's knowledge and what any human being could know.

V

It is very easy to overdraw the contrast between being sorry for one's sins before God and being sorry that one has wronged another person.[4] Of course no human being is omniscient. But sometimes a human being knows as much about the feelings of another human being as is relevant

4. I owe the idea developed in this section and the next to discussions with Stanley Cavell.

to an apology. And then the fact that an omniscient being would know infinitely more is not important to the apology.

Suppose I have wronged you, and I am sorry for what I have done. I may want to bring it about that you know I have the feelings I in fact have. In order to achieve this result I may apologize by saying, "I'm sorry."

But of course you may already know that I am sorry. You may know by the sound of my voice, by the look on my face. Furthermore, I may know that you know I am sorry. In such a case I do not need to bring about the result that you know I have the feelings of sorrow I have. I do not need to bring about that result because it is already achieved. In such a case you are like God insofar as he, too, already knows; and I know that he knows.

Still, there may be a place for me to tell you what you already know, namely, that I am sorry. That is, there may yet be a place for apology. Here are some reasons why an apology may yet be important.

1. I need to acknowledge my wrongdoing. I have done you wrong. I know it. You know it. But unless and until I acknowledge my guilt, there is something important to both of us that has gone unsaid. It needs to be said. Our relationship cannot be put right until I have "owned up" to what I have done.

2. I need to ask for forgiveness. And I cannot ask for forgiveness without owning up to what I need to be forgiven for. Of course you may be able and willing to forgive me without an apology. "He didn't know what he was doing," you may say; or, "He is not aware how his actions strike others." But you cannot excuse me like this as a general thing. Or at least if you do, you will not be treating me as a moral agent, responsible for what I do; you will be treating me as a child, or perhaps as a case study.

3. I may want to commiserate with you. You have been hurt by my misdeed. As your friend, I want to express sympathy for your hurt. But, since it was I who wronged you, I cannot commiserate sincerely, or successfully, without apologizing.

4. I may need to share the burden of my guilt. To apologize is to invite a response from you. By responding in a forgiving way you accept me, wrongdoing and all, and so relieve me of some of the burden of my guilt.

I think it is clear that there are theological analogues to most, if not all, these four points. I shall try to bring them out by reference to the Prayer of General Confession from the Episcopalian *Book of Common Prayer* (1928 version). This is the way the prayer goes:

> Almighty God, Father of our Lord Jesus Christ,
> Maker of all things, judge of all men;
> We acknowledge and bewail our manifold sins and wickedness,
> Which we, from time to time, most grievously have committed,
> By thought, word, and deed,

Against thy Divine Majesty,
Provoking most justly thy wrath and indignation against us.
We do earnestly repent.
And are heartily sorry for these our misdoings;
The remembrance of them is grievous unto us;
The burden of them is intolerable.
Have mercy upon us,
Have mercy upon us, most merciful Father;
For thy Son our Lord Jesus Christ's sake,
Forgive us all that is past;
And grant that we may ever hereafter
Serve and please thee
In newness of life,
To the honour and glory of thy Name;
Through Jesus Christ our Lord. Amen.

1. The importance of acknowledging one's sins is made clear in the opening statement, "We acknowledge and bewail our manifold sins and wickedness . . ." It is not enough to be sorry. One must acknowledge one's sins.

2. The connection between being sorry, acknowledging one's sins, and asking for forgiveness is brought out in this sequence: "We do earnestly repent, And are heartily sorry for these our misdoings; . . . Have mercy upon us, . . . Forgive us all that is past; And grant that we may ever hereafter Serve and please thee In newness of life . . ."

3. One might question whether there is any place in the believer's relations with God for commiserating with God. To attempt to commiserate with God might seem to be attempting something presumptuous and inappropriate. Still, there is a recognition in the Prayer of General Confession that one's misdeeds are an affront to the Divine Majesty (". . . our manifold sins and wickedness, Which we, from time to time, most grievously have committed . . . Against thy Divine Majesty . . ."). To recognize that affront is, perhaps, to offer a kind of commiseration.

4. Finally, the request to share one's burdens is suggested in the lines, "The remembrance of [our misdeeds] is grievous unto us; The burden of them is intolerable." God is conceived as not merely lifting the burden of one's guilt, but sharing it. This is the point of the doctrine of the atonement. ("Surely he hath borne our griefs, and carried our sorrows" [Isa. 53.4].)

It is clear now that our Augustinian puzzle—Why is it necessary to express sorrow for one's sins, when God knows already? Why isn't it enough to have feelings of sorrow?—arises from an over-simplified picture of what it is to have such feelings and of what could be the point in expressing them. Certainly there may be point, even profound point, in saying that one is sorry for a misdeed even when one's hearer already knows how one feels, and one knows that one's hearer knows.

VI

Can something similar be said about other religious feelings? I think so. Consider gratitude to God for one's blessings. Here, as before, it is easy to overdraw the contrast between relations with God and relations with a human being. If A has done a favor to B, other things being equal, this fact needs to be acknowledged by B. It will not, in general, be enough that B is grateful, even if A knows that B is grateful and B knows that A knows. B needs to say, "Thank you."

To get an idea of the importance of B's saying, "Thank you," we might think of possible explanations for B's failure to do so.

One explanation might be that B, though grateful, is too proud to admit any indebtedness to A. Another possible explanation would be the very opposite, namely, that B lacks sufficient self-respect to be able to admit any gratitude to A; saying "Thank you" might threaten the little self-esteem B has. In both these situations it will be important to B, as well as to B's relationship to A, that B say "Thank you."

There are, of course, all sorts of ways that saying "Thank you" may go wrong. The "Thank you" may be grudging, servile, resentful, patronizing or automatic. But it may be appropriately spoken and appropriately received. My point is that saying "Thank you" is not usually simply doing something to bring about the result that another person knows one has feelings of gratitude. It is acting in a way appropriate to the receipt of a gift or favor.

Most of this carries over to the theological case. The believer needs to acknowledge God's blessings. It may be hard to do this, and especially hard to do it in the right spirit. But to do it in the right spirit is to offer a kind of return gift; it is to give thanks, which is an act of worship.

I turn now to feelings of joy. "My soul shall be joyful in the Lord," says the psalmist. One religious feeling of joy is joy in God. We do not ordinarily think of ourselves as rejoicing or being joyful in other people (though we certainly delight in our children, or take delight in them); but we do rejoice in the good fortune, success or happiness of other people. Perhaps an interhuman analogue to being joyful in God is therefore being joyful in the success, happiness, or good fortune of another person.

We often express joy in the good fortune of another person by a celebration. We throw a party. Suppose I have a friend who has just passed a difficult examination. I have shared her ordeal with her. I am overjoyed by her success. Since she is a good friend, she can easily tell how elated I am. And I know she can tell. Yet it would be ridiculous to say there is no need for me to throw a party for her, since she knows already how happy I am at her success, perhaps even how pleased everyone else is who would come to the party. The role of the celebration is in no way usurped by someone's prior knowledge of the feelings of joy it is meant to express.

So it is also with joy in God. The Bible enjoins us to be joyful in God. We are to "make a joyful noise unto the Lord," to "make a loud noise, and rejoice, and sing praise" (Ps. 98.4). Among the many recommended noise-makers are the harp, the voice, trumpets, and a cornet (Ps. 98.5–6). The role of such a celebration is in no way usurped by a prior knowledge—whether Divine or human—of the feelings of joy it is meant to express.

Thus the idea that God knows already the secrets of one's heart does not make it inappropriate to rejoice in God, to express gratitude to him for one's blessings or to express sorrow to him for one's sins. In fact, almost the reverse is true; the idea that God knows already cancels out a range of considerations that might otherwise be thought to justify one in hiding one's feelings. To see that this is so let us first remind ourselves of non-religious cases in which it might be appropriate to hide one's feelings.

I may want to hide my feelings of jealousy and frustration when I lose a game or contest lest the winner be unable to enjoy her well-earned satisfaction. Again, to express to my child the rage I experience when I learn that he has been slighted, or unfairly dealt with, may bewilder and confuse him; it may be best to hide these feelings.

There certainly are occasions on which one would not express one's religious feelings before others. Thus, for example, it may be wrong to express my gratitude to God for a healthy child in the presence of someone with a deformed child. Or again, it may be inappropriate or wrong to rejoice in God in a public school, lest the religious sensibilities of others be offended.

But there can be no point in hiding one's feelings from God, lest God be offended; God knows already. The idea that God knows already what is in one's heart—far from being a reason for not expressing religious feelings—may actually be a good reason for not hiding them. Concealment has no point when we are dealing with one "unto whom all hearts are open, all desires known, and from whom no secrets are hid" (Opening Collect from the service of Holy Communion, *The Book of Common Prayer*).

VII

I have argued that Augustine's idea of engaging in ritual to enhance one's religious feelings is, in his own dualistic terms, misconceived. I have also argued that the puzzle this idea is meant to solve, is misconceived. But mightn't it still be the case that some people sometimes engage in religious ritual to enhance their feelings toward God? And suppose someone had that project? Mightn't it be a reasonable one, or would it be inevitably phony and in bad faith?

Consider gratitude to God for one's blessings. Imagine thinking that by going to church or synagogue to join in a service of praise and thanksgiving one might arouse or enhance one's feelings of gratitude toward God. Either one now has no such feelings at all or one has them only to degree n. Isn't the project of doing something "with the members of one's body" to arouse those feelings or to enhance them beyond degree n, inevitably phony—phony because one's motivation to join in the service must go beyond any feelings of gratitude one now has?

I am inclined to think that this project is indeed a phony one. (If I am right, that point, too, counts against what Augustine says in the passage from "On the Care of the Dead.") But there is a similar project, one that might easily be confused with the project Augustine outlines, that need not be phony.

I have already mentioned that other-directed feelings, such as gratitude, carry with them the recognition of some truth, or alleged truth (in the case of gratitude, the truth, or alleged truth, that someone has benefited one). Now religious feelings are feelings such that having them carries with it the recognition of alleged truths (e.g., that God is gracious, that one is a sinner, etc.) which are such that one who leads a religious life will think it important to find regular occasions on which to rehearse and acknowledge them. To provide a regular opportunity to rehearse these putative truths is also to provide opportunity to feel afresh the gratitude, the joy and the sorrow that carry with them the recognition of these alleged truths. It may, of course, be the case that on a given occasion, or for an extended period of time, even for life, one in fact feels no gratitude, no sorrow, no joy—no matter how many times one says the familiar words and makes the familiar movements. But one can make a place in one's life for the feeling of religious feelings without seeking to manipulate or force those feelings. One can do this by making a place for the dramatic rehearsal, "with the members of one's body," of what one regards as life's most important truths. Put briefly, that is the justification for religious ritual in the life of a believer.

VIII

Both the puzzle Augustine begins with in the passage cited from "On the Care of the Dead" and the puzzle he ends up with have turned out to be specious. The puzzle he ends up with is this: How can the mere motions of the body in ritual intensify religious feelings and attitudes? This puzzle is specious because it is not the mere motions of the body that have such an effect; what has, or may have, such an effect is (among other things)

the sincere and understanding performance of ritual—the dramatic rehearsal of the tenets of one's faith, including the story of salvation.

The puzzle Augustine begins with is then this: Why need one express, as well as simply have, feelings such as sorrow for one's sins, since
God knows already what feelings one has? This puzzle is specious because
it presupposes that the only (or at least the primary) reason for saying
(e.g.) that I am sorry for having done something wrong is to bring about
the result that someone else knows (or thinks) that I have certain feelings.
But this is not so. An apology may have real point even when the person
it is directed toward already knows, and I know that she or he knows,
what is in my heart. And so, for that matter, may a banquet. And so may a
ritual in which people rehearse, dramatically, the tenets of their faith and
in which, as Augustine says, they "do with the members of their bodies
what befits suppliants—when they bend their knees and stretch out their
hands, or even prostrate themselves."

God and Human Attitudes

JAMES RACHELS

> Kneeling down or grovelling on the ground,
> even to express your reverence for heavenly
> things, is contrary to human dignity.
>
> KANT

1. It is necessarily true that God (if He exists) is worthy of worship.[1] Any being who is not worthy of worship cannot be God, just as any being who is not omnipotent, or who is not perfectly good, cannot be God. This is reflected in the attitudes of religious believers who recognize that, whatever else God may be, He is a being before whom men should bow down. Moreover, He is unique in this; to worship anyone or anything else is blasphemy. In this paper I shall present an a priori argument against the existence of God which is based on the conception of God as a fitting object of worship. The argument is that God cannot exist, because no being could ever *be* a fitting object of worship.

However, before I can present this argument, there are several preliminary matters that require attention. The chief of these, which will hopefully have some independent interest of its own, is an examination of the concept of worship. In spite of its great importance this concept has received remarkably little attention from philosophers of religion; and when it has been treated, the usual approach is by way of referring to God's awesomeness or mysteriousness: to worship is to "bow down in silent awe" when confronted with a being that is "terrifyingly mysterious."[2] But

---

1. Hartshorne and Pike suggest that the formula "that than which none greater can be conceived" should be interpreted as "that than which none more worthy of worship can be conceived." Charles Hartshorne, *Anselm's Discovery* (LaSalle, Illinois, 1966), pp. 25–26; and Nelson Pike, *God and Timelessness* (London, 1970), pp. 149–160.
2. These phrases are from John Hick, *Philosophy of Religion* (Englewood Cliffs, New Jersey, 1963), pp. 13–14.

Reprinted from *Religious Studies* 7 (1971) by permission of Cambridge University Press. © Cambridge University Press 1971. Footnotes have been renumbered for convenience.

neither of these notions is of much help in understanding worship. Awe is certainly not the same thing as worship; one can be awed by a performance of *King Lear,* or by witnessing an eclipse of the sun or an earthquake, or by meeting one's favourite film-star, without worshiping any of these things. And a great many things are both terrifying and mysterious that we have not the slightest inclination to worship—I suppose the Black Plague fits that description for many people. The account of worship that I will give will be an alternative to those which rely on such notions as awesomeness and mysteriousness.

2. Consider McBlank, who worked against his country's entry into the Second World War, refused induction into the army, and was sent to jail. He was active in the "ban the bomb" movements of the fifties; he made speeches, wrote pamphlets, led demonstrations, and went back to jail. And finally, he has been active in opposing the war in Vietnam. In all of this he has acted out of principle; he thinks that all war is evil and that no war is ever justified. I want to make three observations about McBlank's pacifist commitments. (*a*) One thing that is involved is simply his recognition that certain facts are the case. History is full of wars; war causes the massive destruction of life and property; in war men suffer on a scale hardly matched in any other way; the large nations now have weapons which, if used, could destroy the human race; and so on. These are just facts which any normally informed man will admit without argument. (*b*) But of course they are not *merely* facts, which people recognise to be the case in some indifferent manner. They are facts that have special importance to human beings. They form an ominous and threatening backdrop to people's lives—even though for most people they are a backdrop only. But not so for McBlank. He sees the accumulation of these facts as having radical implications for his conduct; he behaves in a very different way from the way he would behave were it not for these facts. His whole style of life is different; his conduct is altered, not just in its details, but in its pattern. (*c*) Not only is his overt behaviour affected; so are his ways of thinking about the world and his place in it. His *self-image* is different. He sees himself as a member of a race with an insane history of self-destruction. He *is* an opponent of militarism just as he is a father or a musician. When some existentialists say that we "create ourselves" by our choices, they may have something like this in mind.

Thus, there are at least three things that determine McBlank's role as an opponent of war: first, his recognition that certain facts are the case; second, his taking these facts as having important implications for his conduct; and third, his self-image as living his life (at least in part) in response to these facts. My first thesis about worship is that the worshiper has a set of beliefs about God[3] which function in the same way as McBlank's beliefs about war.

First, the worshiper believes that certain things are the case: that the world was created by an all-powerful, all-wise being who knows our every thought and action; that this being, called God, cares for us and regards us as his children; that we are made by him in order to return his love and to live in accordance with his laws; and that, if we do not live in a way pleasing to him, we may be severely punished. Now these beliefs are certainly not shared by all reasonable people; on the contrary, many thoughtful persons regard them as nothing more than mere fantasy. But these beliefs are accepted by religious people, and that is what is important here. I do not say that this particular set of beliefs is definitive of religion in general, or of Judaism or Christianity in particular; it is meant only as a sample of the sorts of belief typically held by religious people in the West. They are, however, the sort of beliefs about God that are required for the business of worshiping God to make any sense.

Second, like the facts about warfare, these are not merely facts which one notes with an air of indifference; they have important implications for one's conduct. An effort must be made to discover God's will both for people generally and for oneself in particular; and to this end, the believer consults the church authorities and the theologians, reads the scripture, and prays. The degree to which this will alter his overt behaviour will depend, first, on exactly what he decides God would have him do, and second, on the extent to which his behaviour would have followed the prescribed pattern in any case.[4]

Finally, the believer's recognition of these "facts" will influence his self-image and his way of thinking about the world and his place in it. The world will be regarded as made for the fulfilment of divine purposes; the hardships that befall men will be regarded either as "tests" in some sense or as punishments for sin; and most important, the believer will think of himself as a "Child of God" and of his conduct as reflecting either honour or dishonour upon his Heavenly Father.

What will be most controversial in what I have said so far (to some philosophers, though perhaps not to most religious believers) is the treatment of claims such as "God regards us as his children" as in some sense

3. In speaking of "beliefs about God" I have in mind those typical of Western religions. I shall construct my account of worship in these terms, although the account will be adaptable to other forms of worship such as Satan-worship (see footnote 10).
4. For example, one religious believer who thinks that his conduct must be very different on account of his belief is P. T. Geach: see his essay "The Moral Law and the Law of God," in *God and the Soul* (London, 1969).

factual. Wittgenstein[5] is reported to have thought this a total misunderstanding of religious belief; and others have followed him in this.[6] Religious utterances, it is said, do not report putative facts; instead, we should understand such utterances as revealing the speaker's *form of life*. To have a form of life is to accept a language-game; the religious believer accepts a language-game in which there is talk of God, creation, Heaven and Hell, a Last Judgment, and so forth, which the sceptic does not accept. Such language-games can only be understood on their own terms; we must not try to assimilate them to other sorts of games. To see how this particular game works we need only to examine the way the language of religion is used by actual believers—in its proper habitat the language-game will be "in order" as it is. We find that the religious believer uses such utterances for a number of purposes, e.g. to express reasons for action, to show the significance which he attaches to various things, to express his attitudes, etc.—but not to "state facts" in the ordinary sense. So when the believer makes a typically religious assertion, and a nonbeliever denies the same, *they are not contradicting one another*; rather, the nonbeliever is simply refusing to play the believer's (very serious) game. Wittgenstein (as recorded by his pupils) said:

> "Suppose that someone believed in the Last Judgment, and I don't, does this mean that I believe the opposite to him, just that there won't be such a thing? I would say: 'not at all, or not always.'
>
> Suppose I say that the body will rot, and another says 'No. Particles will rejoin in a thousand years, and there will be a Resurrection of you.'
>
> If some said: 'Wittgenstein, do you believe in this?' I'd say: 'No.' 'Do you contradict the man?' I'd say: 'No.' "[7]

Wittgenstein goes on to say that the difference between the believer and the sceptic is not that one holds something to be true that the other thinks false, but that the believer takes certain things as "guidance for life" that the sceptic does not, e.g. that there will be a Last Judgment. He illustrates this by reference to a person who "thinks of retribution" when he plans his conduct or assesses his condition:

> "Suppose you had two people, and one of them, when he had to decide which course to take, thought of retribution, and the other did not. One person might, for instance, be inclined to take everything that happened

5. Ludwig Wittgenstein, *Lectures and Conversations on Aesthetics, Psychology, and Religious Belief* (Berkeley, 1966). Edited by Cyril Barrett from notes taken by Yorick Smythies, Rush Rhees, and James Taylor.
6. For example, Rush Rhees, in *Without Answers* (London, 1969), ch. 13.
7. Wittgenstein, p. 53.

to him as a reward or punishment, and another person doesn't think of this at all.

If he is ill, he may think: 'What have I done to deserve this?' This is one way of thinking of retribution. Another way is, he thinks in a general way whenever he is ashamed of himself: 'This will be punished.'

Take two people, one of whom talks of his behaviour and of what happens to him in terms of retribution, the other does not. These people think entirely differently. Yet, so far, you can't say they believe different things.

Suppose someone is ill and he says: 'This is punishment,' and I say: 'If I'm ill, I don't think of punishment at all.' If you say: 'Do you believe the opposite?'—you can call it believing the opposite, but it is entirely different from what we would normally call believing the opposite.

I think differently, in a different way. I say different things to myself. I have different pictures."[8]

I will limit myself to three remarks about this very difficult view.[9] First it is not at all clear that this account is true to the intentions of those who actually engage in religious discourse. If a believer (at least, the great majority of those whom I have known or read about) says that there will be a Last Judgment, and a sceptic says that there will not, the believer certainly will think that he has been contradicted. Of course, the sceptic might not think of denying such a thing except for the fact that the believer asserts it; and in this trivial sense the sceptic might "think differently" from the believer—but this is completely beside the point. Moreover, former believers who become sceptics frequently do so because they come to believe that religious assertions are *false;* and then, they consider themselves to be denying exactly what they previously asserted. Second, a belief does not lose its ordinary factual import simply because it occupies a central place in one's way of life. McBlank takes the facts about war as "guidance for life" in a perfectly straightforward sense; but they remain facts. I take it that just as the man in Wittgenstein's example "thinks of retribution" often, McBlank thinks of war often. So, we do not need to assign religious utterances a special status in order to explain their importance for one's way of life. Finally, while I realise that my account is very simple and mundane, whereas Wittgenstein's is "deep" and difficult, nonetheless this may be an advantage, not a handicap, of my view. If the impact of religious belief on one's conduct and thinking can be explained by appeal to nothing more mysterious than putative facts and their impact on

8. Wittgenstein, pp. 54–5.
9. The whole subject is explored in detail in Kai Nielsen, "Wittgensteinian Fideism," *Philosophy,* XLII (1967), pp. 191–209 [this volume, pp. 237–54—Eds.].

conduct and thinking, then the need for a more obscure theory will be obviated. And if a man believes that, *as a matter of fact,* his actions are subject to review by a just God who will mete out rewards and punishments on a day of final reckoning, that will explain very nicely why he "thinks of retribution" when he reflects on his conduct.

3. Worship is something that is *done;* but it is not clear just *what* is done when one worships. Other actions, such as throwing a ball or insulting one's neighbour, seem transparent enough. But not so with worship: when we celebrate Mass in the Roman Catholic Church, for example, what are we doing (apart from eating a wafer and drinking wine)? Or when we sing hymns in a protestant church, what are we doing (other than merely singing songs)? What is it that makes these acts acts of *worship?* One obvious point is that these actions, and others like them, are ritualistic in character; so, before we can make any progress in understanding worship, perhaps it will help to ask about the nature of ritual.

First we need to distinguish the ceremonial form of a ritual from what is supposed to be accomplished by it. Consider, for example, the ritual of investiture for an English Prince. The Prince kneels; the Queen (or King) places a crown on his head; and he takes an oath: "I do become your liege man of life and limb and of earthly worship, and faith and trust I will bear unto thee to live and die against all manner of folks." By this ceremony the Prince is elevated to his new station; and by this oath he acknowledges the commitments which, as Prince, he will owe the Queen. In one sense the ceremonial form of the ritual is quite unimportant: it is possible that some other procedure might have been laid down, without the point of the ritual being affected in any way. Rather than placing a crown on his head, the Queen might break an egg into his palm (that could symbolise all sorts of things). Once this was established as the procedure to be followed, it would do as well as the other. It would still be the ritual of investiture, so long as it was understood that by the ceremony a Prince is created. The performance of a ritual, then, is in certain respects like the use of language: in speaking, sounds are uttered and, thanks to the conventions of the language, something is said, or affirmed, or done, etc.: and in a ritual performance, a ceremony is enacted and, thanks to the conventions associated with the ceremony, something is done, or affirmed, or celebrated, etc.

How are we to explain the point of the ritual of investiture? We might explain that certain parts of the ritual symbolise specific things, for example that the Prince kneeling before the Queen symbolises his subordination to her (it is not, for example, merely to make it easier for her to place the crown on his head). But it is essential that, in explaining the point of the ritual as a whole, we include that a Prince is being created, that he is henceforth to have certain rights in virtue of having been made a Prince, and that he is to have certain duties which he is now acknowledging, among which are complete loyalty and faithfulness to the Queen, and so on. If the listener already knows about the complex relations between Queens, Princes, and subjects, then all we need to tell him is that a Prince is being installed in office; but if he is unfamiliar with this social system, we must tell him a great deal if he is to understand what is going on.

So, once we understand the social system in which there are Queens, Princes, and subjects, and therefore understand the role assigned to each within that system, we can sum up what is happening in the ritual of investiture in this way: someone is being made a Prince, and he is accepting that role with all that it involves. (Exactly the same explanation could be given, *mutatis mutandis,* for the marriage ceremony.)

The question to be asked about the ritual of worship is what analogous explanation can be given of it. The ceremonial form of the ritual may vary according to the customs of the religious community; it may involve singing, drinking wine, counting beads, sitting with a solemn expression on one's face, dancing, making a sacrifice, or what-have-you. But what is the point of it?

As I have already said, the worshiper thinks of himself as inhabiting a world created by an infinitely wise, infinitely powerful, perfectly good God; and it is a world in which he, along with other men, occupies a special place in virtue of God's intentions. This gives him a certain role to play: the role of a "Child of God." My second thesis about worship is that in worshiping God one is acknowledging and accepting this role, and that this is the primary function of the ritual of worship. Just as the ritual of investiture derives its significance from its place within the social system of Queens, Princes, and subjects, the ritual of worship gets its significance from an assumed system of relationships between God and men. In the ceremony of investiture, the Prince assumes a role with respect to the Queen and the citizenry; and in worship, a man affirms his role with respect to God.

Worship presumes the superior status of the one worshiped. This is reflected in the logical point that there can be no such thing as mutual or reciprocal worship, unless one or the other of the parties is mistaken as to his own status. We can very well comprehend people loving one another or respecting one another, but not (unless they are misled) worshiping one another. This is because the worshiper necessarily assumes his own inferiority; and since inferiority is an asymmetrical relation, so is worship. (The nature of the "superiority" and "inferiority" involved here is of course problematic; but on the account I am presenting it may be understood on the model of superior and inferior positions within a social system. More on this later.) This is also why *humility* is necessary on the part of the worshiper. The role to which he commits himself is that of the humble servant, "not worthy to touch the hem of His garment." Compared to God's gloriousness, "all our righteousnesses are as filthy rags" (Isaiah 64: 6). So, in committing oneself to this role, one is acknowledging God's greatness and one's own relative worthlessness. This humble attitude is not a mere embellishment of the ritual: on the contrary, worship, unlike love or respect, *requires* humility. Pride is a sin, and pride before God is incompatible with worshiping him.

On the view that I am suggesting, the function of worship as "glorifying" or "praising" God, which is usually taken to be its primary function, may be regarded as derivative from the more fundamental nature of worship as commitment to the role of God's Child. "Praising" God is giving him the honour and respect due to one in his position of eminence, just as one shows respect and honour in giving fealty to a King.

In short, the worshiper is in this position: He believes that there is a being, God, who is the perfectly good, perfectly powerful, perfectly wise Creator of the Universe; and he views himself as the "Child of God," made for God's purposes and responsible to God for his conduct. And the ritual of worship, which may have any number of ceremonial forms according to the customs of the religious community, has as its point the acceptance of, and commitment to, one's role as God's Child, with all that this involves. If this account is accepted, then there is no mystery as to the relation between the act of worship and the worshiper's other activity. Worship will be regarded not as an isolated act taking place on Sunday morning, with no necessary connection to one's behaviour the rest of the week, but as a ritualistic expression of and commitment to a role which dominates one's whole way of life.[10]

4. An important feature of roles is that they can be violated; we can act and think consistently with a role, or we can act and think inconsistently with it. The Prince can, for example, act inconsistently with his role as Prince by giving greater importance to his own interests and welfare than to the Queen's; in this case, he is no longer her "liege man." And a father who does not attend to the welfare of his children is not acting consistently with his role as a father (at least as that role is defined in our society), and so on. The question that I want to raise now is, What would count as violating the role to which one is pledged in virtue of worshiping God?

10. This account of worship, specified here in terms of what it means to worship God, may easily be adapted to the worship of other beings such as Satan. The only changes required are (*a*) that we substitute for beliefs about God analogous beliefs about Satan, and (*b*) that we understand the ritual of worship as committing the Satan-worshiper to a role as Satan's servant in the same way that worshiping God commits theists to the role of His servant.

In Genesis there are two familiar stories, both concerning Abraham, that are relevant here. The first is the story of the near-sacrifice of Isaac. We are told that Abraham was "tempted" by God, who commanded him to offer Isaac as a human sacrifice. Abraham obeyed without hesitation: he prepared an altar, bound Isaac to it, and was about to kill him until God intervened at the last moment, saying "Lay not thine hand upon the lad, neither do thou any thing unto him; for now I know that thou fearest God, seeing thou hast not withheld thy son, thine only son from me" (Genesis 22: 12). So Abraham passed the test. But how could he have failed? What was his "temptation"? Obviously, his temptation was to disobey God; God had ordered him to do something contrary to both his wishes and his sense of what would otherwise be right and wrong. He could have defied God; but he did not—he subordinated himself, his own desires and judgments, to God's command, even when the temptation to do otherwise was strongest.

It is interesting that Abraham's record in this respect was not perfect. We also have the story of him bargaining with God over the conditions for saving Sodom and Gomorrah from destruction. God had said that he would destroy those cities because they were so wicked; but Abraham gets God to agree that if fifty righteous men can be found there, then the cities will be spared. Then he persuades God to lower the number to forty-five, then forty, then thirty, then twenty, and finally ten. Here we have a different Abraham, not servile and obedient, but willing to challenge God and bargain with him. However, even as he bargains with God, Abraham realises that there is something radically inappropriate about it: he says, "Behold now, I have taken upon me to speak unto the Lord, which am but dust and ashes . . . O let not the Lord be angry . . ." (Genesis 18: 27, 30).

The fact is that Abraham could not, consistently with his role as God's subject, set his own judgment and will against God's. The author of Genesis was certainly right about this. We cannot recognise any being *as God,* and at the same time set ourselves against him. The point is not merely that it would be imprudent to defy God, since we certainly can't get away with it; rather, there is a stronger, logical point involved—namely, that if we recognise any being *as God,* then we are committed, in virtue of that recognition, to obeying him.

To see why this is so, we must first notice that "God" is not a proper name like "Richard Nixon" but a title like "President of the United States" or "King."[11] Thus, "Jehovah is God" is a nontautological statement in which the title "God" is assigned to Jehovah, a particular being—just as "Richard Nixon is President of the United States" assigns the title "Presi-

11. Cf. Nelson Pike, "Omnipotence and God's Ability to Sin," *American Philosophical Quarterly,* VI (1969), pp. 208–9; and C. B. Martin, *Religious Belief* (Ithaca, 1959), ch. 4.

dent of the United States" to a particular man. This permits us to understand how statements like "God is perfectly wise" can be logical truths, which is highly problematic if "God" is regarded as a proper name. Although it is not a logical truth that any particular being is perfectly wise, it nevertheless is a logical truth that if any being is God (i.e. if any being properly holds that title) then that being is perfectly wise. This is exactly analogous to saying: although it is not a logical truth that Richard Nixon has the authority to veto congressional legislation, nevertheless it is a logical truth that if Richard Nixon is President of the United States then he has that authority.

To bear the title "God," then, a being must have certain qualifications. He must, for example, be all-powerful and perfectly good in addition to being perfectly wise. And in the same vein, to apply the title "God" to a being is to recognise him as one to be obeyed. The same is true, to a lesser extent, of "King"—to recognise anyone as King is to acknowledge that he occupies a place of authority and has a claim on one's allegiance as his subject. And to recognise any being as God is to acknowledge that he has *unlimited* authority, and an unlimited claim on one's allegiance.[12] Thus, we might regard Abraham's reluctance to defy Jehovah as grounded not only in his fear of Jehovah's wrath, but as a logical consequence of his acceptance of Jehovah *as God*. Camus was right to think that "From the moment that man submits God to moral judgment, he kills Him in his own heart."[13] What a man can "kill" by defying or even questioning God is not the being that (supposedly) *is* God, but *his own conception of that being as God*. That God is not to be judged, challenged, defied, or disobeyed, is at bottom a truth of logic; to do any of these things is incompatible with taking him as One to be worshiped.

12. This suggestion might also throw some light on the much-discussed problem of how we could, even in principle, *verify* the existence of God. Sceptics have argued that, even though we might be able to confirm the existence of an all-powerful cosmic superbeing (if one existed), we still wouldn't know what it means to verify that this being is *divine*. And this, it is said, casts doubt on whether the notion of divinity, and related notions such as "Christ" and "God," are intelligible. (Cf. Kai Nielsen, "Eschatological Verification," *The Canadian Journal of Theology*, IX, 1963.) Perhaps this is because, in designating a being as God, we are not only describing him as having certain factual properties (such as omnipotence), but also *ascribing* to him a certain place in our devotions, and taking him as one to be obeyed, worshiped, praised, etc. If this is part of the logic of "God," then we shouldn't be surprised if God's existence, in so far as that includes the existence of divinity, is not entirely confirmable—for only the "factual properties" such as omnipotence will be verifiable in the usual way. But once the reason for this is understood, it no longer seems such a serious matter.

13. Albert Camus, *The Rebel*, translated by Anthony Bower (New York, 1956), p. 62.

5. So the idea that any being could be *worthy* of worship is much more problematical than we might have at first imagined. For in admitting that a being is worthy of worship we would be recognising him as having an unqualified claim on our obedience. The question, then, is whether there could be such an unqualified claim. It should be noted that the description of a being as all-powerful, all-wise, etc., would not automatically settle the issue; for even while admitting the existence of such an awesome being we might still question whether we should recognise him as having an unlimited claim on our obedience.

In fact, there is a long tradition in moral philosophy, from Plato to Kant, according to which such a recognition could never be made by a moral agent. According to this tradition, to be a moral agent is to be an autonomous or self-directed agent; unlike the precepts of law or social custom, moral precepts are imposed by the agent upon himself, and the penalty for their violation is, in Kant's words, "self-contempt and inner abhorrence."[14] The virtuous man is therefore identified with the man of integrity, i.e. the man who acts according to precepts which he can, on reflection, conscientiously approve in his own heart. Although this is a highly individualistic approach to morals, it is not thought to invite anarchy because men are regarded as more or less reasonable and as desiring what we would normally think of as a decent life lived in the company of other men.

On this view, to deliver oneself over to a moral authority for directions about what to do is simply incompatible with being a moral agent. To say "I will follow so-and-so's directions no matter what they are and no matter what my own conscience would otherwise direct me to do" is to opt out of moral thinking altogether; it is to abandon one's role as a moral agent. And it does not matter whether "so-and-so" is the law, the customs of one's society, or God. This does not, of course, preclude one from seeking advice on moral matters, and even on occasion following that advice blindly, trusting in the good judgment of the adviser. But this is to be justified by the details of the particular case, e.g. that you cannot in that case form any reasonable judgment of your own due to ignorance or inexperience in dealing with the types of matters involved. What *is* precluded is that a man should, while in possession of his wits, adopt this style of decision-making (or perhaps we should say this style of *abdicating* decision-making) as a general strategy of living, or abandon his own best judgment in any case where he can form a judgment of which he is reasonably confident.

What we have, then, is a conflict between the role of worshiper, which by its very nature commits one to total subservience to God, and the role

14. Immanuel Kant, *Foundations of the Metaphysics of Morals*, translated by Lewis White Beck (New York, 1959), p. 44.

of moral agent, which necessarily involves autonomous decision-making. The point is that the role of worshiper takes precedence over every other role which the worshiper has—when there is any conflict, the worshiper's commitment to God has priority over any other commitments which he might have. But the first commitment of a moral agent is to do what in his own heart he thinks is right. Thus the following argument might be constructed:

(a) If any being is God, he must be a fitting object of worship.

(b) No being could possibly be a fitting object of worship, since worship requires the abandonment of one's role as an autonomous moral agent.

(c) Therefore, there cannot be any being who is God.

6. The concept of moral agency underlying this argument is complex and controversial; and, although I think it is sound, I cannot give it the detailed treatment here that it requires. Instead, I will conclude by answering some of the most obvious objections to the argument.

(1) What if God lets us go our own way, and issues no commands other than that we should live according to our own consciences? In that case, there would be no incompatibility between our commitment to God and our commitments as moral agents, since God would leave us free to direct our own lives. The fact that this supposition is contrary to major religious traditions (such as the Christian tradition) doesn't matter, since these traditions could be mistaken. The answer here is that this is a mere contingency, and that even if God did not require obedience to detailed commands, the worshiper would still be committed to the abandonment of his role as a moral agent, *if* God required it.

(2) It has been admitted as a necessary truth that God is perfectly good; it follows as a corollary that He would never require us to do anything except what is right. Therefore in obeying God we would only be doing what we should do in any case. So there is no incompatibility between obeying him and carrying out our moral commitments. Our primary commitment as moral agents is to do right, and God's commands *are* right, so that's that.

This objection rests on a misunderstanding of the assertion that (necessarily) God is perfectly good. This can be intelligibly asserted only because of the principle that *No being who is not perfectly good may bear the title "God."*[15] We cannot determine whether some being is God without first checking on whether he is perfectly good;[16] and we cannot decide whether

---

15. See above, section 4.

16. Of course we cannot ever know that such a being is *perfectly* good, since this would require an examination of *all* his actions and commands, etc., which is impos-

he is perfectly good without knowing (among other things) whether his commands to us are right. Thus our own judgment that some actions are right, and others wrong, is logically prior to our recognition of any being as God. The upshot of this is that we cannot justify the suspension of our own judgment on the grounds that we are deferring to God's command (which, as a matter of logic, *must* be right); for if, by our own best judgment, the command is wrong, this gives us good reason to withhold the title "God" from the commander.

(3) The following expresses a view which has always had its advocates among theologians: "Men are sinful; their very consciences are corrupt and unreliable guides. What is taken for conscientiousness among men is nothing more than self-aggrandisement and arrogance. Therefore, we cannot trust our own judgment; we must trust God and do what he wills. Only then can we be assured of doing right."

This view suffers from a fundamental inconsistency. It is said that we cannot know for ourselves what is right and what is wrong; and this is because our judgment is corrupt. But how do we know that our judgment is corrupt? Presumably, in order to know that, we would have to know (*a*) that some actions are morally required of us, and (*b*) that our own judgment does not reveal that these actions are required. However, (*a*) is just the sort of thing that we can*not* know, according to this view. Now it may be suggested that while we cannot know (*a*) by our own judgment, we can know it as a result of God's revelation. But even setting aside the practical difficulties of distinguishing genuine from bogus revelation (a generous concession), there is still this problem: if we learn that God (i.e. some being that we take to be God) requires us to do a certain action, and we conclude on this account that the action is morally right, then we have *still* made at least one moral judgment of our own, namely that whatever this being requires is morally right. Therefore, it is impossible to maintain the view that we do have some moral knowledge, and that *all* of it comes from God's revelation.

(4) Many philosophers, including St. Thomas, have held that the voice of individual conscience *is* the voice of God speaking to the individual, whether he is a believer or not.[17] This would resolve the alleged conflict

---

sible. However, if we observed many good things about him and no evil ones, we would be justified in putting forth the hypothesis that he is perfectly good and acting accordingly. The hypothesis would be confirmed or disconfirmed by future observations in the usual way.

17. Cf. Geach, pp. 124–125: "The rational recognition that a practice is generally undesirable and that it is best for people on the whole not even to think of resorting to it is thus *in fact* a promulgation to a man of the Divine law forbidding the practice, even if he does not realise that this is a promulgation of the Divine law, even if he does not believe there is a God."

because in following one's conscience one would at the same time be discharging his obligation as a worshiper to obey God. However, this manoeuvre is unsatisfying, since if taken seriously it would lead to the conclusion that, in speaking to us through our "consciences," God is merely tricking us: for he is giving us the illusion of self-governance while all the time he is manipulating our thoughts from without. Moreover, in acting from conscience we are acting under the view that our actions are right and not merely that they are decreed by a higher power. Plato's argument in the *Euthyphro* can be adapted to this point: If, in speaking to us through the voice of conscience, God is informing us of what is right, then there is no reason to think that we could not discover this for ourselves—the notion of "God informing us" is eliminable. On the other hand, if God is only giving us arbitrary commands, which cannot be thought of as "right" independently of his promulgating them, then the whole idea of "conscience," as it is normally understood, is a sham.

(5) Finally, someone might object that the question of whether any being is *worthy* of worship is different from the question of whether we *should* worship him. In general, that X is worthy of our doing Y with respect to X does not entail that we should do Y with respect to X. For example, Mrs. Brown, being a fine woman, may be worthy of a marriage proposal, but we ought not to propose to her since she is already married. Or, Seaman Jones may be worthy of a medal for heroism but perhaps there are reasons why we should not award it. Similarly, it may be that there is a being who is worthy of worship and yet we should not worship him since it would interfere with our lives as moral agents. Thus God, who is worthy of worship, may exist; and we should love, respect, and honor him, but not worship him in the full sense of the word. If this is correct, then the argument of section 5 is fallacious.

This rebuttal will not work because of an important disanalogy between the cases of proposing marriage and awarding the medal, on the one hand, and the case of worship on the other. It may be that Mrs. Brown is worthy of a proposal, yet there are circumstances in which it would be wrong to propose to her. However, these circumstances are contrasted with others in which it would be perfectly all right. The same goes for Seaman Jones's medal: there are *some* circumstances in which awarding it would be proper. But in the case of worship—if the foregoing arguments have been sound— there are *no* circumstances under which anyone should worship God. And if one should *never* worship, then the concept of a fitting object of worship is an empty one.

The above argument will probably not persuade anyone to abandon belief in God—arguments rarely do—and there are certainly many more points which need to be worked out before it can be known whether this argument is even viable. Yet it does raise an issue which is clear enough.

Theologians are already accustomed to speaking of theistic belief and commitment as taking the believer "beyond morality," and I think they are right. The question is whether this should not be regarded as a severe embarrassment.[18]

18. A number of people read earlier versions of this paper and made helpful comments. I have to thank especially Kai Nielsen, William Ruddick, Jack Glickman, and Steven Cahn.

Life After Death

TERENCE PENELHUM

TWO CONCEPTS OF SURVIVAL

The doctrine of the immortality of the soul certainly predates Christianity. It finds its classic expression in Plato's dialogue, the *Phaedo*. This dialogue has as its dramatic setting the last day in the life of Socrates. Socrates has been condemned to death by the Athenians for allegedly corrupting the youth of the city with his philosophical questioning, and when the sun sets he must drink the cup of poison that will kill him. As Plato portrays his last day in prison before the carrying out of the sentence, Socrates devotes his final hours to discussion of whether the soul can survive the death of the body and whether death is to be feared. His conclusion is that the soul will survive and that the wise man need have no fear of death but should welcome it as a release of the soul from the bondage of the body. The arguments that Plato puts into the mouth of Socrates are based upon his belief that the human soul shows an awareness of a higher and nonmaterial realm of forms or ideas, of which it could not learn through the body and its sensory apparatus alone. The soul shows this awareness through its capacity to use general concepts and in particular through its powers of mathematical and moral reflection. It is thus identified primarily with the reason of man and is held to be alien to the body and essentially imprisoned within it. The philosopher is the man who is able to recognize the soul's higher kinship and attempts as far as he can to free the soul from the shackles of physical concerns. For him, at least, death will complete what he has par-

Reprinted by permission of the author from *Religion and Rationality* (New York: Random House, 1971), pp. 334–355. Footnotes have been renumbered for convenience.

tially succeeded in achieving during his lifetime. It is clear from the doctrine of the parts of the soul in the *Republic* that Plato recognizes the desires as parts of the soul also and not merely as functions of bodily states;
but he thinks of the satisfaction of physical desires as alien to the natural
concerns of the soul, which has its own, immaterial objects to seek after.

This doctrine has been enormously influential, and many have thought
that it, or something like it, is also the Christian doctrine. Certain elements
in the Platonic view (such as Plato's suggestion that the soul's higher as-
pirations reveal its preexistence and his belief that matter is a fundamentally negative, and even evil, principle) would have to be abandoned or
amended for the two doctrines to be assimilated. But many Christians have
thought that their belief is in essence the same as the doctrine we find in
Plato. This obscures the fact that the doctrine of the resurrection of the
body clearly seems to be a distinctively Christian contribution. When this
fact is emphasized, it becomes important to decide how far the two beliefs
are irreconcilable.

Some thinkers certainly hold that they are. Professor Oscar Cullmann,
for example, has recently argued that there is a fundamental divergence
between the Platonic and Christian doctrines and that this can be seen
when we compare the serenity with which Socrates' doctrines enable him
to face his approaching death in the *Phaedo,* with the agony that Jesus
undergoes when faced with the approach of death in the Gospel narra-
tives.[1] The primitive Christian tradition, he argues, does not present death
as a welcome passage from one realm to another, but as the most elemental
and horrifying reality that man confronts, because death is the destruction
of the person, not his release. The distinctive Christian hope, expressed in
the doctrines of the Resurrection of Christ and the final resurrection of
men, is the hope that God will literally re-create what he has permitted
death to destroy. This interpretation has been challenged by H. A. Wolfson, who has argued that the early Christian Church believed both in the
survival of the soul and in the resurrection of the body, and that this combination of beliefs can readily accommodate all the original New Testament attitudes toward death.[2] The final doctrinal issue between them seems
to be whether or not the soul continues in a disembodied state between
death and resurrection. If so, then at the resurrection the person is made
whole again by the soul's being reunited with the body (or, perhaps, by its
being united with another body). If not, then the resurrection is indeed
the reappearance of a person from annihilation.

I cannot comment profitably on the historical question that Cullmann

1. Oscar Cullmann, *Immortality of the Soul or Resurrection of the Dead?* (London:
Epworth, 1958).
2. H. A. Wolfson, "Immortality and Resurrection in the Philosophy of the Church
Fathers," in *Religious Philosophy* (Cambridge: Harvard University Press, 1961).

and Wolfson debate; though some of the later discussion will bear on the logic of the two competing alternatives. There can be no doubt that the doctrine of the immortality of the soul, even though Greek in origin, has been held by many members of the Christian tradition, whether it belonged originally to that tradition or not. The doctrine of the resurrection of the body, certainly authentically a part of the Christian tradition (since some form of it is clearly held by St. Paul),[3] is part of the most widely used creed of the Christian Church. Let us leave aside their historical relationship and look at the logical possibilities they present. I shall begin with the doctrine of the immortality of the soul, or, as I prefer to word it, the doctrine of disembodied survival. Before doing so, however, I shall attempt to clear the ground a little by indicating the major sources of difficulty that philosophers have discovered in these doctrines.

These difficulties divide themselves naturally into two groups. There are, first of all, difficulties about envisaging the kind of life that survivors of death in either sense could be said to lead. It is not enough to say that the nature of this life is totally unknown, for if this is taken seriously to the extent of our being unable to say that these beings will possess personal characteristics as we now understand these, it seems to leave the belief that they will survive without any content. If one wishes to avoid this pitfall, one has to ascribe to the survivors some characteristics that persons as we know them possess. This does not seem impossible in the case of the doctrine of the resurrection of the body; though it can be made impossible if unlimited stress is placed on the claim that the body of the survivor is transformed. Radical transformation is to be expected as part of such a doctrine, but total transformation would rob the notion of survival of all clear meaning, for it is part of that notion that the *person* survives, and this seems to entail that the resulting being is a person also. But if the doctrine of the resurrection of the body is expressed in ways that avoids this danger, it is clearly possible for us to form a rough notion (which is all one can reasonably demand) of what such a future state would be like.

The difficulty seems much greater, however, when we consider the doctrine of disembodied survival. For it is not obviously intelligible to ascribe personal characteristics to a being that is denied to have any physical ones. The notion of human intelligence, for example, seems closely bound up with the things men can be seen to do and heard to say; the notion of human emotion seems closely bound up with the way men talk and behave; and the notion of human action seems closely bound up with that of physical movement. There is plenty of room for disagreement over the nature of these connections, but they cannot even exist in the case of an allegedly disembodied being. So can we understand what is meant by talk of dis-

3. See I Corinthians, Chapter 15.

embodied intelligences, or disembodied sufferers of emotion, or disembodied agents? A natural answer to our present problem is: Disembodied survivors might have mental lives. They might, that is, think, imagine, dream, or have feelings. This looks coherent enough. On the other hand, for them to have anything to think *about* or have feelings *toward*, it might be necessary for them also to have that which supplies us with our objects of reflection or emotion, namely, perception. Some might also want to add the notion of agency (especially if they wish to use the doctrine of disembodied survival to offer explanations of the phenomena of psychical research). We must bear in mind, further, that disembodied persons could, of course, never perceive or meet each other, in any normal sense of these words. What we need to do, even at the risk of spinning fantasies, is to see how severely the belief in their disembodiment restricts the range of concepts that we can apply to them.

The second group of difficulties affects both doctrines, though in different ways. These are difficulties about the self-identity of the survivors. The belief that people survive is not merely the belief that after people's deaths there will be personal beings in existence. It is the belief that those beings will be the same ones that existed before death. One of the reasons for concern about the nature of the life a disembodied person might lead is that if this mode of life were *too* radically different from the sort of life we lead, those beings leading it could not be identified with us. This difficulty is critical, for even if we can readily understand what the future life that is spoken of would be like, its coming to pass would only be an interesting cosmic hypothesis, lacking any personal relevance, if the beings living that life were not ourselves.[4] This requirement connects with another. We have to be able to form some concept of what it is for the future, post-mortem being to remain the same through time in the future life, quite apart from his also being identifiable with some previous person who existed in *this* life. If, for instance, our being able to identify a person whom we meet now as some person we knew previously depends on our being able to discern some feature that he still possesses; and if that feature is something that a being in the future life could not possess, then it needs to be shown that there could be post-mortem persons who persist through time at all. There would have to be some substitute, in the case of post-mortem persons, for the feature that establishes identity for pre-mortem persons. If we are not able to indicate what this would be, we have no adequately clear concept of what talk of post-mortem persons means.

4. The emphasis on the importance of this is a most valuable feature of Antony Flew's contributions to this subject. See *A New Approach to Psychical Research* (London: Watts & Co., 1953) and his article "Immortality," in Paul Edwards (ed.), *Encyclopedia of Philosophy* (New York: Macmillan and Free Press, 1967), Vol. 4, pp. 139–150.

These problems about identity arise in quite different ways for the two doctrines of disembodied survival and bodily resurrection. A proponent of the doctrine of disembodied survival has to face the problem of the continuing identity of the disembodied person through time, by showing that what makes that person identical through time could be some wholly *mental* feature and that the absence of a body does not render the notion of a body inapplicable. (He may or may not do this by claiming that we use mental rather than physical features to identify pre-mortem beings through time.) This task may not be hopeless, though it looks as though we depend on the physical continuity of people for our ability to reidentify them. He must also succeed in showing that some purely mental feature will serve to identify the post-mortem person with his pre-mortem predecessor.

In the case of the doctrine of the resurrection of the body, the problem of how the post-mortem, resurrected person can remain identical through time in the future state does not look very difficult, since the sort of life envisaged for this being is an embodied one, similar in enough respects (one may suppose) to our own. So even if we decided that the continuity of the body is a necessary condition of the continuance of a person through time, this condition could easily be said to be satisfied in the case of a resurrected person. Yet we still have a difficulty: Could a post-mortem person, even in this embodied state, be identified with any pre-mortem person? For if the doctrine of resurrection is presented in a form that entails the annihilation of a person at death, it could reasonably be argued that what is predicted as happening at the resurrection is not, after all, the reappearance of the original person but the (first) appearance of a *duplicate* person—no doubt resembling the former one but not numerically identical with him. If this can be argued and cannot be refuted, we are in the odd position of being unsure whether or not to say that the future persons are the former ones. Philosophers have often noted the extent to which problems of identity seem to involve not discoveries but decisions—decisions on what to *call* a particular situation. The literature of personal identity is full of actual and imagined stories introduced to help us discover, by deciding how to talk of them, what the conditions of application of our concepts are. The doctrine of the resurrection of the body seems to present us with just such a matter of decision—namely, would this admittedly conceivable future state properly be described as the reappearance of a former person or as the first appearance of a duplicate of him?

DISEMBODIED PERSONALITY

Let us now look at the first group of difficulties, those connected with the possibility of applying our normal concepts of personal life to post-mortem beings. These seem to arise, as we have seen already, only in connection with the belief that men survive without their bodies, and I shall therefore only discuss them in this connection.

These difficulties raise the most fundamental issues in the philosophy of mind. There is no doubt that the belief that the soul continues after physical death is one of the major causes of the famous "Cartesian dualism" of mind and matter. The dualist position, formulated by Descartes in the seventeenth century, restated a metaphysical position very close in many ways to that of Plato. Descartes' position is, roughly, that the soul (or mind) and the body are two distinct substances that have no common properties and have a purely causal and contingent relationship with one another. The mind occupies no space, is free, and indivisible; whereas the body does occupy space, is incapable of spontaneous motion, and can be divided. Further, each person cannot fail to be aware of the contents of his own mind, whereas the possibility of knowledge of the external physical world needs philosophical demonstration in view of the fact that our senses sometimes deceive us.

In the *Meditations* Descartes argues for his metaphysical dualism on epistemological grounds like these. But whatever its surface and deep causes are, its strengths and weaknesses as a theory about the composition of the human person have dominated philosophical discussion for over two centuries. Only recently, through the work of Wittgenstein and Ryle, have philosophers freed themselves from this dominance.[5] It is not necessary to hold the dualistic view of the nature of embodied persons in order to maintain the post-mortem existence of *dis*embodied persons, but a combination of the two is natural and is very common on a popular level. If we can make sense of the view that the mind or soul is essentially independent of the body it is "in," then there would seem to be no real difficulty about understanding the belief that it can continue when its occupancy of that body ceases. It has become very clear, however, that the dualistic picture of the structure of a person forces its adherents into the view that a person's mental life and mental qualities are features of the history of his mind and have at best a causal relationship with what his body is seen to do. In fact the greater part of what we say about people commits us to certain expectations about their physical performances. This does not mean, as some over-enthusiastic behaviorists seem at times to suggest, that people do not have private mental images, wishes, and thoughts. It means rather that their intelligence, will, and emotions do not consist only, or even mainly, in the occurrence of those private experiences. It is therefore very doubtful indeed

5. See Ludwig Wittgenstein, *Philosophical Investigations*, trans. by G. E. M. Anscombe (Oxford: Basil Blackwell, 1953); Gilbert Ryle, *The Concept of Mind* (London: Hutchinson, 1949).

that dualism could hope to do justice to the variety of people's mental lives; it is also doubtful that this mental life could continue without a body. The only way of seeing whether or not the latter can be made plausible seems to be the slow and tedious process of wondering, case by case, how much of what we now can ascribe to embodied persons could be ascribed to disembodied ones without absurdity. If little or nothing can be so ascribed, we cannot attach any content to the phrase "disembodied person." If some characteristics can be ascribed to such a person, we may be able to attach some content to this notion, although the concept of a person will be much attenuated in the process.

Disembodied persons can conduct no physical performances. They cannot walk or talk (or, therefore, converse), open and close their eyes or peer (or, therefore, look), turn their heads and incline their ears (or, therefore, listen), raise their hands in anger or weep (or, therefore, give bodily expression to their emotions), or touch or feel physical objects. Hence they cannot perceive each other or be perceived by us. Can they, still, be said without absurdity to perceive physical things? Perhaps we could say so if we were prepared to allow that a being having a set of visual images corresponding to the actual disposition of some physical things was thereby *seeing* those things. We could say so if we were prepared to allow that a being having a sequence of auditory experiences that made him think correctly that a certain object was giving off a particular sound was thereby *hearing* that object. The notions of seeing and hearing would be attenuated, since they would not, if applied in such cases, entail that the person who saw was physically in front of the object he saw with his face turned toward it or that the person who heard was receiving sound waves from the object that was giving them off. On the other hand, many philosophers hold that such implications are at most informal ones that are not essential to the concepts in question. Perhaps we could also say even that disembodied percipients could *do* things to the objects (or persons) they see and hear. We might be able to say this if we imagined that sometimes these percipients had wishes that were immediately actualized in the world, without any natural explanation for the strange things that occurred; though obviously such fantasies would involve the ascription of occult powers to the spirits.[6] We might prefer to avoid all talk of interaction between the world of the spirits and ours, however, by denying that a disembodied being can see or hear or act in our world at all. Perhaps their lives consist exclusively of internal processes—acts of imagination and reflection. Such a life would be life in a dream world; and each person would have his own private dream. It might include dream images "of" others, though

6. These suggestions and alternatives to some of them are discussed in Chapters 2, 3, and 4 of my book *Survival and Disembodied Existence* (London: Routledge & Kegan Paul, 1970).

the accuracy of any reflections they occasioned would be purely coincidental.[7]

These informal suggestions indicate that it might be possible, given a good deal of conceptual elasticity, to accord to disembodied persons at least some of the forms of mental life with which we are familiar. It therefore seems overdoctrinaire to refuse to admit that such beings could be called persons. We must bear in mind, however, that they could hardly be said to have an *inter*personal existence. Not only would we be unable to perceive a disembodied person; but a disembodied person, being unable to perceive another disembodied person, could have no more reason than we have to believe that others besides himself existed. Only if he can perceive embodied persons would he be in a position to know from anything other than memory that they exist or that they act in particular ways. The logic of the concept of disembodied persons clearly rules out the possibility of there being a community of such persons, even though by exercising conceptual care and tolerance we do seem able to ascribe some sort of life to disembodied individuals. In response to this, a verificationist might demand that before we can understand the ascriptions we have considered we should be able to say how we would *know* that a disembodied individual was having some experience or performing some act. But since we are dealing with a possible use of predicates that we have already learned, this verificationist demand seems too stringent.

We have also had to put aside another question whose bearing cannot be disputed, since it casts doubt on our ability to think of disembodied individuals. In asking whether some of the notions of a personal mental life can be applied, we have had to assume that there is a continuing, non-physical subject to whom they can be applied, who has the experience or who does the action. This notion is essential to our understanding of the suggestion that there is a plurality of distinct individuals (whether they form a community or not), that on some occasion an experience is had by one of them rather than another, and that on another occasion a second experience is had by the same individual (or, indeed, a different individual) as had the first. In daily life the distinction between individuals and the continuing identity of individuals through time seems to depend upon the fact that each individual person has a distinguishable and persisting body. In the absence of a body are we able to form any notion of what has the experience or does the actions, has certain other experiences or actions in its past, and will have others in its future? In what follows, in order to retain

7. See H. H. Price, "Survival and the Idea of 'Another World,'" *Proceedings of the Society for Psychical Research,* 50 (1952); reprinted in J. R. Smythies (ed.), *Brain and Mind* (London: Routledge & Kegan Paul, 1965). For comments on Price see the Smythies volume and Penelhum, *Survival and Disembodied Existence,* Chapter 4.

some degree of clarity and simplicity in a philosophical area where obscurity is especially easy, I shall concentrate on trying to provide some account of what it might be for a disembodied person to retain identity through time. The philosophical theories we shall look at are usually also intended to offer some answer to the problem of distinguishing between two or more contemporaries—the problem, that is, of individuation. It is in any case hard to see how that question could have an answer if the problem of identity through time does not. I shall now turn, then, to the second, and more fundamental, of our two problems in the logic of the concept of survival.

THE PROBLEM OF IDENTITY: HUME'S SKEPTICISM

The logical problems one has to contend with when examining the concept of survival are to a large extent extensions of those that have puzzled philosophers when they have tried to analyze the notion of personal identity.[8] We all recognize one another; we are all familiar enough with the experience of wondering who someone is; and most of us know the embarrassment that follows when one makes a mistake about who someone is. Our day-to-day thinking about these matters suggests that we take it for granted that there are clearly understood factors that determine whether the man before us is Smith or not, or is who he says he is or not, even though we may be unable to decide sometimes, through lack of information, whether these factors obtain. Philosophers have been puzzled, however, when they have tried to say what these factors are. Skeptical philosophers have even wondered whether any such factors can be isolated; and if they cannot be, they have suggested, our assumption that people do retain their identities from one period of time to the next may be an illusion.

We do not need to spend much time here on this sort of skepticism. Its most famous exponent is Hume, who confessed himself unable to detect any stability in the mental life of men and therefore thought that the incessant changes that human minds undergo make it plainly false that they retain any identity at all.[9] Our belief that they do retain an identity is a convenient fiction but nothing better. This skepticism rests on an unstated assumption that there is some sort of logical conflict between the notions

8. For a general discussion of the problems of personal identity, see my article of that title in *Encyclopedia of Philosophy,* Vol. 6. This contains, besides a more rigorous treatment of issues raised briefly here, some extended discussion of the implications of the "puzzle cases," which I have had to omit from a short treatment of these topics. The latter part of my *Survival and Disembodied Existence* is intended to be a more thorough examination of the issues introduced in this chapter.

9. See Hume's *Treatise of Human Nature,* Book I, Part 4, Section 6. The criticisms I make here are more informal versions of those I raised in "Hume on Personal Identity," *The Philosophical Review,* 44, No. 4 (1955), 571–589, reprinted in V. C. Chappell (ed.), *Hume* (New York: Doubleday, 1967), pp. 213–239.

of sameness and change. If this were so, then in order to be sure that any type of being retained identity through time, we would have to be sure that it, or at least the essential part of it, remained unchanged through that time. If this is true, then of course Hume would be quite justified in relapsing into skepticism about personal identity. But once the assumption is exposed, its gratuitousness becomes apparent. Sameness or identity is an ambiguous notion; borrowing vocabulary found in Hume himself, we can distinguish between "numerical identity" and "specific identity." Two things are identical in the specific sense if they are exactly alike in some or all respects. This can only be true if they are, nevertheless, two distinct things—if, that is, they are *not* identical in the numercial sense. Two numerically different things may or may not be the same in the specific sense. One and the same thing (in the numerical sense) may be the same at one time as it was at an earlier time, or it may not. If it is not, it has changed. To say that just because it has changed it cannot be numerically the same is to confuse the two sorts of identity.

Certain changes, however, may destroy a thing—that is, whatever remains of it is no longer sufficient to entitle us to say that that thing has continued in existence, and we are forced to say that something else is there, as when a house crumbles and a mere heap of stones remains. Even though Hume is wrong in thinking that the mere fact of change destroys numerical identity, it is still the case that for each *sort* of thing, certain changes will destroy that identity and certain others will not. Reducing all parts of a chair to ashes in a fire will destroy its identity, whereas changing the color of its surface by painting it will not. This suggests, once again, that the proper philosophical task is to discover, at least in the case of those classes of things that are of philosophical interest to us, what factors have to remain for a thing of that sort to continue in being and which ones do not. The problem of personal identity consists, in part, of trying to clarify this in the case of persons.

When we try to do this we are confronted with another oddity in a discussion like Hume's. He restricts himself, without any apparent recognition of the need to justify this restriction, to a consideration of only the mental factors that make up the being of a person and ignores the physical ones. If one makes this restriction, one is immediately confronted with the following facts that Hume stresses: first, he notes that the changes we can introspect within the mind succeed one another very rapidly; and second, he points out that one cannot detect any more stable element. Since we usually conceive of *things* as entities that change fairly slowly unless catastrophe strikes them and do not normally change nearly as rapidly as the contents of the mind seem to do, our ascription of identity to the person is apt to seem puzzling. But what needs to be questioned here is Hume's restriction. One of the major reasons for it is that Hume inherits the dualism that Descartes passed down from Plato into modern philosophy. It is a characteristic part of that tradition not merely to divide the human person into two parts but to identify the real person with the mind and assume that the body is merely a place that this person inhabits. If this identification is presupposed, then Hume's bewilderment in the face of the rapidity of mental change is understandable enough.

MENTAL AND BODILY CRITERIA OF IDENTITY

One way of trying to avoid this confusion is to resort to a doctrine that Hume recognizes to be without value: the doctrine of spiritual substance. This is the doctrine that in spite of the changingness of our mental lives, there is some hidden core to it that persists unchanged throughout, thus providing a backdrop against which the changes occur. This backdrop need not be *un*changing: It could be subject only to gradual change. The tacit assumption that it cannot change at all is only the result of assuming that identity and change are always inconsistent. But even if we allow that the spiritual substance to which the occurrences in our mental lives belong might itself be subject to gradual change, the doctrine is without value. For if the doctrine implies that we can find this relatively permanent core within by looking into ourselves, then it is false; for we cannot, as Hume emphasizes. If on the other hand, it is admitted that the doctrine postulates something that is not accessible to observation, there is another difficulty: It can at best be a matter of happy accident that when we judge someone before us to be the same person as someone we knew before, we are right. For the only thing that would make this judgment reliable is the knowledge that the features possessed by the present and the past person belonged to the same substance. Yet when the substance is inaccessible even to the person himself, how could we ever know that an identity judgment was true? It is obvious that our basis for such judgments must be something other than what the doctrine requires it to be, for how, otherwise, could we learn to make such judgments in the first place?

We base our identity judgments, at least of others, upon the observation of their physical appearance. This fact, plus the mysteriousness of the doctrine of spiritual substance, has made it very tempting for philosophers to say that what makes a person the same from one period to the next is the continuance of his body throughout the two periods. The human body has the relative stability that we associate with a great many observable material objects and is not usually subject to the rapid changes that go on in the human mind. The plausibility of the claim that bodily continuity is a necessary and sufficient condition of personal identity derives also from the fact that our judgments about the identity of persons are in the vast majority of cases based on our having looked at them, talked to them, and recognized them. This may be why even philosophers who have tacitly identified the person with his mind have assumed that a person cannot consist only of thoughts, feelings, images, and other fleeting and changing phenomena, but must consist, beneath this, of something more stable. For they have, perhaps, been looking within the mind itself for something that has the relative stability of the body, even though they have officially abandoned any belief that the body provides persons with their continuing identity.

Suppose, however, that they were to abandon body surrogates like spiritual substance. Suppose they were not to assume that the identity of a person consists in the persistence of some relatively stable element such as his body, but were to concentrate their attention solely upon what they consider to be the contents of his mental life. If they were to do this, it would seem that their only hope of giving an account of the self-identity of persons would be to suggest the existence of some relationship among the fleeting elements of which human mental life is composed. An appropriate relationship does seem available. Some of the later experiences in a man's life history are, the story might go, memories of the earlier ones. And only the same person who had the earlier experiences could have a memory of one of them among his later experiences. So we have here the possibility of a purely mental standard of identity: that person A at time T_2 is the same as person B at some earlier time T_1 if and only if, among the experiences that person A has at T_2 there are memories of experiences that person B had at T_1. In the literature of the subject these two criteria of identity (bodily continuity and memory) have contended for priority.

The claim that personal identity can be understood solely in terms of memory can be accepted by someone who does not believe that a person can be identified with his mind or that anyone ever survives physical death. A philosopher who does not believe these things might still believe that the embodied person before him can be identified with Smith, whom he used to know, only if the person before him has the appropriate memories. But it is clear that someone who does believe those things must reject the thesis that only bodily continuity can be a criterion of personal identity. For if it is a necessary condition of a person's continuing that his body should continue, no one could survive in a disembodied form. Someone who accepts the doctrine of disembodied survival, therefore, will naturally incline toward the view that memory is the one necessary and sufficient condition of personal identity, since he must reject the traditional alternative position.

There is an artificiality about speaking, as I have, about two competing positions here. For in daily life it looks as though we use both standards of identity, resorting to one or the other depending on circumstances. Sometimes we decide who someone is by ascertaining facts about their physical appearance, height, weight, and the rest. Sometimes we decide who someone is by trying to determine whether or not they can remember certain past events that the person they claim to be could not fail, we think, to recall. Indeed, the barrier between these two methods becomes less clear than it first seems, when we reflect that we might try to reach our decision by seeing what skills a person has retained or what performances he can carry out. But although both standards are used, one might still have priority over the other. This would be the case if the other would not be available to us if the one were not or if the description of the one required some reference to the other.

It might look as though the use of the bodily criterion of identity presupposes that of memory in some way. For we cannot know, without resorting to our own or someone else's memory of the person in question, whether the body before us is the same one that the person we think he is had in the past. This is true, but it does not show that the man's own memories determine who he is. It only shows that other people could not determine the necessary physical facts about him unless they could rely on their own memories to do it, and this is not the same thing.

There are two arguments that tend to show, I think, that the bodily criterion has priority over the memory criterion. The first one, which is the less fundamental, rests on the fact that people forget things. We cannot say that the man before us is the man who performed some past action if and only if he remembers doing that action, for people forget actions they have done. But one might object on two counts that this need not refute the claim that his having the memory of that action is what makes that action his rather than someone else's. For, first, all we mean by this is that he *could* remember doing it, not that he *does* remember doing it; and, second, all we need is that he be able to remember doing some action or having some experience that the person who did the original action also did, or had.

Let us take these objections in order. The first will not do, for what do we mean when we say that he could remember doing the action in question? If we mean that it is in practice possible to get him to recall doing it, for instance, by psychoanalysis, then the retort is that all practicable methods might fail without thereby showing that the action was not done by him. If, on the other hand, we merely mean that it is in theory possible, then this requires further elucidation: Something that is possible in theory but not in practice is possible in virtue of some condition that in practice cannot bring it about. And this condition can only be the very fact that we are trying to elucidate, namely, the fact that the action was done by him and not by someone else. The other objection does not hold either, for a similar sort of reason. If we say that although the man before us cannot remember doing the action in question, he did do it because he can remember having some experience that the past person who did that action had, this presupposes that we understand what makes the past person who had that experience the same past person who did the original action. There must therefore be some standard of identity, actually satisfied, that we are appealing to in order to presuppose this. To say that this standard is itself that of memory is to raise our original question all over again.

The second and more fundamental argument rests on the fact that the notion of remembering is ambiguous. To say that someone remembers some action or event may mean merely that he believes he did it or witnessed it (without, at least consciously, basing this belief upon being told about it). It is possible, of course, for someone to remember something in this sense without what he remembers having happened at all and without its having happened to *him* even if it did occur. The more common use of the notion of remembering, however, concedes the truth of the man's belief, so that to say that the man remembers some action or event is to say that his claim to know about it is correct. Let us call these sense (i) and sense (ii) of "remember." Then we can say that to remember in sense (i) is to believe that one remembers in sense (ii).

It is apparent that memory in sense (i) cannot provide a criterion of personal identity. It is certainly not a sufficient condition of a man before us being the person that he claims to be that he remembers, in sense (i), doing or experiencing something done or experienced by the man he claims to be. For he could believe that he remembered doing something in this sense, even if nobody had done it. So we have to lean on sense (ii) of "remember." But this leads into a deeper problem. Let us simplify our discussion by concentrating solely upon a person's remembering doing an action or having an experience or witnessing an event and leave aside the complexities involved in someone's remembering some fact, such as that Caesar was murdered. To say that someone, in sense (ii), remembers, is not merely to report that he believes something, but to accept his belief to be true. But an integral part of his belief is not only that some action was done, some experience had, or some event witnessed, but that it was done or had or witnessed *by him*. In other words, to say that he remembers in sense (ii) is not just to say that he now has some mental image or some conviction, even though it is likely to include this; it is to say that the past action, experience, or event that he refers to is part of his own past. But it now becomes clear that we cannot even state the memory criterion of identity without having some prior (and therefore independent) notion of the identity of the person. So the identity of the person must in the end rest upon some other condition, and the claim that it could rest solely upon memory must be false. The bodily criterion of identity is the natural one to refer to here. If, because of some commitment to dualism, one refuses to resort to it, it becomes wholly mysterious what the criterion of personal identity can be.[10]

IDENTITY AND SURVIVAL

We can now return to the problem of survival. We were considering how far it is possible to make sense of the notion of the persistence of a disembodied person through time and of the claim that some particular future disembodied person will be identical with one of us in this world here and now. We can also ask how far the doctrine of the resurrection of the body frees us from the difficulties that the doctrine of disembodied survival encounters.

If bodily continuity is a necessary condition of the persistence of a person through time, then we cannot form any clear conception of the persistence of a person through time without a body nor of the identity of such a person with some previous embodied person. The previous reflections about the notion of personal identity leave us with two results: first, that to attempt to understand the self-identity of a person solely in terms of memory is impossible and, second, that when we are considering the case of flesh-and-blood persons there seems no alternative but to conclude that bodily continuity is a necessary condition of personal identity. These conclusions by themselves do not show that no substitute for bodily continuity could be invented when discussing the case of disembodied personality. But some substitute for it would have to be supplied by invention, and until it is, the notion of disembodied personal identity makes no sense.

The main line of argument is now plain, but for greater completeness it may be desirable to apply it to the doctrine of disembodied survival in a little more detail. An adherent of this doctrine, anxious to avoid admitting the necessity of the bodily criterion of personal identity, might perhaps claim that a survivor of death would intelligibly be said to be identical with someone who had died, because he remembered the actions and experiences of that person. And he might be said intelligibly to persist through time in his disembodied state because later and earlier experiences in the afterlife could be similarly connected by memories.

Let us take the latter suggestion first. It is that the disembodied person who has some experience at some future time FT_2 will be identical with the disembodied person who will have had some experience at an earlier future time FT_1 if, along with the experience at FT_2, there is a memory of the one he had at FT_1. The difficulty is to make sense not only of a phrase like "along with the experience there is a memory," but also, of what it

10. On this topic see Antony Flew, "Locke and the Problem of Personal Identity," *Philosophy*, 26 (1951), 53–68, and Sydney Shoemaker, "Personal Identity and Memory," *Journal of Philosophy*, 56 (1959), 868–882.

means to speak of a memory here at all. For it will have to be a memory in sense (ii). And to say that the disembodied person has a memory at FT_2 in sense (ii) of some experience had at FT_1 is to assume that the two experiences will have been had by the same person; and this time, since we have no bodily criterion of identity to fall back on, we have no way of interpreting this claim.

If we turn now to the problem of identifying the disembodied person with some person who has died, we find the same difficulty. To say that he can be so identified because he remembers the deeds or experiences of that person is once again to use the notion of remembering in sense (ii). But to do this is to presuppose that we understand what it is for the remembering to be identical with the person who did those deeds or had those experiences. And we do not actually understand this. For although the person who did those deeds had a body, the rememberer, by hypothesis, does not have one and therefore cannot have the same body. It does not seem possible, therefore, to find any answer to the problem of self-identity for disembodied persons.

What about the doctrine of the resurrection of the body? Given that we are talking of the future existence of persons with bodies, the notion of their lasting through time in their future state does not seem to present any logical difficulties. But what of their identity with ourselves? If we assume some one-to-one correspondence between the inhabitants of the next world and of this (that is, assume at least that the inhabitants of the next world each resemble, claim to be, and claim to remember the doings of inhabitants of this one), it might seem foolish to deny that they will be identical with ourselves. But foolishness is not logical absurdity. It is conceivable that there might be a future existence in which there were large numbers of persons each resembling one of us and having uncanny knowledge of our pasts. And if that world does come to be in the future, we shall not be in it. What would make it a world with us in it, rather than a world with duplicates of us in it and not ourselves? Unless we can give a clear answer to this, it seems, very paradoxically, to be a matter of arbitrary choice whether to say these future people are us or not.

Surely, the answer might run, they will have the same bodies that we now have. But this is precisely what is not obvious. Apart from questions about whether the future bodies are like ours in youth, maturity, or old age, the dissolution of the earthly body means that the future body will be in some sense new. To say that it is the old one re-created is merely to say it is the same one without giving any reason for saying it is identical with the original body rather than one very much like it. To answer this way, then, seems merely to face the same puzzle again. To say that the future beings will remember in sense (ii) our doings and feelings is to raise the same questions here as before. The only possible solution seems to be to insist that in spite of the time gap between the death of the old body and the appearance of the new one, something persists in between. But what? The person disembodied? If so, then the doctrine of the resurrection of the body does not avoid the difficulties that beset the doctrine of disembodied survival, for the simple reason that it falls back upon that very doctrine when its own implications are understood.

This argument does not show that the doctrine of the resurrection of the body is absurd in the way in which the doctrine of disembodied survival is. It shows rather that the doctrine of resurrection is merely one way, and a question-begging way, of describing a set of circumstances that can be described equally well in another fashion. Yet the difference between the two alternative descriptions is a vital one. For it comes to no less than the original question, namely, do we survive? It is a question that the doctrine provides an answer to but one that seems to have no conclusive grounds, even if the circumstances envisaged in the doctrine were admitted to be forthcoming.

The belief in survival, then, at least in this version, does not run into insuperable difficulties of logic. But it does not seem possible to describe a set of future circumstances that will unambiguously show it to be true. I have previously argued[11] that if the doctrine is agreed to be coherent, it can offer a suitable answer to the difficulties about the verification of religious beliefs. I do not consider the present puzzle to show that it is not coherent. But it does show its status to be very baffling.

11. [In ch. 11 of the book from which this selection is taken—Eds.]

The Life Everlasting
and the
Bodily Criterion of Identity

GEORGE I. MAVRODES

"I believe in . . . the resurrection of the body and the life everlasting. Amen." With these words the Apostle's Creed comes to a close, and with them also it expresses, I think, an important element in the orthodox Christian faith. As a very minimum this element involves the claim that the lives of at least some human beings do not come to a permanent end with their bodily deaths here, but that these individuals will either continue their lives beyond the incident of death or else that they will resume their lives at some point in the future, and that this continued or resumed life will be everlasting. An additional element seems to be the claim that this continued or resumed life will be a bodily life, and that it involves the resurrection—presumably somehow or other a reconstitution—of the body which died here.

Naturally, one might think of critical questions to ask about this belief, such as that of what reason or justification might be given in favor of supposing that it is true, or that of how such an apparently difficult operation might be accomplished. I think that Christians have usually been inclined to answer the former of these questions by saying that one knows of such things primarily by the revelation of God. And they usually have not thought of much of interest to say about the second question beyond saying that the resurrection of the body and the life everlasting are gifts of God, who is presumably able to do such things. In this paper I do not intend to pursue these questions at all, and so I will say nothing either in support or in criticism of such answers.

Reprinted by permission of the author and of the editor of NOÛS from Vol. XI, 1 (1977):27–39. The format of the references has been altered for convenience.

I turn, instead, to a somewhat different question, one which some philosophers apparently think is somehow prior to the questions I have just mentioned. This is the question of what, if any, sense can be made out of the identification of the persons who live the life everlasting with persons who began their careers in this world and died here. Some philosophers not only think that this question is prior to the others I have just mentioned—they apparently think it is the only philosophical question about immortality and similar topics. John Passmore, for example, writes, "As for immortality, there have often been doubts about whether this is really a question for philosophy. But insofar as it is, the question is whether it is possible to identify the being who is said to live after death with the living being by any of the ordinary means used in identification—that is, the means by which we determine whether we are both talking about the same person."[1]

Antony Flew asserts both the priority and the enormity of the difficulty involved in this question. He writes, "Any reconstitution doctrine is confronted with the question 'How is the reconstituted person on the last day to be identified as the original me, as opposed to a mere replica, an appropriately brilliant forgery?' There seems to be no satisfactory answer to this question, at least for a pure reconstitution theory. This question is, however, logically prior to all questions about the reasons, if any, that might be brought forward in support of such a doctrine.

"This decisive objection seems rarely to have been raised, and when it has been, its force has not usually been felt. . . . Notwithstanding the form of the original question, the difficulty is not one of 'How do you know?' but of 'What do you know?' The objection is that the reconstituted people could only be mere replicas of and surrogates for their earthly predecessors. Neither the appeal to the cognitive and executive resources of Omnipotence nor the appeal to the supposed special status of the person in question does anything at all to meet this contention."[2]

In a somewhat similar spirit, but with a different twist, Terence Penelhum argues that if there is a temporal gap between the death of a person and the appearance of an apparently resurrected person much like him, then it is open to us to *decide*, whichever way we want, whether to consider these to be just one person or two distinct persons. If I understand him correctly, he means to claim that, since ordinary bodily continuity has been broken, the claim that the new person is identical with the old one is neither true nor false *prior to our decision about how to speak of it*. And after our decision it will have whatever value our decision has ascribed to it. So he writes that in ordinary, this-worldly, cases of the identification of

1. John Passmore, "Philosophy," in *The Encyclopedia of Philosophy*, edited by Paul Edwards (New York: Macmillan Publishing Co. & The Free Press), Vol. 6, p. 223.
2. Antony Flew, "Immortality," in *The Encyclopedia of Philosophy*, Vol. 4, p. 140.

persons, even after comas, failures of memory, etc., "there are bodily facts which establish who it is. The absence of those facts, though perhaps . . . not a fatal barrier to identification on memory-claims alone, certainly renders it optional. With the gap between the death of the one body and the appearance of the resurrection-body all necessity for saying Smith's successor is Smith disappears, however possible it is. And it does not seem that Smith *need* concern himself with being his own successor unless that successor *has* to be identified with Smith. And without the continuity of the body, the identification does not *have* to be performed. The critical difference between a person's looking forward to his own resurrected future and his predicting the future existence of a being like himself seems to depend on a decision which can, in default of bodily continuance, be taken equally well one way or the other."[3]

If we were to put the objection we are here considering in its bluntest form it would come to something like this: We can know from the outset, and before we get into questions and claims about revelation, omnipotence, and the like, that the beliefs to which I referred in the first paragraph of this paper are false. Not even the omnipotence of God can bring about the state of affairs envisioned in those beliefs. For that state of affairs is conceptually impossible. That is a blunt statement of the position but it is perhaps not exactly accurate. More accurately, this position holds that there is a conceptual incompatibility between the state of affairs envisioned in his belief and some empirical facts about this world, facts which we know to be plainly true. While therefore it is abstractly possible that an omnipotent God could actualize the state of affairs in question, it is not possible for him to do so *given what actually happens in the world.* And it may also be held that it is now too late for God to alter the course of this world in such a way as to make possible the life of the world to come, at least in a way which would be importantly relevant to these Christian beliefs.

The conceptual incompatibility alleged here is supposed to be generated by a criterion of personal identity. As I understand it, the person who urges such an incompatibility need not deny that there may be a "world to come," perhaps a better world than this one, nor that there may be human beings in it living an everlasting life. What he denies is that any of those fortunate people could be identical with any person who has lived and died in this world, or at least with any person who has died in this world some considerable time ago. This sort of objector—I will call him the Criterial Sceptic—holds that in order for the person in the world to come to be identical with a person who has died in this world they, or he, would have to satisfy a criterion of identity. They, or he, would have to have the

3. Terence Penelhum, *Survival and Disembodied Existence* (New York: Humanities Press, 1970), pp. 96–7. [See also Penelhum's article in this volume, especially pp. 197–98—Eds.]

very same body. But we know perfectly well that the bodies of many of those to whom this doctrine is supposed to apply have already decayed and passed out of existence. So no person in the world to come could have *that* body. And so no person in the world to come could be identical with that long-dead resident of this world.

At this juncture we might formulate the relevant aspect of the bodily criterion of identity as follows:

> (1) For any x and y, x is the same person (human being) as y only if x has the same body as y.

More accurately, we should say that either (1) is the bodily criterion, or that it is a (conjunctive) part of that criterion, or that the criterion entails (1). The latter claim is the minimum which is acceptable for this position. For unless the criterion at least entails (1) it will not serve to rule out the possibility that some person who lived and died in this world is identical with a person who will live again in the world to come.

The objection which is based on this criterion, if it holds good, cuts to the heart of the beliefs in question. For the Christian does not merely hold that there shall be people living a blessed life in the world to come, nor even that such people will in some way or other be very much like some people who have lived here. He believes that it is these very people themselves, the people who have begun their careers in this world and here suffered the agony of death, who will share that blessed life. And when he believes in or hopes for that destiny for himself it is indeed *for himself*. He hopes that it shall be *he,* and not another, who will "attain unto the resurrection of the dead." If, therefore, the Criterial Sceptic should be right, then a major element in what the last sentence of the creed expresses will be false, and the Christian faith will be severely impoverished. In this paper I want to examine some aspects of the position which the Criterial Sceptic holds.

Let us begin by considering a state of affairs which only partially represents what the Christian believes, and which seems to differ from that belief in one, perhaps important, respect. This state of affairs is described as

> (2) At a certain time there exists in this world a person, x, who has a body, A, and the life of this person extends through time t_1. At some future time, perhaps in the world to come, there exists a person, y, with a body, B, and the life of this person extends through t_2. *And A is in no sense the same body as B.*

And suppose too that

> (3) It is claimed that x is the same person as y.

Now, the claim referred to in (3) may be puzzling to some of us. Perhaps this puzzlement will be expressed in questions to the one who makes the claim, questions such as "What do you mean by claiming that y is the same person as x?" or "What is it that makes y the same person as x?" But the import of such questions may also be unclear and puzzling. The one who hears them may be at a loss to understand just what it is the questioner wants. And for that reason, or perhaps for some other, he may be at a loss as to just how to respond. So he may reply essentially by repeating the original claim, perhaps with extra emphasis. "They just *are* the same person, that's all! Or to put it another way, you've been calling that person in the world to come by the name 'y.' But it's old x, after all, and you shouldn't let the new name confuse you." Such a reply may seem singularly unilluminating, simply restating, as it does, the original claim. Perhaps we shall nevertheless have to make do with some such reply in the end. But at any rate we are not at that end yet.

A person, I said, might be at a loss as to how to explain his identity claim in this case. But perhaps not everyone will be at such a loss. Someone with philosophical inclinations might, for example, think of replying something like this. "When I say that y is identical with x I mean something which in conjunction with any true statement which predicates a given property of x will entail a true statement predicating that property of y. So, for example, if it is true that x was born in Biloxi, Mississippi, then my claim, in conjunction with that fact, entails that y was born in Biloxi, Mississippi." And perhaps this reply goes further than the previous one.

This reply probably reminds us of what is sometimes called "Leibniz' Law," and it is intended to do so. A first stab at formulating that law might go like this:

(4) For any entities x and y, x is identical with y IFF x has every property which y has, and vice versa.

As it stands, this has some difficulties. First, it may suggest, in conjunction with certain empirical facts, that I had no youth. For one of my properties is that of being gray-haired. But the only plausible candidate for Mavrodes-as-youth did not have gray hair. So perhaps this formulation entails that I am not identical with that candidate. This difficulty can be remedied. While it is true of me now that I have gray hair it is also true of me now that in 1950 I had brown hair. It is also true of the candidate for Mavrodes-as-youth that he had brown hair in 1950, and there is no empirical reason to think that it is not true of him that he has gray hair now. Probably if we want a version of Leibniz' Law which applies to diachronic, as well as synchronic, identity then we need to formulate it in terms of properties such as these.

Some properties are such that even if a given thing has them at some time it need not have them at every time at which it has any property at all (i.e., at any time at which it exists). Having brown hair is apparently such a property. Let us call these the "time-variable properties." There are other properties such that if an entity has one of them at some time then it has that property at all times that it has any properties at all. Call these the "time-stable properties." Now we can propound the thesis that to every property which a thing has at an arbitrarily chosen time, t, there corresponds a time-stable property which it has at all times. For take any arbitrarily chosen property, P, which the thing has at t. If P is time-stable then it is itself the corresponding property, and the thing will have P whenever it exists. If P is time-variable, then *having P at t* is the corresponding time-stable property which the thing will have as long as it exists. And if we want a version of Leibniz' Law which will apply to diachronic identity then we should formulate it in terms of time-stable properties only.

A second difficulty is that Leibniz' Law may not apply to what we may call "intensional" properties. Consider, for example, the property of *being thought by Porphyry to be a different heavenly body from the Morning Star*. Now, it seems possible that Porphyry thought that the Evening Star was a different heavenly body from the Morning Star. But it seems very unlikely that he thought that the Morning Star was a different heavenly body from the Morning Star. In conjunction with the stated version of Leibniz' Law this may suggest that the Morning Star is not identical with the Evening Star. I am not sure how this should be handled. Perhaps there is some correct analysis of intensional predicates which will show that the two statements about Porphyry's beliefs do necessarily have the same truth value after all. If so, well and good. If not, then I suppose that Leibniz' Law should be restricted to cover non-intensional predicates only. Since only non-intensional predicates function in the remainder of my discussion that is the procedure I adopt here.

The third difficulty grows out of a suggestion by Peter Geach.[4] He holds, if I understand him correctly, that expressions of the form "x and y are the same entity," "x is the same thing as y," etc., are ill-formed. The corresponding well-formed expression would be "x is the same s as y," where "s" is a variable ranging over sorts or kinds. So we should say that Samuel Clemens is the same *person* as Mark Twain, that the Evening Star is the same *planet* as the Morning Star, and so on. I do not know whether Geach's view of this matter is correct, or, if it is, just how Leibniz' Law might be amended to take it into account. Assuming that his view is correct, however, the following conjecture seems to me to have a good bit of plausibility. We begin by observing that to any property which a thing

4. Peter Geach, "Identity," *The Review of Metaphysics* 21(1967): 3–12.

has, and for any sort to which that thing belongs, there corresponds a property which that thing has and which can be possessed only by a thing of that sort. For consider any arbitrarily chosen property, P, which a certain thing has, and any arbitrarily chosen sort, S, to which that thing belongs. Then that thing will have the property of *being an S which has P,* and this is a property which only S can have. Call such properties in general "sort-bound properties," and call properties which are bound to a given sort, S, "S-bound properties." Then Leibniz' Law can be reformulated in terms of being the same thing-of-a-sort and in terms of sort-bound properties.

Taking these difficulties and possible difficulties into account, a more cautious formulation of Leibniz' Law might be

(5) For any x, y, and z, where x and y are individuals and z is a sort or kind, x is the same z as y IFF x has every time-stable, non-intensional, z-bound property which y has, and vice versa.

And now a person who is inclined to accept the claim in (3) may say that x and y satisfy the right hand part of (5) (where the sort in question is that of human being), and that is the explanation which he can give of the claim that they are the same person. I will call a person who responds in this way a "Leibnizian Believer."

The Criterial Sceptic, however, will deny that x and y can be the same person, and so he will deny the claim in (3). He denies this because he holds that the criterion for any x and y being the same human person is that they have the same body. But in description (2) it is stipulated that the bodies A and B, which belong to x and y, are in no sense the same body. (This, of course, is the respect in which this situation differs from the one which the Christian expects to be actualized.) Because their bodies are not identical, says the Criterial Sceptic, the x and y referred to in (2) cannot be the same person.

It may be important to notice here that the Leibnizian Believer can maintain that in a certain sense x and y do have the same body after all, despite the explicit disclaimer in (2). In fact, his Leibnizian position requires him to claim that x and y have the same *two* bodies. He must hold that since it is true of x that he has body A at t_1 then it must also be true of y that he has body A at t_1. And in the same way it must be true of both x and y that he has body B at t_2. What the Leibnizian Believer does here, of course, is to admit—indeed, to insist—that x and y have the same body at *any given time.* This is just one of the many time-stable properties which they share. The Criterial Sceptic must also insist that if x and y are to be identical then they must have the same body at any given time. But he cannot be satisfied to leave it at that, for, if he were so satisfied, he would have no reason to reject the claim put forward in (3). He must insist that if x and y are to be identical then if x has a certain body at some time then

y has that very same body at every time at which y exists. And that is a requirement which the situation described in (2) does not satisfy.

What options do these disputants have? Assuming that they restrict
themselves to the situation envisioned in (2), the Leibnizian Believer who
accepts the claim in (3) seems compelled to reject the bodily Criterion of
identity. The Criterial Sceptic, on the other hand, seems to have two options as he rejects the claim in (3). He might just reject Leibniz' Law and
be done with it. But he could also do something else. He could accept
Leibniz' Law and then go on to point out that, on his view, the property
of *having body* α is a time-stable property (or, at least, that *being a human
being who has body* α is a time-stable property). For if this is so then it is
not hard to show that there is a time-stable property which either x or y
must have if they are to be identical but which they cannot both have if
the description in (2) is to be satisfied. So, on this interpretation, even
Leibniz' Law will show that x and y are not identical. So perhaps the
Criterial Sceptic has the more flexible position.

But perhaps, too, we were too hasty in thinking that the Leibnizian
Believer has only one option. Inspired by the versatility of his opponent
why should he not say that he, in his turn, can accept the bodily criterion
of identity. Only, he will insist, the phrase "has the same body" must be
interpreted to mean "has the same body at any particular time t." Interpreted in that way the bodily criterion of identity is perfectly compatible
with the x and y described in (2) being the same person. If the Criterial
Sceptic is to reject the claim in (3) then he must reject this interpretation
of his criterion. He must insist that (1) be read as

(6) For any x and y, x is the same person as y only if x has, at every
time at which x exists, the same body which y has at any time at
which y exists.

And so the Criterial Sceptic needs a sense of "same" (in the phrase "same
body") which is diachronic.

So much, then, for the discussion of the situation envisioned in (2).
Many Christians, at least, will think that it is not a crucial case nor the
strongest case. For they profess to believe in the resurrection of the body,
the body which ran through its career in this world and then died, and not
merely in the production of a new body for the world to come. So they believe that if y, in the world to come, is identical with some this-worldly x,
then the body which y has in that world to come *is,* in some sense, the
same body which x had in this world. Does this improve their position
vis à vis the Criterial Sceptic?

Such a sceptic, I think, is likely to say that the believer's position is not
thereby strengthened, at least not with respect to many of those who are
supposed to share in the life everlasting. For as a matter of fact they have

already died, long ago, and their bodies have already decayed and totally ceased from existing. And so it is not possible that there should be a body, now or in the future, which is identical with the one they had during their earthly career. But why should this last consequence be thought to follow upon the former undisputed facts? Why should it be impossible that a certain body should perish, decay, and cease from existing, and then that later on that same body should be resurrected and take its place again in the realm of existing things?

The Sceptic will not be embarrassed by these questions, and will take them as a welcome opportunity to clarify further his sense of the diachronic identity of bodies. He has a criterion for such identity. The relevant part of it is as follows:

(7) For any x and y, x is the same body as y only if x is spatio-temporally continuous with y.

But if a body has decayed and ceased to exist by t_1 then there is a time immediately after t_1 during which it does not exist. If it were to be resurrected and brought again into existence at some later time, t_2, then it would suffer from a temporal gap between t_1 and t_2. The body which existed at t_2 would not be spatio-temporally continuous with the body which existed before t_1. And so, according to (7), they could not be identical.

Now, a Leibnizian Believer who accepts the resurrection of the body might simply challenge (7) at this point. And perhaps that is what he should do in the end. At this point, however, it might be useful to accept (7) provisionally, and to request some further account of it. After all, if there are criteria for identity for persons and for bodies, should there not also be a criterion for spatio-temporal continuity? And what is spatio-temporal continuity anyway? Is not this a technical notion much less familiar to us than the notions of person and body? If, as the sceptic seems to suggest, a whole host of believers have been mistaken and confused over what these familiar notions allow as possible should we not be even more wary of supposing that we can handle correctly this technical and unfamiliar notion? What more can be said to guide us?

Here again the sceptic will probably not be embarrassed. Whether it is a criterion or not, he will offer us a further explanation of what he is getting at. Informally, the idea seems to be something like this: Body x occupies some set of spatio-temporal points, and body y similarly occupies a set of points. These sets of points may be isolated from each other in the following sense. It may be that every continuous path through space and time from any point in the first set to any point in the second set passes through some spatio-temporal location in which there is no body at all. And if the locations of x and y are isolated from each other in that way then x and y are not spatio-temporally continuous. I put this here as only a necessary condition for spatio-temporal continuity, and not a sufficient condition. For there may possibly be other necessary conditions. It may, for example, be necessary that the bodies which "bridge the gap" between x and y be of a certain sort if x and y are to be continuous. But those further conditions, if there are any, are irrelevant to my argument here.

Perhaps we could state this necessary condition more formally as follows:

(8) For any x and y, if x and y are bodies, then x is spatio-temporally continuous with y if and only if there is a spatio-temporal point, ST_1, at which x is located, and a point, ST_2, at which y is located, and there is a compact series of points including ST_1 and ST_2 such that there is a body located at every point in this series.

Well, perhaps so. This explanation does not seem to have escaped from technicality, but maybe if we work through it carefully it will be clear enough. Except for one point. Or perhaps even that is clear enough. At any rate it is this. The expression "ST_1" appears twice in the formula above. What is the relation between the point referred to in its first occurrence and that referred to in its second occurrence?

But of course the answer is obvious, isn't it? These two uses of "ST_1" refer to the same point. Of course they do. But this answer, though obvious, is crucial. For if we allow these two uses to refer to two different points then (8) will not rule out the claim that the resurrection body is spatio-temporally continuous with some long perished earthly body. So it would seem that the sceptic cannot afford to abandon this answer. And this reply invites us to ask about the criterion of identity for spatio-temporal points. This question bodes more embarrassment for the sceptic than did the earlier ones.

It may be important to notice here that we cannot avoid this question merely by stylistic changes which eliminate the word "same" from the answer, or which eliminate the double use of "ST_1" in (8). I suppose that we can make such changes. (We can, for that matter, restate the Christian hope of enjoying the life everlasting so that it does not require the word "same.") These words are not crucial, but the fact which lies behind them is. If (8) is to be applicable to the diachronic identity of bodies then we must say two things about a single point. We must state its relation to the body in question and we must state its relation to another point. And in doing this we must understand that we are saying these two things about the very same point. And so, it would seem, we must understand what it is for something to be "the very same point."

Here, I think, the line of inquiry which we have been following begins to draw to a close. For it is hard to think of a criterion of identity for spatio-temporal points which will be attractive to the Criterial Sceptic. What seem to be the options? Well, I suppose that a feeble step forward might be taken by saying that x and y are the same point if and only if they have the same spatio-temporal coordinates. But of course the question will be asked again, and the sceptic will be wedged even more tightly in the constricting corner. Or the sceptic may simply opt for a Leibnizian account of sameness here. But surely the believer will seize on this to justify his reliance on Leibniz' Law from the beginning. If, after all, even the sceptic comes to nothing better than this is in the end. . . .

On the other hand, the sceptic may here formulate a criterion which does not depend on bodies, times and spaces, but which makes use of some other notions. I do not know what such a criterion might be. But any such attempt seems likely to give aid and comfort to the believer. For if there is such a criterion for points, and if the identity of bodies depends in the end upon such a criterion, then why should there not also be a non-spatio-temporal, non-physical criterion for persons too, thus avoiding all the difficulties which the Criterial Sceptic has raised? Or, finally, the sceptic may simply say that no criterion is available here, nor is any needed. Spatio-temporal points, he might say, are "criterially primitive." We understand what is meant by "same" here without the use of criteria. Point x just is the same as y, and there is no more to be said about it. I suspect that this is correct. But correct or not, will it not almost surely incite the believer to reply that we understand "same person" at least as well as "same spatio-temporal point"? And if we understand the one without criteria then why should we not also understand the other in the same way? It looks suddenly as though whatever the sceptic says opens up a plausible position for the believer to occupy.

This concludes the body of my argument. In some sense, I have not solved the problem posed by people such as Flew, Passmore, and Penelhum. I have not shown that the resurrection body satisfies the continuity criterion for identity with the this-worldly body, and hence I have not shown that the resurrected person satisfies the bodily identity criterion for identity with some pre-mortem person. What I have argued, essentially, is that the problem cannot have the gravity which philosophers such as these are inclined to assign to it. Either it must be much more serious, infecting all of our ordinary judgments about the identity of this-worldly persons with the incoherence or arbitrariness which they ascribe to resurrection judgments, or it is less serious, having, in all likelihood, the same sort of solution which validates our ordinary judgments. In the first case the Christian's faith, though perhaps rather bad off, would not be worse off than the more prosaic faith of his non-religious colleagues, and he and they could survey the dismal logical prospects together. In the second case, too, the Christian's faith would seem to be no worse off than that of his secular counterparts. But in the second case the prospects, or some of them at least, are more cheerful. The believer might even invite his counterpart to consider some of them with him. But who knows whether that is philosophy?

PART III

FAITH, RATIONALITY, AND WORLD RELIGIONS

Kierkegaard's Arguments Against Objective Reasoning in Religion

ROBERT MERRIHEW ADAMS

It is sometimes held that there is something in the nature of religious faith itself that renders it useless or undesirable to reason objectively in support of such faith, even if the reasoning should happen to have considerable plausibility. Søren Kierkegaard's *Concluding Unscientific Postscript* is probably the document most commonly cited as representative of this view. In the present essay I shall discuss three arguments for the view. I call them the Approximation Argument, the Postponement Argument, and the Passion Argument; and I suggest they can all be found in the *Post-script*. I shall try to show that the Approximation Argument is a bad argument. The other two will not be so easily disposed of, however. I believe they show that Kierkegaard's conclusion, or something like it, does indeed follow from a certain conception of religiousness—a conception which has some appeal, although for reasons which I shall briefly suggest, I am not prepared to accept it.

Kierkegaard uses the word "objective" and its cognates in several senses, most of which need not concern us here. We are interested in the sense in which he uses it when he says, "it is precisely a misunderstanding to seek an objective assurance," and when he speaks of "an objective uncertainty held fast in the appropriation-process of the most passionate inwardness" (pp. 41, 182).[1] Let us say that a piece of reasoning, R, is *objective reason-*

1. Søren Kierkegaard, *Concluding Unscientific Postscript*, translated by David F. Swenson; introduction, notes, and completion of translation by Walter Lowrie (Princeton: Princeton University Press, 1941). Page references in parentheses in the body of the present paper are to this work.

Reprinted from *The Monist*, Vol. 60, No. 2, 1977, with the permission of the author and the publisher.

ing just in case every (or almost every) intelligent, fair-minded, and sufficiently informed person would regard *R* as showing or tending to show (in the circumstances in which *R* is used, and to the extent claimed in *R*) that *R*'s conclusion is true or probably true. Uses of "objective" and "objectively" in other contexts can be understood from their relation to this one; for example, an objective uncertainty is a proposition which cannot be shown by objective reasoning to be certainly true.

1. THE APPROXIMATION ARGUMENT

"Is it possible to base an eternal happiness upon historical knowledge?" is one of the central questions in the *Postscript,* and in the *Philosophical Fragments* to which it is a "postscript." Part of Kierkegaard's answer to the question is that it is not possible to base an eternal happiness on objective reasoning about historical facts.

> For nothing is more readily evident than that the greatest attainable certainty with respect to anything historical is merely an *approximation.* And an approximation, when viewed as a basis for an eternal happiness, is wholly inadequate, since the incommensurability makes a result impossible. [p. 25]

Kierkegaard maintains that it is possible, however, to base an eternal happiness on a belief in historical facts that is independent of objective evidence for them, and that that is what one must do in order to be a Christian. This is the Approximation Argument for the proposition that Christian faith cannot be based on objective reasoning.[2] (It is assumed that some belief about historical facts is an essential part of Christian faith, so that if religious faith cannot be based on objective historical reasoning, then Christian faith cannot be based on objective reasoning at all.) Let us examine the argument in detail.

Its first premise is Kierkegaard's claim that "the greatest attainable certainty with respect to anything historical is merely an approximation." I take him to mean that historical evidence, objectively considered, never completely excludes the possibility of error. "It goes without saying," he claims, "that it is impossible in the case of historical problems to reach an objective decision so certain that no doubt could disturb it" (p. 41). For

2. The argument is not original with Kierkegaard. It can be found in works of G. E. Lessing and D. F. Strauss that Kierkegaard had read. See especially Thulstrup's quotation and discussion of a passage from Strauss in the commentary portion of Søren Kierkegaard, *Philosophical Fragments,* translated by David F. Swenson, second edition, translation revised by Howard V. Hong, with introduction and commentary by Niels Thulstrup (Princeton: Princeton University Press, 1962), pp. 149–51.

Kierkegaard's purposes it does not matter how small the possibility of error is, so long as it is finitely small (that is, so long as it is not literally infinitesimal). He insists (p. 31) that his Approximation Argument makes no appeal to the supposition that the objective evidence for Christian historical beliefs is weaker than the objective evidence for any other historical belief. The argument turns on a claim about *all* historical evidence. The probability of error in our belief that there was an American Civil War in the nineteenth century, for instance, might be as small as $10^{\frac{1}{2,000,000}}$; that would be a large enough chance of error for Kierkegaard's argument.

It might be disputed, but let us assume for the sake of argument that there is some such finitely small probability of error in the objective grounds for all historical beliefs, as Kierkegaard held. This need not keep us from saying that we "know," and it is "certain," that there was an American Civil War. For such an absurdly small possibility of error is as good as no possibility of error at all, "for all practical intents and purposes," as we might say. Such a possibility of error is too small to be worth worrying about.

But would it be too small to be worth worrying about if we had an *infinite* passionate interest in the question about the Civil War? If we have an infinite passionate interest in something, there is no limit to how important it is to us. (The nature of such an interest will be discussed more fully in section 3 below.) Kierkegaard maintains that in relation to an infinite passionate interest *no* possibility of error is too small to be worth worrying about. "In relation to an eternal happiness, and an infinite passionate interest in its behalf (in which latter alone the former can exist), an iota is of importance, of infinite importance . . ." (p. 28). This is the basis for the second premise of the Approximation Argument, which is Kierkegaard's claim that "an approximation, when viewed as a basis for an eternal happiness, is wholly inadequate" (p. 25). "An approximation is essentially incommensurable with an infinite personal interest in an eternal happiness" (p. 26).

At this point in the argument it is important to have some understanding of Kierkegaard's conception of faith, and the way in which he thinks faith excludes doubt. Faith must be decisive; in fact it seems to consist in a sort of decision-making. "The conclusion of belief is not so much a conclusion as a resolution, and it is for this reason that belief excludes doubt."[3] The decision of faith is a decision to disregard the possibility of error—to act on what is believed, without hedging one's bets to take account of any possibility of error.

To disregard the possibility of error is not to be unaware of it, or fail to

3. Kierkegaard, *Philosophical Fragments*, p. 104; cf. pp. 102–03.

consider it, or lack anxiety about it. Kierkegaard insists that the believer must be keenly *aware* of the risk of error. "If I wish to preserve myself in faith I must constantly be intent upon holding fast the objective uncertainty, so as to remain out upon the deep, over seventy thousand fathoms of water, still preserving my faith" (p. 182).

For Kierkegaard, then, to ask whether faith in a historical fact can be based on objective reasoning is to ask whether objective reasoning can justify one in disregarding the possibility of error which (he thinks) historical evidence always leaves. Here another aspect of Kierkegaard's conception of faith plays its part in the argument. He thinks that in all genuine religious faith the believer is *infinitely* interested in the object of his faith. And he thinks it follows that objective reasoning cannot justify him in disregarding *any* possibility of error about the object of faith, and therefore cannot lead him all the way to religious faith where a historical fact is concerned. The farthest it could lead him is to the conclusion that *if* he had only a certain finite (though very great) interest in the matter, the possibility of error would be too small to be worth worrying about and he would be justified in disregarding it. But faith disregards a possibility of error that *is* worth worrying about, since an infinite interest is involved. Thus faith requires a "leap" beyond the evidence, a leap that cannot be justified by objective reasoning (cf. p. 90).

There is something right in what Kierkegaard is saying here, but his Approximation Argument is a bad argument. He is right in holding that grounds of doubt which may be insignificant for most practical purposes can be extremely troubling for the intensity of a religious concern, and that it may require great decisiveness, or something like courage, to overcome them religiously. But he is mistaken in holding that objective reasoning could not justify one in disregarding any possibility of error about something in which one is infinitely interested.

The mistake, I believe, lies in his overlooking the fact that there are at least two different reasons one might have for disregarding a possibility of error. The first is that the possibility is too small to be worth worrying about. The second is that the risk of not disregarding the possibility of error would be greater than the risk of disregarding it. Of these two reasons only the first is ruled out by the infinite passionate interest.

I will illustrate this point with two examples, one secular and one religious. A certain woman has a very great (though not infinite) interest in her husband's love for her. She rightly judges that the objective evidence available to her renders it 99.9 per cent probable that he loves her truly. The intensity of her interest is sufficient to cause her some *anxiety* over the remaining 1/1,000 chance that he loves her not; for her this chance is not too small to be worth worrying about. (Kierkegaard uses a similar example to support his Approximation Argument; see p. 511.) But she (very reasonably) wants to *disregard* the risk of error, in the sense of not hedging her bets, if he does love her. This desire is at least as strong as her desire not to be deceived if he does not love her. Objective reasoning should therefore suffice to bring her to the conclusion that she ought to disregard the risk of error, since by not disregarding it she would run 999 times as great risk of frustrating one of these desires.

Or suppose you are trying to base your eternal happiness on your relation to Jesus, and therefore have an infinite passionate interest in the question whether he declared Peter and his episcopal successors to be infallible in matters of religious doctrine. You want to be committed to whichever is the true belief on this question, disregarding any possibility of error in it. And suppose, just for the sake of argument, that objective historical evidence renders it 99 per cent probable that Jesus did declare Peter and his successors to be infallible—or 99 per cent probable that he did not—for our present discussion it does not matter which. The one per cent chance of error is enough to make you *anxious*, in view of your infinite interest. But objective reasoning leads to the conclusion that you ought to commit yourself to the more probable opinion, *disregarding* the risk of error, if your strongest desire in the matter is to be so committed to the true opinion. For the only other way to satisfy this desire would be to commit yourself to the less probable opinion, disregarding the risk of error in it. The first way will be successful if and only if the more probable opinion is true, and the second way if and only if the less probable opinion is true. Surely it is prudent to do what gives you a 99 per cent chance of satisfying your strong desire, in preference to what gives you only a one per cent chance of satisfying it.

In this argument your strong desire to be committed to the true opinion is presupposed. The reasonableness of this desire may depend on a belief for which no probability can be established by purely historical reasoning, such as the belief that Jesus is God. But any difficulties arising from this point are distinct from those urged in the Approximation Argument, which itself presupposes the infinite passionate interest in the historical question.

There is some resemblance between my arguments in these examples and Pascal's famous Wager argument. But whereas Pascal's argument turns on weighing an infinite interest against a finite one, mine turn on weighing a large chance of success against a small one. An argument closer to Pascal's will be discussed in section 4 below.

The reader may well have noticed in the foregoing discussion some unclarity about what sort of justification is being demanded and given for religious beliefs about historical facts. There are at least two different types of question about a proposition which I might try to settle by objective reasoning: (1) Is it probable that the proposition is true? (2) In view of the evidence which I have for and against the proposition, and my interest in the matter, is it prudent for me to have faith in the truth of the proposition, disregarding the possibility of error? Correspondingly, we may distinguish two ways in which a belief can be *based on* objective reasoning. The proposition believed may be the conclusion of a piece of objective reasoning, and accepted because it is that. We may say that such a -belief is *objectively probable*. Or one might hold a belief or maintain a religious faith because of a piece of objective reasoning whose conclusion is that it would be prudent, morally right, or otherwise desirable for one to hold that belief or faith. In this latter case let us say that the belief is *objectively advantageous*. It is clear that historical beliefs can be objectively probable; and in the Approximation Argument, Kierkegaard does not deny Christian historical beliefs can be objectively probable. His thesis is, in effect, that in view of an infinite passionate interest in their subject matter, they cannot be objectively advantageous, and therefore cannot be fully justified objectively, even if they are objectively probable. It is this thesis that I have attempted to refute. I have not been discussing the question whether Christian historical beliefs are objectively probable.

2. THE POSTPONEMENT ARGUMENT

The trouble with objective historical reasoning, according to the Approximation Argument, is that it cannot yield complete certainty. But that is not Kierkegaard's only complaint against it as a basis for religious faith. He also objects that objective historical inquiry is never completely finished, so that one who seeks to base his faith on it postpones his religious commitment forever. In the process of historical research "new difficulties arise and are overcome, and new difficulties again arise. Each generation inherits from its predecessor the illusion that the method is quite impeccable, but the learned scholars have not yet succeeded . . . and so forth. . . . The infinite personal passionate interest of the subject . . . vanishes more and more, because the decision is postponed, and postponed as following directly upon the result of the learned inquiry" (p. 28). As soon as we take "an historical document" as "our standard for the determination of Christian truth," we are "involved in a parenthesis whose conclusion is everlastingly prospective" (p. 28)—that is, we are involved in a religious digression which keeps religious commitment forever in the future.[4]

Kierkegaard has such fears about allowing religious faith to rest on *any*

4. Essentially the same argument can be found in a plea, which has had great influence among more recent theologians, for making Christian faith independent of the results of critical historical study of the Bible: Martin Kähler's famous lecture, first delivered in 1892, *Der sogenannte historische Jesus und der geschichtliche biblische Christus* (München: Christus Kaiser Verlag, 1961), p. 50f.

empirical reasoning. The danger of postponement of commitment arises not only from the uncertainties of historical scholarship, but also in connection with the design argument for God's existence. In the *Philosophical Fragments* Kierkegaard notes some objections to the attempt to prove God's existence from evidence of "the wisdom in nature, the goodness, the wisdom in the governance of the world," and then says, "even if I began I would never finish, and would in addition have to live constantly in suspense, lest something so terrible should suddenly happen that my bit of proof would be demolished."[5] What we have before us is a quite general sort of objection to the treatment of religious beliefs as empirically testable. On this point many analytical philosophers seem to agree with Kierkegaard. Much discussion in recent analytical philosophy of religion has proceeded from the supposition that religious beliefs are not empirically testable. I think it is far from obvious that that supposition is correct; and it is interesting to consider arguments that may be advanced to support it.

Kierkegaard's statements suggest an argument that I call the Postponement Argument. Its first premise is that one cannot have an authentic religious faith without being totally committed to it. In order to be totally committed to a belief, in the relevant sense, one must be determined not to abandon the belief under any circumstances that one recognizes as epistemically possible.

The second premise is that one cannot yet be totally committed to any belief which one bases on an inquiry in which one recognizes any possibility of a future need to revise the results. Total commitment to any belief so based will necessarily be postponed. I believe that this premise, suitably interpreted, is true. Consider the position of someone who regards himself as committed to a belief on the basis of objective evidence, but who recognizes some possibility that future discoveries will destroy the objective justification of the belief. We must ask how he is disposed to react in the event, however unlikely, that the objective basis of his belief is overthrown. Is he prepared to abandon the belief in that event? If so, he is not totally committed to the belief in the relevant sense. But if he is determined to cling to his belief even if its objective justification is taken away, then he is not basing the belief on the objective justification—or at least he is not basing it solely on the justification.[6]

The conclusion to be drawn from these two premises is that authentic religious faith cannot be based on an inquiry in which one recognizes any

5. Kierkegaard, *Philosophical Fragment*, p. 52.
6. Kierkegaard notes the possibility that in believing in God's existence "I make so bold as to defy all objections, even those that have not yet been made." But in that case he thinks the belief is not really based on the evidence of God's work in the world; "it is not from the works that I make my proof" (*Philosophical Fragments*, p. 52).

possibility of a future need to revise the results. We ought to note that this conclusion embodies two important restrictions on the scope of the argument.

In the first place, we are not given an argument that authentic religious faith cannot *have* an objective justification that is subject to possible future revision. What we are given is an argument that the authentic believer's holding of his religious belief cannot *depend* entirely on such a justification.

In the second place, this conclusion applies only to those who *recognize* some epistemic possibility that the objective results which appear to support their belief may be overturned. I think it would be unreasonable to require, as part of total commitment, a determination with regard to one's response to circumstances that one does not recognize as possible at all. It may be, however, that one does not recognize such a possibility when one ought to.

Kierkegaard needs one further premise in order to arrive at the conclusion that authentic religious faith cannot without error be based on any objective empirical reasoning. This third premise is that in every objective empirical inquiry there is always, objectively considered, some epistemic possibility that the results of the inquiry will need to be revised in view of new evidence or new reasoning. I believe Kierkegaard makes this assumption; he certainly makes it with regard to historical inquiry. From this premise it follows that one is in error if in any objective empirical inquiry one does not recognize any possibility of a future need to revise the results. But if one does recognize such a possibility, then according to the conclusion already reached in the Postponement Argument, one cannot base an authentic religious faith on the inquiry.

Some philosophers might attack the third premise of this argument; and certainly it is controversial. But I am more inclined to criticize the first premise. There is undoubtedly something plausible about the claim that authentic religious faith must involve a commitment so complete that the believer is resolved not to abandon his belief under any circumstances that he regards as epistemically possible. If you are willing to abandon your ostensibly religious beliefs for the sake of objective inquiry, mightn't we justly say that objective inquiry is your real religion, the thing to which you are most deeply committed?

There is also something plausible to be said on the other side, however. It has commonly been thought to be an important part of religious ethics that one ought to be humble, teachable, open to correction, new inspiration, and growth of insight, even (and perhaps especially) in important religious beliefs. That view would have to be discarded if we were to concede to Kierkegaard that the heart of commitment in religion is an unconditional determination not to change in one's important religious beliefs. In fact I think there is something radically wrong with this conception of religious commitment. Faith ought not to be thought of as unconditional devotion to a belief. For in the first place the object of religious devotion is not a belief or attitude of one's own, but God. And in the second place it may be doubted that religious devotion to God can or should be completely unconditional. God's love for sinners is sometimes said to be completely unconditional, not being based on any excellence or merit of theirs. But religious devotion to God is generally thought to be based on His goodness and love. It is the part of the strong, not the weak, to love unconditionally. And in relation to God we are weak.

3. THE PASSION ARGUMENT

In Kierkegaard's statements of the Approximation Argument and the Postponement Argument it is assumed that a system of religious beliefs might be objectively probable. It is only for the sake of argument, however, that Kierkegaard allows this assumption. He really holds that religious faith, by its very nature, needs objective *im*probability. "Anything that is almost probable, or probable, or extremely and emphatically probable, is something [one] can almost know, or as good as know, or extremely and emphatically almost *know*—but it is impossible to *believe*" (p. 189). Nor will Kierkegaard countenance the suggestion that religion ought to go beyond belief to some almost-knowledge based on probability. "Faith is the highest passion in a man. There are perhaps many in every generation who do not even reach it, but no one gets further."[7] It would be a betrayal of religion to try to go beyond faith. The suggestion that faith might be replaced by "probabilities and guarantees" is for the believer "a temptation to be resisted with all his strength" (p. 15). The attempt to establish religious beliefs on a foundation of objective probability is therefore no service to religion, but inimical to religion's true interests. The approximation to certainty which might be afforded by objective probability is rejected, not only for the reasons given in the Approximation Argument and Postponement Argument, but also from a deeper motive, "since on the contrary it behooves us to get rid of introductory guarantees of security, proofs from consequences, and the whole mob of public pawnbrokers and guarantors, so as to permit the absurd to stand out in all its clarity—in order that the individual may believe if he wills it; I merely say that it must be strenuous in the highest degree so to believe" (p. 190).

As this last quotation indicates, Kierkegaard thinks that religious belief ought to be based on a strenuous exertion of the will—a passionate striving. His reasons for thinking that objective probability is religiously undesirable have to do with the place of passion in religion, and constitute what I

7. Søren Kierkegaard, *Fear and Trembling,* trans. Walter Lowrie, 2d ed. (Princeton: Princeton University Press, 1970; published in one volume with *The Sickness unto Death*), p. 131. Cf. *Postscript,* p. 31f.

call the Passion Argument. The first premise of the argument is that the most essential and the most valuable feature of religiousness is passion, indeed an infinite passion, a passion of the greatest possible intensity. The second premise is that an infinite passion requires objective improbability. And the conclusion therefore is that that which is most essential and most valuable in religiousness requires objective improbability.

My discussion of this argument will have three parts. (a) First I will try to clarify, very briefly, what it is that is supposed to be objectively improbable. (b) Then we will consider Kierkegaard's reasons for holding that infinite passion requires objective improbability. In so doing we will also gain a clearer understanding of what a Kierkegaardian infinite passion is. (c) Finally I will discuss the first premise of the argument—although issues will arise at that point which I do not pretend to be able to settle by argument.

(a) What are the beliefs whose improbability is needed by religious passion? Kierkegaard will hardly be satisfied with the improbability of just any one belief; it must surely be at least an important belief. On the other hand it would clearly be preposterous to suppose that every belief involved in Christianity must be objectively improbable. (Consider, for example, the belief that the man Jesus did indeed live.) I think that what is demanded in the Passion Argument is the objective improbability of at least one belief which must be true if the goal sought by the religious passion is to be attained.

(b) We can find in the *Postscript* suggestions of several reasons for thinking that an infinite passion needs objective improbability. The two that seem to me most interesting have to do with (i) the risks accepted and (ii) the costs paid in pursuance of a passionate interest.

(i) One reason that Kierkegaard has for valuing objective improbability is that it increases the *risk* attaching to the religious life, and risk is so essential for the expression of religious passion that "without risk there is no faith" (p. 182). About the nature of an eternal happiness, the goal of religious striving, Kierkegaard says "there is nothing to be said . . . except that it is the good which is attained by venturing everything absolutely" (p. 382).

> But what then does it mean to venture? A venture is the precise correlative of an uncertainty; when the certainty is there the venture becomes impossible. . . . If what I hope to gain by venturing is itself certain, I do not risk or venture, but make an exchange. . . . No, if I am in truth resolved to venture, in truth resolved to strive for the attainment of the highest good, the uncertainty must be there, and I must have room to move, so to speak. But the largest space I can obtain, where there is room for the most vehement gesture of the passion that embraces the infinite, is uncertainty of knowledge with respect to an

eternal happiness, or the certain knowledge that the choice is in the finite sense a piece of madness: now there is room, now you can venture! [pp. 380–82]

How is it that objective improbability provides the largest space for the most vehement gesture of infinite passion? Consider two cases. (A) You plunge into a raging torrent to rescue from drowning someone you love, who is crying for help. (B) You plunge into a raging torrent in a desperate attempt to rescue someone you love, who appears to be unconscious and *may* already have drowned. In both cases you manifest a passionate interest in saving the person, risking your own life in order to do so. But I think Kierkegaard would say there is more passion in the second case than in the first. For in the second case you risk your life in what is, objectively considered, a smaller chance that you will be able to save your loved one. A greater passion is required for a more desperate attempt.

A similar assessment may be made of the following pair of cases. (A′) You stake everything on your faith in the truth of Christianity, knowing that it is objectively 99 per cent probable that Christianity is true. (B′) You stake everything on your faith in the truth of Christianity, knowing that the truth of Christianity is, objectively, possible but so improbable that its probability is, say, as small as $\dfrac{1}{10^{2,000,000}}$. There is passion in both cases, but Kierkegaard will say that there is more passion in the second case than in the first. For to venture the same stake (namely, everything) on a much smaller chance of success shows greater passion.

Acceptance of risk can thus be seen as a *measure* of the intensity of passion. I believe this provides us with one way of understanding what Kierkegaard means when he calls religious passion "infinite." An *infinite* passionate interest in x is an interest so strong that it leads one to make the greatest possible sacrifices in order to obtain x, on the smallest possible chance of success. The infinity of the passion is shown in that there is no sacrifice so great one will not make it, and no chance of success so small one will not act on it. A passion which is infinite in this sense requires, by its very nature, a situation of maximum risk for its expression.

It will doubtless be objected that this argument involves a misunderstanding of what a passionate interest is. Such an interest is a disposition. In order to have a great passionate interest it is not necessary actually to make a great sacrifice with a small chance of success; all that is necessary is to have such an intense interest that one *would* do so if an appropriate occasion should arise. It is therefore a mistake to say that there *is* more passion in case (B) than in case (A), or in (B′) than in (A′). More passion is *shown* in (B) than in (A), and in (B′) than in (A′); but an equal passion may exist in cases in which there is no occasion to show it.

This objection may well be correct as regards what we normally mean by "passionate interest." But that is not decisive for the argument. The crucial question is what part dispositions, possibly unactualized, ought to play in religious devotion. And here we must have a digression about the position of the *Postscript* on this question—a position that is complex at best and is not obviously consistent.

In the first place I do not think that Kierkegaard would be prepared to think of passion, or a passionate interest, as primarily a disposition that might remain unactualized. He seems to conceive of passion chiefly as an intensity in which one actually does and feels. "Passion is momentary" (p. 178), although capable of continual repetition. And what is momentary in such a way that it must be repeated rather than protracted is presumably an occurrence rather than a disposition. It agrees with this conception of passion that Kierkegaard idealizes a life of "persistent striving," and says that the religious task is to "exercise" the God-relationship and to give "existential expression" to the religious choice (pp. 110, 364, 367).

All of this supports the view that what Kierkegaard means by "an infinite passionate interest" is a pattern of actual decision-making, in which one continually exercises and expresses one's religiousness by making the greatest possible sacrifices on the smallest possible chance of success. In order to actualize such a pattern of life one needs chances of success that are as small as possible. That is the room that is required for "the most vehement gesture" of infinite passion.

But on the other hand Kierkegaard does allow a dispositional element in the religious life, and even precisely in the making of the greatest possible sacrifices. We might suppose that if we are to make the greatest possible sacrifices in our religious devotion, we must do so by abandoning all worldly interests and devoting all our time and attention to religion. That is what monasticism attempts to do, as Kierkegaard sees it; and (in the *Postscript*, at any rate) he rejects the attempt, contrary to what our argument to this point would have led us to expect of him. He holds that "resignation" (pp. 353, 367) or "renunciation" (pp. 362, 386) of *all* finite ends is precisely the first thing that religiousness requires; but he means a renunciation that is compatible with pursuing and enjoying finite ends (pp. 362–71). This renunciation is the practice of a sort of detachment; Kierkegaard uses the image of a dentist loosening the soft tissues around a tooth, while it is still in place, in preparation for pulling it (p. 367). It is partly a matter of not treating finite things with a desperate seriousness, but with a certain coolness or humor, even while one pursues them (pp. 368, 370).

This coolness is not just a disposition. But the renunciation also has a dispositional aspect. "Now if for any individual an eternal happiness is his highest good, this will mean that all finite satisfactions are volitionally relegated to the status of what may have to be renounced in favor of an eternal happiness" (p. 350). The volitional relegation is not a disposition but an act of choice. The object of this choice, however, appears to be a dispositional state—the state of being such that one *would* forgo any finite satisfaction *if* it *were* religiously necessary or advantageous to do so.

It seems clear that Kierkegaard, in the *Postscript,* is willing to admit a dispositional element at one point in the religious venture, but not at another. It is enough in most cases, he thinks, if one is *prepared* to cease for the sake of religion from pursuing some finite end; but it is not enough that one *would* hold to one's belief in the face of objective improbability. The belief must actually be improbable, although the pursuit of the finite need not actually cease. What is not clear is a reason for this disparity. The following hypothesis, admittedly somewhat speculative as interpretation of the text, is the best explanation I can offer.

The admission of a dispositional element in the religious renunciation of the finite is something to which Kierkegaard seems to be driven by the view that there is no alternative to it except idolatry. For suppose one actually ceases from all worldly pursuits and enters a monastery. In the monastery one would pursue a number of particular ends (such as getting up in the middle of the night to say the offices) which, although religious in a way ("churchy," one might say), are still finite. The absolute *telos* or end of religion is no more to be identified with them than with the ends pursued by an alderman (pp. 362–71). To pretend otherwise would be to make an idolatrous identification of the absolute end with some finite end. An existing person cannot have sacrificed everything by actually having ceased from pursuing *all* finite ends. For as long as he lives and acts he is pursuing some finite end. Therefore his renouncing *everything* finite must be at least partly dispositional.

Kierkegaard does not seem happy with this position. He regards it as of the utmost importance that the religious passion should come to expression. The problem of finding an adequate expression for a passion for an infinite end, in the face of the fact that in every concrete action one will be pursuing some finite end, is treated in the *Postscript* as the central problem of religion (see especially pp. 386–468). If the sacrifice of everything finite must remain largely dispositional, then perhaps it is all the more important to Kierkegaard that the smallness of the chance for which it is sacrificed should be fully actual, so that the infinity of the religious passion may be measured by an actuality in at least one aspect of the religious venture.

(ii) According to Kierkegaard, as I have argued, the intensity of a passion is measured in part by the smallness of the chances of success that one acts on. It can also be measured in part by its *costliness*—that is, by how much one gives up or suffers in acting on those chances. This second measure can also be made the basis of an argument for the claim that an infinite passion requires objective improbability. For the objective improbability of a religious belief, if recognized, increases the costliness of holding it. The risk involved in staking everything on an objectively improbable belief gives rise to an anxiety and mental suffering whose acceptance is itself a sacrifice. It seems to follow that if one is not staking everything on a belief one sees to be objectively improbable, one's passion is not infinite in Kierkegaard's sense, since one's sacrifice could be greater if one did adhere to an improbable belief.

Kierkegaard uses an argument similar to this. For God to give us objective knowledge of Himself, eliminating paradox from it, would be "to lower the price of the God-relationship."

> And even if God could be imagined willing, no man with passion in his heart could desire it. To a maiden genuinely in love it could never occur that she had bought her happiness too dear, but rather that she had not bought it dear enough. And just as the passion of the infinite was itself the truth, so in the case of the highest value it holds true that the price is the value, that a low price means a poor value. . . . [p. 207]

Kierkegaard here appears to hold, first, that an increase in the objective probability of religious belief would reduce its costliness, and second, that the value of a religious life is measured by its cost. I take it his reason for the second of these claims is that passion is the most valuable thing in a religious life and passion is measured by its cost. If we grant Kierkegaard the requisite conception of an infinite passion, we seem once again to have a plausible argument for the view that objective improbability is required for such a passion.

(c) We must therefore consider whether infinite passion, as Kierkegaard conceives of it, ought to be part of the religious ideal of life. Such a passion is a striving, or pattern of decision-making, in which, with the greatest possible intensity of feeling, one continually makes the greatest possible sacrifices on the smallest possible chance of success. This seems to me an impossible ideal. I doubt that any human being could have a passion of this sort, because I doubt that one could make a sacrifice so great that a greater could not be made, or have a (nonzero) chance of success so small that a smaller could not be had.

But even if Kierkegaard's ideal is impossible, one might want to try to approximate it. Intensity of passion might still be measured by the greatness of sacrifices made and the smallness of chances of success acted on, even if we cannot hope for a greatest possible or a smallest possible here. And it could be claimed that the most essential and valuable thing in religiousness is a passion that is very intense (though it cannot be infinite) by this standard—the more intense the better. This claim will not support an argument that objective improbability is absolutely required for religious passion. For a passion could presumably be very intense, involving great sacrifices and risks of some other sort, without an objectively improbable belief. But it could still be argued that objectively improbable religious beliefs enhance the value of the religious life by increasing its sacrifices and diminishing its chances of success, whereas objective probability detracts from the value of religious passion by diminishing its intensity.

The most crucial question about the Passion Argument, then, is whether maximization of sacrifice and risk are so valuable in religion as to make objective improbability a desirable characteristic of religious beliefs. Certainly much religious thought and feeling places a very high value on sacrifice and on passionate intensity. But the doctrine that it is desirable to increase without limit, or to the highest possible degree (if there is one) the cost and risk of a religious life is less plausible (to say the least) than the view that *some* degree of cost and risk may add to the value of a religious life. The former doctrine would set the religious interest at enmity with all other interests, or at least with the best of them. Kierkegaard is surely right in thinking that it would be impossible to live without pursuing some finite ends. But even so it would be possible to exchange the pursuit of better finite ends for the pursuit of worse ones—for example, by exchanging the pursuit of truth, beauty, and satisfying personal relationships for the self-flagellating pursuit of pain. And a way of life would be the costlier for requiring such an exchange. Kierkegaard does not, in the *Postscript*, demand it. But the presuppositions of his Passion Argument seem to imply that such a sacrifice would be religiously desirable. Such a conception of religion is demonic. In a tolerable religious ethics some way must be found to conceive of the religious interest as inclusive rather than exclusive of the best of other interests—including, I think, the interest in having well-grounded beliefs.

4. PASCAL'S WAGER AND KIERKEGAARD'S LEAP

Ironically, Kierkegaard's views about religious passion suggest a way in which his religious beliefs could be based on objective reasoning—not on reasoning which would show them to be objectively probable, but on reasoning which shows them to be objectively advantageous. Consider the situation of a person whom Kierkegaard would regard as a genuine Christian believer. What would such a person want most of all? He would want above all else to attain the truth through Christianity. That is, he would desire both that Christianity be true and that he himself be related to it as a genuine believer. He would desire that state of affairs (which we may call S) so ardently that he would be willing to sacrifice everything else to obtain it, given only the smallest possible chance of success.

We can therefore construct the following argument, which has an obvious analogy to Pascal's Wager. Let us assume that there is, objectively, some chance, however small, that Christianity is true. This is an assumption which Kierkegaard accepts (p. 31), and I think it is plausible. There are two possibilities, then: either Christianity is true, or it is false. (Others might object to so stark a disjunction, but Kierkegaard will not.) If Christianity is false it is impossible for anyone to obtain S, since S includes the truth of Christianity. It is only if Christianity is true that anything one does will help one or hinder one in obtaining S. And if Christianity is true, one will obtain S just in case one becomes a genuine Christian believer. It seems obvious that one would increase one's chances of becoming a genuine Christian believer by becoming one now (if one can), even if the truth of Christian beliefs is now objectively uncertain or improbable. Hence it would seem to be advantageous for anyone who can to become a genuine Christian believer now, if he wants S so much that he would be willing to sacrifice everything else for the smallest possible chance of obtaining S. Indeed I believe that the argument I have given for this conclusion is a piece of objective reasoning, and that Christian belief is therefore *objectively* advantageous for anyone who wants S as much as a Kierkegaardian genuine Christian must want it.

Of course this argument does not tend at all to show that it is objectively probable that Christianity is true. It only gives a practical, prudential reason for believing, to someone who has a certain desire. Nor does the argument do anything to prove that such an absolutely overriding desire for S is reasonable.[8] It does show, however, that just as Kierkegaard's position has more logical structure than one might at first think, it is more difficult than he probably realized for him to get away entirely from objective justification.[9]

8. It is worth noting, though, that a similar argument might still provide some less overriding justification of belief to someone who had a strong, but less overriding, desire for S.

9. Versions of this paper have been read to philosophical colloquia at Occidental College and California State University, Fullerton. I am indebted to participants in those discussions, to students in many of my classes, and particularly to Marilyn McCord Adams, Van Harvey, Thomas Kselman, William Laserow, and James Muyskens, for helpful comment on the ideas which are contained in this paper (or which would have been, had it not been for their criticisms).

Pascal's Wager

JAMES CARGILE

A. Pascal's statement of his wager argument[1,2] is couched in terms of the theory of probability and the theory of games, and the exposition is unclear and unnecessarily complicated. The following is a "creative" reformulation of the argument designed to avoid *some* of the objections which have been or might be raised against the original.

B. Premises:

1. "If there is a God, we are incapable of knowing either what he is, or whether he exists" (Pascal). And further, we have no way of knowing that God does not exist.

2. If you perform religious rites with enthusiasm, and never question the claims of some religion, you will come to be devoutly religious. "Go then and take holy water, and have masses said; belief will come and stupefy your scruples" (William James' version[3] of a remark by Pascal).

3. If you are devoutly religious—Christian, Jew, Moslem, Hindu, polytheist, etc.—and there is a God, then he will send you to heaven when you die.

Conclusion: Solely on grounds of rational self-interest, you should participate in religious rites, refrain from sceptical thoughts, etc.

1. *Pascal's Pensées,* bilingual edition, trans. H. F. Stewart, D.D., no. 223.
2. Georges Brunet, in *Le Pari de Pascal,* pp. 62–3, points out that Pascal was not the originator of the wager argument. Other writings on the background of Pascal's argument are *Le Pari de Pascal,* by A. Ducas, and "Le Fragment Infini-Rien et ses Sources," by M. J. Orcibal, in *Blaise Pascal, L'Homme et L'Oeuvre,* section V.
3. William James, *The Will to Believe* (New York, 1897), pp. 5–6.

Reprinted from *Philosophy* 41 (1966) by permission of Cambridge University Press. © The Royal Institute of Philosophy 1966. Footnotes have been renumbered for convenience.

Proof: Consider the following case: A very rich man who is fond of jazz promises that in two years, he is going to toss an unbiased coin. If it lands heads, he will give each devoted jazz fan a million dollars. If it lands tails, he won't do anything. Every Sunday for the next two years, a one-hour jazz concert is scheduled. It is known to be highly likely that if you attend these concerts religiously, and avoid listening to classical music, you will become a devoted jazz fan.

This case is clearly analogous to the situation of the man who is reflecting as to whether or not he should take up religious observances. And in either case the answer is obvious: you had better start listening uncritically to a lot of jazz. You may return to classical music as a millionaire, and you may get to heaven and not have to listen to sermons any more.

It may be objected that the person who "wagers" by attending concerts loses, if he loses, only two years of classical music, while the person who "wagers" by participating in religious rites and avoiding sceptical thoughts loses, if he loses, the only chance for thinking he will ever have. But after all, what is thinking? You have only to pass up philosophical quibbling which everyone knows is silly anyway. You can keep your mind exercised on mathematics or formal logic or approved scientific topics. Concession to religion needn't be much, even when you strive for real faith. Look what subtle reasoners even fanatics can be!

It may be objected that God may save atheists and agnostics as well as religious people. And the rich man *might* give a million dollars to a lover of classical music—but why depend on *kindness* when you can get a *contract* (or rather, a covenant)?

Someone might plan to delay attending the concerts until the second year so as to get in as much classical music as possible. Similarly, someone might plan to follow the advice of Pascal's argument in forty years, after enjoying his scepticism as long as he can. But if the rich man announces that he *may* exclude people who are not jazz fans from his offer if they delay attending the concerts, it would obviously be foolish to delay. And if you plan to delay religious observance, you may not live that long. It is foolish to be even a little careless with an opportunity for infinite gain.

C. This argument is designed to convince an open-minded agnostic acting out of rational self-interest that he ought to take up religious practices in the hope of becoming religious. Pascal has other arguments which will then be brought forward to bring the newly-won religious sympathiser into Pascal's own particular church, but the wager argument is not one of these. William James (*loc. cit.*) criticises Pascal's argument on the grounds that it would not convert a Moslem to Catholicism. But it wasn't intended to. James has probably been misled by Pascal's comment about holy water and masses. But this needn't occur in the presentation of the wager argument; the point which the reference to holy water and masses is designed to illustrate could be made just as well with respect to Moslem rituals. The argument is aimed at convincing sceptics, whose coolness about their prospects for immortality horrifies Pascal, that they should become *involved* on the side of those committed to belief in immortality.

James also criticises Pascal's argument as immoral, and says indignantly, "We feel that a faith in masses and holy water adopted wilfully after such a mechanical calculation would lack the inner soul of faith's reality: and if we were ourselves in the place of the Deity, we should probably take particular pleasure in cutting off believers of this pattern from their infinite reward." It seems that James is overlooking the fact that *"believers* of this pattern" are going to be just the same as other believers. Their belief isn't *sustained* by the argument, nor is it acquired by simply deciding to believe—James rightly regards the idea of "believing by our volition" as "simply silly"—rather, their faith is acquired as a result of actions which they were persuaded by the argument to perform. Once belief comes, the believer may genuinely despise his old sceptical self and shudder to think that such considerations as self-interest ever moved him. He may sincerely perform acts of faith, with no thought of his ultimate reward. A cynic may decide that the most convenient arrangement is a death-bed conversion; but if he is really converted, no one will despise this cynicism more than he.

Since James says that he is presenting Pascal's words "translated freely" it seems fair to protest against his representing Pascal as saying that "any finite loss is reasonable, even a certain one is reasonable, if there is but the possibility of infinite gain." Pascal's exposition is unclear, but he doesn't make such a mistake as this. James also presents the choice as one between belief and unbelief, which is probably one reason why he considers the argument immoral. But Pascal doesn't put it as a choice between belief and unbelief. He speaks obscurely of "risking your life," where he seems to be asking, not that you believe, but that you observe religious rites and abstain from criticism in the hope of being led to belief.

James also presents Pascal's argument as starting with the claim that human reason can't tell us what to do and ending with the claim that a certain course is obviously the reasonable one. This is especially reprehensible when presented as a translation. Jean Mesnard makes the same mistake in paraphrasing Pascal's argument,[4] apparently with approval, as starting with the claim that "reason cannot determine our choice" and ending with "Our reason therefore commands us to bet on the existence of God!" Pascal actually starts by saying that reason cannot settle the question

4. Jean Mesnard, *Pascal, His Life and Works,* trans. by G. S. Fraser (London, 1952), pp. 156–7.

as to whether or not there *is* a God, and concludes by saying that reason does clearly advise us to *"bet"* that there is a God—which for Pascal means being religious or sincerely trying to become so.

D. Various presentations of the wager argument defend it against the charge that it is an immoral argument. But no presentation I know of notices that the argument, which is presented as an appeal to a self-interested, rational sceptic who is completely uncommitted,[5] is simply invalid, because no such person could accept the premises.

Premise 1 might not be acceptable to an agnostic because it considers only the possibility of a transcendent God. The agnostic might think that investigation of occult phenomena *could* answer the God question, though of course only an affirmative answer would be so obtainable. Still, the sceptic would certainly admit that the God question is pretty much up in the air. So with "could not know" changed to "do not know," premise 1 would be acceptable to a sceptic.

The sceptic might doubt that he is the sort of person of whom the factual claim of premise 2 is true. But he would probably admit that there are measures sufficient to bring him into a religious frame of mind, even if the measures required were somewhat more severe than are needed by the average man. So he might accept premise 2 while still preserving his title as a sceptic or agnostic.

However, no self-respecting sceptic could accept premise 3. For one thing, if he accepts premise 1 as stated, that is, accepts that if there is a God, then "we are incapable of knowing what he is," then he cannot consistently agree with premise 3 that one thing we can be sure of about the possible owner-operator of the universe is that he is the sort of being who will send religious people to heaven. And premise 1 apart, why should not the neutral sceptic think it just as likely that God will save atheists and agnostics as that he will save believers? He might hope that it is more likely, either purely for his own sake, or on moral grounds.

The fact that, say, Christianity or Mohammedanism *promise* their adherents an infinite reward, while, say, dialectical materialism does not, cannot be produced as a good reason for a neutral adopting one of the former positions rather than the latter. The argument, "If you become devoutly religious, and religion is right about there being a God, then you will get an infinite reward," is just invalid. It would be all right to argue

5. M. L. Goldmann ("Le Pari, est-il Ecrit 'Pour le Libertin'?" in *Blaise Pascal, L'Homme et L'Oeuvre,* section IV) argues that the argument is not for the sceptic who is *satisfied* with this world, but is rather for the man who is conscious of the miserable human condition. It is certainly consistent for a self-interested, rational sceptic to feel unhappy with man's lot. But even if he has the appropriate human longings, the rational sceptic must find Pascal's argument invalid.

"If you become devoutly religious, and religion is right about there being a God and religion is right about one claim it makes about his character, then you will get an infinite reward." But with these premises, there are no longer just the two possibilities, "Religion is right about there being a God or it isn't right about there being a God." There are three possibilities: Religion is right about there being a God and right about his character; or religion is right about there being a God and wrong about his character; or religion is wrong about there being a God.

E. However, an attempt might be made to reinstate the wager argument in spite of the observations in D, as follows:

Either (a) there is a god who will send only religious people to heaven or (b) there is not. To be religious is to wager for (a). To fail to be religious is to wager for (b). We can't settle the question whether (a) or (b) is the case, at least not at present. But (a) is clearly vastly better than (b). With (a), infinite bliss is *guaranteed*, while with (b) we are still in the miserable human condition of facing death with no assurance as to what lies beyond. So (a) is clearly the best wager.

This arrangement does indeed appeal to a self-interested, *uncommitted* sceptic—it does not *presuppose* anything about the nature of god—the assumption about the nature of god is explicit in the argument. A sceptic might accept this argument and still deserve the title of "sceptic," but he would not deserve the title of "clear thinker."

The argument just presented is formally similar to the following:

Either (a) there is a god who will send you to heaven only if you commit a painful ritual suicide within an hour of first reading this, or (b) there is not. We cannot settle the question whether (a) or (b) is the case or it is at least not settled yet. But (a) is vastly preferable to (b), since in situation (a) infinite bliss is *guaranteed*, while in (b) we are left in the usual miserable human condition. So we should wager for (a) by performing the suicidal ritual.

It might be objected that we can be sure that there is not a god who will send us to heaven only if we commit suicide but we can't be sure that there is not a god who will send us to heaven only if we are religious. However, a sceptic would demand proof for this.

Both the foregoing arguments might gain plausibility through confusing possibility with probability. Certainly Pascal's application of probability theory could be severely criticised. However, my purpose has not been to criticise this aspect of the argument, but only to point out that the argument cannot stand as an appeal to someone who subscribes to no religious presuppositions.

F. Though my criticism of Pascal's argument has not been based on attacking his use of probability theory, it may be worth noting that if his use of probability theory were right, probability theory would be in a bad way.

Pascal uses a certain method from probability theory for calculating whether a given bet is a good one, to support his argument. The method is as follows: given a bet on whether or not an event E will happen, you multiply the probability of E by the odds offered (with the largest number in the odds, if there is one, in the numerator). If this product exceeds one, and you are getting the high end of the odds, then the bet is a good one for you no matter how low the probability of E may be.

The limitations of this method are well known and Pascal's application of it creates a situation somewhat like the Petersburg Paradox.[6] But I think we need not go as far as the Petersburg Paradox to criticise Pascal's application of this method. It is enough to observe that in applying the method, Pascal takes for granted that the hypothesis that there is a God has some non-zero probability.

The only support Pascal could have for this is the so-called "Principle of Indifference," the fallaciousness of which is well known.[7] Pascal assumes that if a proposition is logically possible and not known to be false, then it has some non-zero probability. But the propositional function "There exists a God who prefers contemplating the real number x more than any other activity" provides us with a set of mutually incompatible propositions, each of which is logically and epistemically possible, such that there could not be a non-zero probability for each member of the set. Even if this "propositional function" is rejected as nonsense, such a function as "There are n rabbits in the universe" would provide a set of mutually incompatible propositions infinitely many of which would be both logically and epistemically possible. They could all be assigned probability numbers, e.g., from the series ½, ¼, ⅛, . . . , but such an assignment would be absurd.

G. Of course, there remains the argument that if you become devoutly religious (and not a Calvinist!) you will *think* that you are going to get an infinite reward, and this is pleasanter than not thinking so. Whether Pascal would have stooped to this is a question outside the scope of the present essay.

H. It must be emphasised that my criticisms have not been intended to suggest that religious belief is unreasonable. It is one thing to hold that reason directs us to be religious, quite another to hold that it is (perfectly) reasonable to be religious.

Even in this connection, it is not the belief in an infinite gain which

6. See, for example, Harold Cramer, *The Elements of Probability Theory*, p. 95, or William Feller, *Introduction to Probability Theory and its Applications*, pp. 199–201.
7. See William Kneale, *Probability and Induction*, pp. 184–5.

makes it reasonable to be religious. I may get the idea into my head that setting fire to the bus station will get me into heaven, but this belief does not make it *reasonable* for me to perform this religious act. *How I got the belief* would be crucial in determining whether the religious act of setting fire to the bus station is reasonable.

For example, if someone were dressed as an angel in a very convincing way, and lowered by an invisible wire to hang in front of me as I was climbing a cliff where I had every reason to think no one else was present, and this "angel" told me to burn the bus station, and I did, and the judge found out about the prank, and found out how diabolically convincing it had been, he might well dismiss my case, calling my action reasonable. Or again, if a heavenly host actually appeared to me and to all mankind, and promised us all eternal bliss if I burn down the bus station, my fellow men might consider me irrational to refuse.

On the other hand, if I were talked into burning the bus station by some sleazy prophet, my religious observance might well be called irrational.

I. There remains one way of reconstruing the wager argument so as to make the preceding criticisms inapplicable. It might be observed that many professed sceptics have lingering tendencies to believe in some religion, and that proposing a wager is an effective way to exploit these tendencies to bring them back into the fold.

Thus a lapsed Christian might feel that there is a 1/100 chance that Christianity is right, while assigning no likelihood at all to the claims of other religions. Furthermore, he may be sure that if Christianity is right, then however ordinary sinners and believers in other religions may fare, hard-boiled atheists will fare very badly indeed. For such a person as this, the wager might be thought to exert a powerful attraction to return to active Christianity.

However, this doesn't seem to be true in actual practice, and there are good reasons why this should be so. For one thing, if someone is a hard-boiled atheist, he won't assign any positive probability to Christian claims about God. And if he isn't a hard-boiled atheist and does assign a positive probability to Christian claims, he is likely to imagine the Christian God as too nice to be stingy with rewards for people in his category, so the wager won't lead him to change his schedule.

Furthermore, lingering religiosity is not in itself enough to make the wager appetising. It has to be lingering religiosity which the agent will express in a positive probability estimate, or otherwise the wager won't get started. And many people who have superstitious tendencies would still not attach any positive probability to these superstitions.

And finally, even when someone does attach a positive probability to some religion's god-claims (and to no other's) the wager argument is not sure to bind him. Let us very roughly distinguish between objective and subjective theories of probability by noting that on an objective theory, it is not necessary that someone's judgment of a probability have any connection with his wagering behaviour; while on a subjective view, given the person's value scheme, his wagering behaviour is essential to determining his probability judgments. Then on the objective view, even given a positive probability estimate for some religion and a definite preference for heaven, being willing to make the wager doesn't follow and it is even a vexed question (at least) to show that wager-reluctance in such circumstances would even be less than reasonable. And on the subjective view, the probability estimate won't be of much use in persuading the agent to wager, considering that willingness to wager was an essential feature in determining the probability estimate.

Wittgensteinian Fideism

KAI NIELSEN

I

Wittgenstein did not write on the philosophy of religion.[1] But certain strands of his later thought readily lend themselves to what I call Wittgensteinian Fideism. There is no text that I can turn to for an extended statement of this position, but certain remarks made by Winch, Hughes, Malcolm, Geach, Cavell, Cameron and Coburn can either serve as partial statements of this position, or can be easily used in service of such a statement.[2] Some of their contentions will serve as targets for my argumentation, for as much as I admire Wittgenstein, it seems to me that the fideistic

1. This now turns out to be inaccurate. Since this was first written, the following book has been announced: Ludwig Wittgenstein, *Lectures and Conversations on Aesthetics, Psychology and Religious Belief.* [Ed. Cyril Barrett, Berkeley, 1966—Eds.]
2. The scattered but central sources here are as follows: Peter Winch, *The Idea of a Social Science* (London: 1958); "Understanding a Primitive Society," *American Philosophical Quarterly*, vol. I (October, 1964), pp. 307–25; G. E. Hughes, "Martin's Religious Belief," *Australasian Journal of Philosophy*, vol. 40 (August, 1962), pp. 211–19; Norman Malcolm, "Anselm's Ontological Arguments," *The Philosophical Review* (1960); "Is it a Religious Belief That 'God Exists'?" *Faith and the Philosophers*, John Hick (ed.) (New York: 1964); Peter Geach, "Nominalism," *Sophia*, vol. III, No. 2 (1964); Stanley Cavell, "Existentialism and Analytic Philosophy," *Daedalus*, vol. 93 (Summer, 1964); J. M. Cameron, *The Night Battle* (Baltimore: 1962); "What Is a Christian?" *The New York Review of Books*, vol. VI (May 26, 1966); Robert Coburn, "A Neglected Use of Theological Language," *Mind*, vol. LXXII (July, 1963).

Reprinted from *Philosophy* 42 (1967) by permission of Cambridge University Press. © The Royal Institute of Philosophy 1967. Footnotes have been renumbered for convenience.

conclusions drawn by these philosophers from his thought are often absurd. This leads me back to an inspection of their arguments and the
premisses in these arguments.

These philosophers call attention to the linguistic regularities concerning "God" that Ziff notes, but beyond anything Ziff claims they stress that
religious concepts can only be understood if we have an insider's grasp of
the form of life of which they are an integral part.[3] As Malcolm puts it,
the very genesis of the concept of God grows out of a certain "storm in the
soul." Only within a certain form of life could we have the idea of an "un-
bearably heavy conscience" from which arises the Judaeo-Christian concept of God and of a "forgiveness that is beyond all measure." If, as Malcolm maintains, one does not have a grasp of that form of life from "the
inside not just from the outside" and, if as an insider, one does not have "at
least some inclination to *partake* in that religious form of life," the very
concept of God will seem "an arbitrary and absurd construction." There
cannot be a deep understanding of the concept of God without "an understanding of the phenomena of human life that gave rise to it."[4]

Certainly much of what Malcolm says here is unquestionably true.
Anthropologists for years have stressed, and rightly, that one cannot gain
a deep understanding of the distinctive features of a tribe's culture without
a participant's understanding of the way of life of that culture. Concepts
cannot be adequately understood apart from a grasp of their function in the
stream of life. If a man has no experience of religion, has never learned
God-talk where the "engine isn't idling," he will not have a deep understanding of religion. But having such an understanding of religion is perfectly compatible with asserting, as did the Swedish philosopher Axel
Hägerström, that the concept of God is "nothing but a creation of our own
confused thought" growing out of our need to escape "from the anxiety
and wearisomeness of life."[5] And this comes from a philosopher who, as
C. D. Broad's biographical remarks make evident, was once thoroughly
immersed in the religious stream of life.

Malcolm's above contention is only one of the Wittgensteinian claims
that I shall examine. The following cluster of dark sayings have, when
they are accepted, a tendency to generate what I call Wittgensteinian
fideism:

  1. The forms of language are the forms of life.
  2. What is *given* are the forms of life.

3. Paul Ziff, "About God" in *Religious Experience and Truth*, Sidney Hook (ed.)
(New York: 1961).
4. Norman Malcolm, "Anselm's Ontological Arguments," *The Philosophical Review*
(1960).
5. Axel Hägerström, *Philosophy and Religion* (London: 1964), p. 216.

3. Ordinary language is all right as it is.

4. A philosopher's task is not to evaluate or criticise language or the forms of life, but to describe them where necessary and to the extent necessary to break philosophical perplexity concerning their operation.

5. The different modes of discourse which are distinctive forms of life all have a logic of their own.

6. Forms of life taken as a whole are not amenable to criticism; each mode of discourse is in order as it is, for each has its own criteria and each sets its own norms of intelligibility, reality and rationality.

7. These general, dispute-engendering concepts, i.e., intelligibility, reality and rationality are systematically ambiguous; their exact meaning can only be determined in the context of a determinate way of life.

8. There is no Archimedean point in terms of which a philosopher (or for that matter anyone else) can relevantly criticise whole modes of discourse or, what comes to the same thing, ways of life, for each mode of discourse has its own specific criteria of rationality/irrationality, intelligibility/unintelligibility, and reality/unreality.[6]

A Wittgensteinian Fideist who accepted such contentions could readily argue that religion is a unique and very ancient form of life with its own distinctive criteria. It can only be understood or criticised, and then only in a piecemeal way, from within this mode by someone who has a participant's understanding of this mode of discourse. To argue, as I do and as C. B. Martin has, that the very first-order discourse of this form of life is incoherent or irrational can be nothing but a confusion, for it is this very form of life, this very form of discourse itself, that sets its own criteria of coherence, intelligibility or rationality. Philosophy cannot relevantly criticise religion; it can only display for us the workings, the style of functioning, of religious discourse.

I agree with such Wittgensteinians that to understand religious discourse one must have a participant's understanding of it. However, this certainly does not entail that one is actually a participant, that one *accepts* or *believes* in the religion in question. But I do *not* agree that the first-order discourse of religion is in order as it is, and I do not agree that philosophy cannot relevantly criticise religions or forms of life. I shall examine these issues by examining some Wittgensteinian defences of the above approach to religion.

Let me remark at the outset that I am not sure to what extent Wittgenstein himself would have accepted a Wittgensteinian Fideism. But Witt-

6. I do not necessarily lay all these aperçu at Wittgenstein's door, but all of them can clearly be found in one or another of his disciples.

genstein's work has been taken in that way and it is thought in many quarters that such an approach will give us a deep grasp of religion and will expose the shallowness of scepticism. For this reason I shall carefully examine the view I call Wittgensteinian Fideism. But do not forget, what I indeed hope would be true, that Wittgenstein might well wish to say of Wittgensteinians what Freud said of Freudians. I shall start with G. E. Hughes who presents the most direct confrontation with my view.

II

In his discussion of C. B. Martin's *Religious Belief,* Hughes has defended in an incisive way the claim that, as a whole, rock-bottom, religious utterances or propositions are in order as they are.[7] He does not claim that they are *all* in order but only that generally speaking they are.

He starts by asking what are our criteria for conceptual confusion when we claim that *en bloc* first-order religious propositions are in conceptual disarray. He remarks, "I should guess that it is possible to show any category of statements or expressions to be conceptually confused if one is allowed to insist that they must conform to the logic of some other category or categories of statements or expressions if they are to be said to make sense."[8] Certainly, Max Black and a host of others have made it evident that if we try to treat inductive reasonings as if they were deductive ones, we would make nonsense of them. Similarly, if we try to construe moral statements as if they were empirical statements, and moral reasoning as if it were scientific reasoning, we would make nonsense out of morality. We have learned to treat these concepts and modes of reasoning as being sui generis; inductive reasonings and moral reasoning have, in the sense Ryle uses "logic," a logic of their own. Our job as philosophers is to come to understand and display that logic, not to distort it by trying to reduce it to the logic of some other preferred type of discourse or to try to interpret it in terms of some ideal language like that found in *Principia Mathematica.* We should, Hughes argues, in doing the philosophy of religion adopt "an alternative programme for meta-theology . . . that . . . consists in allowing the actual use of religious terms and statements to determine their logic, rather than trying to force an alien logic upon them."[9] Hughes remarks that if we adopt this programme rather than the one Martin adopts (a programme similar to the one I have adopted) our philosophical arguments about religion can be seen in a quite different light. Arguments which show how religious statements generate contradictions

7. G. E. Hughes, "Martin's *Religious Belief,*" *Australasian Journal of Philosophy,* vol. 40 (August, 1962), pp. 211–19.
8. Ibid., p. 214.
9. Ibid.

when they are construed on the model of other types of statements "can now be construed as showing some of the peculiarities of their own logic."[10]

Hughes illustrates his argument with an example from Chapter Four of Martin's *Religious Belief*. Martin argues there (pp. 40–1) that "God" may be used in either of two ways: as a proper name referring to a particular being (a name such as "Charles" or "Sven") or as a descriptive term. Martin tries to show that using it in both ways at once leads to a contradiction. Hughes then remarks that Martin "makes out a massive and powerful case for this contradictoriness *provided that the alternatives are as he states them*."[11] That is to say, Martin's remarks are well taken about "proper names and descriptive phrases *as applied to particular things*."[12] But these acute remarks are all beside the point, Hughes contends, for God is not thought of as a "particular thing" within orthodox Jewish and Christian thought. The "patterns of what makes sense and what does not, in the case of names and descriptions of particular things, does not fit the pattern of usage of the word "God" on the lips of believers."[13] It is about as sensible to speak of God as a particular being, as it is to speak of the number 18 or perfect moral virtue as a particular being. Moreover, it is worth remembering in this context that one piece of meta-theology which has won wide acceptance among the orthodox is that "God" is not a substance-word (Aquinas in the formal mode).

On my approach and on Martin's approach "the fact that the pattern of usage of a term such as 'God' does not accord with that of other non-theological terms with which it is taken to be analogous, is made a basis for the charge that the use of the term is logically incoherent."[14] But on Hughes' programme—a good programme for a Wittgensteinian fideist—the "same non-accordance is regarded as showing that the terms are not as analogous as they have at first appeared, and the actual usage of religious terms within religious language is taken as normative for the logical type and the kind of meaning they have."[15] Hughes goes on to remark that "which of these programmes is preferable is perhaps the most important question for meta-theology (even, *mutatis mutandis*, for all meta-theorising)."[16]

Hughes defends his crucial Wittgensteinian methodological preference on the grounds that religious language is a long-established *fait accompli*, and something which does a job which no other segment of language can

10. Ibid.
11. Ibid., pp. 214–15.
12. Ibid., p. 215.
13. Ibid.
14. Ibid.
15. Ibid.
16. Ibid.

do. It is because of this that he is tempted to think that religious statements are in order just as they are, i.e. in their own kind of order and, as a whole, in a coherent order.[17] This is a significant claim the ramifications of which I will later consider in detail, but for now I will content myself with a brief sociological remark. We should counterpose against the fact that religious language is a *fait accompli* another fact, namely, that at all times and at all places, even among the most primitive tribes, there have been sceptics and scoffers, people who though perfectly familiar with the religious language game played in their culture would not play the religious language game, not because they could not, but because, even though they were perfectly familiar with it, even though they had an insider's understanding of it, they found it incoherent. But our first-order operations with what some *philosophers* call "material object talk" and our actual operation with arithmetic are not in this state of controversy. (Meta-mathematics may be in a shambles, but not arithmetic or algebra.) But in this respect religion is very different. There are people who can play the language game, even people who *want* very much to go on playing the language game of religion, but they morally and intellectually speaking cannot continue this activity because their intellects, not their natural sympathies, make assent to Jewish or Christian doctrine impossible. Moreover their doubts are often much older than their acquaintance with theology or philosophy and they were only reinforced by their acquaintance with these disciplines. There are people—and among the educated a continually growing number of people—who find, or at least think they find, the religious language game they have been taught as children either falderal or at best, in Santayana's celebrated phase, "moral poetry." This seems to me to count heavily, though *surely* not decisively, against thinking that at rock-bottom such talk must have a coherent order.

Hughes' other consideration, i.e., that religious language does a job which no other segment of language can do, is more troubling. The truth of this very claim could be challenged, but this is not the tack I now want to take. Rather I want simply to point out that in a culure like ours, religious discourse is coming to fail to do its distinctive tasks because many people do not find it coherent. Perhaps they are profoundly deceived; perhaps it is after all a perfectly coherent mode of discourse, but, given their beliefs, to point out to them that such a language game is played is not enough. They perfectly well know how to use this discourse; they know that it is an ancient and venerated part of their culture; they know that it has a distinctive role in their culture. Knowing so well how to play the language game, their very perplexity is over the apparent incoherence of just this familiar discourse. It is not that they are like Moore, who was

17. Ibid., pp. 215–16.

puzzled by what Bradley and other philosophers said about time but was not puzzled about time himself. (He could be puzzled about the correct analysis of "time" without being puzzled about time.) But, characteristically at any rate, they are puzzled first and primarily about the very first-order God-talk itself and only secondarily about the theologian's or philosopher's chatter about this chatter. Moreover, if one looks over the range of practices that have counted as religions (if one looks at Confucianism and Therevada Buddhism for example) one finds functioning in cultures, and very ancient cultures at that, religions that in terms of our religions (not just in terms of our theologies) are atheistic or agnostic. Given this, it is perfectly possible that certain *Ersatz* religions, e.g., Spinoza's, Fromm's and perhaps even Comte's "atheistical Catholicism," could, given certain cultural conditions, become religions. But given these facts and these possibilities, the fact—if it is a fact—that religious language does a job no other segment of language can do, does little to show that Christian or Islamic or Jewish first-order God-talk or God-talk at all is in a coherent order just as it is.

Hughes could reply that the part of religious talk that is in order just as it is, is what is really alive in religion; it is that which is essential to religion, constitutive of True Religion, i.e. that which is shared by all these religions and by *Ersatz* religions as well. But if this reply is made we are likely to end up (1) with a very unWittgensteinian essentialist bogey-man, and (2) with treating religion or True Religion as little more than "morality touched with emotion," i.e. Santayana's "moral poetry." Given that the Christian Creed as well as the Christian code is crucial to Christianity, as understood by the orthodox, such a conclusion would be most unwelcome, and would, in effect, be a capitulation to the meta-theologian who claimed that Christian discourse, as it stands, is incoherent and not a vindication of the meta-theological claim that the bulk of Christian language is perfectly in place if only metaphysicians and theologians would not tinker with it.

I do not want to claim that anything I have said so far settles anything. So far, I have only tried to show that there is something to be settled and that we cannot take this short Wittgensteinian way with the concepts of religion. The central considerations here are (1) is the first-order God-talk of Judaism, Christianity or Islam actually, for the most part, anyway, in order as it is, or is it in some way fundamentally incoherent, and (2) how could we decide this issue? These issues need a careful conceptual investigation.

III

These issues come up in an unsettling and probing way in the writings of Peter Winch. He does not directly attack the problem of the intelligibility of God-talk. Rather, Winch, in examining what it is to understand concepts radically different from our own, brings to the fore considerations which are central to an understanding and appraisal of Wittgensteinian Fideism.[18]

In trying to understand what it is to understand a primitive society, Winch examines the Azande conception of magic and subjects Evans-Pritchard's methodological remarks concerning it to a careful critical scrutiny. Evans-Pritchard indeed insists that in order to understand the Azande conceptions, we must understand them in terms of how they are taken by the Azande themselves and in terms of their own social structure, i.e., forms of life. But he ceases to make common cause with Wittgenstein and Winch when he argues that nonetheless the Azande are plainly labouring under an illusion. There is no magic and there are no witches. We know that we, with our scientific culture, are right about these matters and the Azande are wrong. Our scientific account of these matters is in accord with objective reality while the Azande magical beliefs are not.

This certainly seems like a scarcely disputable bit of common sense, but Winch is not satisfied with such an answer. While trying to avoid what he calls a Protagorean relativism "with all the paradoxes that involves," Winch still maintains that, though Evans-Pritchard is right in stressing that "we should not lose sight of the fact that men's ideas and beliefs must be checkable by reference to something independent—some reality," he is "wrong, and crucially wrong, in his attempt to characterise the scientific in terms of that which is in accord with objective reality."[19] Evans-Pritchard is mistaken in thinking that, while the Azande have a different conception of reality from ours, our scientific conception agrees with what reality actually is like while theirs does not.[20]

Winch, moving from counter-assertion to argument, contends that "the check of the independently real is not peculiar to science."[21] It is a mistake to think, as Evans-Pritchard and Pareto do, that scientific discourse provides us with "a paradigm against which to measure the intellectual respectability of other modes of discourse."[22] At this point in his argumentation Winch uses an example from religious discourse to drive home his point. God, when he speaks to Job out of the whirlwind, takes Job to task for having lost sight of the reality of God. Winch remarks that we would badly misunderstand that passage if we thought that Job had made some

18. The central essay here is his "Understanding a Primitive Society," *American Philosophical Quarterly*, vol. I (October, 1964), pp. 307–25. But see also Peter Winch, *The Idea of a Social Science* (London: 1958).
19. Peter Winch, "Understanding a Primitive Society," p. 308.
20. Ibid.
21. Ibid.
22. Ibid.

kind of theoretical mistake, which he might have corrected by further observation and experiment. Yet, Winch argues, God's reality is independent
of human whim or of what any man cares to think about it.

It is here that Winch makes a very revealing remark—a remark that
could readily be used to put a Wittgensteinian Fideism into orbit. What
God's reality amounts to, Winch says, "can only be seen from the religious
tradition in which the concept of God is used."[23] Such a religious context
is very unlike a scientific context in which we can speak of theoretical entities. Yet only within the religious use of language does "the conception
of God's reality have its place."[24] As the concept of what is real or what is
unreal vis-à-vis magic is only given within and only intelligible within the
Azande form of life in which the Azande magical practices are embedded,
so the concept of God's reality is only given within and only intelligible
within the religious form of life in which such a conception of God is embedded. In both cases there is an ongoing form of life that guarantees intelligibility and reality to the concepts in question. God and Azande magic
are not *simply* my ideas or Jewish or Azande ideas. Here we have baldly
stated a major motif in Wittgensteinian Fideism.

"What is real?" or "What is reality?", like "What is there?", do not
have a clear sense. When asked in a completely general way they are
meaningless. We can only raise the problem of the reality of something
within a form of life. There is no completely extra-linguistic or context-
independent conception of reality in accordance with which we might
judge forms of life.

> Reality is not what gives language sense. What is real and what is un-
> real shows itself in the sense that language has. Further, both the dis-
> tinction between the real and the unreal and the concept of agreement
> with reality themselves belong to our language.[25]

Yet these distinctions, though surely not the words used to make them,
would, Winch argues, have to be a part of any language. Without such
distinctions we could not have a system of communication and thus we
could not have a language. But how exactly the distinction between the
real and the unreal is to be drawn is determined by the actual linguistic
usage of some *particular* language. Evans-Pritchard and the man who
would reject the whole mode of God-talk as unintelligible or incoherent
are both unwittingly saying something that does not make sense, for their
own conceptions of reality are *not* determined by the actual usage of "reality" and they are mistakenly assuming that their very specialised use of

23. Ibid., p. 309.
24. Ibid.
25. Ibid.

"reality" is something they can use as a yardstick with which to appraise any and every form of life. But they have given us no reasons for adopting this procedure or making this assumption.

If we have been brought up in a certain tradition and understand scientific discourse, we can, while working in that discourse, ask whether a certain scientific hypothesis agrees with reality. We can, given an understanding of science, test this claim; but when Evans-Pritchard makes the putative statement that "Criteria applied in scientific experimentation constitute a true link between our ideas and an independent reality," he has *not* asserted a scientific hypothesis or even made an empirical statement. His putative assertion is not open to confirmation or disconfirmation; and if "true link" and "independent reality" are explained by reference to the scientific universe of discourse, we would beg the question of whether scientific experimentation, rather than magic or religion, constitutes a true link between our ideas and an independent reality. There seems to be no established use of discourse by means of which the expressions "true link" and "independent reality" in Evans-Pritchard's assertion can be explained. At any rate—and to put Winch's contention in a minimal way—Evans-Pritchard does not give these expressions a use or show us that they have a use. Thus when we try to say that the idea of God makes no true link with an independent reality we are using "true link" and "independent reality" in a meaningless or at least a wholly indeterminate way.

This argument is reinforced by a further claim made by Winch in his *The Idea of a Social Science*. There Winch sets forth a central plank in any Wittgensteinian Fideism. Logic, as a formal theory of order, must, given that it is an interpreted logic (an interpreted calculus), systematically display the forms of order found in the modes of social life. What can and cannot be said, what follows from what, is dictated by the norms of intelligibility embedded in the modes of social life. These finally determine the criteria of logical appraisal. Since this is so, "one cannot apply criteria of logic to modes of social life as such."[26] Science is one such mode and religion another; "each has criteria of intelligibility peculiar to itself." Within science or religion an action can be logical or illogical. It would, for example, be illogical for a scientist working in a certain area to refuse to take cognisance of the results of a properly conducted experiment; and it would also be illogical for a man who believed in God to try to pit his strength against God. But it makes no sense at all to assert that science or religion is logical or illogical, any more than it would make sense to speak of music as either well-coloured or ill-coloured or of stones as either married or divorced.

Winch's view here has rightly been taken to involve a claim to con-

26. Peter Winch, *The Idea of a Social Science*, p. 200.

ceptual self-sufficiency for all of the forms of life. It has also been thought that it involves a kind of compartmentalisation of the modes of discourse or forms of life. Winch is indeed saying that we cannot criticise science or ethics by criteria appropriate to religion, and vice-versa. Like Hughes, Winch is claiming that each mode of discourse must be understood in its own terms and that relevant criticism of that mode of discourse cannot be made,from outside of that discourse, but can take place only from within it, when some specific difficulty actually arises in science or in religion.

There is much here that is very perceptive, but there is much that needs close scrutiny as well. Let me assume here what in reality is quite open to question, namely, that Winch is correct about the Azande. That is, let me assume that given the radically different conceptual structure embedded in their language, and given the role magic and witchcraft play in their lives, we can have no good grounds for saying, as Evans-Pritchard does, that our concept of reality is the correct one and theirs is not. But even making this very questionable assumption, it does not at all follow that in our tribe religion and science are related as Azande magic is related to our scientific beliefs. There is no "religious language" or "scientific language." There is rather the international notation of mathematics and logic; and English, French, German and the like. In short, "religious discourse" and "scientific discourse" are part of the same overall conceptual structure. Moreover, in that conceptual structure there is a large amount of discourse, which is neither religious nor scientific, that is constantly being utilised by both the religious man and the scientist when they make religious or scientific claims. In short, they share a number of key categories. This situation differs from the Azande situation in a very significant sense, for in the former situation, we do not have in the same literal sense two *different* conceptual structures exemplifying two different ways of life. C. P. Snow to the contrary notwithstanding, we do not have two cultures here but only one.

Sometimes it is indeed tempting to think there really are two cultures. When I read a certain kind of religious literature—as in a recent reading of Simone Weil's *Waiting for God*—I have the *feeling* that I belong to another tribe: that what she can understand and take as certain I have no understanding of at all, beyond a Ziffian sense of her linguistic regularities. Leslie Fiedler tells us that Miss Weil "speaks of the problems of belief in the vocabulary of the unbeliever," but that is not how I read her.[27] I find her unabashedly talking about religious matters in a way that I find nearly as incredible as some of the things the Azande say. She blithely accepts what I find unintelligible. Yet this initial impression is in a way misleading,

27. Leslie Fiedler, "Introduction" to Simone Weil's *Waiting For God* (New York: 1951), pp. 3–4.

for, as I read on, I discover that she is sensitive to *some* of the conceptual perplexities that perplex me. I find her saying "There is a God. There is no God. Where is the problem? I am quite sure that there is a God in the sense that I am sure my love is no illusion. I am quite sure there is no God, in the sense that I am sure there is nothing which resembles what I can conceive when I say that word. . . ." When I ponder this, I realise that as much as we might differ, we are in the same universe of discourse. Miss Weil is not, after all, to me like the Azande with his witchcraft substance. We both learned "the language" of Christian belief; only I think it is illusion-producing while she thinks that certain crucial segments of it are our stammering way of talking about ultimate reality. A very deep gulf separates us; we are not even like Settembrini and Naphta. But all the same, there remains a sense in which we do understand each other and in which we share a massive background of beliefs and assumptions. Given that, it is not so apparent that we do *not* have common grounds for arguing about which concepts of reality are correct or mistaken here.

Winch, as we have seen, argues against Pareto's and Evans-Pritchard's claim that scientific concepts alone can characterise objective reality. He is correct in his claim that their claim is an incoherent one. "Scientific concepts alone make a true link with objective reality" is neither analytic nor empirical. No use has been given to "true link" or "objective reality." When a plain man looks at a harvest moon and says that it is orange, or says that the sun rises in the east and sets in the west, or that his vineyard posts are solid, he is not making scientific statements, but he is not making *subjective* statements either. His statements can be perfectly objective; they can be about how things are, and they can be objectively testable (publicly verifiable) without being scientific or without conflicting with science. But when it is claimed—as presumably people who seriously utter certain religious propositions claim—that the *facts* asserted by these religious propositions are such and such, their claims must be open to some possible confirmation or disconfirmation: their claims must be publicly testable. As Austin puts it, they are making some assertion or trying to make some assertion about how things-are-in-the-world. But a claim like "God created the heavens and the earth," when "God" is used non-anthropomorphically, is not testable. That is to say, it is a claim that purports to assert a fact, yet it is devoid of truth-value. People who use such religious talk—partake of such a form of life—cannot determine how, even in principle, they would establish or disestablish such religious claims, but they still believe that they are factual assertions: that is to say that they have truth-values. It is a fact that there is a God; it is a fact that He created the world; it is a fact that He protects me and the like. Yet, how could we say what it would be like for God to create the world, if it is impossible in principle to say what would have to transpire for it to be false that God created the world? Or to put this verificationist point in a weaker and more adequate way, if we cannot even say what *in principle* would count as *evidence* against the putative statement that God created the world, then "God created the world" is devoid of factual content.

This verificationist argument can, perhaps, be successfully rebutted, but it is far less vulnerable than the claim that only scientific ideas correspond with reality. That is to say, given the concept of objective reality that plain men, including plain religious men, utilise in everyday life, a statement asserts a fact, actually has factual content, only if it is confirmable or disconfirmable in principle. To count as a factual statement, it must assert a certain determinate reality (a pleonasm); that is, its descriptive content includes one set of empirically determinable conditions and excludes others.[28] People who argue for this would, or at least should, claim that these last remarks are what Wittgenstein called grammatical remarks, i.e., they hold in virtue of the linguistic conventions governing the crucial terms in question. But key religious utterances, though they purport to be factual statements, do not succeed in making what actually counts as a genuine factual statement. That is, as Strawson puts it, they are not actually part of that type of discourse we call a fact-stating type of discourse. Thus they lack the kind of coherence they must have to make genuinely factual claims.

I shall not here, though I have elsewhere, assess such a controversial claim.[29] Here I want only to note that even if it turns out to be mistaken, it is a far more powerful counter-thrust against Winchian claims to the conceptual self-sufficiency and the coherence of God-talk, than is the simplistic claim that only scientific ideas are in accord with objective reality. Such a verificationist claim—a claim utilised by Ayer and Flew—stands here as an unmet challenge to Wittgensteinian Fideism.

IV

Someone who wanted to use Winch to defend a Wittgensteinian Fideism might reply that a key religious claim like "God created the heavens and the earth" does indeed have something to do with understanding the

28. That "determinate reality" is a pleonasm has been argued in a powerful way by Axel Hägerström in his *Philosophy and Religion* (London: 1964). It is surely to be hoped that the rest of Hägerström's writings in Swedish will soon be made available to non-Swedish readers.

29. Kai Nielsen, "On Speaking of God," *Theoria* vol. XXVIII (1962, Part 2); "Religion and Commitment," *Problems of Religious Knowledge and Language,* W. T. Blackstone and R. H. Ayers (eds.); "Eschatological Verification," *Canadian Journal of Theology,* vol. IX (1963); "God and Verification Again," *Canadian Journal of Theology,* vol. XI (1965); "On Fixing the Reference Range of 'God'," *Religious Studies* (October, 1966).

world. We could not have a deep understanding of our world if we did not understand *that,* but it must be realised that the understanding in question is not the narrowly factual or empirical one I have just been talking about. Supernatural facts are a *sui generis* kind of fact. They are not, as Austin would put it, "a special kind of something in the world"; and they cannot be modelled on the garden variety concept of a fact. My argument, my critic might say, only shows that such religious statements are not factual in the way commonsensical, scientific and empirical statements are factual. It does not show religious statements are incoherent or pseudo-factual. Moreover, it in effect confirms the Wittgensteinian claim that religious discourse is one kind of discourse with its own distinctive logic while science and common sense are forms of life that constitute other quite distinct modes of discourse with their own unique criteria.

My reply is that the phrase "logic of discourse" is a dangerous metaphor and that these discourses are not in actual life nearly so compartmentalised as the above argument would have it. The man perplexed about God is not like the man perplexed by Azande beliefs in witchcraft substance. He is not an outsider who does not know the form of life but an insider who does. So God spoke to Job out of the whirlwind. So how did he do it? Nobody, or at least nobody who matters, believes any more in a sky God up there, who might have done it in a very loud voice. But what did happen? How are we to understand "God spoke to Job"? Maybe it was all Job's tortured imagination? Yet how do we even understand what it is that he was supposed to have imagined? And how are we to understand "I am who am"? A man may be puzzled about the *nature* of time, but when his alarm clock rings at 5.30 a.m. and a little later the weather comes on over the radio at 6.00 and his clock shows 6.00 too, he does not, unless he is excessively neurotic, doubt what time it is. He is painfully aware what time it is. But perfectly sane men in a tribe where God-talk is an established practice, part of an ancient and venerated form of life, can and do come to wonder to whom or to what they are praying, or what is being talked about when it is said that "God spoke to Job." God is a person, but we can't identify Him; God acts in the world but has no body. Words here are put together in a strange way. What could it possibly mean to speak of "action" or "a person" here? These terms cut across activities; they are at home in religious and non-religious contexts. It is also true that some logical rules (the laws of contradiction, excluded middle and the like) most certainly seem to cut across forms of life. The forms of life are not as compartmentalised as Winch seems to imply, and as a Wittgensteinian Fideism requires. Insiders can and do come to doubt the very coherence of this religious mode of life and its first-order talk.

They indeed do, it will be replied, but in doing that they are philosophically confused. Careful attention to the concept of reality, and to the systematic ambiguity of norms of intelligibility, will show why. It is just here, it will be claimed, that Wittgenstein's insights are most enlightening. This takes us to what I regard as the heart of the matter, and here we need to consider some very fundamental arguments of Winch's.

Winch makes one central point which seems to me unassailable: to understand religious conceptions we need a religious tradition; without a participant's understanding of that form of life, there can be no understanding of religion. To understand it we must learn the rules of conceptual propriety distinctive of that form of life. Without a knowledge by *wont* of the norms of conceptual propriety associated with God-talk, we can have no grasp of the concept of God, and thus, without such knowledge by *wont,* there can be no quest for God or even a rejection of God. If "we are to speak of difficulties and incoherencies appearing and being detected in the way certain practices have hitherto been carried on in a society, surely this can only be understood in connection with problems arising in the carrying on of the activity."[30]

Surely we must start here. There could not even be a *problem* about God if we could not. But to start at this point is one thing, to end there is another. The need to start from "inside" need not preclude the recognition of clefts, inconsistencies, and elements of incoherence in the very practice (form of life). Once magic and belief in fairies were ongoing practices in our stream of life. By now, by people working from the inside, the entire practice, the entire "form of life," has come to be rejected as incoherent.

We have seen, however, that Winch, after the fashion of a Wittgenstein Fideist, argues that we cannot intelligibly assert the incoherence, illogicality, irrationality or unintelligibility of a form of life itself. The forms of life, he argues, have a conceptual self sufficiency; operating with them, we can say that something does or does not make sense, is logical or illogical, e.g., that was an illogical chess move. But we cannot say of the whole activity itself that it is illogical, irrational, unintelligible or incoherent, e.g., chess is illogical.

The tide of metaphysics is running high here. Our everyday discourse, which is so important for a Wittgensteinian, will not support such a Winchian claim. "An ongoing but irrational form of life" most certainly does *not appear* to be a contradiction. "Foot-binding was for a long time an established institution but it was really cruel and irrational" may be false but it is not nonsense. "Primogeniture had a definite rationale" and "Magical practices are essential for the Azande" are not grammatical remarks, but this means that their denials are significant and this means that we can make judgements about the rationality of forms-of-life. Similarly, we can say, without *conceptual* impropriety, that gambling is illogical. We might

30. Peter Winch, "Understanding a Primitive Society," p. 319.

even say that French is illogical because of its haphazard use of gender, or that the irregularities of English grammar make it illogical. All of these statements may be false, they may even be absurdly false, but they certainly do not appear to be self-contradictory or senseless. It is not at all evident that language has gone on a holiday here. But to establish his thesis Winch must show that, appearances notwithstanding, they are all either senseless or metaphorical.

It can be replied: how do you deal (1) with Winch's specific argument that "the criteria of logic . . . arise out of, and are only intelligible in the context of, ways of living or modes of social life as such"[31] and (2) his further contention that "formal requirements tell us nothing about what in particular is to count as consistency, just as the rules of the propositional calculus limit, but do not themselves determine what are to be proper values of p, q, etc."?[32] I cannot consistently assert p and not-p, but what range of values the variable p takes is not uniquely determined by purely formal considerations. If I know that to say x is a bachelor entails x is not-married, I know, by purely formal considerations, that I cannot assert x is a married bachelor. But what counts as "a bachelor" or "a married man" can only be determined by reference to the actual usage embedded in the form of life of which they are a part.

Unless we are prepared to accept the compartmentalisation thesis, dear to Wittgensteinian Fideists, the acceptance of the above claim about logic need not commit one to the paradoxical thesis that modes of social life cannot be appraised as logical or illogical, rational or irrational. Religion, morality and science may indeed each have "criteria of intelligibility peculiar to itself." This means that the criteria of application for "God," "Divine Person," "perfect good," and the like is set by the first-order religious discourse itself. However, it also remains true that (1) discourse concerning God goes on in Swedish, German, English, French and the like, and (2) that there is no separate religious language. Given these two facts and given the overall universe of discourse of which religious discourse is a part, it may still be found that religious discourse, like discourse about fairies, is incoherent, e.g., "God is three and one," "God is a person that one *encounters* in prayer but God is utterly *transcendent*." Seemingly contradictory statements may indeed turn out not to be contradictory. When fully stated and understood, in terms of their distinctive contextual use, what *appears* to be contradictory or paradoxical may be seen to be straightforward and non-contradictory. Religious discourse is not something isolated, sufficient unto itself; "sacred discourse" shares categories with, utilises the concepts of, and contains the syntactical structure of, "profane discourse." Where

31. Peter Winch, *The Idea of a Social Science*, pp. 100–1.
32. Peter Winch, "Understanding a Primitive Society," p. 319.

there is what at least appears to be a contradiction, or where words are put together in a way fluent speakers *cannot* understand, a case must be made out for the contention that the contradiction is *only apparent*. What appears to be unintelligible, must be shown to have a use in the discourse or it must be given a use. That is to say, the words must be given an employment or shown to have an employment so that fluent speakers can grasp what is being said.

Many key religious statements at least appear to be contradictory or incoherent. That a *case* needs to be made out and perhaps even can be made out to show that they are not really contradictory or incoherent, shows that such a question can be raised about religious discourse. Given this fact and given the centrality of some of these religious statements, it becomes apparent that Winch's argument does not succeed in establishing that it is impossible to appraise whole ways of life as rational or irrational, intelligible or unintelligible. Furthermore, that we can ask questions about "God is three and one" and "A *transcendent* God is *encountered* in prayer" that involve appealing to criteria from the discourse as a whole and not just from religious talk, indicates that Winch's argument does not show that we can compartmentalise religious talk. In short, the Winchian arguments that we have examined do not show that we cannot raise questions about the rationality of a form of life or that religious discourse is so sui generis that its criteria of intelligibility are contained within itself.

We are not yet at the bottom of the barrel. The question "What is real?" has no determinate sense. What is real and what is unreal is a very context-dependent notion. What in a specific context counts as "real" or "reality" as in "a real trout," "a real champion," "an unreal distinction," "the realities of the economic situation," "a sense of reality," "the reality of death" or "the reality of God," can only be determined with reference to the particular matter we are talking about. We have no antecedent understanding of reality such that we could determine whether language agreed with reality, whether a specific language agreed with reality or whether a given form of discourse agreed with reality. With the exception of the *very last bit*, I agree with Winch about such matters, but alas it is this very last bit that is essential for a Wittgensteinian Fideism.

However, with this last Wittgensteinian claim, there are very real difficulties similar to ones we have already discussed. "Reality" may be systematically ambiguous, but what constitutes evidence, or tests for the truth or reliability of specific claims, is not completely idiosyncratic to the context or activity we are talking about. Activities are not that insulated. As I have already remarked, once there was an ongoing form of life in which fairies and witches were taken to be real entities, but gradually, as we reflected on the criteria we actually use for determining whether various entities, including persons, are or are not part of the spatio-temporal world of experience, we came to give up believing in fairies and witches. That a language-game was played, that a form of life existed, did not preclude our asking about the coherence of the concepts involved and about the reality of what they conceptualised.

Without a participant's understanding of God-talk, we could not raise the question of the reality of God, but with it, this is perfectly possible and perfectly intelligible.

Indeed we sometimes judge the reality of one thing in terms of something utterly inappropriate, e.g., moral distinctions are unreal because moral utterances do not make factual assertions. Here we do commit a howler. But, as my above examples show, this need not always be the case. "Johnson ought to be impeached" can be seen, by an examination of the relevant forms of life, not to describe a certain happening. It is not a bit of fact-stating discourse asserting some actual occurrence, but rather it tells us to make something occur. "Witches are out on Hallowe'en" is a putative factual statement. It supposedly does assert that a certain identifiable state-of-affairs obtains. It supposedly is like saying "The Klan is out on Hallowe'en." But the factual intelligibility of the former is not evident, for it is not clear what counts as a witch. To say that "witch" refers to a unique kind of reality only intelligible within a distinctive form of life is an incredible piece of evasion. To reason in such a manner is to show that one is committed to a certain metaphysical theory, come what may. But, if one wants to be realistic and non-evasive, one will surely say that it gradually became apparent, vis-à-vis forms of life in which talk of witches was embedded, that in light of the meanings of "fact" and "evidence" in the overall discourse of which witch-talk was a part, that witch-talk was incoherent. Though there was a form of life in which the existence of witches was asserted, such a way of life is and was irrational. And even if for some baroque reason I am mistaken in saying that it is or was irrational to believe in witches, the fact that such a question can be intelligently raised about one form of life plainly demonstrates that Winch's a priori arguments against such an appraisal of a form of life as a whole will not wash.

Perhaps God-talk is not as incoherent and irrational as witch-talk; perhaps there is an intelligible concept of the reality of God, and perhaps there is a God, but the fact that there is a form of life in which God-talk is embedded does not preclude our asking these questions or our giving, quite intelligibly, though perhaps mistakenly, the same negative answer we gave to witch-talk.

Rationality and Religious Belief

ALVIN PLANTINGA

What I mean to discuss in this paper is the question: "Is it rational, or reasonable, or rationally acceptable, to believe in God?" I mean to *discuss* this question, not answer it. My initial aim is not to argue that religious belief *is* rational (although I think it is) but to try to understand this question.

The first thing to note is that I have stated the question misleadingly. What I really want to discuss is whether it is rational to believe that God exists—that there is such a person as God. Of course there is an important difference between believing that God exists and believing *in* God. To believe that God exists is just to accept a certain proposition—the proposition that there really is such a person as God—as true. According to the book of James (2:19) the devils believe this proposition, and they tremble. To believe *in* God, however, is to trust him, to commit your life to him, to make his purposes your own. The devils do not do that. So there is a difference between believing in God and believing that he exists; for purposes of economy, however, I shall use the phrase "belief in God" as a synonym for "belief that God exists."

I. THE EVIDENTIALIST OBJECTION

Our question, therefore, is whether belief in God is rational. This question is widely asked and widely answered. Many philosophers—most prominently, those in the great tradition of natural theology—have argued that

Published for the first time. Parts of this paper appeared in C. F. Delaney (ed.), *Rationality and Religious Belief* (Notre Dame: University of Notre Dame Press, 1978) and in NOÛS 15 (1981):41–51.Used by permission of University of Notre Dame Press, the editor of NOÛS, and the author.

belief in God *is* rational; they have typically done so by providing what they took to be *demonstrations* or *proofs* of God's existence. Many others have argued that belief in God *is* *irrational*. If we call those of the first group "natural theologians," perhaps we should call those of the second "natural atheologians." (That would at any rate be kinder than calling them "unnatural theologians.") J. L. Mackie, for example, opens his statement of the problem of evil as follows: "I think, however, that a more telling criticism can be made by way of the traditional problem of evil. Here it can be shown, not merely that religious beliefs lack rational support, but that they are positively irrational."[1] And a very large number of philosophers take it that a central question—perhaps *the* central question—of philosophy of religion is the question whether religious belief in general and belief in God in particular is rationally acceptable.[2]

Now an apparently straightforward and promising way to approach this question would be to take a definition of rationality and see whether belief in God conforms to it. The chief difficulty with this appealing course, however, is that no such definition of rationality seems to be available. If there *were* such a definition, it would set out some conditions for a belief's being rationally acceptable—conditions that are severally necessary and jointly sufficient. That is, each of the conditions would have to be met by a belief that is rationally acceptable; and if a belief met all the conditions, then it would follow that it is rationally acceptable. But it is monumentally difficult to find any non-trivial necessary conditions at all. Surely, for example, we cannot insist that S's belief that p is rational only if it is *true*. For consider Newton's belief that if x, y and z are moving colinearly, then the motion of z with respect to x is the sum of the motions of y with respect to x and z with respect to y. No doubt Newton was rational in accepting this belief; yet it was false, at least if contemporary physicists are to be trusted. And if they aren't—that is, if they are wrong in contradicting Newton—then *they* exemplify what I'm speaking of; they rationally believe a proposition which, as it turns out, is false.

Nor can we say that a belief is rationally acceptable only if it is possibly true, not necessarily false in the broadly logical sense.[3] For example, I might do the sum $735 + 421 + 9,216$ several times and get the same answer: $10,362$. I am then rational in believing that $735 + 421 + 9,216 = 10,362$, even though the fact is I've made the same error each time—failed

---

1. "Evil and Omnipotence," *Mind* 64 (1955), pp. 203–4.

2. See, for example, T. McPherson, *The Philosophy of Religion* (London: D. Van Nostrand, 1965); T. Penelhum, *Religion and Rationality* (New York: Random House, 1971); J. Ross, *Philosophical Theology* (Indianapolis: Bobbs Merrill, 1969); A. Plantinga, *God and Other Minds* (Ithaca, N.Y.: Cornell University Press 1967), and many others.

3. See my book *The Nature of Necessity* (Oxford: Clarendon Press, 1974), chap. 1.

to carry a "1" from the first column—and thus believe what is necessarily false. Or I might be a mathematical neophyte who hears from his teacher that every continuous function is differentiable. I need not be irrational in believing this, despite the fact that it is necessarily false. Examples of this sort can be multiplied.

So this question presents something of an initial enigma in that it is by no means easy to say what it is for a belief to be rational. And the fact is those philosophers who ask this question about belief in God do not typically try to answer it by giving necessary and sufficient conditions for rational belief. Instead, they typically ask whether the believer has *evidence* or *sufficient evidence* for his belief; or they may try to argue that in fact there is sufficient evidence for the proposition that there is *no* God; but in any case they try to answer this question by finding evidence for or against theistic belief. Philosophers who think there are sound arguments for the existence of God—the natural theologians—claim there is good evidence *for* this proposition; philosophers who believe that there are sound arguments for the non-existence of God naturally claim that there is evidence *against* this proposition. But they concur in holding that belief in God is rational only if there is, on balance, a preponderance of evidence for it—or less radically, only if there is not, on balance, a preponderance of evidence against it.

The nineteenth-century philosopher W. K. Clifford provides a splendid if somewhat strident example of the view that the believer in God must have evidence if he is not to be irrational. Here he does not discriminate against religious belief; he apparently holds that a belief of any sort at all is rationally acceptable only if there is sufficient evidence for it. And he goes on to insist that it is wicked, immoral, monstrous, and perhaps even impolite to accept a belief for which one does not have sufficient evidence:

> Whoso would deserve well of his fellows in this matter will guard the purity of his belief with a very fanaticism of jealous care, lest at any time it should rest on an unworthy object, and catch a stain which can never be wiped away.

He adds that if a

> belief has been accepted on insufficient evidence, the pleasure is a stolen one. Not only does it deceive ourselves by giving us a sense of power which we do not really possess, but it is sinful, because it is stolen in defiance of our duty to mankind. That duty is to guard ourselves from such beliefs as from a pestilence which may shortly master our body and spread to the rest of the town.

And finally:

To sum up: it is wrong always, everywhere, and for anyone to believe anything upon insufficient evidence.[4]

(It is not hard to detect, in these quotations, the "tone of robustious pathos" with which William James credits him.) Clifford finds it utterly obvious, furthermore, that those who believe in God do indéed so believe on insufficient evidence and thus deserve the above abuse. A believer in God is, on his view, at best a harmless pest and at worst a menace to society; in either case he should be discouraged.

Here Clifford is urging *the evidentialist objection to theistic belief*—the claim that belief in God is irrational, or unreasonable, or noetically substandard because, so goes the claim, there is insufficient evidence for it. Suppose we take a deeper look at this position. What is essential to it is the claim that we must evaluate the rationality of belief in God by examining its relation to *other* propositions. We are directed to estimate its rationality by determining whether we have *evidence* for it—whether we know, or at any rate rationally believe, some other propositions which stand in the appropriate relation to the proposition in question. And belief in God is rational, or reasonable, or rationally acceptable, on this view, only if there are other propositions with respect to which it is thus evident.

According to the Cliffordian position, then, there is a set of propositions E such that my belief in God is rational if and only if it is evident with respect to E—if and only if E constitutes, on balance, evidence for it. But what propositions are to be found in E? Do we know that belief in God is not itself in E? If it *is*, of course, then it is certainly evident with respect to E. How does a proposition get into E anyway? How do we decide which propositions are the ones such that my belief in God is rational if and only if it is evident with respect to them? Should we say that E contains the propositions that I *know*? But then, for our question to be interesting, we should first have to argue or agree that I don't know that God exists—that I only *believe* it, whether rationally or irrationally. This position is widely taken for granted, and indeed taken for granted by theists as well as others. But why should the latter concede that he doesn't know that God exists— that at best he rationally believes it? The Bible regularly speaks of *knowledge* in this context—not just rational or well-founded belief. Of course it is true that the believer has *faith*—faith in God, faith in what He reveals— but this by no means settles the issue. The question is whether he doesn't also *know* that God exists. Indeed, according to the Heidelberg Catechism, knowledge is an essential element of faith, so that one has true faith that *p* only if he knows that *p*:

4. W. K. Clifford, "The Ethics of Belief," from *Lectures and Essays* (London: Macmillan, 1979).

True faith is not only a certain (i.e., sure) knowledge whereby I hold for truth all that God has revealed in His word, but also a deep-rooted assurance created in me by the Holy Spirit through the gospel that not only others but I too have had my sins forgiven, have been made forever right with God and have been granted salvation. (Q 21)

So from this point of view a man has true faith that p only if he knows that p, and also meets a certain further condition: roughly (where p is a universal proposition) that of accepting the universal instantiation of p with respect to himself. Now of course the theist may be unwilling to concede that he does not have true faith. But if he does have true faith, then, at least according to the Catechism, he has a "certain (i.e., sure) knowledge" of such revealed truths as that, e.g., "God so loved the world that he gave his only son, that whoever believes in him should not perish but have everlasting life" (John 3:16)—a truth that self-evidently entails that God exists. Accordingly the theist may be unwilling to concede that he does not know but only believes that God exists.

II. CLASSICAL FOUNDATIONALISM

Now of course the evidentialist will not be at all eager to agree that belief in God belongs in E. But why not? To answer we must take a deeper look at his position. The evidentialist objection is nearly always rooted in *classical foundationalism*, an enormously popular picture or total way of looking at faith, knowledge, justified belief, rationality and allied topics. This picture has had a long and distinguished career in the history of philosophy, including among its adherents Plato, Aristotle, Aquinas, Descartes, Leibniz, Locke, and, to leap to the present, Professor Roderick Chisholm; its near relatives, perhaps, remain the dominant ways of thinking about these topics. We may think of the classical foundationalist as beginning with the observation that some of one's beliefs may be *based upon* others; it may be that there are a pair of propositions A and B such that I believe A *on the basis of B*. Although this relation isn't easy to characterize in a revealing and non-trivial fashion, it is nonetheless familiar. I believe that the word "umbrageous" is spelled u-m-b-r-a-g-e-o-u-s: this belief is based on another belief of mine; the belief that that's how the dictionary says it's spelled. I believe that $72 \times 71 = 5112$. This belief is based upon several other beliefs I hold: that $1 \times 72 = 72$; $7 \times 2 = 14$; $7 \times 7 = 49$; $49 + 1 = 50$; and others. Some of my beliefs, however, I accept but don't accept on the basis of any other beliefs. Call these beliefs *basic*. I believe that $2 + 1 = 3$, for example, and don't believe it on the basis of other propositions. I also believe that I am seated at my desk, and that there is a mild pain in my right knee. These too are basic for me; I don't believe them on the basis of any

other propositions. According to the classical foundationalist, some propositions are *properly* or *rightly* basic for a person and some are not. Those that
are not, are rationally accepted only on the basis of *evidence,* where the
evidence must trace back, ultimately, to what is properly basic.

Suppose we say that the assemblage of beliefs a person holds, together
with the various logical and epistemic relations that hold among them, constitutes that person's noetic structure; and let's say that the *foundations* of
S's noetic structure (call it "F") is the set of propositions that are *basic* for
S and *properly* basic for him.

And from the foundationalist point of view, our question must be restated: Is belief in God evident with respect to the foundations of my noetic
structure? Clifford, as I say, takes it to be obvious that the answer is no.
But is this obvious? To restate my earlier question: Might it not be that my
belief in God is itself in the foundations of my noetic structure? Perhaps it
is a member of F, in which case, of course, it will automatically be evident
with respect to F.

Here the classical foundationalist goes further. Not just any belief can
properly be in the foundations of a person's noetic structure; to be in F a
belief must meet some fairly specific conditions. It must be capable of
functioning foundationally; it must be capable of bearing its share of the
weight of the entire noetic structure. The propositions in F, of course, are
not inferred from other propositions and are not accepted on the basis of
other propositions. I *know* the propositions in the foundations of my noetic
structure, but not by virtue of knowing other propositions; for these are
the ones I start with. And so the question the foundationalist asks about
belief in God—namely, what is the evidence for it?—is not properly asked
about the members of F; these items don't require to be evident with respect to other propositions in order to be rationally believed. Accordingly,
says the foundationalist, not just any proposition is capable of functioning
foundationally; to be so capable, with respect to a person S, a proposition
must not need the evidential support of other propositions; it must be such
that it is possible that S know *p* but have no evidence for *p.*

Well, suppose all this is so; what kind of propositions can function
foundationally? Here different foundationalists give different answers.
Aristotle and Aquinas, for example, held that self-evident propositions—ones
like *all black dogs are black*—belong in the foundations. Aquinas, at least,
seems also to hold that propositions "evident to the senses," as he puts it—
propositions like *some things change*—belong there. For he believed, of
course, that the existence of God is demonstrable; and by this I think he
meant that God's existence can be deduced from foundational propositions.
He holds, furthermore, that God's existence can be demonstrated "from his
effects"—from sensible objects; and in each of the five ways there is a
premise that, says Aquinas, is "evident to the senses." I therefore believe

Aquinas meant to include such propositions among the foundations. You may think it strange, incidentally, to count Aquinas among the Cliffordians. On this point, however, he probably belongs with them; he held that belief in God is rational only if supported by the foundations. Of course he differs from Clifford in holding that in fact God's existence *is* supported by them; he thinks it follows from members of F by argument forms that are themselves in F. This, indeed, is the burden of his five ways.

According to Aquinas, therefore, self-evident propositions and those evident to the senses belong in the foundations. And when he speaks of propositions of the latter sort, he means such propositions as

(1) there's a tree over there,
(2) there is an ashtray on my desk,
(3) that tree's leaves have turned yellow,

and

(4) this fender has rusted through.

Modern foundationalists—Descartes, for example—argue that what goes into the foundations, in addition to self-evident propositions, are not propositions that, like (1)–(4), entail the existence of such material objects as ashtrays, trees, leaves, and fenders, but more cautious claims; for example:

(5) I seem to see a red book,
(6) it seems to me that I see a book with a red cover,
(7) I seem to see something red,

or even, as Professor Chisholm put it,

(8) I am appeared redly to.

The modern foundationalist who opts for propositions like (5)–(8) rather than (1)–(4) has a prima facie plausible reason for doing so: Belief in a proposition of the latter sort seems to have a sort of immunity from error not enjoyed by belief in one of the former. I may believe that there is a red ashtray on my desk, or that I see a red ashtray on my desk, when the fact is there is no red ashtray there at all: I am color-blind, or hallucinating, or the victim of an illusion of some sort or other. But it is at the least very much harder to see that I could be wrong in believing that I *seem* to see a red ashtray on my desk—that, in Chisholm's language, I am appeared redly (or red-ashtrayly) to. There are plenty of possible worlds in which I mistakenly believe that there is a red book on my desk; it is at least plausible to hold that there are no possible worlds in which I mistakenly believe that I seem to see a red book there. And this immunity from error may plausibly be taken to provide a reason for distinguishing between propositions like

(5)–(8) and (1)–(4), admitting the former but not the latter to the foundations.

There is a small problem here, however: Every necessarily true proposition—every proposition true in all possible worlds—is such that there is no possible world in which I mistakenly believe it. Yet presumably the foundationalist will not be inclined to hold that every necessary proposition I believe is in the foundations of my noetic structure. Consider, for example, Goldbach's Conjecture that every even number greater than two is the sum of two primes. This proposition is either necessarily true or necessarily false, although it isn't presently known which. Suppose it is in fact true, and I believe it, but not because I have found a proof of it; I simply believe it. The foundationalist will presumably hold, in this case, that my belief in Goldbach's Conjecture is necessarily true but not a good candidate for the foundations. Here I truly believe but do not know the proposition in question; so it does not belong among the foundations, and this despite the fact that there is no possible world in which I mistakenly believe it.

Presumably, then, the modern foundationalist will not hold that just any necessarily true belief is automatically among the foundations. He may argue instead that what characterizes propositions like (5)–(8) is not just that it is not possible to believe them mistakenly, but that it is not possible to be mistaken about them. That is to say, a proposition of this sort is like a necessary proposition in that it is not possible for me to believe it mistakenly; it is unlike a necessary proposition, however, in that it is also not possible for me to believe its *denial* mistakenly. If I believe that I am appeared to redly, then it follows that I *am* appeared to redly; but if I believe that I am not appeared to redly, it follows equally that I am not thus appeared to. We might say that propositions meeting this condition are *incorrigible* for me; perhaps we can explain this notion thus:

(9) p is incorrigible for S at t iff there is no possible world in which S mistakenly believes p at t and no possible world in which S mistakenly believes not-p at t.[5]

According to our paradigm Cliffordian, then, a belief is properly in the foundations of my noetic structure only if it is either self-evident or incorrigible for me. So suppose we take a look at self-evidence. What is it? Under what conditions is a proposition self-evident? What kinds of proposi-

5. Philip Quinn has pointed out (in correspondence) that, according to (9), false propositions will be incorrigible for me now: Although I do not now seem to see something green, the proposition *I seem to see something green* is incorrigible for me now. I'm not certain this feature of the definition is a defect; if it is, it can be repaired by adding the clause "p is true" to the definiens or, as Quinn suggests, by adding "S believes p at t."

tions are self-evident? Examples would include very simple arithmetical truths such as

(10) $2 + 1 = 3$,

simple truths of logic such as

(11) no man is both married and unmarried,

perhaps the generalizations of simple truths of logic, such as

(12) for any proposition p, the conjunction of p with its denial is false,

and certain propositions expressing identity and diversity; for example:

(13) Redness is distinct from greenness,
(14) the property of being prime is distinct from the property of being composite,

and

(15) the proposition *all men are mortal* is distinct from the proposition *all mortals are men*.[6]

There are others; Aquinas gives as examples:

(16) the whole is greater than the part,

where, presumably, he means by "part" what we mean by "proper part," and, more dubiously,

(17) man is an animal.[7]

Still other candidates—candidates which may be less than entirely un controversial—come from many other areas; for example:

(18) if p is necessarily true and p entails q, then q is necessarily true,
(19) if e^1 occurs before e^2 and e^2 occurs before e^3, then e^1 occurs before e^3,

and

(20) it is wrong to cause unnecessary (and unwanted) pain just for the fun of it.

What is it that characterizes these propositions? According to the tradition, the outstanding characteristic of a self-evident proposition is that one simply sees it to be true upon grasping or understanding it. Under-

6. Examples of these kinds are given by Locke, *Essay Concerning Human Understanding*, Book IV, chap. 7.
7. *Summa Theologica* 1, Q1 a2; *Summa Contra Gentiles* I, chap. 10.

standing a self-evident proposition is sufficient for apprehending its truth. Of course this notion must be relativized to *persons;* what is self-evident to you might not be to me. Very simple arithmetical truths will be self-evident to nearly all of us; but a truth like $17 + 18 = 35$ may be self-evident only to some. And of course a proposition is self-evident to a person only if he does in fact grasp it; so a proposition will not be self-evident to those who do not apprehend the concepts involved in the proposition. As Aquinas says, some propositions are self-evident only to the learned; his example is the truth that immaterial substances do not occupy space. Among those propositions whose concepts not everyone grasps, some are such that anyone who *did* grasp them would see their truth; for example:

(21) A model of a first order theory T assigns truth to the axioms of T.

Others—$17 + 13 = 30$, for example—may be such that some but not all of those who apprehend them also see that they are true.

But how shall we understand this "seeing that they are true"? Those who speak of self-evidence explicitly turn to this visual metaphor and expressly explain self-evidence by reference to vision. There are two important aspects to the metaphor and two corresponding components to the idea of self-evidence. First, there is the *epistemic* component: a proposition p is self-evident to a person S only if S has *immediate* knowledge of p—i.e., knows p, and does not know p on the basis of his knowledge of other propositions. Consider a simple arithmetic truth such as $2 + 1 = 3$ and compare it with one like $24 \times 24 = 576$. I know each of these propositions; and I know the second but not the first on the basis of computation, which is a kind of inference. So I have immediate knowledge of the first but not the second. The epistemic component of self-evidence, therefore, is immediate knowledge; it follows, of course, that any proposition self-evident to a person is true.

But there is also a phenomenological component. Consider again our two propositions; the first but not the second has about it a kind of luminous aura or glow when you bring it to mind or consider it. Locke speaks, in this connection, of an "evident luster"; a self-evident proposition, he says, displays a kind of "clarity and brightness to the attentive mind." Descartes speaks instead of "clarity and distinctness"; each, I think, is referring to the same phenomenological feature. And this feature is connected with another: Upon understanding a proposition of this sort one feels a strong inclination to accept it; this luminous obviousness seems to compel or at least impel assent. Aquinas and Locke, indeed, held that a person, or at any rate a normal well-formed human being, finds it impossible to withhold assent when considering a self-evident proposition. The phenomenological component of the idea of self-evidence, then, seems to have a double aspect: There is the luminous aura that $2 + 1 = 3$ displays, and there is also an experienced tendency to accept or believe it. Perhaps, indeed, the luminous aura *just is* the experienced impulsion towards acceptance; perhaps these are the very same thing. In that case the phenomenological component would not have the double aspect I suggested it did have; in either case, however, we must recognize this phenomenological aspect of self-evidence.

Now suppose we return to the main question: Why shouldn't belief in God be among the foundations of my noetic structure? Can belief in God be properly basic for a person? If not, why not? The answer, on the part of the modern foundationalist was that even if this belief is *true*, it does not have the characteristics a proposition must have to deserve a place in the foundations. There is no room in the foundations for a proposition that can be known only on the basis of other propositions. A proposition is properly basic for a person only if he knows it immediately—i.e., knows it, and does not know it on the basis of other propositions. The proposition that God exists, however, is at best truly believed, not known, and even if it were known, it wouldn't be known immediately. The only propositions that meet this condition of immediate knowledge are those that are self-evident or incorrigible. Since this proposition is neither, it is not properly basic for anyone; that is, no well-formed, rational noetic structure contains this proposition in its foundations.

But why should the theist concede these things? Suppose he grants that there is a foundation to his noetic structure: a set F of propositions such that (1) he knows each member of F *immediately* and (2) whatever else he knows is evident with respect to the members of F. Suppose he concedes, further, that he does know other things, and knows them on the basis of his knowledge of these basic propositions. Suppose, in a particularly irenic and conciliatory frame of mind, he concedes still further that much of what he believes, he believes but does not know; and that the rationality of these beliefs is to be tested or measured by way of their connections with those propositions that are basic for him. Why should he not combine these concessions with the claim that his belief in God is properly basic for him?

Because, says the modern foundationalist, belief in God is neither self-evident nor incorrigible. But now we must look more closely at this fundamental principle of the foundationalist's position:

(22) a proposition *p* is properly basic for a person S if and only if *p* is either self-evident to S or incorrigible for S;

that is, the foundations of a well-formed, rational noetic structure will contain propositions that are self-evident or incorrigible and will not contain any propositions that do not meet this condition.

And here we must ask a question that has been clamoring for attention. How does the foundationalist know—how does anyone know—that, indeed, a given proposition *is* self-evident? How do we tell? Isn't it possible that a proposition should seem to me to be self-evident when in fact it is not? Consider an analogy. Suppose the theist claims that a proposition *p* is properly basic for a person S if S knows *p* *immediately;* and suppose he adds that one of the things he immediately knows is that God exists. The foundationalist, presumably, will want to reply as follows: you *say* you have immediate knowledge of this proposition, but perhaps you are mistaken; perhaps you only *believe* and do not *know* that God exists; perhaps, indeed, God does *not* exist. How do you know that you have immediate knowledge of this proposition? What leads you to think so?

Here the theist may be hard put to give an answer; but the foundationalist may find a similar question similarly embarrassing. How does he know that a given proposition—7 + 5 = 12, for example—is self-evident? Might we not be mistaken in our judgment of self-evidence? It seems obviously possible that there should be a race of persons—on some other planet, let's say—who think they find *other* propositions self-evident, some of these others being the denials of propositions *we* find self-evident. Perhaps this race invariably makes mistakes about what is self-evident. But might not the same thing be true of us? A proposition is self-evident, after all, only if it is *true;* and it certainly seems possible that we should believe a proposition self-evident when in fact it is not.

Nor need we rest content with the mere possibility that we should mistakenly find a proposition self-evident. Here the Russell paradoxes are peculiarly instructive. It seems self-evident to many that some properties—e.g., that of being a horse—do not exemplify themselves, while others—e.g., that of being a property—do. It seems self-evident, furthermore, that if some properties exemplify themselves and others do not, then there is such a property as *self-exemplification:* a property enjoyed by the properties in the first group but lacked by those in the second. But it also seems self-evident that if there is such a property as *self-exemplification,* then there is such a property as *non-self-exemplification:* the property a property has if and only if it does not exemplify itself. And of course it seems self-evident that if there is such a property as *non-self-exemplification,* then either it exemplifies itself or it does not. But if it does exemplify itself, it has the property of non-self-exemplification, in which case it does not exemplify itself. So if it does exemplify itself, it does not exemplify itself. But of course it is also true that if it does exemplify itself, then it does; so if it exemplifies itself, it both does and does not exemplify itself. Hence it does not exemplify itself. If, on the other hand, non-self-exemplification does not exemplify itself, then it does not have the property of non-self-exemplification, in which case it must have the property of self-exemplification, i.e., it exemplifies itself. So if it does not exemplify itself, it does exemplify itself. But it is also true that if it does not exemplify itself, then it does not exemplify it-self; so if it does not exemplify itself, it both does and does not exemplify itself. Hence it is false that it does not exemplify itself, and true that it does. But now from propositions that seem self-evident we have deduced, by arguments that seem self-evidently right, that non-self-exemplification both exemplifies itself and does not exemplify itself; and this seems self-evidently false. The conclusion must be that at least one proposition that *seems* self-evident, is not *in fact* self-evident.

We must distinguish, therefore, what *appears* to be self-evident from what really *is*. Suppose we say that a proposition *seems* or *appears* self-evident to a person if he understands it, and if it displays the phenomeno-logical feature referred to above—the "evident luster" of which Locke speaks—when he attentively considers it. How, then, does the foundation-alist determine which propositions really *are* self-evident for him? By noting, of course, which ones appear self-evident to him; he has nothing else to go on. Of course he cannot sensibly hold that *whatever* appears self-evident, really is; that is the lesson of the Russell paradoxes. Perhaps, however, he can retreat to a weaker principle; perhaps he can hold that whatever seems self-evident has, as we might put it, the presumption of self-evidence in its favor. What appears to be self-evident ought to be taken to be self-evident unless there are reasons to the contrary—unless, for example, it appears self-evident that the proposition in question con-flicts with *other* apparently self-evident propositions. And perhaps he will support this injunction by appeal to some such principles as

(24) Whatever seems self-evident is very likely true

or

(25) most propositions that *seem* self-evident *are* self-evident (and hence true).

But why should we accept (24) and (25)? Why does the foundational-ist accept them? We should note, first of all, that neither of these proposi-tions seems self-evident. One who understands them can nonetheless won-der whether they are true and in fact reject them. They do not possess that evident luster; and there certainly seem to be thinkable alternatives. Impressed with evolutionary theory, for example, we might suppose that the disposition to find these propositions self-evident is a trait emerging in the course of a long evolutionary development—a trait that has a certain sur-vival value, but is at best fortuitously connected with truth, so that many or most of the propositions that appear self-evident to us are in fact false. Or, remembering our Descartes, we might speculate that we have been created by a being who delights in deception and produces in us a power-ful tendency to accept certain false propositions as self-evident. Or we might speculate, in a Kierkegaardian vein, that our noetic endowment, once pristine and totally reliable, has been corrupted by some primal cataclysm befalling the human race. So (24) and (25) are not themselves apparently self-evident.

The important point here, however, lies in a different direction. Suppose these principles—(24) and (25)—*were* apparently self-evident. That is, suppose the proposition

> (26) most propositions that display the phenomenological feature are true

itself displayed this feature. Would that be a relevant answer to the question of what reason, if any, there is for believing that most propositions displaying this feature are true? It is hard to see how. The question is whether a proposition's displaying this feature is a reason for thinking it true; to reply that (26) itself displays this feature is simply to invite the question again. Here the appeal to self-evidence seems entirely unsatisfactory. It is as if the theist were to reply to the question: "Why believe in God?" by pointing out that God requires us to believe in Him, and requires us to believe only what is true. This may indeed be so; but it does not supply a reason for belief for anyone who does not already believe. Similarly, the claim that (24) and (25) are apparently self-evident, may or may not be true; but it can serve as a reason for accepting them only for someone who already accepts them. And hence it cannot serve as a reason, for the foundationalist, for accepting them.

The fact of the matter is, I think, that the foundationalist has no reason at all for accepting (24) and (25). They do not appear to be self-evident; and of course they are not incorrigible. But if the foundationalist *does* have a reason for them, that reason must trace back, ultimately, to the foundations; that is, the foundationalist has a reason, on his own view, for (24) and (25) only if they are evident with respect to propositions that are properly basic for him—propositions that are self-evident or incorrigible. It is hard to see how (24) or (25) could be evident with respect to such propositions.

Accordingly, the foundationalist accepts (24) and (25) but has no reason for so doing. He isn't *obliged* to accept them; there are alternatives. He simply commits himself to them. We might say that he commits himself to the trustworthiness of his noetic equipment. More elegantly, he commits himself to the reliability of his epistemic endowment. If, with an older tradition, we think of reason as an organ, or power, or faculty—the faculty whereby we discern what is self-evident—then the foundationalist commits himself to the basic reliability of reason. He doesn't do so, of course, as a result of (broadly speaking) scientific or rational investigation; he does so in advance of such investigation. For he has no reasons for accepting (24) and (25); but he does accept them, and he uses them to determine the acceptability of *other* propositions. In other words, (24) and (25) are members of the foundation of his noetic structure.

The foundationalist, therefore, commits himself to the basic reliability of reason. I do not say this by way of criticism; it is a commitment I share. The theist is by no means obliged to reject this commitment. Augustine, indeed, argued that reason is ultimately reliable just because God has created us and is not a deceiver. He has created us in such a way that certain propositions appear self-evident to us; and because he is a God of goodness and truth, he would not create us in such a way that *false* propositions should appear self-evident. Had Augustine been apprised of the Russell paradoxes, he might have expressed himself more guardedly; but his basic point remains. One who believes in God can certainly accept (24) and (25); and he, unlike the foundationalist, can give a reason for doing so.

Since the theist can properly concur with the foundationalist on (24) and (25), he can agree with the latter that apparently self-evident and incorrigible propositions are properly basic for S. But the foundationalist *credo*, we have seen, contains *two* elements, a positive and a negative. The foundationalist holds, positively, that

(27) self-evident and incorrigible propositions are properly basic for S,

and he adds, negatively, that

(28) *only* propositions of those sorts are properly basic for S.

But why should we accept this negative element? What is there to be said in favor of it? Do we have anything more than the foundationalist's word for (28)?

The fact is we have *less* than the foundationalist's word for it. For consider (28). (28) is neither self-evident nor incorrigible; nor does it appear to follow from propositions that are. It is, therefore, basic for the foundationalist. So he holds that self-evident and incorrigible propositions are the only viable candidates for the foundations of his noetic structure, but he himself accepts (28) as basic, which is neither self-evident nor incorrigible. Accordingly, the foundationalist is hoist on his own petard; his characteristic claim is self-referentially incoherent.[8] Is there then any reason at all for believing (28)? If so, it is hard to see what it might be. (28) certainly does not appear to be self-evident; it is certainly not incorrigible. It is very hard to see, furthermore, that it either follows from or is evident with respect to propositions that are self-evident or incorrigible. So it is hard to see that there is any reason for accepting (28), even from a roughly foun-

8. (28), of course, is stated for modern foundationalism, but precisely similar remarks apply to the ancient and medieval foundationalism embraced by Aristotle and Aquinas.

dationalist point of view. Why then should we accept it? Why should the theist feel any obligation to believe it?

The answer, I believe, is that there is no reason at all for accepting (28); it is no more than a bit of intellectual imperialism on the part of the foundationalist. He means to commit himself to reason and to nothing more; he therefore declares irrational any noetic structure that contains more—belief in God, for example—in its foundations. But here there is no reason for the theist to follow his example.

III. IS BELIEF IN GOD PROPERLY BASIC?

Now many Reformed theologians[9] and thinkers have rejected *natural theology* (thought of as the attempt to provide proofs or arguments for the existence of God). They have held not merely that the proffered arguments are unsuccessful, but that the whole enterprise is in some way radically misguided. I've argued elsewhere[10] that the Reformed rejection of natural theology is best construed as an inchoate and unfocused rejection of classical foundationalism. What these Reformed thinkers really mean to hold, I think, is that belief in God need not be based on argument or evidence from other propositions at all. They mean to hold that the believer is entirely within his intellectual rights in believing as he does even if he doesn't know of any good theistic argument (deductive or non-deductive), even if he doesn't believe that there is any such argument, and even if in fact no such argument exists. They hold that it is perfectly rational to accept belief in God without accepting it on the basis of any other beliefs or propositions at all. In a word, they hold that *belief in God is properly basic.* And insofar as they mean to reject classical foundationalism, they are to be applauded; classical foundationalism is eminently rejectable. Of course it does not follow that belief in God *is* properly basic; perhaps the class of properly basic propositions is broader than classical foundationalists think, but still not broad enough to admit belief in God. But why think so? What might be the objections to the Reformed view that belief in God is properly basic? I wish to examine two such objections.

It is sometimes claimed that if I have no evidence for the existence of God, then if I accept that proposition my belief will be groundless, or gratuitous, or arbitrary. I think this is an error; let me explain. Suppose we consider perceptual beliefs, memory beliefs, and beliefs ascribing mental states to other persons: such beliefs as

9. A Reformed theologian is one whose intellectual sympathies lie with the Protestant tradition going back to John Calvin (not someone who was formerly a theologian and has since seen the light).
10. "The Reformed Objection to Natural Theology," *Proceedings of the American Catholic Philosophical Association,* 1980.

(29) I see a tree,
(30) I had breakfast this morning,

and

(31) That person is angry.

Although beliefs of this sort are typically and properly taken as basic, it would be a mistake to describe them as *groundless*. Upon having an experience of a certain sort, I believe that I am perceiving a tree. In the typical case, I do not hold this belief on the basis of other beliefs; it is nonetheless not groundless. My having that characteristic sort of experience—to use Professor Chisholm's language, my being appeared treely to—plays a crucial role in the formation and justification of that belief. We might say this experience, together, perhaps, with other circumstances, is what *justifies* me in holding it; this is the *ground* of my justification, and, by extension, the ground of the belief itself.

If I see someone displaying typical pain behavior, I take it that he or she is in pain. Again, I don't take the displayed behavior as *evidence* for that belief; I don't infer that belief from others I hold; I don't accept it on the basis of other beliefs. Still, my perceiving the pain behavior plays a unique role in the formation and justification of that belief; as in the previous case, it forms the ground of my justification for the belief in question. The same holds for memory beliefs. I seem to remember having breakfast this morning; that is, I have an inclination to believe the proposition that I had breakfast, along with a certain past-tinged experience that is familiar to all but hard to describe. Perhaps we should say that I am appeared to pastly; but perhaps that insufficiently distinguishes the experience in question from that accompanying beliefs about the past not grounded in my own memory. The phenomenology of memory is a rich and unexplored realm; here I have no time to explore it. In this case as in the others, however, there is a justifying circumstance present, a condition that forms the ground of my justification for accepting the memory belief in question.

In each of these cases, a belief is taken as basic, and in each case properly taken as basic. In each case there is some circumstance or condition that confers justification; there is a circumstance that serves as the *ground* of justification. So in each case there will be some true proposition of the sort:

(32) In condition C, S is justified in taking p as basic.

Of course C will vary with p. For a perceptual judgment such as

(33) I see a rose-colored wall before me,

C will include my being appeared to in a certain fashion. No doubt *C* will include more. If I'm appeared to in the familiar fashion but know that I'm wearing rose-colored glasses, or that I am suffering from a disease that causes me to be thus appeared to, no matter what the color of the nearby objects, then I'm not justified in taking (33) as basic. Similarly for memory. Suppose I know that my memory is unreliable; it often plays me tricks. In particular, when I seem to remember having breakfast, then, more often than not, I *haven't* had breakfast. Under these conditions I am not justified in taking it as basic that I had breakfast, even though I seem to remember that I did.

So being appropriately appeared to, in the perceptual case, is not sufficient for justification; some further condition—a condition hard to state in detail—is clearly necessary. The central point here, however, is that a belief is properly basic only in certain conditions; these conditions are, we might say, the ground of its justification and, by extension, the ground of the belief itself. In this sense, basic beliefs are not, or are not necessarily, *groundless* beliefs.

Now similar things may be said about belief in God. When the Reformers claim that this belief is properly basic, they do not mean to say, of course, that there are no justifying circumstances for it, or that it is in that sense groundless or gratuitous. Quite the contrary. Calvin holds that God "reveals and daily discloses himself in the whole workmanship of the universe," and the divine art "reveals itself in the innumerable and yet distinct and well ordered variety of the heavenly host." God has so created us that we have a tendency or disposition to see his hand in the world about us. More precisely, there is in us a disposition to believe propositions of the sort *this flower was created by God* or *this vast and intricate universe was created by God* when we contemplate the flower or behold the starry heavens or think about the vast reaches of the universe.

Calvin recognizes, at least implicitly, that other sorts of conditions may trigger this disposition. Upon reading the Bible, one may be impressed with a deep sense that God is speaking to him. Upon having done what I know is cheap, or wrong, or wicked, I may feel guilty in God's sight and form the belief *God disapproves of what I've done.* Upon confession and repentance, I may feel forgiven, forming the belief *God forgives me for what I've done.* A person in grave danger may turn to God, asking for his protection and help; and of course he or she then forms the belief that God is indeed able to hear and help if he sees fit. When life is sweet and satisfying, a spontaneous sense of gratitude may well up within the soul; someone in this condition may thank and praise the Lord for his goodness, and will of course form the accompanying belief that indeed the Lord is to be thanked and praised.

There are therefore many conditions and circumstances that call forth belief in God: guilt, gratitude, danger, a sense of God's presence, a sense that he speaks, perception of various parts of the universe. A complete job would explore the phenomenology of all these conditions and of more besides. This is a large and important topic; but here I can only point to the existence of these conditions.

Of course, none of the beliefs I mentioned a moment ago is the simple belief that God exists. What we have instead are such beliefs as

(34) God is speaking to me,
(35) God has created all this,
(36) God disapproves of what I have done,
(37) God forgives me,

and

(38) God is to be thanked and praised.

These propositions are properly basic in the right circumstances. But it is quite consistent with this to suppose that the proposition *there is such a person as God* is neither properly basic nor taken as basic by those who believe in God. Perhaps what they take as basic are such propositions as (34)–(38), believing in the existence of God on the basis of propositions such as those. From this point of view, it isn't exactly right to say that it is belief in God that is properly basic; more exactly, what are properly basic are such propositions as (34)–(38), each of which self-evidently entails that God exists. It isn't the relatively high level and general proposition *God exists* that is properly basic, but instead propositions detailing some of his attributes or actions.

Suppose we return to the analogy between belief in God and belief in God and belief in the existence of perceptual objects, other persons, and the past. Here too it is relatively specific and concrete propositions rather than their more general and abstract colleagues that are properly basic. Perhaps such items as

(39) There are trees,
(40) There are other persons,

and

(41) The world has existed for more than five minutes

are not in fact properly basic; it is instead such propositions as

(42) I see a tree,
(43) That person is pleased,

and

(44) I had breakfast more than an hour ago

that deserve that accolade. Of course, propositions of the latter sort immediately and self-evidently entail propositions of the former sort; and perhaps there is thus no harm in speaking of the former as properly basic, even though so to speak is to speak a bit loosely.

The same must be said about belief in God. We may say, speaking loosely, that belief in God is properly basic; strictly speaking, however, it is probably not that proposition but such propositions as (34)–(38) that enjoy that status. But the main point, here, is this: belief in God or (34)–(38), are properly basic; to say so, however, is not to deny that there are justifying conditions for these beliefs, or conditions that confer justification on one who accepts them as basic. They are therefore not groundless or gratuitous.

A second objection I've often heard: If belief in God is properly basic, why can't *just any* belief be properly basic? Couldn't we say the same for any bizarre aberration we can think of? What about voodoo or astrology? What about the belief that the Great Pumpkin returns every Halloween? Could I properly take *that* as basic? And if I can't, why can I properly take belief in God as basic? Suppose I believe that if I flap my arms with sufficient vigor, I can take off and fly about the room; could I defend myself against the charge of irrationality by claiming this belief is basic? If we say that belief in God is properly basic, won't we be committed to holding that just anything, or nearly anything, can properly be taken as basic, thus throwing wide the gates to irrationalism and superstition?

Certainly not. What might lead one to think the Reformed epistemologist is in this kind of trouble? The fact that he rejects the criteria for proper basicality purveyed by classical foundationalism? But why should *that* be thought to commit him to such tolerance of irrationality? Consider an analogy. In the palmy days of positivism, the positivists went about confidently wielding their verifiability criterion and declaring meaningless much that was obviously meaningful. Now suppose someone rejected a formulation of that criterion—the one to be found in the second edition of A. J. Ayer's *Language, Truth and Logic,* for example. Would that mean she was committed to holding that

(45) " 'Twas brillig; and the slithy toves did gyre and bymble in the wabe,"

contrary to appearances, makes good sense? Of course not. But then the same goes for the Reformed epistemologist; the fact that he rejects the classical foundationalist's criterion of proper basicality does not mean that he is committed to supposing just anything is properly basic.

But what then is the problem? Is it that the Reformed epistemologist not only rejects those criteria for proper basicality, but seems in no hurry to produce what he takes to be a better substitute? If he has no such criterion, how can he fairly reject belief in the Great Pumpkin as properly basic?

This objection betrays an important misconception. How do we rightly arrive at or develop criteria for meaningfulness, or justified belief, or proper basicality? Where do they come from? Must one have such a criterion before one can sensibly make any judgments—positive or negative—about proper basicality? Surely not. Suppose I don't know of a satisfactory substitute for the criteria proposed by classical foundationalism; I am nevertheless entirely within my rights in holding that certain propositions are not properly basic in certain conditions. Some propositions seem self-evident when in fact they are not; that is the lesson of some of the Russell paradoxes. Nevertheless it would be irrational to take as basic the denial of a proposition that seems self-evident to you. Similarly, suppose it seems to you that you see a tree; you would then be irrational in taking as basic the proposition that you don't see a tree, or that there aren't any trees. In the same way, even if I don't know of some illuminating criterion of meaning, I can quite properly declare (45) meaningless.

And this raises an important question—one Roderick Chisholm has taught us to ask. What is the status of criteria for knowledge, or proper basicality, or justified belief? Typically, these are universal statements. The modern foundationalist's criterion for proper basicality, for example, is doubly universal:

(46) For any proposition A and person S, A is properly basic for S if and only if A is incorrigible for S or self-evident to S.

But how could one know a thing like that? What are its credentials? Clearly enough, (46) isn't self-evident or just obviously true. But if it isn't, how does one arrive at it? What sorts of arguments would be appropriate? Of course a foundationalist might find (46) so appealing, he simply takes it to be true, neither offering argument for it, nor accepting it on the basis of other things he believes. If he does so, however, then, as we have seen in connection with (28), his noetic structure will be self-referentially incoherent. (46) itself is neither self-evident nor incorrigible; hence in accepting (46) as basic, the modern foundationalist violates the condition of proper basicality he himself lays down in accepting it. On the other hand, perhaps the foundationalist will try to produce some argument for it from premises that are self-evident or incorrigible; it is exceedingly hard to see, however, what such an argument might be like. And until he has produced such arguments, what shall the rest of us do—we who do not find (46) at all obvious or compelling? How could he use (46) to show us that belief in God, for example, is not properly basic? Why should we believe (46), or pay it any attention?

The fact is, I think, that neither (46) nor any other revealing necessary and sufficient condition for proper basicality follows from clearly self-evident premisses by clearly acceptable arguments. And hence the proper way to arrive at such a criterion is, broadly speaking, *inductive*. We must assemble examples of beliefs and conditions such that the former are obviously properly basic in the latter, and examples of beliefs and conditions such that the former are obviously *not* properly basic in the latter. We must then frame hypotheses as to the necessary and sufficient conditions of proper basicality and test these hypotheses by reference to those examples. Under the right conditions, for example, it is clearly rational to believe that you see a human person before you: a being who has thoughts and feelings, who knows and believes things, who makes decisions and acts. It is clear, furthermore, that you are under no obligation to reason to this belief from others you hold; under those conditions that belief is properly basic for you. But then (46) must be mistaken; the belief in question, under those circumstances, is properly basic, though neither self-evident nor incorrigible for you. Similarly, you may seem to remember that you had breakfast this morning, and perhaps you know of no reason to suppose your memory is playing you tricks. If so, you are entirely justified in taking that belief as basic. Of course it isn't properly basic on the criteria offered by classical foundationalists; but that fact counts not against you but against those criteria.

Accordingly, criteria for proper basicality must be reached from below rather than above; they should not be presented *ex cathedra* but argued and tested by a relevant set of examples. But there is no reason to assume, in advance, that everyone will agree on the examples. The Christian or Jew will of course suppose that belief in God is entirely proper and rational; if he doesn't accept this belief on the basis of other propositions, he will conclude that it is basic for him and quite properly so. Followers of Bertrand Russell and Madelyn Murray O'Hare may disagree, but how is that relevant? Must my criteria, or those of the believing community, conform to their examples? Surely not. The theistic community is responsible to *its* set of examples, not to theirs.

Accordingly, the Reformed epistemologist can properly hold that belief in the Great Pumpkin is not properly basic, even though he holds that belief in God *is* properly basic, and even if he has no full-fledged criterion of proper basicality. Of course he is committed to supposing that there is a relevant *difference* between belief in God and belief in the Great Pumpkin, if he holds that the former but not the latter is properly basic. But this should prove no great embarrassment; there are plenty of candidates. These candidates are to be found in the neighborhood of the conditions I mentioned that justify and ground belief in God. Thus, for example, the Reformed epistemologist may concur with Calvin in holding that God has implanted in us a natural tendency to see his hand in the world around us; the same cannot be said for the Great Pumpkin, there being no Great Pumpkin and no natural tendency to accept beliefs about the Great Pumpkin.

By way of conclusion then, the evidentialist objection, insofar as it is based upon classical foundationalism, is bankrupt; being self-evident, or incorrigible, or evident to the senses is not a necessary condition of proper basicality. Furthermore, one who holds that belief in God *is* properly basic is not thereby committed to the idea that belief in God is groundless, or gratuitous, or without justifying circumstances. And even if he lacks a general criterion of proper basicality, he is not obliged to suppose that just any or nearly any belief—belief in the Great Pumpkin, for example— is properly basic. Like everyone should, he begins with examples; and he may take belief in the Great Pumpkin as a paradigm of irrational basic belief.

The New Map
of the Universe of Faiths

JOHN HICK

Let me begin by proposing a working definition of religion as an understanding of the universe, together with an appropriate way of living within it, which involves reference beyond the natural world to God or gods or to the Absolute or to a transcendent order or process. Such a definition includes such theistic faiths as Judaism, Christianity, Islam, Sikhism; the theistic Hinduism of the Bhagavad Gītā; the semi-theistic faith of Mahayana Buddhism and the non-theistic faiths of Theravada Buddhism and non-theistic Hinduism. It does not however include purely naturalistic systems of belief, such as communism and humanism, immensely important though these are today as alternatives to religious faith.

When we look back into the past we find that religion has been a virtually universal dimension of human life—so much so that man has been defined as the religious animal. For he has displayed an innate tendency to experience his environment as being religiously as well as naturally significant, and to feel required to live in it as such. To quote the anthropologist, Raymond Firth, "religion is universal in human societies."[1] "In every human community on earth today," says Wilfred Cantwell Smith, "there exists something that we, as sophisticated observers, may term religion, or a religion. And we are able to see it in each case as the latest development in a continuous tradition that goes back, we can now affirm, for at least

[margin note: HOMO RELIGIOSUS]

1. *Elements of Social Organization,* 3rd ed. (London: Tavistock Publications, 1969), p. 216.

Reprinted by permission of the author from *God and the Universe of Faiths* (London: The Macmillan Press Ltd., 1973), ch. 10.

one hundred thousand years."[2] In the life of primitive man this religious tendency is expressed in a belief in sacred objects, endowed with *mana*, and in a multitude of nature and ancestral spirits needing to be carefully propitiated. The divine was here crudely apprehended as a plurality of quasi-animal forces which could to some extent be controlled by ritualistic and magical procedures. This represents the simplest beginning of man's awareness of the transcendent in the infancy of the human race—an infancy which is also to some extent still available for study in the life of primitive tribes today.

The development of religion and religions begins to emerge into the light of recorded history as the third millennium B.C. moves towards the period around 2000 B.C. There are two main regions of the earth in which civilisation seems first to have arisen and in which religions first took a shape that is at least dimly discernible to us as we peer back through the mists of time—these being Mesopotamia in the Near East and the Indus valley of northern India. In Mesopotamia men lived in nomadic shepherd tribes, each worshipping its own god. Then the tribes gradually coalesced into nation states, the former tribal gods becoming ranked in hierarchies (some however being lost by amalgamation in the process) dominated by great national deities such as Marduk of Babylon, the Sumerian Ishtar, Amon of Thebes, Jahweh of Israel, the Greek Zeus, and so on. Further east in the Indus valley there was likewise a wealth of gods and goddesses, though apparently not so much tribal or national in character as expressive of the basic forces of nature, above all fertility. The many deities of the Near East and of India expressed man's awareness of the divine at the dawn of documentary history, some four thousand years ago. It is perhaps worth stressing that the picture was by no means a wholly pleasant one. The tribal and national gods were often martial and cruel, sometimes requiring human sacrifices. And although rather little is known about the very early, pre-Aryan Indian deities, it is certain that later Indian deities have vividly symbolised the cruel and destructive as well as the beneficent aspects of nature.

These early developments in the two cradles of civilisation, Mesopotamia and the Indus valley, can be described as the growth of natural religion, prior to any special intrusions of divine revelation or illumination. Primitive spirit-worship expressed man's fears of unknown forces; his reverence for nature deities expressed his sense of dependence upon realities greater than himself; and his tribal gods expressed the unity and continuity of his group over against other groups. One can in fact discern all sorts of causal connections between the forms which early religion took and the material circumstances of man's life, indicating the large part played by

2. *The Meaning and End of Religion* (New York: Mentor Books, 1963) p. 22.

the human element within the history of religion. For example, Trevor Ling points out that life in ancient India (apart from the Punjab immediately prior to the Aryan invasions) was agricultural and was organised in small village units; and suggests that "among agricultural peoples, aware of the fertile earth which brings forth from itself and nourishes its progeny upon its broad bosom, it is the mother-principle which seems important."[3] Accordingly God the Mother, and a variety of more specialised female deities, have always held a prominent place in Indian religious thought and mythology. This contrasts with the characteristically male expression of deity in the Semitic religions, which had their origins among nomadic, pastoral, herd-keeping peoples in the Near East. The divine was known to the desert-dwelling herdsmen who founded the Israelite tradition as God the King and Father; and this conception has continued both in later Judaism and in Christianity, and was renewed out of the desert experience of Mohammed in the Islamic religion. Such regional variations in our human ways of conceiving the divine have persisted through time into the developed world faiths that we know today. The typical western conception of God is still predominantly in terms of the male principle of power and authority; and in the typical Indian conceptions of deity the female principle still plays a distinctly larger part than in the west.

Here then was the natural condition of man's religious life: religion without revelation. But sometimes around 800 B.C. there began what has been called the golden age of religious creativity. This consisted in a remarkable series of revelatory experiences occurring during the next five hundred or so years in different parts of the world, experiences which deepened and purified men's conceptions of the ultimate, and which religious faith can only attribute to the pressure of the divine Spirit upon the human spirit. First came the early Jewish prophets, Amos, Hosea and first Isaiah, declaring that they had heard the Word of the Lord claiming their obedience and demanding a new level of righteousness and justice in the life of Israel. Then in Persia the great prophet Zoroaster appeared; China produced Lao-tzu and then Confucius; in India the Upanishads were written, and Gotama the Buddha lived, and Mahavira, the founder of the Jain religion and, probably about the end of this period, the writing of the Bhagavad Gītā;[4] and Greece produced Pythagoras and then, ending this golden age, Socrates and Plato. Then after the gap of some three hundred

3. *A History of Religion East and West* (London: Macmillan and New York: St. Martin's Press, 1968) p. 27.
4. The dating of the Bhagavad Gītā has been a matter of much debate; but R. C. Zaehner in his recent monumental critical edition says that "One would probably not be going far wrong if one dated it at some time between the fifth and second centuries B.C." *The Bhagavad Gītā* (Oxford: Clarendon Press, 1969) p. 7.

years came Jesus of Nazareth and the emergence of Christianity; and after another gap the prophet Mohammed and the rise of Islam.

The suggestion that we must consider is that these were all moments of divine revelation. But let us ask, in order to test this thought, whether we should not expect God to make his revelation in a single mighty act, rather than to produce a number of different, and therefore presumably partial, revelations at different times and places? I think that in seeing the answer to this question we receive an important clue to the place of the religions of the world in the divine purpose. For when we remember the facts of history and geography we realise that in the period we are speaking of, between two and three thousand years ago, it was not possible for God to reveal himself through any human mediation to all mankind. A world-wide revelation might be possible today, thanks to the inventions of printing, and even more of radio, TV and communication satellites. But in the technology of the ancient world this was not possible. Although on a time scale of centuries and millennia there has been a slow diffusion and interaction of cultures, particularly within the vast Euro-Asian land mass, yet the more striking fact for our present purpose is the fragmented character of the ancient world. Communications between the different groups of humanity was then so limited and slow that for all practical purposes men inhabited different worlds. For the most part people in Europe, in India, in Arabia, in Africa, in China were unaware of the others' existence. And as the world was fragmented, so was its religious life. If there was to be a revelation of the divine reality to mankind it had to be a pluriform revelation, a series of revealing experiences occurring independently within the different streams of human history. And since religion and culture were one, the great creative moments of revelation and illumination have influenced the development of the various cultures, giving them the coherence and impetus to expand into larger units, thus creating the vast, many-sided historical entities which we call the world religions.

Each of these religio-cultural complexes has expanded until it touched the boundaries of another such complex spreading out from another centre. Thus each major occasion of divine revelation has slowly transformed the primitive and national religions within the sphere of its influence into what we now know as the world faiths. The early Dravidian and Aryan polytheisms of India were drawn through the religious experience and thought of the Brahmins into what the west calls Hinduism. The national and mystery cults of the mediterranean world and then of northern Europe were drawn by influences stemming from the life and teaching of Christ into what has become Christianity. The early polytheism of the Arab peoples has been transformed under the influence of Mohammed and his message into Islam. Great areas of South-East Asia, of China, Tibet and Japan were drawn into the spreading Buddhist movement. None of these expansions from different centres of revelation has of course been simple and uncontested, and a number of alternatives which proved less durable have perished or been absorbed in the process—for example, Mithraism has disappeared altogether; and Zoroastrianism, whilst it greatly influenced the development of the Judaic-Christian tradition, and has to that extent been absorbed, only survives directly today on a small scale in Parseeism.

Seen in this historical context these movements of faith—the Judaic-Christian, the Buddhist, the Hindu, the Muslim—are not essentially rivals. They began at different times and in different places, and each expanded outwards into the surrounding world of primitive natural religion until most of the world was drawn up into one or other of the great revealed faiths. And once this global pattern had become established it has ever since remained fairly stable. It is true that the process of establishment involved conflict in the case of Islam's entry into India and the virtual expulsion of Buddhism from India in the medieval period, and in the case of Islam's advance into Europe and then its retreat at the end of the medieval period. But since the frontiers of the different world faiths became more or less fixed there has been little penetration of one faith into societies moulded by another. The most successful missionary efforts of the great faiths continue to this day to be "downwards" into the remaining world of relatively primitive religions rather than "sideways" into territories dominated by another world faith. For example, as between Christianity and Islam there has been little more than rather rare individual conversions; but both faiths have successful missions in Africa. Again, the Christian population of the Indian subcontinent, after more than two centuries of missionary effort, is only about 2.7 per cent; but on the other hand the Christian missions in the South Pacific are fairly successful. Thus the general picture, so far as the great world religions is concerned, is that each has gone through an early period of geographical expansion, converting a region of the world from its more primitive religious state, and has thereafter continued in a comparatively settled condition within more or less stable boundaries.

Now it is of course possible to see this entire development from the primitive forms of religion up to and including the great world faiths as the history of man's most persistent illusion, growing from crude fantasies into sophisticated metaphysical speculations. But from the standpoint of religious faith the only reasonable hypothesis is that this historical picture represents a movement of divine self-revelation to mankind. This hypothesis offers a general answer to the question of the relation between the different world religions and of the truths which they embody. It suggests to us that the same divine reality has always been self-revealingly active towards mankind, and that the differences of human response are related to different human circumstances. These circumstances—ethnic, geographical, climatic, economic, sociological, historical—have produced the existing differentiations of human culture, and within each main cultural region the response to the divine has taken its own characteristic forms. In each case the post-primitive response has been initiated by some spiritually outstanding individual or succession of individuals, developing in the course of time into one of the great religio-cultural phenomena which we call the world religions. Thus Islam embodies the main response of the Arabic peoples to the divine reality; Hinduism, the main (though not the only) response of the peoples of India; Buddhism, the main response of the peoples of South-East Asia and parts of northern Asia; Christianity, the main response of the European peoples, both within Europe itself and in their emigrations to the Americas and Australasia.

Thus it is, I think, intelligible historically why the revelation of the divine reality to man, and the disclosure of the divine will for human life, had to occur separately within the different streams of human life. We can see how these revelations took different forms related to the different mentalities of the peoples to whom they came, and developed within these different cultures into the vast and many-sided historical phenomena of the world religions.

But let us now ask whether this is intelligible theologically. What about the conflicting truth-claims of the different faiths? Is the divine nature personal or non-personal; does deity become incarnate in the world; are human beings born again and again on earth; is the Bible, or the Koran, or the Bhagavad Gītā the Word of God? If what Christianity says in answer to these questions is true, must not what Hinduism says be to a large extent false? If what Buddhism says is true, must not what Islam says be largely false?

Let us begin with the recognition, which is made in all the main religious traditions, that the ultimate divine reality is infinite and as such transcends the grasp of the human mind. God, to use our Christian term, is infinite. He is not a thing, a part of the universe, existing alongside other things; nor is he a being falling under a certain kind. And therefore he cannot be defined or encompassed by human thought. We cannot draw boundaries round his nature and say that he is this and no more. If we could fully define God, describing his inner being and his outer limits, this would not be God. The God whom our minds can penetrate and whom our thoughts can circumnavigate is merely a finite and partial image of God.

From this it follows that the different encounters with the transcendent within the different religious traditions may all be encounters with the one infinite reality, though with partially different and overlapping aspects of that reality. This is a very familiar thought in Indian religious literature.

We read, for example, in the ancient Rig-Vedas, dating back to perhaps as much as a thousand years before Christ:

> They call it Indra, Mitra, Varuna, and Agni
> And also heavenly, beautiful Garutman:
> The real is one, though sages name it variously.[5]

We might translate this thought into the terms of the faiths represented today in Britain:

> They call it Jahweh, Allah, Krishna, Param Atma,
> And also holy, blessed Trinity:
> The real is one, though sages name it differently.

And in the Bhagavad Gītā the Lord Krishna, the personal God of love, says, "Howsoever men approach me, even so do I accept them; for, on all sides, whatever path they may choose is mine."[6]

Again, there is the parable of the blind men and the elephant, said to have been told by the Buddha. An elephant was brought to a group of blind men who had never encountered such an animal before. One felt a leg and reported that an elephant is a great living pillar. Another felt the trunk and reported that an elephant is a great snake. Another felt a tusk and reported that an elephant is like a sharp ploughshare. And so on. And then they all quarrelled together, each claiming that his own account was the truth and therefore all the others false. In fact of course they were all true, but each referring only to one aspect of the total reality and all expressed in very imperfect analogies.

Now the possibility, indeed the probability, that we have seriously to consider is that many different accounts of the divine reality may be true, though all expressed in imperfect human analogies, but that none is "the truth, the whole truth, and nothing but the truth." May it not be that the different concepts of God, as Jahweh, Allah, Krishna, Param Atma, Holy Trinity, and so on; and likewise the different concepts of the hidden structure of reality, as the eternal emanation of Brahman or as an immense cosmic process culminating in Nirvana, are all images of the divine, each expressing some aspect or range of aspects and yet none by itself fully and exhaustively corresponding to the infinite nature of the ultimate reality?

Two immediate qualifications however to this hypothesis. First, the idea that we are considering is not that any and every conception of God or of the transcendent is valid, still less all equally valid; but that every conception of the divine which has come out of a great revelatory religious

5. I 164.
6. IV II.

experience and has been tested through a long tradition of worship, and
has sustained human faith over centuries of time and in millions of lives,
is likely to represent a genuine encounter with the divine reality. And second, the parable of the blind men and the elephant is of course only a
parable, and like most parables it is designed to make one point and must
not be pressed as an analogy at other points. The suggestion is not that the
different encounters with the divine which lie at the basis of the great religious traditions are responses to different *parts* of the divine. They are
rather encounters from different historical and cultural standpoints with
the same infinite divine reality and as such they lead to differently focused
awarenesses of that reality. The indications of this are most evident in worship and prayer. What is said about God in the theological treatises of the
different faiths is indeed often widely different. But it is in prayer that a
belief in God comes alive and does its main work. And when we turn from
abstract theology to the living stuff of worship we meet again and again
the overlap and confluence of faiths.

Here, for example, is a Muslim prayer at the feast of Ramadan:

> Praise be to God, Lord of creation, Source of all livelihood, who
> orders the morning, Lord of majesty and honour, of grace and
> beneficence. He who is so far that he may not be seen and so
> near that he witnesses the secret things. Blessed be he and for
> ever exalted.[7]

And here is a Sikh creed used at the morning prayer:

> There is but one God. He is all that is.
> He is the Creator of all things and He is all-pervasive.
> He is without fear and without enmity.
> He is timeless, unborn and self-existent.
> He is the Enlightener
> And can be realised by grace of Himself alone.
> He was in the beginning; He was in all ages.
> The True One is, was, O Nanak, and shall forever be.[8]

And here again is a verse from the Koran:

> To God belongs the praise, Lord of the heavens and Lord of the
> earth, the Lord of all being. His is the dominion in the heavens
> and in the earth: he is the Almighty, the All-wise.[9]

7. Kenneth Cragg, *Alive to God: Muslim and Christian Prayer* (London and New
York: Oxford University Press, 1970) p. 65.
8. Harbans Singh, *Guru Nanak and Origins of the Sikh Faith* (Bombay, London
and New York: Asia Publishing House, 1969), pp. 96–7.
9. *Alive to God*, p. 61 (Surah of the Kneeling, v. 35).

Turning now to the Hindu idea of the many incarnations of God, here is a verse from the Rāmāyana:

> Seers and sages, saints and hermits, fix on Him their reverent gaze,
> And in faint and trembling accents, holy scripture hymns His praise.
> He the omnipresent spirit, lord of heaven and earth and hell,
> To redeem His people, freely has vouchsafed with men to dwell.[10]

And from the rich literature of devotional song here is a Bhakti hymn of the Vaishnavite branch of Hinduism:

> Now all my days with joy I'll fill, full to the brim
> With all my heart to Vitthal cling, and only Him.
>
> He will sweep utterly away all dole and care;
> And all in sunder shall I rend illusion's snare.
>
> O altogether dear is He, and He alone,
> For all my burden He will take to be His own.
>
> Lo, all the sorrow of the world will straightway cease,
> And all unending now shall be the reign of peace.[11]

And a Muslim mystical verse:

> Love came a guest
> Within my breast,
> My soul was spread,
> Love banqueted.[12]

And finally another Hindu (Vaishnavite) devotional hymn:

> O save me, save me, Mightiest,
>   Save me and set me free.
> O let the love that fills my breast
>   Cling to thee lovingly.
>
> Grant me to taste how sweet thou art;
>   Grant me but this, I pray,
> And never shall my love depart
>   Or turn from thee away.

10. *Sacred Books of the World*, edited by A. C. Bouquet (London: Pelican Books, 1954) p. 226 (The Rāmāyana of Tulsi Das, Canto 1, Chandha 2, translated by F. S. Growse).
11. Ibid., p. 245 (A Hymn of Namdev, translated by Nicol MacNicol).
12. *Alive to God*, p. 79 (From Ibn Hazm, "The Ring of the Dove").

> Then I thy name shall magnify
> And tell thy praise abroad,
> For very love and gladness I
> Shall dance before my God.[13]

Such prayers and hymns as these must express, surely, diverse encounters with the same divine reality. These encounters have taken place within different human cultures by people of different ways of thought and feeling, with different histories and different frameworks of philosophical thought, and have developed into different systems of theology embodied in different religious structures and organisations. These resulting large-scale religio-cultural phenomena are what we call the religions of the world. But must there not lie behind them the same infinite divine reality, and may not our divisions into Christian, Hindu, Muslim, Jew, and so on, and all that goes with them, accordingly represent secondary, human, historical developments?

There is a further problem, however, which now arises. I have been speaking so far of the ultimate reality in a variety of terms—the Father, Son and Spirit of Christianity, the Jahweh of Judaism, the Allah of Islam, and so on—but always thus far in theistic terms, as a personal God under one name or another. But what of the non-theistic religions? What of the non-theistic Hinduism according to which the ultimate reality, Brahman, is not He but It; and what about Buddhism, which in one form is agnostic concerning the existence of God even though in another form it has come to worship the Buddha himself? Can these non-theistic faiths be seen as encounters with the same divine reality that is encountered in theistic religion?

Speaking very tentatively, I think it is possible that the sense of the divine as non-personal may indeed reflect an aspect of the same infinite reality that is encountered as personal in theistic religious experience. The question can be pursued both as a matter of pure theology and in relation to religious experience. Theologically, the Hindu distinction between Nirguna Brahman and Saguna Brahman is important and should be adopted into western religious thought. Detaching the distinction, then, from its Hindu context we may say that Nirguna God is the eternal self-existent divine reality, beyond the scope of all human categories, including personality; and Saguna God is God in relation to his creation and with the attributes which express this relationship, such as personality, omnipotence, goodness, love and omniscience. Thus the one ultimate reality is both Nirguna and non-personal, and Saguna and personal, in a duality which is in principle acceptable to human understanding. When we turn

13. *Sacred Books of the World,* p. 246 (A Hymn of Tukaram).

to men's religious awareness of God we are speaking of Saguna God, God in relation to man. And here the larger traditions of both east and west report a dual experience of the divine as personal and as other than personal. It will be a sufficient reminder of the strand of personal relationship with the divine in Hinduism to mention Iswara, the personal God who represents the Absolute as known and worshipped by finite persons. It should also be remembered that the characterisation of Brahman as *satcitananda,* absolute being, consciousness and bliss, is not far from the conception of infinitely transcendent personal life. Thus there is both the thought and the experience of the personal divine within Hinduism. But there is likewise the thought and the experience of God as other than personal within Christianity. Rudolph Otto describes this strand in the mysticism of Meister Eckhart. He says:

> The divine, which on the one hand is conceived in symbols taken from the social sphere, as Lord, King, Father, Judge—a person in relation to persons—is on the other hand denoted in dynamic symbols as the power of life, as light and life, as spirit ebbing and flowing, as truth, knowledge, essential justice and holiness, a glowing fire that penetrates and pervades. It is characterized as the principle of a renewed, supernatural Life, mediating and giving itself, breaking forth in the living man as his nova vita, as the content of his life and being. What is here insisted upon is not so much an "immanent" God, as an "experienced" God, known as an inward principle of the power of new being and life. Eckhart knows this *deuteros theos* besides the personal God. . . .[14]

Let me now try to draw the threads together and to project them into the future. I have been suggesting that Christianity is a way of salvation which, beginning some two thousand years ago, has become the principal way of salvation in three continents. The other great world faiths are likewise ways of salvation, providing the principal path to the divine reality for other large sections of humanity. I have also suggested that the idea that Jesus proclaimed himself as God incarnate, and as the sole point of saving contact between God and man, is without adequate historical foundation and represents a doctrine developed by the church. We should therefore not infer, from the christian experience of redemption through Christ, that salvation cannot be experienced in any other way. The alternative possibility is that the ultimate divine reality—in our christian terms, God—has always been pressing in upon the human spirit, but always in ways which leave men free to open or close themselves to the divine presence. Human life has developed along characteristically different lines in the main areas of civilisation, and these differences have naturally entered into the ways in

14. Rudolph Otto, *Mysticism East and West,* trans. Bertha L. Bracey and Richenda C. Payne (New York: Meridian Books, 1957), p. 131.

which men have apprehended and responded to God. For the great religious figures through whose experience divine revelation has come have each been conditioned by a particular history and culture. One can hardly imagine Gotama the Buddha except in the setting of the India of his time, or Jesus the Christ except against the background of Old Testament Judaism, or Mohammed except in the setting of Arabia. And human history and culture have likewise shaped the development of the webs of religious creeds, practices and organisations which we know as the great world faiths.

It is thus possible to consider the hypothesis that they are all, at their experiential roots, in contact with the same ultimate reality, but that their differing experiences of that reality, interacting over the centuries with the different thought-forms of different cultures, have led to increasing differentiation and contrasting elaboration—so that Hinduism, for example, is a very different phenomenon from Christianity, and very different ways of conceiving and experiencing the divine occur within them.

However, now that the religious traditions are consciously interacting with each other in the "one world" of today, in mutual observation and dialogue, it is possible that their future developments may be on gradually converging courses. For during the next few centuries they will no doubt continue to change, and it may be that they will grow closer together, and even that one day such names as "Christianity," "Buddhism," "Islam," "Hinduism," will no longer describe the then current configurations of men's religious experience and belief. I am not here thinking of the extinction of human religiousness in a universal wave of secularisation. This is of course a possible future; and indeed many think it the most likely future to come about. But if man is an indelibly religious animal he will always, even in his secular cultures, experience a sense of the transcendent by which he will be both troubled and uplifted. The future I am thinking of is accordingly one in which what we now call the different religions will constitute the past history of different emphases and variations within a global religious life. I do not mean that all men everywhere will be overtly religious, any more than they are today. I mean rather that the discoveries now taking place by men of different faiths of central common ground, hitherto largely concealed by the variety of cultural forms in which it was expressed, may eventually render obsolete the sense of belonging to rival ideological communities. Not that all religious men will think alike, or worship in the same way or experience the divine identically. On the contrary, so long as there is a rich variety of human cultures—and let us hope there will always be this—we should expect there to be correspondingly different forms of religious cult, ritual and organisation, conceptualised in different theological doctrines. And so long as there is a wide spectrum of human psychological types—and again let us hope that there will always be this—we should expect there to be correspondingly different emphases between, for example, the sense of the divine as just and as merciful, between *karma* and *bhakti;* or between worship as formal and communal and worship as free and personal. Thus we may expect the different world faiths to continue as religio-cultural phenomena, though phenomena which are increasingly influencing one another's development. The relation between them will then perhaps be somewhat like that now obtaining between the different denominations of Christianity in Europe or the United States. That is to say, there will in most countries be a dominant religious tradition, with other traditions present in varying strengths, but with considerable awareness on all hands of what they have in common; with some degree of osmosis of membership through their institutional walls; with a large degree of practical co-operation; and even conceivably with some interchange of ministry.

Beyond this the ultimate unity of faiths will be an eschatological unity in which each is both fulfilled and transcended—fulfilled in so far as it is true, transcended in so far as it is less than the whole truth. And indeed even such fulfilling must be a transcending; for the function of a religion is to bring us to a right relationship with the ultimate divine reality, to awareness of our true nature and our place in the Whole, into the presence of God. In the eternal life there is no longer any place for religions; the pilgrim has no need of a way after he has finally arrived. In St. John's vision of the heavenly city at the end of our christian scriptures it is said that there is no temple—no christian church or chapel, no jewish synagogue, no hindu or buddhist temple, no muslim mosque, no sikh gurdwara. . . . For all these exist in time, as ways through time to eternity.

PROBLEM?
THIS 'EARLY' ESSAY BY HICK TOO SUPERFICIAL; IT MAKES
US 'ANONYMOUS ——— "(X'IANS, JEWS, ETC) SO THAT THE
RESPECTIVE RELIGIONS ARE COLLAPSED INTO A COMMON
ONENESS. DOES THIS CALL INTO QUESTION THE CLAIMS
OF OTHERS? — YES!

Truth and Religions

NINIAN SMART

Is there a problem about how the truth-claims of Christianity can be reconciled with those of other religions?

The first question about the question is about truth-claims. Not just *truth*-claims, surely? There can be imperatival incompatibilities. Religions appear to recommend or command different paths. For the Christian pacifist, "Turn the other cheek" is vitally right; for the Muslim, it is better to say something like "Act honourably, but there is no need to turn the other cheek." Again, different rituals are commended or commanded. For the Catholic, the Mass; for the Muslim, daily prayers and the pilgrimage to Mecca.

So we are not merely concerned with possible incompatibilities as to truth-claims; but also with possible incompatibilities in *practice*-claims.

The next problem about the question has to do with the *identification* of truth-claims and practice-claims as being Christian. The Christian tradition is variegated, as we all know; and we need no reminding that in this age as in many previous epochs Christianity is in flux. It is highly fluctuating in regard to theology, as it happens. How then do we identify the core of Christian truth-claims?

We sometimes operate on the assumption that though there are many Christianities there is only one Christian faith. Thus the great task of theology is to penetrate to this one faith and articulate it and express it. This assumption of the single faith is unaffected by the recognition that there are changing cultural circumstances—that modern man, for instance,

From *Truth and Dialogue in World Religions: Conflicting Truth-Claims,* ed. John Hick (London: Sheldon Press; Philadelphia: The Westminster Press, 1974). © 1974 University of Birmingham. Used by permission.

may find some elements of traditional expression of the faith (miracle stories, for instance) unacceptable. The programme of demythologization itself is a phase in the never-ending supposed task of relating the one faith to the changing cultural milieu. It is a case of adapting the one to the many. Different times, different theologies—but always the one faith. Different climes, different theologies—but always the one faith. This is the pervasive model at the back of our minds, when we ask about the compatibility or otherwise of Christian truth-claims and those of other faiths. Similar remarks apply, perhaps, to the practice-claims: there is, so to say, a single divine imperative, could we but find it.

The model of a single faith is reinforced by the historical accident (or is it an accident?) that the churches recognize in the New Testament the single platform upon which they all stand. The task of the theologian then becomes importantly to extract the single faith from its pages. Paul here stands as a looming figure, for the more the historicity of the Gospels is called in question (and a century and a half of scientific history is bound to plaster the text with queries), the greater the significance of the great theologian of the risen Christ.

Naturally, there is a similar question about other faiths. Is there a single substance of the Buddhist dharma, for instance? Even in Islam, pegged to the glorious revelation of the Qur'ān, there are variations, developments. Is there then a single Islam?

The question of identifying the one faith in Christianity is made harder by a feeling that often accompanies the model of the one faith—namely that necessarily the focus of faith transcends the concepts which we use to try to express it. If it were not so, the task of identifying the one faith might not be too hard. For one could ask: If Augustine, Aquinas, Luther, and Barth each expressed, in differing cultural milieus, the one faith, then let us state that faith and see the correlation. But it seems that each new theology takes a given core of faith and then elaborates it; rather each new theology is an expression of the theology-transcending X. There is, so to say, no going behind each theology to discover what it is about. It tells you what it is about; it is so to say the glass through which we see the X, and the X can only be seen through one glass or another. If this is so, then the "one faith" is very much a construct, and one without content. In this respect, the quest of the historical Jesus has been a way of trying to get back to a content, round the glasses which filter our vision.

If what I have said on this score is correct, it presents us with one way of talking about Christian truth- and practice-claims, namely to take the whole exhibition of coloured windows through which the Christian tradition has looked out and back on the theology-transcending focus of faith. Or if it be not possible to treat seriously the whole gallery of theologies, then at least a selection of them. However, the very fact (if it is so) that the focus of faith transcends theologies means that the theological traditions can never be fixed. What is to preclude a new theology being devised, to set alongside the others? In this case, though, there is one sort of identification question which can profitably be asked, namely what is the norm whereby some new theology is adjudged to be *Christian*? Some resemblance, presumably, to earlier theologies. But how much? These things seem to be settled by an informal method of acceptance in the community. For example, Paul van Buren's *The Secular Meaning of the Gospel* expresses an atheistic Christology; but a number of Christians took this with sufficient seriousness to deem it as genuinely a *Christian* theology, despite its formal atheism.

[margin note: ? WORD GOD' IS DEAD]

Since new theologies await us over the horizon, it is also necessary to recall that the very situation of interplay between religions, which so markedly characterizes contemporary religious culture, may itself have an impact on theologizing: so that a new theology now beyond the horizon might in theory dissolve some of the incompatibilities between earlier theologies and received non-Christian theologies. For instance, there seems to be a conflict of *Weltanschauung* between theistic Christianity and non-theistic Buddhism; but the incompatibility is less obvious the more existentialist Christian theology becomes. So new syntheses may await us over the horizon; and they cannot be ruled out a priori.

However, there is another check upon indiscriminate synthesizing; this arises from the relation between truth-claims and practice-claims (to put it crudely). It is very obvious that the ritual, experiential and institutional aspects of a religion, and its ethical prescriptions, are not always well coordinated to the theologies being purveyed within it. For example, the meaning of the Eucharist, in Anglicanism, is shaped by the milieu of liturgy, architecture, custom, style of life of those engaged: it is not merely determined theologically, still less by the most avant garde theology. Attitudes to the Buddha in Theravāda Buddhism are not simply determined by doctrines, but by the whole temple-cultus, etc. Thus there is always the possibility of a lack of co-ordination between truth-claims, and actual practice-claims. In one way, this is doubtless a good thing, for it might be held to be the task of the theologian to criticize, where necessary, the actual practices of the church. But how is this legitimate critical tension to be preserved while at the same time theology is to escape the charge of disingenuousness? For it is a cheat if the theologian does not relate the ideal church to the actual church—if he recommends a faith that has no purchase on the received tradition.

For these and other reasons, the question of incompatibilities between one faith and another is a complex matter. In a way we are concerned with the elasticity of a faith—whether certain kinds of stretching the concepts and practices result in a snap. Let us try out a thought-experiment here, by considering what is to be said about Hindu attitudes to Christianity.

The modern Hindu ideology, if one may so dub it, consists in a neo-Sankaran theology in which all religions, albeit existing at different levels, ultimately point to the one truth. This is an appealing doctrine to many; for it suggests that religions are held apart by externals, institutional narrownesses, rather than by any essential conflict. It is the obverse of the conclusion sometimes drawn from conflicts of revelations and teachings, namely that they are all false; the modern Hindu ideology declares that they are all true. The best religion, however, is one which is explicitly synthesizing, all-embracing (this being the merit of Hinduism). It follows from the modern Hindu ideology that there is no incompatibility between Hinduism and Christianity: they both ultimately have the same focus, though symbolized and concretized differently (Christ and Krishna, for example, are different manifestations of the one God). Should Christianity resist this synthesis? Not just on the ground that the Christian tradition is unique—for every tradition is. Let us consider some of the reasons for resisting the synthesis that might be advanced.

"The Hindu conception of deity is different from that revealed to the Christian tradition." *Comment:* it is true that God in the main Christian tradition is conceived in a more personal way than is the neo-Advaitin *Brahman;* but in *this* respect the ultimate reality of Tillich and John Robinson is similarly "impersonal" (compare also pseudo-Dionysius, Meister Eckhart, Dean Mansel). The anti-synthesis argument thus becomes a means of shutting off certain kinds of theological development within Christianity.

"Christ is uniquely Son of God: there are no other incarnations." *Comment:* this point can be stated if there is a prior monotheism and an identification of sorts of Christ with the one God; but the anti-synthesis argument here will not work in the following conditions: (i) if Christ is seen as a "window on ultimate reality" (for there can be many windows); (ii) if Christ is seen, liberal theology-wise, as an exemplar of moral values (for there could be other exemplars, such as the Buddha); (iii) if Christ is simply the preached Christ—the historical anchor of an imperative *kerygma* (for there could be a variety of other historical and mystical anchors of existential challenge). In brief, the appeal to the uniqueness of the incarnation implies a rather conservative ontology. But can't it somehow be done by making a practice-claim? Thus:

"Christ alone is to be worshipped." The Hindu synthesis here seems to be rejected (unless secretly Krishna and others can be *identified* with Christ: to this sort of identification theme we shall return). *Comment:*

the practice-claim could simply be a surd imperative, like a surd revelation. But it is usual in the Christian tradition to advance some grounds for the claim—that the risen Christ provides the key to liberation; that it is through sacramental participation in the death and resurrection of Christ that sin and death are overcome; and negatively that other gods do not have liberating power, are phantasms leading men astray, do not exist. It is thus difficult to give grounds for the practice-claim which does not imply some ontology: some account of the human predicament and of the way in which it is overcome. Historically, moreover, the worship of Christ in part arises from the background of worship of the one God. Here is another respect in which the Christian rejection of synthesis rests upon a particular theism. But as I said earlier, there is no knowing what the future may bring: yet at the present time it seems that Christianity, to maintain its incompatibility with Hinduism, would have to appeal to a particular theism as constituting part of its essence. I shall return to this point after a brief excursus on the paradox of a situation in which incompatibility is regarded as a good thing.

Why should there be a motive for standing out against the noble Hindu synthesis? It is partly a matter of having a *raison d'être*. A movement, religious or otherwise, which does not have a distinctive message tends (rightly) to wither. Still, couldn't Christianity have a more modest *raison d'être*—to nurture those within it and those who find that it chimes in with their spiritual and moral condition? It could be, so to speak, a loosely knit tribal religion, but where the tribe is a new Israel, not ethnically determined (although well rooted in certain, mainly western cultures). One must here, however, understand the logical and cultural predicament of a tribal religion in an intercultural situation (this too will cast light upon the reason for the evolution of the new Hindu ideology).

A tribal religion, like other religions, contains a doctrinal element, woven into the whole practical side: a certain picture of the world and of spirit is drawn. Consider the predicament of the tribal folk when it is faced with a new culture, with a transethnic religion. Is it possible for the tribal folk long to maintain that their world-picture is for them, the other world-picture for others? It is hard to say (from a logical point of view) that P is true for one group and not-P for another, unless all that is meant is that the one group *believes* P and the other believes not-P. Various devices have to be employed if the tribal picture is to remain itself at all. One option is hard—to claim that the tribal picture is of universal validity, for it was always meant for those initiated into tribal lore, and wasn't meant at all for other tribes. This secretive non-universalism could be carried with equanimity when the tribe constituted the real world, the values of other men being a mere shadowy penumbra. Even very big groups have felt like this: for the Chinese, barbarian values were shadowy until Buddhism crept in and destroyed the illusion; for expansionist Europe, the beliefs of colonized folk tended to be curiosities, oddities; in India over a long period the real world was the subcontinent, until Buddhism began to flicker outwards. So then our tribal folk will find the universalist option hard to maintain, because of the tight connection between the picture of the world and the secret sacraments of the tribe. Another option it may not want to face— namely to abandon entirely its own picture and assimilate that of the new culture, though even here unconsciously the old gods can be smuggled in. A *via media* is called for: one in which an adjusted world-picture is seen as a contribution to the store of myths and insights which point towards the transcendent. We may call this option: unity through conscious pluralism, or in short "the pluralistic solution."

We can now return to the question of whether Christianity can regard itself modestly as a loosely-knit tribal religion, nurturing those who participate in its sacraments. Faced with other trans-cultural faiths, it would be essentially in the tribal predicament, if so; and truth is no respecter of groups. To retain its modesty, without losing its *raison d'être,* it would have itself to adopt the pluralistic solution, and this would be virtually to accept the Hindu synthesis. In the context of the variety of faiths and of the virtual certainty that they will continue substantially in a plural world, the pluralistic solution seems sound common sense. Hence its appeal (a wide appeal, even among many Christians, who express this pluralism through a scepticism about missions, though not about hospitals in alien climes).

I have made something in this argument of the tightness of the connection between the tribal world-picture and their secret sacraments. This point is highly relevant to problems of meaning and understanding. Crudely one can distinguish between an initiatory and a non-initiatory view of understanding religious concepts. From the initiatory point of view, understanding God can only be approached via the sacramental or analogous activities, or can only be gained by the initiation constituted by the experience of grace. Full-bloodedly, the initiatory view is a sort of conceptual fideism: only those who can say "I know that my redeemer liveth" know what "redeemer" means. A thin-blooded view would be that we can imaginatively enter into initiations (hence the possibility of coming to understand something of other faiths). Those espousing a hardheaded natural theology would hold that at least some key concepts in religion could be understood metaphysically, without specific religious initiation.

There is a tension here. The more conceptually initiatory a religion is, the more it takes on the character of a tribal religion, except that it may be the religion of an open rather than a closed tribe, adding new members as it can. But though it could be thus universal evangelically, in the sense that any man or all men might join the faith-community, it could, if thus conceptually initiatory, give no reasons why men should join, save "Come and see," maybe. In *practice,* of course, men who join use reasons: the fruits are good—you can see peace on their faces, and so forth. This is a kind of practical natural theology, adding some rationality to the otherwise surd initiation. But by contrast, if a religion seems to be hardly initiatory at all, for the understanding of its concepts, it takes on the guise of a metaphysics, and the link between belief and sacrament is ruptured.

Extreme conceptual fideism as an account of the Christian faith does, I think, have to be rejected, if the aim at any rate is to avoid the pluralistic solution. For paradoxically conceptual fideism can give no account of what other faiths mean (e.g. the Hindu synthesis): for it is implied that initiation is necessary for understanding. Given the further premiss that one cannot be initiated properly into more than one faith (*pace* Ramakrishna), then the Christian conceptual fideist can have no ground for rejecting any other faith. All faiths have this rather negative equal status. This being so, there can be no reason to reject the Hindu claim that all faiths point to the same Truth. Initiatory conceptual fideism slides in to acceptance of a polytheism, or rather a polyfideism, if one may coin so barbarous a hybrid.

But *should* the extra premise, that one cannot be properly initiated into more than one faith, be accepted? Is it that no man can serve two masters? But how are we to know that they *are* two masters? Is it that a person cannot be converted from one faith to another? We know that this happens empirically, so to speak; but could he really have had his earlier faith if he were converted? These are questions which extreme conceptual fideism is not in a position to answer.

As a postscript to the discussion of extreme conceptual fideism, it is worth noting that whereas truth and falsity do not admit, in any straightforward way, at least, of degrees, understanding does. One person can show greater, deeper, etc., understanding than another. It may be that a very deep understanding of the concepts of a given faith is not accessible to the adherent of another faith; but this does not at all show that *some* level of understanding is impossible for him; and it can of course well be that the adherent of a faith has a less profound understanding of it than some person of another faith.

The pluralistic solution, as we have outlined it, is not absolute pluralism: there is at least the notion that there is a single truth towards which different religions point—in line with the modern Hindu ideology, which itself constitutes the response of a sophisticated, variegated cultural tradition faced by an incoming transethnic faith, accompanied by aggressive European values. This attempt at making differing traditions compatible by

postulating a single focus of aspiration does, however, depend on identifi-
cations—identifying one divine focus of faith with another. Can such iden-
tifications be justified?

Let us begin with a relatively simple example. What justifies one in
saying that the Christian and Muslim worship the same God? As far as
the concepts and practices go, the two foci of faith are different. Among
other things, the Christian worships Christ as a person of the Trinity: the
Christian concept of God is thus organically related to God's manifestation
in history and to his representation of himself in the sacraments. These are
elements not present in the Muslim's conception of Allah. Thus conceptually the Christian God and Allah are different. This does not entail that
the concepts do not refer to the same Being: far from it, a major point
about identity statements is that the concepts are different (not all identity
statements, but many, e.g., "Tomorrow is Friday"). The statement "The
Christian and the Muslim worship the same God" is not just to be interpreted intentionally, with phenomenological brackets as it were: rather, it
is itself a theological statement, assuming the existence of a single God for
both Christians and Muslims to worship. But if it is a theological claim,
then from within which tradition? Or does it stand outside both? It could
do, e.g., if it is part of the expression of the modern Hindu ideology. But
let us consider more narrowly the reasons that a *Christian* theologian might
give for the assertion. Let us assume too that he here as elsewhere is presenting a glass through which one can look on the focus of faith—there
being no independent access to that focus. The only ground, one supposes,
for the identification is that there is a sufficient degree of resemblance between the Christian and Muslim conceptions of God. Since, however,
there is a certain degree of elasticity in Christian theology itself, for the
focus of faith is theology-transcending, it is unlikely that it would take
very strict account of what constitutes a sufficient degree of resemblance.

However, this way of discussing the issue might seem overly conceptual. After all, is it not largely upon the practical side of religion that
the theologian feeds? Does his concept of God not articulate what is given
in experience, ritual, history? Not surprisingly, those who espouse the
pluralistic solution tend to stress the unity of religious *experience*. Thus an
important part of the task of trying to establish a sufficient degree of resemblance is the attempt to evaluate the existential and experiential impact
of different foci of faith. Strictly, there are two things to do: first, to arrive
at a sensible and sensitive phenomenology of religious experience (basically a descriptive task this, though not without its conceptual pitfalls);
and second, to see whether the results contribute to the judgement that
there is a sufficient degree of resemblance to justify the identification of
one focus of faith with another.

The phenomenological judgement as to whether there is a basic common core of religious experience must be based on the facts, and not determined a priori by theology. I do not wish to argue the point here: but my own view is that there is no such common core, but rather that there are different sorts of religious experience which recur in different traditions, though not universally. From a phenomenological point of view it is not possible to base the judgement that all religions point to the same truth upon religious *experience*. Nor is it reasonable to think that there is sufficient conceptual resemblance between God and nirvānā (as conceived in Theravāda Buddhism) to aver that the Theravādin and the Christian are worshipping the same God (for one thing, the Theravādin is not basically *worshipping*). Thus it is hard to justify the pluralistic solution, at least as elaborated in the modern Hindu ideology—save by saying that Christians and Buddhists are really aspiring towards the same focus of faith, even though they cannot know that they are. But what then are the criteria of identity of aspiration? Is there a conceptual baptism of desire?

In brief, there are problems about the pluralistic solution, mainly problems of identification of the religious ultimate. It still remains, however, that there is something to commend the solution: to put the matter in a nasty nutshell, the more evangelical Christianity is, the more it approximates to an open tribal faith, for the truth has to be experienced through the forms of Christian faith; but by the same token there is less ground for dismissing the truth of other initiations. On the other hand, the less evangelical Christianity becomes, the less motive it will have for resisting the pluralistic solution.

But *still* the argument may be over-conceptual, over-theological. Can the practical natural theology mentioned earlier come in to provide the test? It would be something of an irony if human fruits were invoked to decide the interpretation of divinity. But this is not a simple affair, as can be imagined; for what counts as fruits is in part determined by the theologies and the institutions. For example, a Christian might bring sustenance to villagers by getting things done, notably by getting folk to hunt birds; but the fruits of Christian dynamism have to be judged by attitudes to animal life. The Buddhist might not be unqualified in his praise of the dynamism. This indicates that the problem of compatibility is not just to do with the religious ultimate, but with the diagnosis of the worldly situation, including importantly the human situation.

The pluralistic situation is attractive, but it is doubtful whether it could work in the present state of religious traditions, because it is phenomenologically unsound. In an important way, then, there is incompatibility (at present) between religious truth-claims. There is also divergence in practice-claims. It is a further question as to the *criteria* for resolving

SMART DENIES COMMON CORE OF RELIGIOUS EXPERIENCE

PLURALISTIC SOLUTION NOT WORKABLE TODAY BECAUSE

"PHENOMENO-LOGICALLY UNSOUND"

questions of truth and practice. There are, however, certainly grounds for arguing both for and against the monotheism which makes sense of Christ's exclusive claim as liberator. As I have attempted to argue elsewhere, these criteria importantly have to do with religious experience and cultus. For the rest, we must accept that every religion has a given starting point, each unique. The pictures in the gallery are different, have different atmospheres and messages; they cannot be aligned in the same pictorial perspective. And for most men only one picture can be a real focus of loyalty.

— RESPONSE: UNLIKE HICK'S ARTICLE SMART FINDS DIFFICULTIES IN FINDING ALL RELIGIONS HAVE COMMON CORE, HE DENIES THIS!

Selected Bibliography
1965-1980

The works cited below relate closely to issues raised in the selections. For a more complete bibliography, see William J. Wainwright, *Philosophy of Religion: An Annotated Bibliography of Twentieth-Century Writings in English* (New York: Garland Press, 1978). Also consult *The Encyclopedia of Philosophy,* ed. Paul Edwards (New York: Macmillan, 1967) under the heading "Religion, Philosophy of" for references to a variety of articles dealing with virtually all aspects of the philosophy of religion.

KEY TO ABBREVIATIONS

AJP	*The Australasian Journal of Philosophy*
APQ	*American Philosophical Quarterly*
CJP	*Canadian Journal of Philosophy*
IJPR	*International Journal for Philosophy of Religion*
IPQ	*International Philosophical Quarterly*
JAAR	*Journal of the American Academy of Religion*
JP	*The Journal of Philosophy*
JR	*The Journal of Religion*
JRE	*Journal of Religious Ethics*
JVI	*The Journal of Value Inquiry*
NS	*The New Scholasticism*
PAS	*Proceedings of the Aristotelian Society*
PPR	*Philosophy and Phenomenological Research*

PQ   *The Philosophical Quarterly*
PR   *The Philosophical Review*
PS   *Philosophical Studies*
RS   *Religious Studies*
SJP   *Southern Journal of Philosophy*
SWJP   *Southwestern Journal of Philosophy*

References to other periodicals are given in full.

I. THE ATTRIBUTES OF GOD

The Problem of Evil and the Moral Attributes

Adams, Marilyn McCord. "Hell and the God of Justice." *Rs* 11(1975): 433–47.
Adams, Robert Merrihew. "Existence, Self-Interest, and the Problem of Evil." *NOÛS* 13(1979): 53–65.
———. "Middle Knowledge and the Problem of Evil." *APQ* 14(1977): 109–17.
———. "Must God Create the Best?" *PR* 81(1972): 317–32.
Ahern, M. B. *The Problem of Evil.* New York: Schocken Books, 1971.
Barnhart, J. E. "Theodicy and the Free Will Defence: Response to Plantinga and Flew." *RS* 13(1977): 439–53.
Bennett, Philip W. "Evil, God, and the Free Will Defense." *AJP* 51(1973): 39–50.
Botterill, George. "Falsification and the Existence of God: A Discussion of Plantinga's Free Will Defense." *PQ* 27(1977): 114–34.
Cahn, Steven M. "The Book of Job: The Great Dissent." *The Reconstructionist* 31(1965): 14–19.
Clark, Stephen. "God, Good, and Evil." *PAS* 77(1976–77): 247–64. (Also relevant to the topic of divine commands.)
Davis, Stephen T. "A Defence of the Free Will Defence." *RS* 8(1972): 335–43.
Dore, Clement. "An Examination of the 'Soul-Making' Theodicy." *APQ* 7(1970): 119–30.
———. "Do Theodicists Mean What They Say?" *Philosophy* 49(1974): 357–74.
———. "Do Theodicists Need to Solve the Problem of Evil?" *RS* 12(1976): 383–89.
———. "Ethical Supernaturalism." *Sophia* 15(1976): 19–25.
Feinberg, John S. *Theologies and Evil.* Washington, D.C.: University Press of America, 1979.
Flew, Antony. *The Presumption of Atheism.* New York: Harper & Row, 1976, ch. 7.
Geach, Peter. *Providence and Evil.* Cambridge: Cambridge University Press, 1977, chs. 2, 4–7.
Hare, Peter, and Madden, Edward H. *Evil and the Concept of God.* Springfield, Ill.: Charles C. Thomas, 1968.
Hick, John. *Evil and the God of Love.* Revised edition. New York: Harper & Row, 1978.
Kane, Stanley G. "The Failure of Soul-Making Theodicy." *IJPR* 6(1975): 1–22.
———. "The Free-Will Defense Defended." *NS* 50(1976): 435–46.
King-Farlow, John. "Cacodaemony and Devilish Isomorphism." *Analysis* 38(1978): 59–61. (Reply to the article by Cahn in this volume.)

LaFollette, Hugh. "Plantinga on the Free Will Defense." *IJPR* 11(1980): 123–32.

La Para, Nicholas. "Suffering, Happiness, and Evil." *Sophia* 4(1965): 10–16. (Reply to an earlier formulation of the views found in Schlesinger's article in this volume.)

Lewis, Meirlys. "On Forgiveness." *PQ* 30(1980): 236–45. (Reply to the article by Minas in this volume.)

Mann, William E. "The Divine Attributes." *APQ* 12(1975): 151–59. (Also relevant to the topics of omnipotence and omniscience.)

Martin, M. "Is Evil Evidence Against the Existence of God?" *Mind* 87(1978): 429–32.

McCloskey, H. J. *God and Evil.* The Hague: Martinus Nijhoff, 1974.

McGuinness, Frank, and Tomberlin, James E. "God, Evil, and the Free Will Defense." *RS* 13(1977): 455–75.

Pargetter, Robert. "Evil as Evidence Against the Existence of God." *Mind* 85 (1976): 242–45.

Penelhum, Terence. "Divine Goodness and the Problem of Evil." *RS* 2(1966): 95–107.

———. *Religion and Rationality.* New York: Random House, 1971, chs. 16–17.

Pike, Nelson. "Plantinga on Free Will and Evil." *RS* 15(1979): 449–73.

Plantinga, Alvin. *God and Other Minds.* Ithaca, N.Y.: Cornell University Press, 1967, chs. 5–6.

———. *God, Freedom, and Evil.* New York: Harper & Row, 1974, Pt. Ia.

———. *The Nature of Necessity.* Oxford: Clarendon Press, 1974, ch. IX.

———. "The Probabilistic Argument from Evil." *PS* 35(1979): 1–53. (Also relevant to Section III.)

———. "Which Worlds Could God Have Created?" *JP* 70(1973): 539–52.

Purtill, Richard. "Flew and the Free Will Defense." *RS* 13(1977): 477–83.

Quinn, Philip L. *Divine Commands and Moral Requirements.* Oxford: Clarendon Press, 1978, ch. VI. (Pp. 136–46 include a reply to the article by Minas in this volume.)

Reichenbach, Bruce. "Must God Create the Best Possible World?" *IPQ* 19(1979): 203–12.

Resnick, Lawrence. "God and the Best of All Possible Worlds." *APQ* 10(1973): 313–17.

Richman, Robert J. "The Argument from Evil." *RS* 4(1968): 203–11.

Rosenberg, Jay F. "The Problem of Evil Revisited: A Reply to Schlesinger." *JVI* 6(1970): 212–18. (Reply to an earlier formulation of the views found in Schlesinger's article in this volume.)

Ross, James F. *Philosophical Theology.* Indianapolis: Bobbs-Merrill, 1969, ch. 6.

Rowe, William L. "The Problem of Evil and Some Varieties of Atheism." *APQ* 16(1979): 335–41. (Also relevant to Section III.)

Schlesinger, George N. "On the Possibility of the Best of All Possible Worlds." *JVI* 4(1970): 229–32. (Reply to the articles by Rosenberg and Shea under this heading.)

———. *Religion and Scientific Method.* Dordrecht: D. Reidel, 1977, Pt. I.

Shea, Winslow. "God, Evil, and Professor Schlesinger." *JVI* 4(1970): 219–28. (Reply to an earlier formulation of the views found in Schlesinger's article in this volume.)

Swinburne, Richard. "Natural Evil." *APQ* 15(1978): 295–301.

Wainwright, William J. "God and the Necessity of Physical Evils." *Sophia* 11 (1972): 16–19.

Yandell, Keith. *Basic Issues in the Philosophy of Religion*. Boston: Allyn and Bacon, 1971, ch. II.

――――. "Ethics, Evils, and Theism." *Sophia* 8(1969): 18–28.

――――. "The Greater Good Defense." *Sophia* 13(1974): 1–16.

Omnipotence

Cargile, James. "On Omnipotence." *NOÛS* 1(1967): 201–5.

Cowan, Joseph L. "The Paradox of Omnipotence Revisited." *CJP* 3(1974): 435–45.

Englebretsen, George. "The Powers and Capacities of God." *Sophia* 18(1979): 29–31.

Geach, Peter. "An Irrelevance of Omnipotence." *Philosophy* 48(1973): 327–33.

――――. "Can God Fail to Keep Promises?" *Philosophy* 52(1977): 93–95. (Reply to Harrison's 1976 article under this heading.)

Gellman, Jerome. "Omnipotence and Impeccability." *NS* 51(1977): 21–37.

――――. "The Paradox of Omnipotence, and Perfection." *Sophia* 14(1975): 31–39.

Gibbs, Benjamin. "Can God Do Evil?" *Philosophy* 50(1975): 466–69. (Reply to the article by Geach in this volume.)

Harrison, Jonathan. "Geach on God's Alleged Inability to Do Evil." *Philosophy* 51 (1976): 208–15. (Reply to the article by Geach in this volume.)

――――. "Geach on Harrison on Geach on God." *Philosophy* 52(1977): 223–26. (Reply to Geach's 1977 article under this heading.)

Hoffman, Joshua. "Can God Do Evil?" *SJP* 17(1979): 213–20.

―――― and Rosenkrantz, Gary. "What an Omnipotent Agent Can Do." *IJPR* 11 (1980): 1–19.

Kenny, Anthony. *The God of the Philosophers*. Oxford: Clarendon Press, 1979, Pt. Three.

Khamara, Edward J. "In Defence of Omnipotence." *PQ* 28(1978): 215–28.

La Croix, Richard. "The Impossibility of Defining Omnipotence." *PS* 32(1977): 181–90.

Mavrodes, George I. "Defining Omnipotence." *PS* 32(1977): 191–202.

Pike, Nelson. "Omnipotence and God's Ability to Sin." *APQ* 6(1969): 208–16.

Plantinga, Alvin. *God and Other Minds*. Ithaca, N.Y.: Cornell University Press, 1967, pp. 168–73.

Reichenbach, Bruce. "Mavrodes on Omnipotence." *PS* 37(1980): 211–14.

Ross, James F. *Philosophical Theology*. Indianapolis: Bobbs-Merrill, 1969, ch. 5.

Swinburne, Richard. *The Coherence of Theism*. Oxford: Clarendon Press, 1977, ch. 9.

Urban, Linwood, and Walton, Douglas (eds.). *The Power of God*. New York: Oxford University Press, 1978.

Wolfe, Julian. "Omnipotence." *CJP* 1(1971): 245–47.

Omniscience, Timelessness, Spacelessness

Adams, Marilyn McCord. "Is the Existence of God a 'Hard' Fact?" *PR* 76(1967): 492–503. (Reply to the article by Pike in this volume.)

Cahn, Steven M. *Fate, Logic, and Time*. New Haven: Yale University Press, 1967, ch. 5.

Castañeda, Hector-Neri. "Omniscience and Indexical Reference." *JP* 64(1967): 203–10.

Craig, William Lane. "God, Time, and Eternity." *RS* 14(1978): 497–503.

Davis, Stephen T. "Divine Omniscience and Human Freedom." *RS* 15(1979): 303–16.

Dyck, Grace. "Omnipresence and Incorporeality." *RS* 13(1977): 85–91.

Geach, Peter. "Omniscience and the Future." In *Providence and Evil*. Cambridge: Cambridge University Press, 1977, ch. 3.

Helm, Paul. "Divine Foreknowledge and Facts." *CJP* 4(1974): 305–15. (Includes reply to the article by Pike in this volume.)

———. "Foreknowledge and Possibility." *CJP* 6(1976): 731–34.

———. "God and Whatever Comes to Pass." *RS* 14(1978): 315–23.

———. "Timelessness and Foreknowledge." *Mind* 84(1975): 516–27.

Hoffman, Joshua. "Pike on Possible Worlds, Divine Foreknowledge, and Human Freedom. *PR* 88(1979): 433–42. (Discussion of the 1977 article by Pike under this heading.)

Holt, Dennis C. "Foreknowledge and the Necessity of the Past." *CJP* 6(1976): 721–30.

Jantzen, Grace M. "On Worshipping An Embodied God." *CJP* 8(1978): 511–19. (Also relevant to the topic of worship.)

Kane, R. H. "Divine Foreknowledge and Causal Determinism." *SWJP* 9(1978): 69–76.

Kenny, Anthony. "Divine Foreknowledge and Human Freedom." In *Aquinas: A Collection of Critical Essays*. Anthony Kenny, ed. Notre Dame, Ind.: University of Notre Dame Press, 1976, pp. 255–70.

———. *The God of the Philosophers*. Oxford: Clarendon Press, 1979, Pts. One, Two.

Kretzmann, Norman. "Omniscience and Immutability." *JP* 63(1966): 409–21.

La Croix, Richard. "Omniprescience and Divine Determinism." *RS* 12(1976): 365–81.

Penelhum, Terence. *Religion and Rationality*. New York: Random House, 1971, ch. 21.

Pike, Nelson. "Divine Foreknowledge, Human Freedom, and Possible Worlds." *PR* 8(1977): 209–16. (Reply to the work by Plantinga under this heading.)

———. *God and Timelessness*. New York: Schocken Books, 1970.

Plantinga, Alvin. *God, Freedom, and Evil*. New York: Harper & Row, 1974, pp. 66–73. (Reply to the article by Pike in this volume.)

Rowe, William L. *Philosophy of Religion: An Introduction*. Belmont, Calif.: Wadsworth, 1978, ch. 11.

Saunders, John Turk. "Of God and Freedom." *PR* 75(1966): 219–25. (Reply to the article by Pike in this volume.)

Sturch, Richard L. "The Problem of the Divine Eternity." *RS* 10(1974): 487–93.

Sutherland, Stewart R. "God, Time, and Eternity." *PAS* 79(1978): 103–21.

Swinburne, Richard. *The Coherence of Theism*. Oxford: Clarendon Press, 1977, chs. 7, 10, 12.

Wainwright, William J. "God's Body." *JAAR* 42(1974): 470–81.

Young, Robert. *Freedom, Responsibility, and God*. New York: Harper & Row, 1975, especially chs. 12–14.

II. GOD AND HUMAN EXPERIENCE

Religious Experience

Almond, Philip. "On the Varieties of Mystical Experience." *Sophia* 19(1979): 1–9.

Carloyle, Jack C. "The Truth of Mysticism." *RS* 16(1980): 1–13.

Conway, David Alton. "Mavrodes, Martin, and the Verification of Religious Experience." *IJPR* 2(1971): 156–71.
Ewing, Alfred C. "Awareness of God." *Philosophy* 40(1965): 1–17.
Flew, Antony. *God and Philosophy*. New York: Dell, 1966, ch. 6.
Helm, Paul. "Religious Experience." *Sophia* 16(1977): 1–6.
Hick, John. *Arguments for the Existence of God*. New York: Herder and Herder, 1971, ch. 7. (Also relevant to Section III.)
————. *Faith and Knowledge*. 2nd edition. Ithaca, N.Y.: Cornell University Press, especially Pt. II. (Also relevant to section III.)
————. "Religious Faith as Experiencing-As." In *Talk of God*. Royal Institute of Philosophy Lectures, Volume 2. G. N. A. Vesey, ed. London: Macmillan, 1968, pp. 20–35. (Also relevant to section III.)
Katz, Steven T. (ed.). *Mysticism and Philosophical Analysis*. New York: Oxford University Press, 1978.
Kellenberger, J. "The Ineffabilities of Mysticism." *APQ* 16(1979): 307–15.
Kvastad, Nils Bjorn. "Philosophical Problems of Mysticism." *IPQ* 13(1973): 191–207.
Mavrodes, George I. *Belief in God: A Study in the Epistemology of Religion*. New York: Random House, 1970, ch. III.
Melchert, Norman. "Mystical Experience and Ontological Claims." *PPR* 37(1977): 445–63.
Miles, T. R. *Religious Experience*. New York: St. Martin's Press, 1972.
The Monist, vol. 59, no. 4 (October 1976). "The Philosophy of Mysticism."
Oakes, Robert A. "Mediation, Encounters, and God." *IJPR* 2(1971): 148–55.
————. "Religious Experience and Rational Certainty." *RS* 12(1976): 311–18.
————. "Religious Experience, Self-Authentication, and Modality *De Re*: A Prolegomenon." *APQ* 16(1979): 217–24.
Penelhum, Terence. *Religion and Rationality*. New York: Random House, 1971, chs. 13–14.
Pletcher, Galen. "Agreement Among Mystics." *Sophia* 11(1972): 5–15.
————. "Mysticism, Contradiction, and Ineffability." *APQ* 10(1973): 201–11.
Robbins, J. Wesley. "John Hick on Religious Experience and Perception." *IJPR* 5(1974): 108–18.
Shiner, Roger. "A Defence of Encounters." *Sophia* 12(1973): 1–6.
Smart, Ninian. "Interpretations of Mystical Experience." *RS* 1(1965): 75–87.
————. *Philosophers and Religious Truth*. 2nd edition. New York: Macmillan, 1969, ch. 5.
Smith, John E. *Experience and God*. New York: Oxford University Press, 1968.
Swinburne, Richard. *The Existence of God*. Oxford: Clarendon Press, 1979, ch. 13.
Wainwright, William J. "Stace and Mysticism." *JR* 50(1970): 139–54.
Wilson, Kirk Dallas. "John Hick on 'Total Interpretation'." *NS* 52(1978): 280–84.
Yandell, Keith. "The Ineffability Theme." *IJPR* 10(1979): 209–31.
————. "Religious Experience and Rational Appraisal." *RS* 10(1974): 173–87.
————. "Some Varieties of Ineffability." *IJPR* 6(1975): 167–79.

Miracles

Ahern, Dennis M. "Hume on the Evidential Impossibility of Miracles." In *Studies in Epistemology, APQ* Monograph No. 9 (Oxford: Basil Blackwell, 1975), pp. 1–31.
————. "Miracles and Physical Impossibility." *CJP* 7(1977): 71–79.
Basinger, David. "Christian Theism and the Concept of Miracle: Some Epistemological Perplexities." *SJP* 18(1980): 137–50.

Cherry, Christopher. "Miracles and Creation." *IJPR* 5(1974): 234–45.

Erlandson, Douglas K. "A New Look at Miracles." *RS* 13(1977): 417–28.

Flew, Antony. *God and Philosophy*. New York: Dell, 1966, ch. 7.

Gaskin, J. C. A. "Miracles and the Religiously Significant Coincidence." *Ratio* 16 (1975): 72–81.

Hambourger, Robert. "Belief in Miracles and Hume's Essay." *NOÛS* 14(1980): 587–604.

Holland, R. F. "The Miraculous." *APQ* 2(1965): 43–51.

Kellenberger, J. "Miracles." *IJPR* 10(1979): 155–62.

MacKinnon, Alastair. " 'Miracle' and 'Paradox'." *APQ* 4(1967): 308–14.

Penelhum, Terence. *Religion and Rationality*. New York: Random House, 1971, ch. 19.

Robinson, Guy. "Miracles." *Ratio* 9(1967): 155–66.

Schlesinger, George N. *Religion and Scientific Method*. Dordrecht: D. Reidel, 1977, ch. 22.

Smart, Ninian. *Philosophers and Religious Truth*. 2nd edition. New York: Macmillan, 1969, ch. 2.

Swinburne, Richard. *The Concept of Miracle*. New York: St. Martin's Press, 1970.

Yandell, Keith. "Miracles, Epistemology, and Hume's Barrier." *IJPR* 7(1976): 391–417.

Young, Robert. "Miracles and Epistemology." *RS* 8(1972): 115–26.

Ritual, Worship, and Divine Commands

Adams, Robert Merrihew. "Autonomy and Theological Ethics." *RS* 15(1979): 191–94.

Brody, Baruch A. "Morality and Religion Reconsidered." In *Readings in the Philosophy of Religion*. Baruch A. Brody, ed. Englewood Cliffs, N.J.: Prentice-Hall, 1974, pp. 592–603.

Cahn, Steven M. *A New Introduction to Philosophy*. New York: Harper & Row, 1971, ch. 6.

Geach, Peter. "Praying for Things to Happen." In *God and the Soul*. New York: Schocken Books, 1969, ch. 7.

Green, Ronald. "Religious Ritual: A Kantian Perspective." *JRE* 14(1979): 229–38.

Helm, Paul. "Omnipotence and Change." *Philosophy* 51(1976): 454–61.

Mayberry, Thomas C. "God and Moral Authority." *The Monist* 54(1970): 106–23.

Mitchell, Basil. *Morality: Religious and Secular*. Oxford: Clarendon Press, 1980.

Oakes, Robert A. "Reply to Professor Rachels." *RS* 8(1972): 165–67. (Reply to the article by Rachels in this volume.)

Outka, Gene, and Reeder, John P., Jr. (eds.). *Religion and Morality*. Garden City, N.Y.: Anchor Books, 1973, especially Pt. III.

Penelhum, Terence. *Religion and Rationality*. New York: Random House, 1971, ch. 20.

Phillips, D. Z. *The Concept of Prayer*. New York: Schocken Books, 1966.

Price, H. H. *Essays in the Philosophy of Religion*. Oxford: Clarendon Press, 1972, chs. 1, 3.

Quinn, Philip L. *Divine Commands and Moral Requirements*. Oxford: Clarendon Press, 1978. (Ch. I includes a reply to the article by Rachels in this volume.)

Smart, Ninian. *The Concept of Worship*. New York: St. Martin's Press, 1972.

Stump, Eleanor. "Petitionary Prayer." *APQ* 16(1979): 81–93.

Swinburne, Richard. *The Coherence of Theism*. Oxford: Clarendon Press, 1977, chs. 11, 15.

Young, Robert. "Petitioning God." *APQ* 11(1974): 193–201.
———. "Theism and Morality." *CJP* 7(1977): 341–51.

Immortality and Resurrection

Audi, Robert. "Eschatological Verification and Personal Identity." *IJPR* 7(1976): 391–408.
Erlandson, Douglas K. "Timelessness, Immutability, and Eschatology." *IJPR* 9 (1978): 129–45.
Flew, Antony. *The Presumption of Atheism.* New York: Harper & Row, 1976, Pt. III.
Geach, Peter. *God and the Soul.* New York: Schocken Books, 1969, chs. 1–2.
Helm, Paul. "A Theory of Disembodied Survival and Re-embodied Existence." *RS* 14(1978): 15–26. (Reply to views found in Penelhum's article in this volume.)
Herbert, R. T. *Paradox and Identity in Theology.* Ithaca, N.Y.: Cornell University Press, 1979, chs. 1, 6.
Hick, John. *Death and Eternal Life.* New York: Harper & Row, 1976.
Lewis, Hywel D. *Persons and Life After Death: Essays by Hywel D. Lewis and some of his critics.* New York: Harper & Row, 1978.
Penelhum, Terence (ed.). *Immortality.* Belmont, Calif.: Wadsworth, 1973.
———. *Survival and Disembodied Existence.* New York: Humanities Press, 1970.
Phillips, D. Z. *Death and Immortality.* New York: St. Martin's Press, 1970. (Also relevant to Section III.)
Price, H. H. *Essays in the Philosophy of Religion.* Oxford: Clarendon Press, 1972, chs. 5, 6.
Purtill, Richard. "Disembodied Survival Again." *CJP* 7(1977): 125–32.
Quinn, Philip L. "Personal Identity, Bodily Continuity, and Resurrection." *IJPR* 9(1978): 101–13. (Reply to the article by Mavrodes in this volume.)
———. "Some Problems About Resurrection." *RS* 14(1978): 343–59.
Reichenbach, Bruce. *Is Man the Phoenix? A Study of Immortality.* Grand Rapids: Wm. B. Eerdmans, 1978.
———. "Price, Hick, and Disembodied Existence." *RS* 15(1979): 317–25.
Schlesinger, George N. *Religion and Scientific Method.* Dordrecht: D. Reidel, 1977, ch. 5.
Swinburne, Richard. *The Coherence of Theism.* Oxford: Clarendon Press, 1977, ch. 7.
Van Inwagen, Peter. "The Possibility of Resurrection." *IJPR* 9(1978): 114–21. (Reply to the article by Mavrodes in this volume.)
Young, Robert. "Professor Penelhum on the Resurrection of the Body." *RS* 9(1973): 181–87. (Reply to views found in Penelhum's article in this volume.)
———. "The Resurrection of the Body." *Sophia* 9(1970): 1–15.

III. FAITH, RATIONALITY, AND WORLD RELIGIONS

Rationality and Religious Commitment

Allen, Diogenes. "Motives, Rationales, and Religious Beliefs." *APQ* 3(1966): 111–27.
Barbour, Ian. *Myths, Models, and Paradigms.* New York: Harper & Row, 1974.
Christensen, William Niels, and King-Farlow, John. *Faith and the Life of Reason.* Dordrecht: D. Reidel, 1973.

Clegg, J. S. "Faith." *APQ* 16(1979): 225–32.

Dalton, Peter C. "Pascal's Wager: The First Argument." *IJPR* 7(1976): 346–68.

———. "Pascal's Wager: The Second Argument." *SJP* 13(1975): 31–46.

Davis, Stephen T. *Faith, Skepticism, and Evidence.* Lewisburg, Penn.: Bucknell University Press, 1978.

Delaney, C. F. (ed.). *Rationality and Religious Belief.* Notre Dame, Ind.: University of Notre Dame Press, 1978.

Dilley, Frank. "The Status of Religious Beliefs." *APQ* 13(1976): 41–47.

Evans, Stephen C. "Kierkegaard on Subjective Truth: Is God an Ethical Fiction?" *IJPR* 7(1976): 288–99.

Flew, Antony. *God and Philosophy.* New York: Dell, 1966, ch. 9.

———. *The Presumption of Atheism.* New York: Harper & Row, 1976, Pt. I, especially chs. 1, 2, 5.

Gale, Richard M. "William James and the Ethics of Belief." *APQ* 17(1980): 1–14.

Gaskin, J. C. A. "God, Hume, and Natural Belief." *Philosophy* 49(1974): 281–94.

Gellman, Jerome. "The Religious Option Is a Genuine Option." *RS* 14(1978): 505–14.

Gill, Jerry H. *The Possibility of Religious Knowledge.* Grand Rapids: Wm. B. Eerdmans, 1971.

———. "Reasons of the Heart: A Polanyian Reflection." *RS* 14(1978): 143–57.

———. "Tacit Knowing and Religious Belief." *IJPR* 6(1975): 73–88.

Green, Ronald. *Religious Reason.* New York: Oxford University Press, 1978.

Hacking, Ian. "The Logic of Pascal's Wager." *APQ* 9(1972): 186–92.

Harvey, Van. "The Ethics of Belief Reconsidered." *JR* 59(1979): 406–20.

———. *The Historian and the Believer.* New York: Macmillan, 1966, especially ch. VII.

Hick, John. *Faith and Knowledge.* 2nd edition. Ithaca, N.Y.: Cornell University Press, 1966.

Hudson, W. D. "On Two Points Against Wittgensteinian Fideism." *Philosophy* 43(1968): 269–73. (Reply to the article by Nielsen in this volume.)

———. *Wittgenstein and Religious Belief.* London: Macmillan, 1975.

Hughes, G. E. "Plantinga on the Rationality of God's Existence." *PR* 79(1970): 246–52.

Keeling, L. Bryant, and Morelli, Mario F. "Beyond Wittgensteinian Fideism: An Examination of John Hick's Analysis of Religious Faith." *IJPR* 8(1977): 250–62.

Kellenberger, J. "Problems of Faith." *CJP* 6(1976): 417–42.

———. *Religious Discovery, Faith, and Knowledge.* Englewood Cliffs, N.J.: Prentice-Hall, 1972.

Lyas, Colin. "The Groundlessness of Religious Belief." In *Reason and Religion.* Stuart C. Brown, ed. Ithaca, N.Y.: Cornell University Press, 1975, pp. 158–80.

Malcolm, Norman. "The Groundlessness of Belief." In *Reason and Religion.* Stuart C. Brown, ed. Ithaca, N.Y.: Cornell University Press, 1975, pp. 143–57.

Margolis, Joseph. "Religion and Reason." *RS* 12(1976): 429–43.

Mavrodes, George I. *Belief in God: A Study in the Epistemology of Religion.* New York: Random House, 1970.

Martin, Michael. "On Four Critiques of Pascal's Wager." *Sophia* 14(1975): 1–11.

McClendon, James Wm., Jr., and Smith, James M. *Understanding Religious Convictions.* Notre Dame, Ind.: University of Notre Dame Press, 1975.

Mitchell, Basil. "Faith and Reason: A False Antithesis?" *RS* 16(1980): 131–44.

————. *The Justification of Religious Belief*. New York: Oxford University Press, 1981.

Newman, Jay. "Popular Pragmatism and Religious Belief." *IJPR* 8(1977): 94–110.

Nicholl, Larimore Reid. "Pascal's Wager: The Bet Is Off." *PPR* 39(1978): 274–80.

Nielsen, Kai. "Wittgensteinian Fideism: A Reply to Hudson." *Philosophy* 44(1969): 63–65. (Reply to the 1968 article by Hudson under this heading.)

Penelhum, Terence. *Problems of Religious Knowledge*. New York: Herder and Herder, 1971.

————. *Religion and Rationality*. New York: Random House, 1971, ch. 15.

Phillips, D. Z. *Faith and Philosophical Enquiry*. New York: Schocken Books, 1971.

————. *Religion Without Explanation*. Oxford: Basil Blackwell, 1976.

Plantinga, Alvin. *God and Other Minds*. Ithaca, N.Y.: Cornell University Press, 1967, especially Pt. III.

Pojman, Louis. "Kierkegaard on Justification of Belief." *IJPR* 8(1977): 75–93.

————. "Rationality and Religious Belief." *RS* 15(1979): 159–72.

Price, H. H. "Belief 'In' and Belief 'That'." *RS* 1(1965): 5–28.

Resnick, Lawrence. "Evidence, Utility, and God." *Analysis* 31(1971): 87–90.

Ross, James F. *Philosophical Theology*. Indianapolis: Bobbs-Merrill, 1969, ch. 1.

Rowe, William L. *The Cosmological Argument*. Princeton, N.J.: Princeton University Press, 1975, ch. 6.

Schlesinger, George N. *Religion and Scientific Method*. Dordrecht: D. Reidel, 1977, ch. 18.

Shepherd, John J. "Religion and the Contextualization of Criteria." *Sophia* 15 (1976): March 1976, 1–10, July 1976, 1–9.

Sherry, Patrick. *Religion, Truth, and Language-Games*. New York: Harper & Row, 1977.

Swinburne, Richard. "The Christian Wager." *RS* 4(1969): 217–28.

Sykes, Rod. "Soft Rationalism." *IJPR* 8(1977): 51–66.

Tomberlin, James E. "Is Belief in God Justified?" *JP* 67(1970): 531–38.

Trigg, Roger. *Reason and Commitment*. London: Cambridge University Press, 1973.

Winch, Peter. "Meaning and Religious Language." In *Reason and Religion*. Stuart C. Brown, ed. Ithaca, N.Y.: Cornell University Press, 1975, pp. 193–221.

Yandell, Keith. *Basic Issues in the Philosophy of Religion*. Boston: Allyn and Bacon, 1971, ch. VI.

World Religions: Conflicting Truth-Claims

Cahn, Steven M. "The Irrelevance to Religion of Philosophic Proofs for the Existence of God." *APQ* 6(1969): 170–72.

Christian, William A., Jr. *Oppositions of Religious Doctrines*. New York: Herder and Herder, 1972.

Hick, John (ed.). *Truth and Dialogue in World Religions*. Philadelphia: Westminster Press, 1974.

Lipner, Julius. "Does Copernicus Help? Reflections for a Christian Theology of Religions." *RS* 13(1977): 243–58. (Reply to views found in Hick's article in this volume.)

————. "Truth-Claims and Inter-religious Dialogue." *RS* 12(1976): 217–30.

Smart, Ninian. *The Religious Experience of Mankind*. New York: Charles Scribner's Sons, 1969, especially ch. 11.

————. *World Religions: A Dialogue*. Baltimore: Penguin Books, 1966.

Smith, William Cantwell. *Religious Diversity*. Willard G. Oxtoby, ed. New York: Harper & Row, 1976.